Unequal Encounters

Unequal Encounters

A Reader in Early Latin American Political Thought

Katherine Hoyt

LEXINGTON BOOKS
Lanham • Boulder • New York • London

Published by Lexington Books
An imprint of The Rowman & Littlefield Publishing Group, Inc.
4501 Forbes Boulevard, Suite 200, Lanham, Maryland 20706
www.rowman.com

86-90 Paul Street, London EC2A 4NE

British Library Cataloguing in Publication Information Available

Library of Congress Cataloging-in-Publication Data

Names: Hoyt, Katherine, editor.
Title: Unequal encounters : a reader in early Latin American political thought / Katherine Hoyt.
Description: Lanham : Lexington Books, [2022] | Includes bibliographical references and index. | Summary: "This volume presents a selection of the most compelling political writings from early colonial Latin America that address the themes of conquest, colonialism, and enslavement. The anthology centers the voices of Indigenous peoples, whose writings constitute six of the fifteen chapters while also including women's, African, and Jewish perspectives"— Provided by publisher.
Identifiers: LCCN 2021046616 (print) | LCCN 2021046617 (ebook) | ISBN 9781793622525 (cloth) | ISBN 9781793622549 (paper) | ISBN 9781793622532 (epub)
Subjects: LCSH: Political science—Latin America—History. | Indigenous peoples—Latin America—History. | Latin America—History—To 1830. | Latin America—Politics and government—History.
Classification: LCC JA84.L3 U54 2022 (print) | LCC JA84.L3 (ebook) | DDC 320.098—dc23/eng/20211105
LC record available at https://lccn.loc.gov/2021046616
LC ebook record available at https://lccn.loc.gov/2021046617

Contents

Acknowledgments

Chapter 1: Selection excerpted from *The Annals of the Cakchiquels*. Translated from the Cakchiquel Maya by Adrian Recinos and Delia Goetz. Copyright © 1953 by the University of Oklahoma Press. Reprinted by permission.

A shorter version of the introduction to this chapter was published in the book *Cases of Exclusion and Mobilization of Race and Ethnicities in Latin America*, edited by Marc Becker. Reprinted with the permission of Cambridge Scholars Publishing.

Chapter 2: Selection excerpted from Christopher Columbus. *Personal Narrative of the First Voyage of Columbus to America from a manuscript recently discovered in Spain*. Translated with Preface by Samuel Kettell. Boston: Thomas B. Wait and Son: 1827. In the public domain.

Chapter 3: Selection excerpted from Bartolomé de Las Casas. *History of the Indies* [1528], pp. 182–86. Translated by Andrée M. Collard. Copyright © 1971 by Andreé Collard, copyright renewed 1999 by Joyce J. Contrucci. Reprinted with permission of Joyce Contrucci.

Chapter 4: Selection reprinted from *In Defense of the Indians*, by Bartolomé de Las Casas, translated and edited by Stafford Poole, C.M., a Northern Illinois University Press book published by Cornell University Press. Copyright © 1992 by Northern Illinois University Press. Used by permission of the publisher. The material has been edited for length.

Chapter 5: Selection excerpted from Alonso de la Vera Cruz. *The Writings of Alonso de la Vera Cruz: Vol. II. Defense of the Indians: Their Rights*. Original Latin texts with English translation edited by Ernest J. Burrus. (Sources and Studies for the History of the Americas: Vol. IV). Rome and St. Louis, Mo.: Jesuit Historical Institute, 1968. Reproduced with permission.

Chapter 6: Selection excerpted from *Madres del Verbo/Mothers of the Word: Early Spanish-American Women Writers—A Bilingual Anthology*. Translated by Nina A. Scott. Copyright © 2000 by University of New Mexico Press. Reprinted by permission.

Chapter 7: Selection excerpted from "An Indian Town Addresses the King." In *Letters and People of the Spanish Indies: Sixteenth Century*. Translated and edited by James Lockhart and Enrique Otte. Copyright © 1976 by Cambridge University Press. Reprinted by permission of the Licensor through PLSclear.

Chapter 8: Selection excerpted from Bernardino de Sahagún. *Florentine Codex: General History of the Things of New Spain*. Translated from Spanish and Nahuatl to English by Arthur J. O. Anderson and Charles Dibble. Copyright © 1982 by University of Utah Press. Reprinted by permission.

Chapter 9: Selection excerpted from Titu Cusi Yupanqui. *An Inca Account of the Conquest of Peru*. Translated, introduced, and annotated by Ralph Bauer. Copyright © 2005 by University of Colorado Press. Reprinted by permission.

Chapter 10: Selection excerpted from Pedro Sarmiento de Gamboa. *History of the Incas*. Translated and edited by Clements Markham. London: Hakluyt Society, 1907. In the public domain.

Chapter 11: Selection from Alonso de Illescas. "Letter from Don Alonso de Illescas, a Black Man in Esmeraldas (1586)." Translated by Charles Beatty-Medina. In *Afro-Latino Voices: Narratives from the Early Modern Ibero-Atlantic World, 1550–1812*. Edited by Kathryn Joy McKnight and Leo J. Garofalo. Copyright © 2009 by Hackett Publishing Company, Inc. Reprinted by permission of Hackett Publishing Company, Inc. All rights reserved.

Chapter 12: Memoirs excerpted from Martin Cohen, translator. "The Autobiography of Luis de Carvajal, the Younger." *American Jewish History* 55, no. 3 (1966): 282–318. Copyright ©1966 by The American Jewish Historical Society. Reprinted with permission of Johns Hopkins University Press.
  Inquisition documents excerpted from John F. Chuchiak IV, editor and translator. *The Inquisition in New Spain, 1536–1820: A Documentary History*, pp. 240–45. Copyright © 2012 by Johns Hopkins University Press. Reprinted with permission of Johns Hopkins University Press.

Chapter 13: *Royal Commentaries* selection excerpted from Ynca Garcilasso de la Vega. *First part of the Royal commentaries of the Yncas.* Translated and edited with notes and introduction by Clements R. Markham. London: Hakluyt Society, 1869. In the public domain.

General History of Peru selection excerpted from Garcilaso de la Vega, El Inca. *Royal Commentaries of the Incas and General History of Peru.* Translated by Harold V. Livermore. Copyright © 1966 by University of Texas Press. Reprinted by permission.

A shorter version of the introduction to this chapter was published in the book *Cases of Exclusion and Mobilization of Race and Ethnicities in Latin America*, edited by Marc Becker. Reprinted with the permission of Cambridge Scholars Publishing.

Chapter 14: Selection excerpted from Felipe Guamán Poma de Ayala. *The First New Chronicle and Good Government.* Selected, translated and annotated by David Frye. Copyright © 2006 by Hackett Publishing Company. Reprinted by permission of Hackett Publishing Co, Inc. All rights reserved.

A shorter version of the introduction to this chapter was published in the book *Cases of Exclusion and Mobilization of Race and Ethnicities in Latin America*, edited by Marc Becker. Reprinted with the permission of Cambridge Scholars Publishing.

Chapter 15: Selection excerpted from Alonso de Sandoval. *Treatise on Slavery: Selections from "De instauranda Aethiopum salute"* [1627 edition]. Edited and translated with introduction by Nicole Von Germeten. Copyright © 2008 by Hackett Publishing Company, Inc. Reprinted by permission of Hackett Publishing Company. All rights reserved.

Introduction

The field of political theory was defined by scholar George H. Sabine as human "attempts to consciously understand and solve the problems of [their] group life and organization."[1] As taught and studied in the United States, it has expanded in recent years from mainly European thought to include these human attempts at understanding from all regions of the world and there is currently a renewed interest in discussions of conquest, colonialism, and enslavement. The goal of this volume is to present a selection of the most compelling political writings from early colonial Latin America (up to 1630) to address those themes and others. Extensive introductory material introduces readers to the biographies of the writers, their ideas, and the controversies surrounding them. An important feature of this volume is the centering of Indigenous writers. Indeed, Indigenous writings constitute six of the fifteen chapters. The selections in the remainder of the chapters were written primarily by Spanish men who spent time, in many cases most of their lives, in the Americas. However, there is one selection written by a Spanish woman and one written by a writer of African ancestry. The writings range from sermons, logs, histories, treatises, debates, essays, and speeches to official documents, letters, and testimony.

This book, while it is an anthology of political thought, can be used in the study of history as well. Many of the writings will also be of interest to students of anthropology and other fields. While I have included writings that were translated into English as far back as the 1820s, there has been a flurry of translations in the twenty-first century, and it is those translations that have made an English-language volume such as this one possible.

At the same time, the internet has enabled scholars and students to view many original sixteenth-century documents located in libraries scattered around the world, from the annals of the Kaqchikel Maya at the library of

1

the University of Pennsylvania in Philadelphia to the Florentine Codex in (of course) Florence, Italy. I have included in the endnotes and bibliography the links for readers to view them. Some of the later works in this volume were printed on the new printing presses that had spread quickly throughout Western Europe by the early 1500s (and to Mexico in 1539) including the works of El Inca Garcilaso de la Vega and Alonso de Sandoval. Other works such as Friar Alonso de la Vera Cruz's *De dominio infidelium et iusto bello* and Guamán Poma de Ayala's *New Chronicle and Good Government* were not published but rather were "lost" for centuries in private collections or royal libraries and only rediscovered in the late nineteenth or early twentieth centuries. Others were not lost but merely forgotten. And one, the *Memoirs* of Luis de Carvajal the Younger, burned at the stake for "Judaizing" by the Inquisition in Mexico in 1596, was stolen for most of the twentieth century and only returned to the archives in 2017.

The selections included in the book were written in the period that roughly corresponds to the Spanish *Siglo de Oro* or Golden Age. This period is generally considered to have lasted from 1492 (which marked both the completion of what was known as the *Reconquista* and Christopher Columbus's first voyage to the Americas) to the middle of the 1600s. It was a period in which not only art, music and literature flourished, but philosophy as well, both in Spain and in the so-called New World, the region conquered by Spain. In the Americas, Spaniards, Indigenous people, Africans, and mixed-race peoples all contributed to the writing and illustration of books, the design, construction, and decoration of churches, and the composition of music. The Enlightenment or Age of Reason that followed was expressed in Latin America mainly in the sciences in the early years and later, in the 1700s, in the writings of independence proponents and should be the subject of a separate volume.

THE CONTEXT

At the time of the initial encounter of the Spaniards and the Native peoples in what the Spanish called the "New World," the vast majority of the latter were living as sedentary farmers. Semisedentary populations (who spent some of their time hunting and gathering) occupied most of the remaining territory in both North and South America. There were concentrated populations that were completely sedentary in the large cities of the two "great" empires that had arisen in the fifteenth century, that of the Aztecs, in what would become Mexico, and the Inca Empire in South America centered in Peru, as well as in smaller cities such as Iximché, capital city of the Kakchiquel Maya in Guatemala (included in the first chapter of this book), and Huejotzingo in Mexico (in chapter 7). Semisedentary and nomadic peoples lived on the Caribbean islands (as described by Columbus in chapter 2), in the Amazon and Orinoco River basins, and in Southern Argentina and Chile.[2]

Non-Indigenous academics have tended to categorize Indigenous settlements that most resembled European ones (i.e., ones that had a hierarchical social order and an organized religion among other characteristics) as "great civilizations" and have called their transitions to different types of settlements a "decline." According to this way of understanding preconquest history, the earliest "great civilizations" of Mexico and Central America date from about 1200 BCE (Before the Common Era, sometimes called BC) with the rise in southern Mexico of the Olmec culture—best known for its colossal stone heads. The Olmec civilization "declined" after about 400 BCE. The Mayan civilization of Mesoamerica originated as early as 1500 BCE but reached its "glorious" classical period between 200 and 900 CE (Common Era, often called AD) after which it too declined but did not disappear. Contemporaneous with the Mayan civilization were Teotihuacan (near present-day Mexico City) with its massive pyramids, and Monte Albán, a center of both the Zapotec and later the Mixtec peoples. They were followed by the Toltecs and, beginning with the founding of the city of Tenochtitlán, possibly in 1325, the Aztecs, who also claimed Toltec ancestry. The Mexica people, as the Aztecs were called, set up a hierarchical society with a strict educational system.[3] Mexica society was organized for expeditions of military conquests in which the capture of warriors for religious sacrifice was important.[4] There was strong opposition to the Mexicas among some of their neighbors. This helped Hernán Cortés, the Spanish conqueror, convince and/or coerce some Indigenous groups to join him in his battles to defeat the Aztecs, as we see in the letter from the Council of Huejotzingo to King Philip II in chapter 7.

At the time the pyramids were being built in Egypt nearly 5,000 years ago, the desert city of Caral in Peru was a thriving metropolis with pyramids, plazas, and residences. It did not begin its "decline" until about 1,600 BCE.[5] In 2009, the Sacred City of Caral-Supe was added to the UNESCO World Heritage List as the oldest center of civilization in the Americas.[6] Numerous other cultures followed Caral on the coast, in the desert, and in the Andes Mountains. These included the Chavín people (1500–300 BCE) who lived at 10,000 feet above sea level, the desert Nazca people (100 BCE–700 CE) who constructed the famous lines in the desert depicting animals and other forms, and the coastal Moche civilization (100–700 CE) which was noted for pyramids, irrigation works, and fanciful pottery.[7] The Wari and Tiwanaku cultures (500–1000 CE) developed contemporaneously on the coast and in the Bolivian/Peruvian altiplano respectively and were noted for monumental stone structures (in particular at Tiwanaku), irrigation systems, and roads.[8]

The Inca began expanding from their capital at Cusco in about 1300 CE with the greatest growth of their empire under the ninth Inca, Pachacuti Inca Yupanqui, in the mid-fifteenth century. (The term Inca refers both to the people and to their ruler.) The Inca Empire included about nine million inhabitants and covered a territory from present-day Ecuador in the north to central Chile in the south by the time the Spanish arrived there in 1532. Communication and commerce were maintained by a network of 10,000 miles of roadways, and agricultural production—mainly of potatoes, corn, and squash, and the raising of llamas—was organized in each community.[9] Indigenous writers Titu Cusi Yupanqui, El Inca Garcilaso de la Vega, and Guamán Poma in chapters 9, 13, and 14 describe aspects of the Incan rule of this empire.

Recent research has shown that, before the arrival of Columbus in the Americas, the Amazon Basin region was populated by large numbers of semi-sedentary farmers who modified the forests and the soil so that they were able to support numbers of people much greater than had previously been thought. These numbers are more in line, in fact, with the observations of a friar who accompanied the first Spanish expedition to the mouth of the Amazon in 1541 and reported thousands of Indigenous peoples living in villages along much of the route.[10] Archaeologists now believe that between 1200 and 1500 CE, there was an interconnected string of villages along over 1,100 miles of the Amazon River and its tributaries with "ditched enclosures and large habitation mounds with canals, causeways, fish weirs, water reservoirs and raised fields." Archaeologist Jonas Gregorio de Souza and his colleagues have called for a reevaluation of the role of the people of this region in Pre-Columbian cultural developments.[11]

Africans were brought to the "New World" by the Spanish and Portuguese from the beginning of the conquest and most came as enslaved people. The majority of enslaved Africans came from West Africa and West Central Africa, from the Senegal River to the southern part of Angola, a region with many different-sized competing states. In the mid-1400s, the Songhay Empire, with its capitals at Timbuktu and later at Gao, expanded in the interior of the regions of the lower Gambia and Senegal Rivers. The Songhay Empire was known for its manufacturing and for its intellectual life, most particularly for Islamic scholarship.[12] The Kingdom of Benin in West Africa was known for its cotton cloth and its metal work, especially for the world-famous Benin bronzes.[13] The Portuguese trade in African people caused the decline of the Bantu civilization in the Kingdom of Kongo when warfare to capture and enslave workers for the developing sugar plantations in Brazil became continuous. The Kingdom had been noted for its highly productive agriculture and its metallurgical sector.[14]

While enslavement had been a part of life in Africa, the Americas, and Europe for many centuries, what is known as the Atlantic slave trade (from Africa to the Americas) was quantitatively and qualitatively different. The numbers of people trafficked was vastly greater—records of transatlantic slaving voyages between 1501 and 1866 estimate that 12,521,337 enslaved persons were forced onto ships to the New World.[15] People were taken long distances from their homes to alien regions, with different cultures and languages, and the lives of the enslaved people worsened dramatically compared to their lives in Africa. In chapter 11, Alonso de Illescas, an escaped formerly enslaved African and leader of a Maroon community, writes a letter to the king of Spain asking him not to send a military expedition to his territory and, in chapter 15, Jesuit Alonso de Sandoval, who ministered to enslaved Africans arriving by ship to the port of Cartagena, Colombia, condemns their mistreatment.

The Iberian Peninsula, home to the present-day countries of Spain and Portugal, was populated by Celtic and Iberian people before the arrival of the Phoenicians around 800 BCE. The Carthaginians then conquered Iberia in 236 BCE. The Romans invaded in 218 BCE and spent many decades wresting the peninsula from the Carthaginians. Over the next six centuries, the Romans gave Spain and Portugal their languages, the Christian religion, and gave Spain its name, *Hispania*. In turn, Spain gave Rome the Emperors Trajan, Hadrian, and Marcus Aurelius and the poet Seneca. After the Romans destroyed the second Jewish Temple in Jerusalem in 70 CE, the Jewish population (which already existed in the Iberian Peninsula) grew substantially. With the decline of the Roman Empire, the Visigoths, one of the tribes that invaded Rome itself, also established a kingdom in 415 in Iberia with its capital at Toledo.

The Visigoths ruled Iberia until 711 when Islamic Umayyad and North African forces invaded and over a period of ten years conquered much of the peninsula with the exception of several Christian kingdoms in the north. Their rule was followed by the Almoravid and Almohad dynasties. For nearly eight centuries, the history of Iberia would be based on the complicated interactions between Christians, Muslims, and Jews.[16] Among the positive aspects were advances in mathematics, science, architecture, and philosophy. Christian and Muslim kingdoms grew and shrank over the next centuries. And while the people of these two faiths much of the time lived in peace with each other and with the Jewish population, wars broke out between 850 and 1250 in which the Christian kingdoms pushed the Muslims south. In 1250, Portugal became independent kingdom, and the Christians took Seville leaving Granada as the only Islamic kingdom.[17]

In 1469, the young Isabella of Castile and Ferdinand of Aragon married and when they inherited the crowns of their respective kingdoms, they became known as the Catholic monarchs (*los Reyes Católicos*). Although their kingdoms were separate (with Castile being by far the larger of the two) history sees them as having united Spain since they worked closely together.[18] In the pivotal year 1492, the two monarchs accepted the surrender of the last Islamic Kingdom of Granada, expelled from Spain those Jews who refused to convert to Christianity (Muslims would be expelled a decade later), and signed an agreement with mariner Christopher Columbus to explore for new lands and possibly reach Asia by sailing west across the Atlantic. Columbus describes his arrival in the New World in chapter 2 of this volume.

For the first 25 years after arriving in the "new" lands that would eventually be known as the Americas, the Spanish concentrated their efforts on conquering and colonizing the Caribbean Islands and nearby mainland. The mistreatment of the Indigenous peoples on the island of Hispaniola, where Santo Domingo served as the capital city, is denounced by Spanish friar Antonio de Montesinos in chapter 3. It was not until 1519 that the Spaniard Hernán Cortés and his men arrived in Mexico and began what would become a two-year conquest of the Aztec Empire.[19]

After landing on the Mexican coast and founding the town of Vera Cruz, Cortés found allies among the enemies of the Aztecs and coerced into collaboration those who were ambivalent. He led an army of a few Spaniards and thousands of Indigenous fighters into the Aztec capital of Tenochtitlan, where he met the Aztec leader Moctezuma and put him under arrest in spite of being outnumbered by the Mexica. Soon after, Cortés left Tenochtitlan in the hands of the Spaniard Pedro de Alvarado in order to return to Vera Cruz to defeat a force from Cuba sent by the Spanish governor to try to stop his conquest of Mexico, which he was attempting without proper authorization. While Cortés was gone, Alvarado and his men attacked a major religious celebration in Tenochtitlan killing hundreds, including many from among the nobility. When Cortés returned to the capital, he and his men soon found themselves under angry and deadly attack. If any among the Mexica had believed that the Spanish were gods, their brutal actions soon convinced the Mexicas that they were not. Moctezuma himself was killed, reportedly by a stone that hit his head. The Spaniards decided to flee under dark of night but, loaded down with gold and other precious items that they had stolen from the Mexica, they did not get far before they were attacked, losing more than 400 Spaniards and 4,000 native allies in what became known as *La Noche Triste* or the Sorrowful Night.[20]

Cortés regrouped with his allies. He ordered his men to build a fleet of brigantines with which he could blockade the Aztec capital and prevent food from being brought to the residents and their defenders. The brigantines were able to defeat Mexica canoe forces and the Spaniards were also aided by smallpox which had arrived in Mesoamerica for the first time with one of the Spaniards from Cuba who had joined Cortés. The disease entered Tenochtitlan, where the people were weakened by lack of food and killed thousands. Finally, on August 21, 1521, the Spaniards and their Indigenous allies completed their defeat of the Aztec Empire, capturing Moctezuma's successor Cuauhtémoc.[21] The letter from the Council of Huejotzingo to the king in chapter 7 recounts part of the story of their collaboration with Cortés against the Aztecs.

In 2021, Mexico prepared to commemorate the five-hundredth anniversary of the conquest. Mexico City changed the name of Puente de Alvarado Avenue to Mexico-Tenochtitlán Boulevard and President Andrés Manuel López Obrador requested apologies from the king of Spain and the Pope for atrocities committed by Spanish civil, military, and religious authorities during the conquest and afterward.[22]

Even before they had taken over Mexico, the Spanish began the conquest of Panama, establishing towns there in 1508. By 1514, Vasco Núñez de Balboa had become the first European to see the Pacific Ocean and the first Catholic bishop of Panama had been appointed. From Panama, Spanish conquest and settlement proceeded north to Nicaragua where Francisco Hernández de Córdoba founded the cities of León and Granada in 1524. And, at the same time, Pedro de Alvarado went south from Mexico to Guatemala and, over a number of years between 1524 and 1530, conquered the K'iche', the Tz'utuhil, and the Kakchiquel Mayans.[23] The foundation narrative of the Kakchiquel Maya can be read in chapter 1.

Panama also served as the starting point for the conquest of the Inca Empire of Peru. In December of 1530, an expedition led by Francisco Pizarro (who was joined by three brothers and a cousin, all named Pizarro) and Diego de Almagro landed in Ecuador. They discovered that the Inca Empire was immersed in a civil war over the succession to the crown between the two brothers Huascar and Atahualpa, sons of the Inca Huayna Capac who had died a few years earlier from smallpox brought to the continent by the Spaniards. Atahualpa defeated his brother but was captured by the Spanish. He paid a vast ransom in gold and silver but when he demanded his release, the Spanish declared him a traitor and had him strangled and burned at the stake. The Spanish, who had been joined by Andean Indigenous fighters opposed to the Incas, then moved toward the Inca capital at Cusco, entering the city in November of 1533. Another son of Huayna Capac, Manco Inca, then joined the Spaniards[24] and continued collaborating with them until their mistreatment forced him into rebellion. Manco Inca laid siege to Cusco and nearly retook the city for the Incas, but he was finally defeated in 1536 and forced to retreat to Vilcabamba on the eastern side of the Andes with his followers. From there he and his successors harassed the Spanish until the conquistadors finally subdued that last Inca outpost in 1572 and captured and beheaded the Inca Tupac Amaru.[25] Much of this history is covered in chapter 12 in the writings of the Inca Titu Cusi Yupanqui.

The Spanish conquistadors also founded cities in other parts of South America in this period. Bogotá was founded in 1538 and a royal court established there in 1549 while Quito was founded in 1534 and its royal court set up in 1563. The expedition led by the Spaniard Pedro de Mendoza attempted the founding of Buenos Aires in Southern South America in 1536 and, while that attempt failed, the expedition was successful in founding Asunción, Paraguay. The letter written by the Spaniard Isabel de Guevara to Princess Juana of Spain describes those efforts in chapter 6. The second, successful, establishment of Buenos Aires took place in 1580.

Pedro Álvares Cabral of Portugal first landed in what is now Brazil in 1500 and although at the time Portugal was more interested in its trade with East Asia, dyewood (used for dying cloth) and some other products from Brazil found a market in Europe. As demand increased for dyewood, the Portuguese enslaved the local Native peoples, a practice that only increased with the establishment of permanent settlements and the introduction of sugar plantations in 1526. Indigenous peoples revolted against their horrific treatment, killing Brazil's first bishop, but by the early 1570s the Portuguese had defeated many Indigenous communities and eliminated the resistance of a French colony as well. Enslaved Africans were first brought to Brazil early in the sixteenth century, and their numbers greatly increased with the expansion of the sugar plantations in the seventeenth century.[26] Approximately 40 percent of all enslaved Africans were taken by Europeans to Brazil. Like the Indigenous peoples and the enslaved peoples of African descent everywhere in the Americas, enslaved Africans in Brazil rebelled continuously against their enslavers, often running away and in the process creating some of the largest Maroon (runaway) communities in the world.

THE SELECTIONS

The Indigenous writings included in this volume can be divided into two categories: 1) those that give us a picture of preconquest social and political arrangements and 2) those that describe conditions under the Spanish Empire and ask for changes in colonial policy. Among those that treat the preconquest period, the Kaqchikel Chronicles are a foundation narrative telling a story about how the Kaqchikel Maya community of Iximché was established.

Selections from the *General History of the Things of New Spain,* the Florentine Codex, compiled by the Spanish Franciscan Friar Bernardino de Sahagún describe leadership training, social hierarchy and gender relationships among the Mexica people as related to the Friar by Indigenous elders. El Inca Garcilaso de la Vega, one of Peru's first *mestizos* (the term used by the Spanish to refer to those who had a Spanish parent and an Indigenous parent), was influenced by utopian writing. In the selection included here he describes the training of leaders in the Inca Empire as well as the Empire's agricultural political economy, all in a society that was based, he said, on reason and the law of nature.

The letter to King Philip II from the Council of Huejotzingo is part of the second group of Indigenous writings and describes the town's collaboration with the Spanish in the fight against Huejotzingo's enemy, the Aztecs, to support a plea for lowering the high tribute they had been assigned to pay to the Spanish. The narration by Inca Tito Cusi Yupanqui of his father Manco Inca's long resistance to the Spanish conquest is part of a letter to the Spanish King asking for recognition as a prince of Peru under the Spanish crown and for compensation in accord with his status. And the selection chosen here from Guamán Poma de Ayala's vast 1,200-page work, *The First New Chronicle and Good Government,* which he sent to King Philip III, is a listing of the many ways in which Indigenous peoples in Peru were mistreated by the Spanish. Poma de Ayala also makes recommendations for improving Spanish policy. This writing is an example of what is often called "mirror of princes" literature, a genre of advice to rulers that can be found around the world.

Also included in the volume are two shorter politically significant letters, the first by a Spanish woman, Isabel de Guevara, who accompanied the expedition of the Spaniard Pedro de Mendoza to the Rio de La Plata region in South America and the second by Alonso de Illescas, the leader of a successful autonomous community of African and Indigenous peoples in what is now Ecuador. Isabel de Guevara wrote to the Spanish Crown to request compensation in the form of an allotment of Indigenous people for her participation, along with other Spanish women, in the first, unsuccessful, founding of Buenos Aires and the subsequent establishment of Asunción, a journey in which the Spanish men became sick from hunger and illness. Alonso de Illescas, the leader of one of the many communities in the Americas of Africans who had managed to escape from their European enslavers, wrote to the Spanish King Philip II asking him not to send a military mission into his province and saying that he could better pacify the local Indigenous peoples himself.

All of the writers mentioned thus far (as well as Luis de Carvajal, the Jewish convert to Catholicism who is discussed later in the Introduction) could be classified by some as subaltern, that is, writers who were outside the power structures of a colony, given that they were Indigenous and African men, men of Jewish ancestry, or European women. According to scholar Gayatri Spivak, however, the subaltern do not include members of dominant foreign groups (such as European women and men) or dominant Indigenous groups on the national, regional, or local level.[27] Nonetheless, the historian Mónica Díaz argues that defining subaltern in such a way "would easily annul many of the Indigenous subjects who have left a written record in Latin America."[28] Indeed, under Spivak's definition, Indigenous writers and ones of Indigenous or African ancestry in this volume would be considered members of a privileged elite rather than of a subaltern group. The historian Florencia Mallon also objects to Spivak's definition and adds that "no subaltern identity can be pure and transparent; most subalterns are both dominated and dominating subjects, depending on the circumstances of location in which we encounter them."[29]

The remaining writers are Spanish men from various walks of life, including Catholic priests and the explorers Christopher Columbus and Pedro Sarmiento de Gamboa. Columbus kept a log of his first voyage in which he explains how he took possession of the islands that he encountered for the Spanish monarchs. He lay down the principles of what would become known as the Doctrine of Discovery, denounced to this day by Original Peoples around the world for justifying their enslavement and the takeover of their lands.

Friar Antonio de Montesinos' 1511 Advent sermon to the Spanish elite of Santo Domingo in the Caribbean opened the discussion within the Spanish world on the nature of the Indigenous inhabitants of the Americas, their rights, and their treatment and, in fact, the legitimacy of the conquest, albeit all within a European Catholic framework.

These discussions were pursued in the following years by the philosophers and theologians at the University of Salamanca in Spain in what became known as the School of Salamanca under its founder Francisco de Vitoria. Two Spanish friars, Bartolomé de Las Casas and Alonso de la Vera Cruz, were able to add the knowledge gained from their many years of experience in the Americas to the late Scholastic philosophy of natural law they had studied at Salamanca. Las Casas regarded Indigenous peoples as rational creatures made in the image of (a Christian) God and thus as holders of rights under natural law, a position that many Spaniards did not share. Included in this volume are selections from his famous debate against Juan Ginés de Sepúlveda over the future of Spanish policy in the Americas. The debate took place in the Spanish city of Valladolid, and a major point of contention was whether the Indigenous inhabitants of the Americas were barbarians and thus natural slaves as defined by Aristotle, the position taken by Sepulveda.

Alonso de la Vera Cruz was the first theology professor at the University of Mexico when it was founded in 1553, and his first lectures became the basis of his treatise *De dominio infidelium et iusto bello* (On the Dominion of the Infidels and Just War) which defended the rights of Indigenous peoples to their lands. Vera Cruz was a practical philosopher, arguing for the rights of Indigenous peoples in relation to such topics as tributes, land expropriation, and distribution of wealth.

Friar Bernardino de Sahagún compiled information from Mexica individuals along with his own commentary in the *General History of the Things of New* Spain as part of efforts to convert Indigenous peoples to Christianity. At the same time, he admired many of the old customs and the manner in which the wise Indigenous elders were able to educate the young in ways that led to a virtuous society. Here I have counted the *General History* twice, once as Indigenous, and once as Spanish for the commentaries of Friar Bernardino.

Navigator, writer, and soldier Pedro Sarmiento de Gamboa wrote *The History of the Incas* at the direction of Spanish Viceroy of Peru Francisco Toledo in an attempt to prove that the Incas were not natural lords in their lands because their rule was tyrannical, and their customs violated natural law. He was doing his research at the same time Titu Cusi Yupanqui was writing the king asserting the very opposite.

Luis de Carvajal the Younger was the leader of a group of clandestine practitioners of the Jewish faith in New Spain. His writings and accompanying materials from his Inquisition trial are emblematic of a period before the rise of religious toleration in European history in which subjects who did not subscribe to the form of religion of their current monarch were persecuted and frequently condemned to death.

In his manual for the ministry of his fellow Jesuit priests to the enslaved Africans disembarking from the slave ships at Cartagena, Alonso de Sandoval emphasized that Blacks and whites were equal in the eyes of God. Although he described the evils of slavery and the slave trade with abundant detail and strongly condemned mistreatment, ultimately, he stated that he would leave the question of the justice of the institution to others. This position was not at all surprising given that the Jesuits, like most other Catholic religious orders, used enslaved workers themselves on plantations that financially supported their missions.

UNEQUAL ENCOUNTERS

The title of this volume, *Unequal Encounters*, introduces the principal theme of the writings included here: the encounter of the peoples of two continents who had not been aware of the existence of the others, in circumstances where one group (Europeans) were eager to conquer and colonize the other (Indigenous peoples). There were discussions among the Spanish of what kind of beings the Indigenous people were and how they should be treated. Friar Antonio de Montesinos asked rhetorically in 1511 about the Indigenous people, "Are they not human beings? Have they not rational souls?" Decades later, the Inca Titu Cusi Yupanqui described how his father Manco Inca stated that the arriving Spaniards were sons of Viracocha (God) but later their behavior revealed that they were "the sons not of Viracocha but of the Devil."

The encounters were most certainly unequal. Columbus noted that the Indigenous individuals he first encountered in what is today believed to be the Bahamas did not have weapons and did not use iron and steel. He said, "I showed them swords which they grasped by the blades and cut themselves through ignorance." And European diseases eventually killed millions of Indigenous people. Bernardino de Sahagún wrote of the plagues in Mexico of 1520, of 1545 in which he said he personally buried 10,000, and of the plague of 1576 which was raging as he wrote. Almost too obvious to require mention is the appropriateness of the title of historian Jared Diamond's book on the fate of human societies to the situation of the Americas. *Guns, Germs, and Steel*, the title of Diamond's famous book, applies here. Also appropriate is the philosopher Enrique Dussel's point that while we can speak of the encounter of two cultures, "the reality is that the Iberian-European culture tore the indigenous cultures apart."[30]

Not surprisingly, in many early colonial Indigenous writings there was a profound sadness and nostalgia for a time of order, before the arrival of the Spanish, when things were in their proper places. Because it was mainly the Indigenous elites who, after the conquest, were in a position to write, either themselves or through scribes, the nostalgia was for a time when they and their families enjoyed the respect of their people and the tribute that provided them with a comfortable life. The members of the Council of Huejotzingo wrote to the Spanish King, "Of the way in which our fathers and grandfathers and great-grandfathers were rich and honored, there is no longer the slightest trace among us," and, "Now we resemble the commoners; as they eat and dress, so do we."

In some cases, it was more than nostalgia. Some writers showed anger and resistance. Titu Cusi described how his father called his people to rebellion and, when that failed, into exile in Vilcabamba, the famous "lost city of the Incas." Manco Inca asked his people to resist conversion to Christianity saying, "[T]hey may order you to worship what they themselves worship, namely some sort of painted rags [probably a bible or prayerbook] that they claim to be Viracocha. . . . Don't do it but keep with what we have, for, as you can see, the *villcas* speak to us; we can see the sun and the moon with our own eyes. . ."[31] Guamán Poma de Ayala grew angry as he described the mistreatment of the Indigenous peoples by the Spaniards, a situation which he said had turned the earth upside down. He then explained how the Spanish King could bring back order to the kingdom of Peru and have the Indigenous people multiply again. First, he denounced the fact that the local Spanish magistrates became rich, "harming the poor Indians and the [Indian] nobles, scorning them, and taking away their offices and duties." Then he told the king that, "in every province, these Indian men, women and children should be gathered into some old pueblo, for they are lost." He advised further, "Give them cropland and bounded pastures, so that they may serve God and Your Majesty. Let them be called your royal crown Indians."

While the Spaniards were conquering ever more territory in the so-called New World by force of arms, enslaving some Indigenous peoples and assigning allotments of other Indigenous peoples to work for Spaniards without pay, putting them to mine gold and silver, converting them to Christianity, and watching them die by the millions from disease and overwork, they worried about the justice of the conquest and how an angry Catholic God would judge them. Or at least some of the friars worried and, surprisingly, the Spanish monarchs appeared to worry. Queen Isabella said in her will that Indigenous peoples should have the same rights as her Castilian subjects. King Ferdinand called councils to discuss laws for the Indies. King Charles I, their grandson, who was also the Holy Roman Emperor Charles V, temporarily suspended all conquests in 1549 and called theologians to debate their justice in 1550–1551. And King Philip II listened closely to the friars even if he often did not follow their guidance.

It so happened that, whether as a cause or an effect of this questioning of the New World conquests, there was a flowering of the philosophy of natural law in Spain in the sixteenth century, called the Second Scholastic (the first being that of Thomas Aquinas in the thirteenth century). The movement was also affected by Renaissance humanism. Under its teacher, Francisco de Vitoria at the University of Salamanca, it would give rise to a theory of human rights that would be different from, and take place 150 years before, the writings by John Locke and other Enlightenment figures on the law of nature and on natural rights. The contemporary legal scholar Jesús de la Torre states that both Enlightenment thought and the earlier Spanish thought emphasize natural law. De la Torre contends, however, that Enlightenment thought was eminently rationalist and placed the emphasis on individual rights while the Spaniards referred back to Christian thought on the liberation of the oppressed and the treatment of the poor.[32]

Another important question for the Spaniards, Indigenous peoples, and enslaved Africans was conversion to Christianity, and in particular, whether people should be converted by force. This was a time in European history when the accepted idea was that the people had to accept the religion of their monarch at least outwardly, and indeed this principle was formalized with the Peace of Augsburg in 1555. Complicating this, Pope Alexander in 1493 had "given" to Spain and Portugal their sections of the newly "discovered" lands in the Americas based on their promise to convert the inhabitants to Christianity.

In the Americas, the Indigenous population had not previously heard of Christianity, and there was much discussion among the Spanish of how best to convert them from their old religions to Catholicism. There was, however, very little written by the Spanish on whether Indigenous peoples and enslaved Africans had the right to conserve their old religions and reject the new religion, even though most of the friars in charge of ministering to them supposedly believed in free will and believed that acceptance of the faith had to be freely given.

Friar Alonso de la Vera Cruz's argument was more than a little contradictory. He said that unbelievers "may be coerced into accepting baptism and the faith, not so that they pretend to believe but that they will want to believe with all their heart what they formerly rejected." Dussel notes a different contradiction in Bartolomé de Las Casas saying that Las Casas firmly believed that the Spanish had the obligation to preach the Christian Gospel to Indigenous peoples even though he steadfastly maintained that they did not have the obligation to accept it.[33] Alonso de Sandoval, who ministered to the recently arrived enslaved Africans in Cartagena, seemed to believe that interpreters were the answer: "Sometimes, very rarely, the slaves do not want to be baptized. . . . But usually, like bestial people who live among us, such as captured Moors or Englishmen, the slaves simply do not understand our language."

It is important to note the impact of the works we study here on later history and even the present day. Bartolomé de Las Casas (a pariah among some in Spain until fairly recently because of his vivid descriptions of Spanish colonial cruelty) inspired many Latin American revolutionaries, including Simón Bolívar. El Inca Garcilaso de la Vega's works inspired thinkers from the French Encyclopedists of the 1700s to the *Indigenista* movement of the 1930s in Peru and Mexico. On the other hand, repudiation of Columbus and the Doctrine of Discovery has recently led to the changing of the name of Columbus Day to Indigenous Peoples' Day in many places.

Names are also an important issue to address before we conclude. There is no perfect term for the lands that we are discussing. The term "Western Hemisphere" was not in use in the sixteenth century. The term "the Indies" was incorrect at the time and sounds archaic. The term "New World" was evidently coined early but, of course, is Eurocentric; the lands were not new to their inhabitants. As historian Arthur P. Whitaker stated, to the Native Americans "the New World was Europe."[34] In spite of their faults, I use "Indies" and "New World" frequently and interchangeably, sometimes in quotes. I also use "Americas" to refer to the entire continent, from Canada to Argentina. I use "Indigenous people" and "Amerindian" interchangeably to refer to the original inhabitants of the Americas. Peru is Peru. But Mexico I generally refer to as New Spain (unless referring specifically to what we call today in English Mexico City and its surroundings).

The spelling of the transliteration of Indigenous words also requires some attention. Following the guidance of the Academy of Mayan Languages of Guatemala, I use the spelling Kaqchikel for the first selection in this volume, the Kaqchikel Chronicles, except where I am quoting older sources that use the spelling Cakchiquel. In the case of the Council of Huejotzingo, I discuss the issue of names in the introduction to their letter. But, for the Andes, the issue is more complicated. Quechua is a family of languages and different regions have different ways of speaking. As a result, the names of places and of the Inca rulers have been spelled in many different ways in Spanish. I have therefore chosen to follow the most common version of the spelling of Quechua words and names, recognizing that it could be a somewhat controversial choice.

It is my hope that further volumes such as this one will be published in the future on the seventeenth and eighteenth centuries in order to fill important gaps in the study of Latin American political thought. Fortunately, the nineteenth and twentieth centuries have been more thoroughly studied, although subalterns are still sometimes ignored, an ongoing problem since they constitute the vast majority of the population in Latin American societies as they do elsewhere. Given that every region of the world has a history of ideas about how their societies have been structured in the past and prescriptions for how they could better be run in the future, the field of political theory can benefit greatly from their study.

NOTES

1. George H. Sabine and Thomas Landon Thorson, *A History of Political Thought* (Orlando, Holt, Rinehart and Winston, Inc., 1973), 3.

2. Matthew Restall and Kris Lane, *Latin America in Colonial Times* (Cambridge: Cambridge University Press, 2011), 12–16.

3. Carlos Fuentes, *The Buried Mirror: Reflections on Spain and the New World* (Boston: Houghton Mifflin Company, 1992), 96–99.

4. Mark A. Burkholder, Monica Rankin, and Lyman L. Johnson, *Exploitation, Inequality, and Resistance: A History of Latin America since Columbus* (Oxford: Oxford University Press, 2018), 7.

5. Michael A. Malpass, *Ancient Peoples of the Andes* (Ithaca: Cornell University Press, 2016), 54–58; "First City in the New World? Peru's Caral suggests civilization emerged in the Americas 1,000 years earlier than experts believed," *Smithsonian Magazine* (August 2002) https://www.smithsonianmag.com/history/first-city-in-the-new-world-66643778/; Daniel H. Sandweiss, Ruth Shady Solís, Michael E. Moseley, David K. Keefer, and Charles R. Ortloff, "Environmental Change and Economic Development in Coastal Peru between 5,800 and 3,600 Years Ago," *Proceedings of the National Academy of Sciences of the United States of America* 106, no. 5 (2009): 1359.

6. "Cities of Caral-Supe (Peru) and Levoca (Slovakia) added to UNESCO's World Heritage List," *UNESCO News and Events* (June 28, 2009) https://whc.unesco.org/en/news/534/.

7. "Andean Civilizations," Arizona Museum of Natural History: Cultures of the Ancient Americas, accessed June 13, 2021, https://www.arizonamuseumofnaturalhistory.org/explore-the-museum/exhibitions/cultures-of-the-ancient-americas/andean-civilizations; Jason Golomb, "Why the Nasca lines are among Peru's greatest mysteries," National Geographic History and Culture—Reference, accessed June 13, 2021, https://www.nationalgeographic.com/history/article/nasca-lines?loggedin=true.

8. Malpass, *Ancient*, chapters 7 and 8.

9. Burkholder, et al., *Exploitation*, 7–8.

10. Charles C. Mann, *1491: New Revelations of the Americas Before Columbus* (New York: Alfred A. Knopf, 2005), 323–25

11. Jonas Gregorio de Souza and colleagues, "Pre-Columbian earth-builders settled along the entire southern rim of the Amazon," *Nature Communications* (March 27, 2018) https://www.nature.com/articles/s41467–018–03510–7#citeas.

12. Burkholder, et al., *Exploitation*, 11.

13. Burkholder, et al., *Exploitation*, 12–13; The Benin bronzes (which are actually brass) were stolen in the nineteenth century from Benin City and taken to museums in Europe and elsewhere. The Metropolitan Museum in New York announced in June of 2021 that it was returning two bronzes to Nigeria, where Benin City is located. Sarah Bahr, "Met Museum Announces Return of Two Benin Bronzes to Nigeria," *New York Times* (June 9, 2021) https://www.nytimes.com/2021/06/09/arts/design/met-museum-benin-bronzes-nigeria.html.

14. Burkholder, et al., *Exploitation,* 13.

15. "Voyages: The Trans-Atlantic Slave Trade Database," Voyages Database, Emory University, last modified 2009, https://slavevoyages.org/assessment/estimates; Burkholder, *Exploitation*, 15.

16. Roger L. Martínez-Dávila, Josef Díaz, and Ron D. Hart, *Fractured Faiths: Spanish Judaism, the Inquisition, and New World Identities* (Santa Fe: New Mexico History Museum, 2016) 107.

A PBS documentary released in 2019, *The Ornament of the World*, tells of this period "during which the three groups managed for the most part to sustain relationships that enabled them to coexist, collaborate and flourish." https://www.pbs.org/show/ornament-world/.

17. Restall and Lane, *Latin America*, 20.

18. Burkholder, et al., *Exploitation*, 2–3.

19. For readers interested in more about the conquest of Mexico, here are two epic tales. First, from the Indigenous point of view, "Book Twelve" of the *General History of the Things of New Spain: Florentine Codex*, compiled by Bernardino de Sahagún, translated into English by Arthur J. O. Anderson and Charles E. Dibble (Salt Lake City: University of Utah Press, 1982). Second, written by one of the conquerors, Bernal Díaz del Castillo, *The History of the Conquest of New Spain*, translated by Alfred Maudsley and edited by Davíd Carrasco (Albuquerque: University of New Mexico Press, 2008).

20. Burkholder, et al., *Exploitation,* 32–33; Fuentes, *The Buried,* 113–117.

21. Burkholder, et al., *Exploitation,* 32–33; Restall and Lane, *Latin America*, 88–89, 91–92

22. Livia Gershon, "Mexico City Marks 500th Anniversary of the Fall of Tenochtitlán," *Smithsonian Magazine Smart News* (May 24, 2021) https://www.smithsonianmag.com/smart-news/mexico-city-marks-500th-anniversary-fall-tenoch titlan-180977794/; "Mexico Demands Apology from Spain and the Vatican over Conquest," *BBC News* (March 26, 2019) https://www.bbc.com/news/world-latin-america-47701876.

23. Restall and Lane, *Latin America*, 92.

24. Burkholder, et al., *Exploitation*, 36–37.

25. Restall and Lane, *Latin America*, 96.

26. Burkholder, et al., *Exploitation*, 42, 112–113.

27. Gayatri Chakravorty Spivak, "Can the Subaltern Speak?" *Marxism and the Interpretation of Culture*, ed. By Cary Nelson and Lawrence Grossberg (Urbana and Chicago: University of Illinois Press, 1988), 284.

28. Mónica Díaz, *Indigenous Writings from the Convent: Negotiating Ethnic Autonomy in Colonial Mexico* (Tucson: University of Arizona Press, 2010), 17.

29. Florencia E. Mallon, "The Promise and Dilemma of Subaltern Studies: Perspectives from Latin American History," *The American Historical Review* 99, no. 5 (Dec. 1994): 1482.

30. Enrique Dussel, "The Discovery of an Invasion," trans. Gary McEoin in *CrossCurrents* 41, no. 4 (Winter 1991–1992): 444.

31. These quotations and all uncited quotations that follow can be found in the selections included in the reader.

32. Jesús de la Torre Rangel, *Alonso de la Veracruz: amparo de los indios. Su teoría y práctica jurídica* (Aguascalientes: Universidad Autónoma de Aguascalientes, 1998), 93.

33. Enrique Dussel, "Origen de la filosofía política moderna: Las Casas, Vitoria y Suarez," *Caribbean Studies* 33, no. 2 (Jul.–Dec. 2005): 43, 48.

34. Arthur P. Whitaker, "The Origin of the Western Hemisphere Idea," *Proceedings of the American Philosophical Society* 98, no. 5 (Oct. 15, 1954): 323.

Chapter One

The Kaqchikel Maya
"Go To Where You Will See Your Mountains"

The Annals of the Cakchiquels or *Kaqchikel Chronicles* are a combination of legend, of history, and a chronicle of daily life of the Kaqchikel people written in the Kaqchikel Mayan language using the Spanish alphabet. (Except where quoted sources use the spelling Cakchiquel, the spelling used by the Academy of Mayan Languages of Guatemala, Kaqchikel, will be used.) The first part of the Annals describes the founding of the Mayan Kaqchikel community in the highlands of Guatemala and thus can be seen as a foundation narrative—the story of the political beginning of a community often embellished with heroic deeds and miracles.

The *Annals* can be divided into five parts. They are: 1) the founding narrative of the Kaqchikels (where the selection included in this volume can be found); 2) a history of the Kaqchikels up to a 1493 uprising; 3) history from 1493 to the Spanish conquest in 1524; 4) the story of the conquest and Indigenous resistance during the years 1524–1540; and finally, 5) a year by year listing of events in the Kaqchikel community, beginning with the instruction of the members of the community in the Christian faith in 1541, and ending in 1604.

The Annals are believed to have been written during the last half of the sixteenth century by two or possibly three members of the Xahil family, which was one of the ruling families of the Kaqchikels. King Hunyg ruled the Kaqchikels from 1508 to 1521. His son may have begun writing the chronicle before 1560, but what is known for sure is that his grandson, Francisco Hernández Arana, wrote from the 1570s until shortly before his death in 1581. A relative of the previous scribes, Francisco Díaz, continued the writing of the document until 1604, turning it into a history of the yearly events of the community.[1] The pre-Hispanic section was written by the King's grandson Hernández Arana based on stories his forefathers told him.

19

But, as a high-ranking member of Kaqchikels ruling family, he probably had a book or codex from among those not destroyed right after the conquest that served as his primary source for the first part of the chronicle.[2] Anthropologist Robert M. Hill II argues that the original manuscript included drawings, saying that "a significant part of the alphabetic text had been redacted from pictographic documents with origins firmly in the late preconquest highland Mesoamerican tradition."[3]

The document was copied by a professional scribe, probably sometime between 1620 and 1650, and that is the version that has come down to the present day. It was used by church historian Francisco Vázquez between 1714 and 1716 to write his "Papers of the Indians" and then rediscovered by Guatemalan scholar Juan Gavarrete in a Franciscan monastery in 1844. The French Abbot Charles Etienne Brasseur de Bourbourg visited Guatemala in 1855 to study the history and native languages of the country and when Gavarrete showed him the Kaqchikel document, he translated it into French, made a copy of the translation to leave in Guatemala, and took the original document to Europe! While the Abbot maintained that Gavarrete gave him the original, Gavarrete himself wrote, "The original text, nevertheless, remained with him,"[4] giving the impression that he did not willingly give it up. Gavarrete published a Spanish translation of the French copy in 1873.[5]

Nineteenth-century archaeologist Daniel Brinton purchased the original document in France in 1884 following the death of Brasseur and, after translating the *Annals* into English, gave the original to the museum of the library of the University of Pennsylvania in Philadelphia, where it remains to this day.[6]

Historian Adrian Recinos completed a new translation of the document into Spanish in 1950 and collaborated with Delia Goetz on an English version in 1953. The Recinos and Goetz translation is used here. In 2006, Judith Maxwell and Robert M. Hill II published a definitive translation with line-by-line interpretation and explanation of the text[7] which would have made it difficult to use in this reader.

The *Annals* tell us that, at the time of the conquest, there were four nations living in the Guatemalan highlands, the K'iche' (who were the most numerous), the Kaqchikels, the Tz'utujils and the Akahals. Pedro de Alvarado entered the Kaqchikel capital city of Iximché at the head of a Spanish army on April 13, 1524. One of his captains, Bernal Díaz de Castillo, the conquistador and chronicler of the conquest of Mexico, visited the city later that year and noted that "its buildings and residences were fine and rich, as might be expected of chiefs who ruled all the neighboring provinces."[8] The Kaqchikels at first welcomed the Spanish but later rebelled because of oppressive treatment.[9]

The Kaqchikels, along with their neighbors and rivals, formed one branch of the Indigenous Maya whose glorious civilization had its beginnings before

Figure 1.1.   The ruins of the Kaqchiquel capital of Iximché
Photo by Katherine Hoyt

1000 BCE. The Mayan civilization reached its classical period between 200 and 900 CE, when the great city-states of Tikal, Caracol, Copán, and others flourished.[10] The Maya were also influenced by Toltec migration probably between 900 and 1250 CE. The *Annals* begin with a story from this Toltec migration. Daniel Brinton, writing in 1885, maintained that the Toltecs did not exist and that the tale included here of the journey of Kaqchikel founders from the Toltec center of Tola or Tulan or Tollan to the Guatemalan highlands was an imaginative myth with no basis in actual history.[11]

More recent archaeological studies, however, have shown that the Toltecs did, of course, exist. Their civilization flourished between the 900s to the middle of the 1200s in southern and central Mexico. Their inheritance from the Mayan civilization that preceded them can be seen in their capital of Tollan from which the migrants in the story of the Kaqchikel set off. The mixing of Mayan and Toltec civilizations can best be seen at Chichén Itzá on the Yucatan Peninsula in southern Mexico, where current archaeological scholarship indicates that a multiethnic city-state emerged as a "cultural convergence" rather than the imposition of the Toltec culture upon the Mayan.[12]

According to the narrative, the founders of the K'iche' and Kaqchikel communities migrated from the North along the coast of the Gulf of Mexico, then across the Yucatan peninsula, finally settling in the mountains of present-day Guatemala.[13] These travelers' forefathers and mothers could have been part of the out-migration from the Mayan lowlands following the downfall of

the major cities after 900 CE. Scholars do agree that, whatever the veneer
of Toltec influence based on an influx of immigration between the tenth
and thirteenth centuries, the language and culture of the peoples of highland
Guatemala were, at the time of the arrival of the Spaniards, and remain today,
Mayan.[14]

The first part of the *Annals* is a foundation narrative. In that way it differs
from the Popul Vuh, to which it is often compared. The Popul Vuh is a creation narrative that tells how the K'iche Maya people were created from corn.
Foundation narratives tell the stories passed from generation to generation in
oral or written form about how a particular political entity began, what the
inhabitants brought with them from the place from which they had migrated
and what distinguishes their polity from other nations or cities, often their
particular form of government. The most ancient of these tales have usually
included unlikely events (the most famous being the nursing by a she-wolf
of the twins Romulus and Remus who later founded Rome), miracles, and
intervention by sundry oracles, gods, or goddesses. Scholar Walter Wilson
notes that "explicit theological sanction is fundamental to colonization tales,
usually taking the form of oracular consultation, sacrificial divination and/or
dream interpretation"[15] or, as in this case, a talking obsidian stone.

The tales have until recently been assumed to be fictitious. Wilson notes
that "It is not surprising that scholars often speak of foundational accounts as
myths, unified stories formed by traditional narrative patterns that seek to val-
idate certain social arrangements and practices by explaining how they came
into being through the activity of both human and suprahuman entities."[16]

An example, of course, is Brinton's dismissal of the Toltecs (from whose
capital the Kaqchikels supposedly traveled) as being "a purely imaginary
people" and his accusation that those who took the narrative seriously were
"mistaking myth for history."[17] Archaeology and DNA testing, however,
have shown that, in many cases, foundation myths that tell stories hundreds
or even thousands of years old have a basis in fact. In this case, the excava-
tion at Chichén Itzá and other sites has shown the mixing of the Toltec and
Mayan cultures[18] and thus confirmed the possible veracity of the foundation
narrative in the *Annals*.

Today, there are between five and six million Mayan people, speaking
around thirty Mayan languages, living in Guatemala, Mexico, Belize, Hon-
duras, and El Salvador. This is after an estimated 200,000 Mayan Indigenous
people were killed by the military in the Guatemalan civil war that lasted
from 1962 to 1996. This war, in which the Mayans composed 83 percent
of the victims, was one of the conflicts between governments and left-wing
guerrilla forces in Central America in that period that were painted by the
United States as wars against Communism. The UN-sponsored Historical

Clarification Commission (HEC) in its 1999 report stated that US anti-Communism was supported by powerful actors in Guatemala and that the United States showed it was willing to "provide support for strong military regimes in its strategic backyard."[19] The HEC report goes on to describe the conflict and how it affected the Mayans, who were targeted by the government independently of whether they were associated with the guerrillas:

> The massacres, scorched earth operations, forced disappearances and executions of Mayan authorities, leaders and spiritual guides, were not only an attempt to destroy the social base of the guerrillas, but above all, to destroy the cultural values that ensured cohesion and collective action in Mayan communities.[20]

The Maya and their languages and customs survived but their population still suffers from poverty and exploitation. Rigoberta Menchú, a member of the K'iche' Maya and a human rights activist during the most difficult years of the civil war, was awarded the Nobel Peace Prize in 1992. In the year 2000, she said, "Struggles for the rights of poor people, for dignity, for human life, seem to be very, very dark tunnels, but one should always try, in that struggle, to find some light and some hope."[21] With their three-millennia-long cultural history, the Mayans are determined to continue into the future.

The Kaqchikel narrative begins with the story of a gathering in Tulán of the seven Mayan tribes and their departure to find their own "mountains and valleys." The two leaders of the Kaqchikels are Gagavitz and Zactecauh under the high Mayan lords Gekaquch, Baqahol, and Zibakihay. After leading the Kaqchikels in a battle against the Zuyva where they had to fight even the domestic animals, Zactecauh follows Gagavitz over a ravine but missteps and falls into the ravine. Thus one of the leaders is lost. Further adventures follow. Gagavitz enters into an active volcano to put out the fire and emerges safely. Even when they find their new homes, the people suffer from lack of food and clothing until they begin to plant corn. When Gagawitz dies, his two sons Caynoh and Caybatz are still young but, with the support of one of the great lords, the practitioner of witchcraft Tepeuh, they became corulers of the Kaqchikels. And, as the narrative states, "thus our grandfathers completed their government among themselves."

THE ANNALS OF THE CAKCHIQUELS

Here I shall write a few stories of our first fathers and ancestors, those who begot man of old, before these mountains and valleys were inhabited, when there were only rabbits and birds, so they said; when our fathers and grandfathers went to populate the mountains and valleys, oh, my sons! In Tulan.

I shall write the stories of our first fathers and grandfathers, one of whom was called Gagavitz, the other Zactecauh; the stories that they told to us; that from the other side of the sea we came to the place called Tulán, where we were begotten and given birth by our mothers and our fathers, oh, our sons! . . .

[W]e were commanded by our mothers and our fathers to come, we the thirteen clans of the seven tribes, the thirteen groups of warriors. Then we arrived at Tulán in the darkness and in the night. Then we gave the tribute, when the seven tribes and the warriors carried the tribute. We took our places in order at the left part of Tulán. There were the seven tribes. In the right part of Tulán the warriors took their places in order. First the seven tribes paid the tribute, and afterwards the warriors paid the tribute. But this consisted only of precious stones [jade], metal, garlands fastened with green and blue feathers, and paintings and sculptures. They offered flutes, songs, ritual calendars, astronomical calendars, pataxte [a fruit like cocoa], and cocoa. Only with these riches the warriors went to pay tribute to Tulán. Only arrows and shields, only shields of wood were the riches they gave as tribute when they came to Tulán.

Then it was said and commanded to our mothers: "Go, my sons, my daughters, these shall be your tasks, the labor with which we charge you." Thus the Obsidian Stone spoke to them. "Go to where you will see your mountains and your valleys; there on the other side of the sea are mountains and your valleys, oh, my sons! There your countenances shall be gladdened. These are the gifts I shall give to you, your wealth and your domain." Thus they spoke to the thirteen clans of the seven tribes, to the thirteen divisions of warriors. Then they gave to them the deceitful idols [Editor's note: The authors at the time of writing had been converted to Christianity.] of wood and of stone, so they said, our first fathers and ancestors, Gagavitz and Zactecauh. These were their gifts and these were their words also. . . .

The first who arrived were the Quichés. Then the month of Tacaxepeual was fixed for the payment of tribute by the Quichés; then came their companions, one after another, the houses, the families, the clans, each group of warriors, when they arrived at Tulán, when they had all arrived.

The Rabinal arrived, the Zotzils, the Tukuchés, the Tuhalahay, the Vuchabahay, the Ah Chumilahay; the Lamaquis arrived also, the Cumatz and the Akahals. . . . Then we, the Cakchiquels, arrived. Truly, we were the last to arrive at Tulán. And no other came after we arrived, so said Gagavitz and Zactecauh.

In this manner they advised us: "These are your families, your clans," they said to Gekaquch, Baqahol, and Zibakihay. These shall be your chiefs, one is the Ahpop, the other the Ahpop Qamahay. Thus they spoke to Gekaquch, Baqahol, and Zibakihay. "Procreate daughters, engender sons, marry among yourselves, the lords," they said to them. . . . Then we were told: "Truly, your tribute shall be great. Do not sleep and you shall conquer, you shall not be disparaged, my sons. You shall grow great; you shall be powerful. Thus you will possess shields, riches, arrows, and bucklers, and they shall be yours. If they pay you tribute in precious stones, metal, green and blue feathers, songs that you scorn, they shall be yours also; you shall be the most favored, and your countenance shall be gladdened. The stones of jade, the metal, the green and blue feathers, the paintings and sculptures, all things that the seven tribes have paid, shall gladden you in your own country; you shall be favored, and your eyes shall be gladdened with your arrows and your shields. You shall have one principal chief and another younger one. To you the thirteen warriors, to you the thirteen lords, to you the chiefs of equal rank, I will give your bows and your shields. Soon your countenances shall be gladdened by the things you shall receive as tribute, your bows and your shields. There is war there in the east, in the place called Zuyva; there you shall go to prove your bows and your shields that I will give you. Go there, my sons!" Thus they spoke to us when we went to Tulán. . . .

[W]e embarked in the canoes of the Nonoualcas, and turning toward the east, we soon arrived there. They were truly formidable, the city and the houses of the Zuyva, there in the east. When we had reached the edge of the houses, we began to attack them as soon as we arrived. It was indeed terrible when we found ourselves among the houses; there was truly a great clamor. A cloud of dust arose when we arrived; we fought in their houses, we fought with their dogs, with their poultry, we fought with their domestic animals. We attacked once; we attacked twice, until we were routed. Some came from the sky, others walked on the ground, some came down, others climbed up, all of them against us, using their magic art and their incantations.

One by one all the warriors returned to the places of Tapcu and Olomán. "Filled with sadness, we gathered there again and there also we stripped off our feathers and we took off our ornaments, oh, our sons!" Thus spoke Gagavitz and Zactecauh.

Then we asked: "Where is your salvation?" Thus we said to the Quichés. "Since it thunders and resounds in the sky, in the sky is our salvation," they said. Wherefore they were given the name of Tohohils.

And the Zotzils said: "Only in the beak of the macaw can we live and be safe." And therefore they were called the Cakix [macaws].

Then we the Cakchiquels spoke: "Only in the middle of the prairie will be our salvation, when we reach that land." And consequently they called us Chitagah.

Others, called Cucumatz, said that there was salvation only in the water.

The Tukuchés said that salvation was in a high village, and consequently they were called the Ahcic-amag.

And the Akahals said: "We shall only be saved inside a beehive," and so they were given the name of Akahals.

In this way all of them received their [respective] names, and there were many of them. But it is not believed that they were all saved. It should not be forgotten either that the names of all of them came from the east. "It was the devil who came to separate us," said Gagavitz and Zactecauh.

And we said when we inquired for our mountains and our valleys: "Let us test our bows and our shields wherever we have to fight. Now let us seek our homes and our valley." Thus we said. Whereupon we dispersed in the mountains; then we all departed, each tribe took its road, each family followed its own. . . .

Having arrived at the place of Chopi-Ytzel, Gagavitz said to Zactecauh: "We shall cross this ravine." "It is well," he answered. Gagavitz crossed first, and then Zactecauh wished to cross, but he could not do it, and he fell into the ravine. Thus died one of our forefathers; they were separated, and only one, Gagavitz, it was who brought us forth, us the Xahilá.

They soon came for the second time to the places of Zakihuyú and Teyocumán. There they looked upon the volcano called Gagxanul [now called Santa Maria]. The fire which emerged from inside the mountain was truly terrifying. It spouted a long distance. No one could tell how to get inside, because the Gagxanul had been burning for a year and it was impossible to reach the fire. All the warriors of the seven tribes had reached the foot of the mountain, but no one spoke a word because truly their hearts were sore. Nor could they tell how they might capture the fire. There was nothing to do but to wait. And they said to our grandfather Gagavitz when he came to the foot of the volcano, all the warriors said to him: "Oh, you, our brother, you have arrived, and you are our hope. Who will go to bring us the fire and to try our luck in this manner, oh, my brother?" Thus they said. And we answered them: "Who wishes me to go and try our luck? He who does not fear has the heart of a hero." "I will go first"—Gagavitz said to them—"but I do not wish you to be filled with fear so quickly." Truly, it was frightening to look upon the volcano.

Nevertheless there was one Zakitzunún [white sparrow] who wished to go. "I will go with you," said Zakitzunún to Gagavitz. At once they adorned and decorated themselves, and they said one to the other: "No bows or shields!" They took off their clothes, and they covered themselves with gourds, with folded green stalks, and with fresh leaves, and they provided themselves with water. Then they put their heads in, they put in their necks, and [crawling along] with their elbows, their arms and legs went in to put out the fire. So they related. Then Gagavitz descended inside the fire, while Zaquitzunún threw the water over the fire. The green stems of corn mixed with the water that was thrown over the fire. Truly, it was frightening to go down into the mountain, and when the fire of the volcano was extinguished, a great deal of smoke burst forth and spread for a great distance and made darkness and night.

All those who were at the foot of the volcano fled full of terror. Gagavitz stayed for a long time in the volcano, the sun set, and their hearts were filled with anguish. The fire had been captured, but not for them. Some sparks emerged and fell to the foot of the volcano. They went there, but they could not reach them. At last Gagavitz came out from inside the volcano. Truly, his appearance made them afraid when he came out of the mountain called Gagxanul. All the warriors of the seven tribes exclaimed: "Truly, it is terrifying, his magic power, his greatness and majesty: he has destroyed and made captive [the fire]." Thus they said.

As soon as he returned, they set him upon the throne, they did him great honor, and all of them said to him: "You, our brother, have conquered the fire of the mountain and have given us our fire. You are two heroes, one is the first hero and the other the second hero. You are our chiefs, our guiding heads." Thus all the warriors of the seven tribes said to Gagavitz. And he answered them: "The spirit of the mountain has become my slave and my captive, oh, my brothers! When we conquered the spirit of the mountain, we freed the stone of fire, the stone called Zacchog, which is not a precious stone. There are thirteen other stones with it. Hence comes the dance of the Ixtzul, of the spirit of the Volcano Gagxanul." They say that the dance of the Ixtzul was very violent, that it was danced by many groups making an indescribable noise. . . .

When all this happened, the dawn had not yet broken, so they said, but soon after it began to be light. Then they arrived at the place of Pulchich, from which place they left in groups.

This was their Dawn.

The first to go were Gekaquch, Baqahol, Zibakihay, and Cavek, and they went in groups. "You, your families, your clans, be the first to arrive and work, lay the foundations of our buildings because the sun will soon begin to rise. Go!" they said to them. Thereupon they departed, and they came to the places where their sun was to rise, Pantzic, Paraxone, Zimahihay, Pazibakul, Pacavek, and Quehil, as the places were called where their dawn came. They began to build their houses, and there they encountered their chief called Nimahay. The first who built were the first who arrived, Gekaquch, Zibaki-hay, and Cavek. . . .

They became numerous in the place where their sun rose. Three branches of our people saw the dawn there, the Zotzils, the Cakchiquels, and the Tu-kuchés. The Akahals were a little farther off, in the middle of the mountain where the dawn came for the three branches of the people. In the Tohohil Mountain, the dawn broke for the Quichés; in the Zamaneb Mountain came the dawn for the Rabinals. The Zutuhils wished to see their dawn in Tzala, but the tribes had not finished making the fire when the sun rose. They had not yet gone to Tzala when [the sun] rose in the sky and, mounting above the place called Queletat, spread its light and came to Xepoyom.

The warriors and the tribes quickly abandoned [those places] without doing their work, because they wished to go immediately to be united again and to live on the shores of the lake. At that time the tribes were frightened when, as if by magic, the bird of green feathers [the quetzal] crossed the sky, and they heard his loud caws as he crossed the sky. The women of Tzununaa, of Tzololaa, and of Ahachel and Vaiza were watching it in this manner. It was flying over the water, and half of the people hurried to see it.

These are the hardships which they endured while they were there:

"Truly, we endured many hardships when we came to settle in our towns," our grandfathers said of old, oh, my sons! They had brought nothing to eat, to nourish the stomach. Nor did they have anything with which to clothe themselves. Everything was lacking. We lived only on the sap of plants, we smelled the ends of our staffs to satisfy our stomachs.

It was then that we began to sow our corn. We cut down the trees, we burned them, and we sowed the seed. Thus we secured a little nourishment. Thus also we made our clothes; beating the bark of the trees and the maguey leaves, we made our clothing. As soon as we had a little corn, the birds appeared in the sky and swooped down over the corn field, eating a part of our food. This the people of long ago related. . . .

Gagavitz had two sons, the first was called Caynoh and the second Caybatz, both were males. When Gagavitz, he who came from Túlan, died, our grandfathers Caynoh and Caybatz were very young. After their father died, they buried him in Paraxón, there where his dawn had shone.

The two young men arrived then, and as soon as they arrived, Gekaquch, Baqahol, and Zibakahay appeared, and they said to them: "We have come, your mothers and your grandmothers; we are here, the Galel Xahil, the Ahuchán Xahil, those are our titles. We are your Galel, your Ahpop." Thus they told them when they arrived. But those who arrived did not know whether they were descendants of Zatecauh, he who died in the ravine of Chopiytzel. Thus our fathers and grandfathers related, oh, my sons!

The first who became great was Tepeuh, the lord of Cauké, whose residence was called Cuztum Chixna. Tepeuh made himself feared by his witchcraft; the place where he lived trembled, and all the tribes paid tribute to Tepeuh.

Well then, Gekaquch and Baqahol sent their orders to the Galel Xahil. And they said to the Galel and to the Ahuchán Xahil: "Let Caynob and Caybatz first go as your collectors of tribute. We are your lords," they said to the clans. And indeed they were sent by the clans.

They go to present themselves before Tepeuh.

Our grandfathers Caynoh and Caybatz came before Tepeuh. At the first call they set out, leaving the Galel Xahil and the Ahuchán Xahil alone. When they came before Tepeuh, he said to them: "Who are you?" And Caynoh and Caybatz answered: "We are the sons of Gagavitz." Tepeuh was surprised when he heard these words. And so it was that Tepeuh spared their lives because they had come before him with humility.

After that they were sent by Tepeuh to collect tribute, and they went to collect tribute from the people. But they did not have to make the people come in order to collect the tribute. In truth everyone feared the magic power of Caynoh and Caybatz. In the place where they were, a brightness like that of fire shone during the night, and they made the earth tremble like an earthquake. For this reason the people feared them when they came before them. All the people brought them the tribute when they went to receive it. There in the east they were paid with precious objects: metal and cloth. These were the valuable things which the people had to contribute to them. They were truly great. And therefore they became sons of Tepeuh, for the work they had accomplished; they were truly loved by him. . . .

[B]y the vote of all, [the princes] came into power. Caynoh was made Ahpop Xahil and Caybatz was named Ahpop Qamahay. Both lords ruled over all sections after they began to reign.

Caynoh and Caybatz had sons, they had daughters: the first had four sons and the second had five sons. Nine sons Caynoh and Caybatz had. Truly, the magic power of Gagavitz, Zactecauh, Caynoh, and Caybatz was terrible.

Then Caynoh and Caybatz said: "Let our government be completed as our fathers commanded us. Let two of our sons enter into the government," they said. Whereupon one son of the king Caynoh entered, and they made him Ahuchán Xahil of the kingdom; and a son of the king Caybatz entered also and came to be the Galel Xahil of the kingdom. In this manner we have four lords, we the Xahilá, and thus our grandfathers completed their government among themselves.

NOTES

1. Adrian Recinos and Delia Goetz, introduction to *The Annals of the Cakchiquels*, trans. with intro. by Adrian Recinos and Delia Goetz (Norman, OK: University of Oklahoma Press, 1953), 11.

2. Robert M. Carmack, *Quichean Civilization: The Ethnohistoric, Ethnographic and Archaeological Sources* (Berkeley: University of California Press, 1973), 48–49.

It was the policy of the Spanish to destroy Indigenous books because they were considered idolatrous.

3. Robert M. Hill II, *Pictograph to Alphabet—and Back: Reconstructing the Pictographic Origins of the Xajil Chronicle* (Philadelphia: American Philosophical Society, 2012), 3.

4. Daniel Brinton, introduction to *The Annals of the Cakchiquels*. (Philadelphia: Brinton's Library of Aboriginal American Literature, Number VI, 1885).

5. H. B. Nicholson, *Topiltzin Quetzalcoatl: The Once and Future Lord of the Toltecs* (Boulder: University of Colorado Press, 2001), 185.

6. The original document is entitled *Manuscrito Cakchiquel : ó sea memorial de Tecpan-Atitlan (Sololá) Historia del antiquo reino del Cakchiquel, dicho de Guatemala / Escrito en lengua Cakchiquel por don Francisco Ernantez Arana Xahila Xahila y continuado por don Francisco Díaz Gebuta Queh*. Franklin Library, University of Pennsylvania. It can be viewed at https://franklin.library.upenn.edu/catalog/FRANKLIN_9950088663503681. Click on Fascimile. The selection in this volume begins on page 18.

7. Judith Maxwell and Robert M. Hill II, trans. and exegesis, *Kaqchikel Chronicles: The Definitive Edition* (Austin: University of Texas Press, 2006).

8. Quoted in Brinton, introduction, 23.

9. William L. Sherman, "Change in Guatemalan Society, 1470–1620," in *Spaniards and Indians in Southeastern Mesoamerica: Essays on the History of Ethnic Relations,* ed. Murdo J. MacLeod and Robert Wasserstrom (Lincoln: University of Nebraska Press, 1983), 170. See also W. George Lovell, "Surviving Conquest: The Maya of Guatemala in Historical Perspective," *Latin American Research Review* 23, no. 2 (1988): 28.

10. Norman Hammond, "Inside the black box: defining Maya polity," in *Classic Maya Political History: Hieroglyphic and Archeological Evidence*, ed. T. Patrick Culbert (Cambridge: Cambridge University Press, 1996), 253.

11. Brinton, introduction, 11, 59.

12. Linnea H. Wren and Peter Schmidt, "Elite Interaction during the Terminal Classic Period: new evidence from Chichen Itza," in *Classic Maya Political History: Hieroglyphic and Archeological Evidence*, ed. T. Patrick Culbert (Cambridge: Cambridge University Press, 1996), 199–201. See also Alan Knight, *Mexico: From the Beginning to the Spanish Conquest* (Cambridge: Cambridge University Press, 2002), 128–129.

13. Recinos and Goetz, introduction, 4.

14. Recinos and Goetz, introduction, 41.

15. Walter Wilson, "Urban Legends: Acts 10:1–11:18 and the Strategies of Greco-Roman Foundation Narratives," *Journal of Biblical Literature* 120 (Spring 2001): 81.

16. Wilson, "Urban," 80. See also Anthony Douglas Smith, *The Ethnic Origins of Nations* (Oxford, UK: Basil Blackwell, Inc., 1986).

17. Brinton, introduction, 43.

18. Wren and Schmidt, *Elite*, 215.

19. *Guatemala Memory of Silence T'zinil Na 'Tab'al*, Report of the Commission for Historical Clarification. (1999) Human Rights Data Analysis Group. https://hrdag .org/wp-content/uploads/2013/01/CEHreport-english.pdf, 17, 19, 84.

20. *Guatemala Memory*, 23

21. Rigoberta Menchú, "Interview with Kerry Kennedy: Indigenous Rights, Rigoberta Menchú Tum." Robert Kennedy Human Rights, 2000. https://rfkhumanrights .org/work/teaching-human-rights/lessons/rigoberta-mench%C3%BA-tum.

Chapter Two

Christopher Columbus

"Took Possession of That Island for the King and Queen"

Christopher Columbus, the first explorer to sail to the islands and mainland of the Western Hemisphere in modern times, carried out the formal European procedures of his era with cross, flag, and prescribed words to "take possession" of those lands for his queen and king. He is credited with, and blamed for, what is known as the Doctrine of Discovery, the colonization that came with it, and the devastation that it meant for the Indigenous inhabitants who had had their own ordered societies and governments before the arrival of the Europeans.

Columbus was born in the Italian Republic of Genoa in 1451 into a family of wool weavers[1] that had lived in or near the port of Genoa for at least three centuries. Growing up by the sea, Columbus made several voyages as a young man and, in 1476, was shipwrecked off the coast of Portugal. After being rescued, he made his way to Lisbon where he joined a community of Genoese merchants and ship owners. The Portuguese, from the time of Prince Henry the Navigator several decades earlier, had developed improved navigation tools and were exploring the lands along the west coast of Africa.

Historian Felipe Fernández-Armesto states that Columbus may have been developing ideas and evidence in support of making a voyage that would reach the East by sailing to the west as early as the late 1470s[2] and, in 1484, he appealed to Portuguese King John II for ships and support to make such a voyage. For at least a decade these ideas had been developing in several European cities. Early geographer Paolo del Pozzo and fellow Florentine Lorenzo Buonincontri both proposed sailing west to reach Cathay (China) in the East while discovering new lands along the way. Columbus biographer John Noble Wilford says that "The Florentines were providing the theoretical underpinnings for Columbus's inchoate ideas of sailing across the ocean."[3] Columbus had believed that, given Portugal's interest in trade and discovery,

King John II would be receptive to his ideas of reaching Cypango (Japan) by sailing west. However, King John turned him down, and Columbus left for Spain to approach the Spanish monarchs Queen Isabella of Castile and Leon and King Ferdinand of Aragon. After a first meeting in 1486, the monarchs appointed a commission of experts to consider Columbus's proposal. The commission's verdict was negative, but Columbus met again with Isabella in 1489 and she told him to have patience and wait until "the matter of Granada was settled"[4] when she would consider the issue again.

In January of 1492, the forces of Isabella and Ferdinand took the city of Granada and completed the almost 800-hundred-year-long *reconquista* or reconquering of Spain from the Muslims. That year Columbus's supporters at court, Juan de Perez and Luis de Santangel, assisted him with arguments (the former) and funding (the latter), and on April 17, 1492, Queen Isabella signed the document authorizing his voyage. Columbus biographer Kirkpatrick Sale notes, however, that these formal documents nowhere mention Cathay (China), the Indies (Indonesia and other islands in the East Indies), or any other land in Asia; rather they authorized Columbus to "discover and acquire" certain "Islands and Mainlands." Sale adds that if Columbus had expected to encounter the ruler of China, he would have taken better trade goods than the trinkets he later used to trade with the Indigenous people of the islands he encountered, but Sale adds that it may be best to conclude that we will never know exactly what was in his mind.[5]

Columbus set sail with the *Santa Maria*, the *Niña*, and the *Pinta* on May 23, 1492, making landfall in the New World on October 12.[6] On this first voyage, he visited the islands that later were named the Bahamas, Cuba, and Hispaniola. On Christmas Day, the *Santa María* ran aground on Hispaniola and was severely damaged. Materials from the ship were used to build a fort there called La Navidad, which Columbus left three dozen men to defend.[7] The selection included here comes from his log of this first voyage.

His second voyage, which departed from Spain on September 25, 1493, included seventeen ships and 1,200 men, among them soldiers, farmers, and priests. Columbus biographer Samuel Eliot Morison notes that "No European nation had ever undertaken an overseas colonizing expedition on anything approaching this scale" and he explains that the two declared objectives of the crown were the conversion of the natives to Christianity and the estab-lishment of a crown trading colony.[8] But Columbus found that La Navidad on Hispaniola had collapsed. The Spaniards had fought and killed each other over women and gold, and the surviving colonists were killed by the native inhabitants.[9] On this second voyage, Columbus explored more of Cuba, Ja-maica, and Hispaniola and loaded five hundred Taino people from Hispaniola onto his ships to be taken back to Spain[10] beginning in this way the transatlantic slave trade. Fort Isabella, which had replaced La Navidad, was in chaos due to mismanagement and the killing of Indigenous neighbors.[11] Columbus ordered the building of what would be Santo Domingo, and by 1498 Fort Isabella was abandoned.[12]

One objective of the third voyage was to send colonists, among them farmers, to live permanently in the newly discovered land, and another was to discover and explore the mainland that had been theorized to exist in what was called the Western Ocean. The voyage began on May 30, 1498, and while Columbus did briefly sail along the coast of what is now Venezuela, which he suspected was the mainland, he did not have the time to explore it. Upon arriving at Hispaniola, he encountered disorder and mutiny. With the arrival of Francisco de Bobadilla, a chief justice sent by the Crown, Columbus himself was put in chains and sent back to Spain. The king and queen released him but eventually appointed another man to the post of viceroy of the new lands.[13]

Columbus, however, retained some of his wealth and, in 1502, was authorized by the monarchs to make a fourth voyage of exploration to take formal possession of new territories while paying special attention to gold, silver, and pearls. After surviving a massive Atlantic hurricane off Hispaniola, Columbus explored the coast of Central America looking for a strait that would lead to the East Indies. On Aug. 14, 1502, Morison notes, "they anchored off the mouth of a river [in what is now Honduras] which Columbus named Rio de la Posesión, because he there took formal possession of that mainland for his Sovereigns."[14] After twenty-eight days of being unable to move because of foul weather, his ships rounded a cape that he named Cabo Gracias a Dios (Cape Thanks Be to God), a name it retains to this day. Without suspecting that they were near the Pacific Ocean that could give them access to the East of their dreams, Columbus and his sailors spent Christmas and New Year's Day in a harbor where today the Panama Canal begins.[15]

Leaving the mainland coast with damaged ships and difficult currents, Columbus was forced to ground his ships in Jamaica and await rescue. They were marooned for a year, trading with the Indigenous people for food. After a valiant canoe voyage to Santo Domingo by one of his officers to alert the Spaniards, they were rescued in June of 1504, returning to Spain in September. But in November, Queen Isabella, who had always been Columbus's patron, died and with her death any hope of the restoration of his titles. And Columbus himself had been in ill health for some time; he died on May 20, 1506, in Valladolid at age 54 or 55.[16]

Columbus kept a diary of his first voyage, which scholars note was the first known day-by-day log kept by an explorer.[17] The original diary was delivered by Columbus to Isabella and Ferdinand upon his return, but it disappeared

Figure 2.1.   Remains of Columbus in the Cathedral of Seville, Spain
Photo by Katherine Hoyt

after Isabella's death. Columbus, however, had received a copy made by a court scribe before he set off on his second voyage. His older son Diego (who became the governor of Santo Domingo) inherited the copy when his father died in 1506 and, when Diego died in 1526, ownership passed to grandson Luis, although Columbus's second son Ferdinand probably kept it under his care until his death in 1539.[18] This could have been the copy that Ferdinand used when writing his biography of his father[19] and that Bartolomé de Las Casas said he used for his *History of the Indies*. The copy disappeared in about 1554, probably sold by Luis. But the Las Casas multivolume *History* survived and was the principal source of information on the 1492 voyage for Columbus scholars after it was completed in 1561.

Then, in 1790, after a search of Spanish libraries for lost Columbus documents, a lengthy abridgement of Columbus's log in the hand of Las Casas was found in the library of a Spanish duke. Here was likely a copy Las Casas made to use in writing his *History*.[20] It is currently housed at the National Library of Spain in Madrid.[21] The log was transcribed and published in 1824 in Spain. This was soon followed by a translation into English published in Boston in 1827.[22] This translation, which is the version used here, is in the public domain and can be used freely by scholars and students.

Another important surviving document is a letter from Columbus to his supporter Luis de Santangel, in which Columbus summarizes his 1492 voyage. A Barcelona printer obtained a copy shortly after Columbus's return, printed it, and within months ten more editions were published in Antwerp, Basel, and Florence.[23]

Alarmed by Portugal's claims to the new territories based on earlier papal decrees, Isabella and Ferdinand asked Spanish-born Pope Alexander VI for confirmation of Spain's right to the lands. A friend of King Ferdinand, he did not refuse, and, in May of 1493, he issued two bulls, both titled *Inter caetera*, in which he said that he gave, conceded, and assigned to the Catholic monarchs of Spain all lands west of a line he laid out in the Atlantic Ocean as long as those lands were "not actually possessed by some other Christian king or prince." The right of the kings or princes of the lands in question to rule their subjects in peace was not taken into account because they were not Christian. The Pope enjoined the Spanish to send "God-fearing men . . . to instruct the natives and inhabitants in Christian faith and to imbue them with good morals."[24]

Columbus's log can be viewed as an expression of the theory prevailing at the time in Spain and Portugal (and later in other countries) about how rulers could "legitimately" take possession of lands that were new to them. It was also a way to prevent competition and war among European nations (ruled by the "Christian princes") for newly discovered lands.[25] Historian Patricia Seed says that to fulfill the Roman-based conception of possession, a ceremony of arrival witnessed by others and a declaration of the intention to remain were necessary.[26] In his log, Columbus (as copied by Las Casas) describes exactly how he fulfilled these requirements:

> The Admiral bore the royal standard, and the two captains each a banner of the Green Cross, which all the ships had carried; this contained the initials of the names of the King and Queen each side of the cross, and a crown over each letter. . . . The Admiral called upon the two Captains, and the rest of the crew who landed, as also to Rodrigo de Escovedo notary of the fleet, and Rodrigo Sanchez, of Segovia, to bear witness that he before all others took possession (as in fact he did) of that island for the King and Queen his sovereigns, making the requisite declarations, which are more at large set down here in writing.[27]

Another ceremonial aspect of the Spanish ritual of "taking possession" was the renaming of geographical features including islands and rivers. Seed likens it to "the process of baptism practiced upon the peoples of the New World."[28] She also notes that the Spanish believed that they were taking possession of new lands but, equally importantly, establishing authority over people—"articulating a relationship between Europeans and a living, breathing other rather than simply demarcating space,"[29] which was all that the English would do. For the Spanish, Portuguese, and French, the legitimacy of their rule was dependent on their converting the Indigenous people to Christianity, as mandated by the Catholic pope. In contrast, religious conversion was not considered a mandate by the later Protestant English explorers and colonizers in the New World.[30]

Columbus reported to the king in his log on October 12 that he believed the native inhabitants would "very readily become Christians, as they appear to have no religion." Because he could have no reason to believe this as he had just arrived on their island, literary scholar Margarita Zamora says that what he was actually saying was that they had no proper religion, with the standard being European religion.[31] She points out that Columbus goes on to describe other aspects in which the Indigenous people are deficient or inferior which help to establish "the relationship of domination of the Indians by the Spaniards and the establishment of the latter's right of possession."[32] Sales states that it is sad that Columbus was unable to see the virtues of the Taino people he encountered who Sales says were "well fed and well housed, without poverty or serious disease."[33] Columbus describes the new lands as offering opportunities for profit for the Catholic monarchs, not just in gold and pearls, but in crops and pasturage as well. He obviously is thinking to please his queen and king while contemplating the financing of his next voyage to these lands.[34]

Literary historian Stephen Greenblatt emphasizes the public nature of the ceremony of taking possession, the flags, the spoken ritual words, the recording of the actions, and, most importantly, the fact that, as Columbus stated in his letter to Luis de Santangel, they were contradicted by no one.[35] Columbus related how he "found very many islands filled with people innumerable, and of them all I have taken possession for their highnesses, by proclamation made and with the royal standard unfurled, and no opposition was offered me."[36] Greenblatt says that the local natives were not in the "same universe of discourse" as Columbus, given that they could not understand his words and had a different concept of landownership.[37] He notes that, while Columbus's statement that he was not contradicted "is absurd, it is also a sign . . . of an ethical reservation, a sense that the wishes of the native inhabitants should be respected." He adds that, for the Spanish, "legitimation necessarily included an acknowledgement of the existence of the natives and a recognition of values other than superior force."[38] It also acknowledged that the inevitable use of force against the natives needed to be justified even if that was done in a superficial fashion.

In the following years, Catholic philosophers would bring the rights of those native inhabitants to the fore, questioning the legal and moral basis of the Spanish conquest. In fact, before Columbus had made his final voyage, Queen Isabella convened in 1500 a commission of theologians and legal experts to study the question. Scholar Maria del Refugio González notes that, contrary to the general principles of medieval European law that saw non-believers as lacking in all rights, the commission declared the New World Native peoples to be free vassals of the monarchs, equal to the workers of Castille, who could only be enslaved if they were prisoners of war.[39]

As it evolved, the justification for the taking by Europeans of the lands of others came to be known as the Doctrine of Discovery, and this doctrine in recent years has been challenged by Indigenous peoples and repudiated by religious faiths and in international bodies. Robert Miller, a professor of law at Arizona State University and a citizen of the Eastern Shawnee Tribe of Oklahoma, notes that most of the world outside of Europe was colonized based on the Doctrine of Discovery, which was one of the first principles of international law.[40] Miller adds, "Discovery continues to play a very significant role in the lives of Indigenous peoples and it still restricts property, governmental, and self-determination rights."[41]

From October 7 to 12, 1992, an alternative commemoration of the 500th anniversary of Columbus's arrival in the Americas, entitled "500 Years of Indigenous, Black, and Popular Resistance," was held in Managua, Nicaragua, with the participation of 668 delegates from twenty-six American countries. The final statement of the gathering proclaimed that, five hundred years after the beginning of the massacres of their peoples, the occupation of their lands, the extraction of their resources, and exploitation of their labor, "We are still here." Delegates resolved to continue fighting for recognition of the autonomy of Indigenous peoples and for multicultural and multilingual states.[42] While the conference was in session, it was announced that Guatemalan Indigenous leader Rigoberta Menchú, an attendee, was the winner of the Nobel Peace Prize for 1992.[43]

In December 2009, Indigenous peoples from around the world attended the Parliament of the World's Religions and called on Pope Benedict XVI and the Vatican to repudiate the papal bulls that gave legitimacy to the Doctrine of Discovery.[44] In 2012, the World Council of Churches denounced the Doctrine of Discovery "as fundamentally opposed to the gospel of Jesus Christ and as a violation of the inherent human rights that all individuals and peoples have received from God."[45] That same year the Permanent Forum on Indigenous Issues of the United Nations Economic and Social Council said that justifications for the dispossession of Indigenous peoples from their lands, such as the Doctrine of Discovery, contained broader assumptions under which Indigenous peoples were constructed as "inferior and uncivilized," thus laying the bases for the exploitation of Indigenous peoples and their resources.[46]

In 2020, in many parts of the world, systemic racism and the killings by police of Black people and other people of color provoked the removal by protestors of monuments to controversial figures, among them Columbus.[47] A number of places in the United States changed the name of the October 12th Columbus Day holiday to Indigenous Peoples, Day.[48] If it is true, as Wilford says, that it was Columbus's "fate to be the more or less accidental agent of a transcendental discovery," he is "now thrashing in a riptide of conflicting views of his life and his responsibility for almost everything that has happened since."[49]

While there are other documents that could be used to illustrate the principal elements of the Doctrine of Discovery (including early papal bulls), the log of Christopher Columbus was written by a person who made four voyages to the New World and spent time in the hemisphere. Columbus took "possession" of the new lands for the queen and king of Spain with the procedures required by the governing philosophy in Europe in his day and recorded those actions for posterity. In the excerpts included below, the writing is at times in the voice of Las Casas and at times in the voice of Columbus, or as Las Casas says, "the precise words of the Admiral."

CHRISTOPHER COLUMBUS'S LOG
OF HIS FIRST VOYAGE TO AMERICA

At two o'clock in the morning, the land was discovered, at two leagues distance; they took in sail and remained under the square-sail lying to till day, which was Friday [Oct. 12], when they found themselves near a small island, one of the Lucayos, called in the Indian language Guanahani. Presently they descried people, naked, and the Admiral landed in the boat, which was armed, along with Martin Alonzo Pinzon, and Vincent Yanez his brother, captain of the *Niña*.

The Admiral bore the royal standard, and the two captains each a banner of the Green Cross, which all the ships had carried; this contained the initials of the names of the King and Queen each side of the cross, and a crown over each letter. Arrived on shore, they saw trees very green, many streams of water, and diverse sorts of fruits. The Admiral called upon the two Captains, and the rest of the crew who landed, as also to Rodrigo de Escovedo notary of the fleet, and Rodrigo Sanchez, of Segovia, to bear witness that he before all others took possession (as in fact he did) of that island for the King and Queen his sovereigns, making the requisite declarations, which are more at large set down here in writing. Numbers of the people of the island straightway collected together.

Here follow the precise words of the Admiral. "As I saw that they were very friendly to us and perceived that they could be much more easily converted to our holy faith by gentle means than by force, I presented them with some red caps, and strings of beads to wear upon the neck, and many other trifles of small value, wherewith they were much delighted, and became wonderfully attached to us. Afterwards they came swimming to the boats, bringing parrots, balls of cotton thread, javelins, and many other things which they exchanged for articles we gave them, such as glass beads, and hawk's bells; which trade was carried on with the utmost good will.

But they seemed on the whole to me, to be a very poor people. They all go completely naked, even the women, though I saw but one girl. All whom I saw, were young, not above thirty years of age, well made, with fine shapes and faces; their hair short, and coarse like that of a horse's tail, combed toward the forehead, except a small portion which they suffer to hang down behind, and never cut. Some paint themselves with black, which makes them appear like those of the Canaries, neither black nor white; others with white, others with red, and others with such colors as they can find. Some paint the face, and some the whole body; others only the eyes, and others the nose.

Weapons they have none, nor are acquainted with them, for I showed them swords which they grasped by the blades, and cut themselves through ignorance. They have no iron, their javelins being without it, and nothing more than sticks, though some have fish-bones or other things at the ends. They are all of a good size and stature, and handsomely formed. I saw some with scars of wounds upon their bodies, and demanded by signs the cause of them; they answered me in the same way, that there came people from the other islands in the neighborhood who endeavored to make prisoners of them, and they defended themselves. I thought then, and still believe, that these were from the continent. It appears to me, that the people are ingenious, and would be good servants; and I am of opinion that they would very readily become Christians, as they appear to have no religion. They very quickly learn such words as are spoken to them. If it please our Lord, I intend at my return to carry home six of them to your Highnesses, that they may learn our language. I saw no beasts in the island, nor any sort of animals except parrots." These are the words of the Admiral.

Monday, Oct. 15. Stood off and on during the night, determining not to come to anchor till morning, fearing to meet with shoals; continued our course in the morning; and as the island was found to be six or seven leagues distant, and the tide was against us, it was noon when we arrived there. I found that part of it towards San Salvador extending from N. to S. five leagues, and the other side which we coasted along, ran from E. to W. more than ten leagues. From this island espying a still larger one to the W., I set sail in that direction and kept on till night without reaching the western extremity of the island, where I gave it the name of Santa Maria de la Concepcion.

About sunset we anchored near the cape which terminates the island towards the W. to enquire for gold, for the natives we had taken from San Salvador told me that the people here wore golden bracelets upon their arms and legs. I believed pretty confidently that they had invented this story in order to find means to escape from us.

Still I determined to pass none of these islands without taking possession, because being once taken, it would answer for all times. We anchored and remained till Tuesday, when at daybreak I went ashore with the boats armed. The people we found naked like those of San Salvador, and of the same disposition. They suffered us to traverse the island, and gave us what we asked of them. . . .

Tuesday, Nov. 6th. Last night, says the Admiral, the two men whom I had sent into the country returned, and related as follows. After having travelled a dozen leagues, they came to a town containing about fifty houses, where there were probably a thousand inhabitants, every house containing a great number; they were built in the manner of large tents. The inhabitants received them after their fashion with great ceremony; the men and women flocked to behold them, and they were lodged in their best houses. They signified their admiration and reverence of the strangers by touching them, kissing their hands and feet, and making signs of wonder. They imagined them come from heaven, and signified as much to them. They were feasted with such food as the natives had to offer. Upon their arrival at the town they were led by the arms of the principal men of the place to the chief dwelling, here they gave them seats, and the Indians sat upon the ground in a circle round them. The Indians who accompanied the Spaniards explained to the natives the manner in which their new guests lived and gave a favorable account of their character. . . .

The Spaniards on their journey met with great multitudes of people, men and women with firebrands in their hands and herbs to smoke after their custom. [This is probably tobacco.] No village was seen upon the road of a larger size than five houses, but all the inhabitants showed them the same respect. Many sorts of trees were observed, and herbs and odoriferous flowers. Great numbers of birds they remarked, all different from those of Spain except the nightingales, who entertained them with their songs, and the partridges and geese, which were found in abundance. Of quadrupeds they descried none except dumb [non-barking] dogs.

The soil appeared fertile and under good cultivation, producing the aforementioned *names* [probably sweet potatoes] and beans very dissimilar to ours, as well as the grain called panic grass [a genus of grain that includes millet]. They saw vast quantities of cotton, spun and manufactured; a single house contained above five hundred *arrobas* [one *arroba* equals twenty-five pounds]; four thousand quintals [hundredweights] might be collected here per annum. The Admiral says it appears to him that they do not sow it, but that it is productive the whole year round; it is very fine with an exceedingly long staple. Everything which the Indians possessed they were ready to barter at a very low price; a large basket of cotton they would give for a leather thong, or other trifling thing which was offered them. They are an inoffensive, unwarlike people, naked, except that the women wear a very slight covering at the loins; their manners are very decent, and their complexion not very dark, but lighter than that of the inhabitants of the Canary Islands.

"I have no doubt, most serene Princes," says the Admiral, "that were proper devout and religious persons to come among them and learn their language, it would be an easy matter to convert them all to Christianity, and I hope in our Lord that your Highnesses will devote yourselves with much diligence to this object, and bring into the church so many multitudes, inasmuch as you have exterminated those who refused to confess the Father, Son, and Holy Ghost [referring to the Muslims and the Jews], so that having ended your days (as we are all mortal) you may leave your dominions in a tranquil condition, free from heresy and wickedness, and meet with a favorable reception before the eternal Creator, whom may it please to grant you a long life and great increase of kingdoms and dominions, with the will and disposition to promote, as you always have done, the holy Christian religion, Amen."

"This day I launched the ship, and made ready to depart in the name of God, next Thursday, for the SE. in quest of gold and spices, as well as to discover the country." These are the words of the Admiral, who expected to sail on Thursday, but the wind being contrary, detained him till the twelfth day of November. . . .

Friday, Nov. 16. They made it a practice in all those countries and islands, on going on shore, to set up and leave there, a cross. The Admiral went in the boat to the mouth of this port, and upon a point of land, found two large trunks of trees of different sizes laid across each other in the shape of a cross, so exactly that he says a carpenter could not have done the thing with more precision; having paid their adorations to this, he ordered that these trunks should be taken and made into a large and lofty crucifix. . . .

Saturday, Dec. 22. At daybreak they set sail to go in search of the islands where, as the Indians told them, there was much gold, and in some of them more gold than earth; but found the weather unfavorable and returned to their anchorage, when the boat was dispatched with nets for fishing. The sovereign of the country who resided in the neighborhood sent a large canoe full of men, with one of his principal attendants requesting the Admiral to come with the ships to his territory, promising him anything he had. He sent by this messenger a girdle [belt] to which was attached instead of a pouch, a mask having the nose, tongue, and ears of beaten gold. The Indians in the canoe, meeting the boat, gave the girdle to a ship's boy, and proceeded on board the ship with their embassy. Some time passed before they could be understood, the Indians on board not comprehending them, as their language was somewhat different from that of the others; finally they made out to express themselves by signs, and made known their invitation. The Admiral determined to accept it, and came to a resolution to sail the next day, which was Sunday, although he was not accustomed to put to sea on that day; this arose from devotion and not from any superstitious scruples. Besides, entertaining a hope that these people, by the willingness they manifested, would become Christians, and subjects of Castile, and already looking upon them in that light, he was desirous of doing everything to oblige them.

Before quitting this place, he sent six of his men to a very large town, three leagues to the West, the prince of that place having visited the Admiral the preceding day and told him that he had several pieces of gold. With these men he sent his secretary, whom he charged to take care that the Spaniards did nothing wrong to the Indians, for these were so liberal, and the Spaniards so immeasurably greedy; that they were not satisfied with receiving the most valuable of what the inhabitants possessed, in exchange for a leather thong, a bit of glass or earthen ware, or other worthless trifle, and sometimes for nothing at all, which, however, the admiral had always prohibited. Although the articles which the Indians offered were of little value, except the gold, yet the Admiral considering the readiness with which they parted with them, as giving a piece of gold for half a dozen strings of glass beads, ordered that nothing should be taken from them without paying for it.

NOTES

1. John Noble Wilford, *The Mysterious History of Columbus: An Exploration of the Man, the Myth, the Legacy* (New York: Alfred A. Knopf, 1991), 58, 64.

2. Felipe Fernández-Armesto, *Columbus on Himself* (Indianapolis: Hackett Publishing Company, 2010), 23.

3. Wilford, *Mysterious*, 74.

4. Quoted in Wilford, *Mysterious*, 87.

5. Kirkpatrick Sale, *Christopher Columbus and the Conquest of Paradise* (London: I. B. Taurus and Co. Ltd., 2006), 25–26.

6. Wilford, *Mysterious*, 91–93, 101.

7. Samuel Eliot Morison, *Admiral of the Ocean Sea: A Life of Christopher Columbus* (Boston: Little, Brown and Company, 1942), chapters 18–21.

8. Morison, *Admiral*, 390–91.

9. Morison, *Admiral*, 424–28; Wilford, *Mysterious*, 166–68; Laurence Bergreen, *Columbus: The Four Voyages* (New York: Viking, 2011), 147–50.

10. Morison, *Admiral*, 487–88.

11. Bergreen, *Columbus*, 156–57, 166–71.

12. Wilford, *Mysterious*, 175–76.

13. Morison, *Admiral*, 509, 515, 552–53, 571; Bergreen, *Columbus*, chapters 9 and 10.

14. Morison, *Admiral*, chapters 48–49, 582, 597.

15. Morison, *Admiral*, 608.

16. Morison, *Admiral*, 658, 666–69, Wilford, *Mysterious*, 237; Bergreen, *Columbus*, 332–362. For a fascinating discussion of where Columbus's remains are or are not located, see Wilford, *Mysterious*, 241–44 and Bergreen, *Columbus*, 363–64. Wilford summarizes, "It is possible that . . . some of Columbus lies in Santo Domingo and some in Seville."

17. Wilford, *Mysterious*, 37.

18. Robert H. Fuson, introduction to *The Log of Christopher Columbus*, by Christopher Columbus (Camden, Maine: International Marine Publishing Company, 1987), 2.

19. Ferdinand Columbus, *The Life of the Admiral Christopher Columbus by His Son Ferdinand*, translated and annotated by Benjamin Keen (New Brunswick: Rutgers University Press, 1959).

20. Fuson, introduction, 4.

21. The Log can be viewed online at http://www.bne.es/en/Catalogos/Biblioteca DigitalHispanica/Inicio/index.html_Type in *Viajes de Cristóbal Colón*. Click on the title. Then click on "View work." The selection included here begins on page 16.

22. Christopher Columbus, *Personal Narrative of the First Voyage of Columbus to America from a Manuscript Recently Discovered in Spain*. Translated and Preface by Samuel Kettell (Boston: Thomas B. Wait and Son: 1827). The book can be viewed online at: http://babel.hathitrust.org/cgi/pt?id=hvd.32044005032289;seq=7;view=1up; num=i.

23. Wilford, *Mysterious*, 20–21.

24. Pope Alexander VI, "Inter caetera Divinae," in *Church and State through the Centuries*, ed. and trans. by Sidney Z. Ehler and John Morrall (New York: Biblo and Tannen Publishers, 1967), 157–58.

25. Natsu Taylor Saito, "Reflections on Homeland and Security," *The New Centennial Review* 6, no. 1 (Spring 2006): 241.

26. Patricia Seed, "Taking Possession and Reading Texts: Establishing Authority of Overseas Empires," *William and Mary Quarterly* 8, no. 2, (1992): 184.

27. Columbus, *Personal*, 34–35.

28. Seed, *Taking*, 199.

29. Seed, *Taking*, 209.

30. Seed, *Taking*, 189.

31. Margarita Zamora, "Abreast of Columbus: Gender and Discovery," *Cultural Critique* no. 17 (Winter, 1990–1992): 132.

32. Zamora, "Abreast," 143.

33. Sales, *Christopher*, 101.

34. Heike Paul, *Christopher Columbus and the Myth of 'Discovery': The Myths that Made America* (Bielefeld, Germany: Transcript Verlag, 2014), 46–47.

35. Stephen Greenblatt, *Marvelous Possessions: The Wonder of the New World* (Chicago: University of Chicago Press, 1991), 59.

36. Christopher Columbus, "Letter to Luis de Santangel," in *Select Documents Illustrating the Four Voyages of Columbus*, ed. and trans. Cecil Jane (London: Hakluyt Society, 1930), 2.

37. Greenblatt, *Marvelous,* 59.

38. Greenblatt, *Marvelous,* 64.

39. María del Refugio González, "El Descubrimiento de América y el derecho," in *El Descubrimiento de América y su impacto en la historia,* ed. Leopoldo Zea. (México: Fondo de la Cultura Económica, 1991), 102–103.

40. Robert J. Miller, "The International Law of Colonialism: A Comparative Analysis," *Lewis & Clark Law Review* 15, no. 4 (2011): 848.

41. Miller, "International," 921.

42. "III encuentro continental de la resistencia indígena, negra y popular, declaración de Managua," *Boletín de Antropología Americana* 24 (Dec. 1991), 186. This issue was evidently published late. For more on the lead up to the gathering, see Odessa Ramirez, "1992—The Year of Indigenous Peoples," *Social Justice* 19, No. 2 (Summer 1992, Columbus on Trial): 56–62.

43. I attended that conference and stayed in the same guest house as Ms. Menchú. It was an exciting moment!

44. Gale Courey Toensing, "Indigenous delegates ask Pope to repudiate Doctrine of Discovery," *Indian Country Today,* December 21, 2009, https://indiancountrytoday.com/archive/indigenous-delegates-ask-pope-to-repudiate-doctrine-of-discovery.

45. World Council of Churches Executive Committee, *Statement on the doctrine of discovery and its enduring impact on Indigenous Peoples,* February 17, 2012, http://www.oikoumene.org/en/resources/documents/executive-committee/bossey-february-2012/statement-on-the-doctrine-of-discovery-and-its-enduring-impact-on-Indigenous-peoples.html.

46. Permanent Forum on Indigenous Issues of the UN Economic and Social Council, *Discussion on the special theme for the year: "The Doctrine of Discovery: its enduring impact on Indigenous peoples and the right to redress for past conquests,"* May 10, 2012, http://unpfip.blogspot.com/2012/05/recommendations-of-permanent-forum.html.

47. Teresa Machemer, "Christopher Columbus Statues Beheaded, Pulled Down Across America," *Smithsonian Magazine,* June 12, 2020, https://www.smithsonianmag.com/smart-news/christopher-columbus-statues-beheaded-torn-down-180975079/.

48. Leila Fadel, "Columbus Day Or Indigenous Peoples' Day," NPR *Morning Edition,* October 14, 2019, https://www.npr.org/2019/10/14/769083847/columbus-day-or-Indigenous-peoples-day.

49. Wilford, *Mysterious,* 247.

Chapter Three

Antonio de Montesinos

"Are They Not Human Beings?"

Antonio de Montesinos was a priest of the Dominican Order, a Catholic order of religious men and women founded in 1216 by the Spanish priest St. Dominic of Guzman. A sermon Montesinos gave in December of 1511 opened the discussion within the Spanish world of the nature of the Indigenous inhabitants of the Americas, their rights and their treatment.

Montesino's date of birth is unknown, but he made his profession as a Dominican friar in 1502 in Salamanca, Spain, later studying in Valladolid. In 1510, he was sent to the island of Hispaniola along with his superior Pedro de Cordoba and colleagues Bernardo de Santo Domingo and Domingo de Villamayor.

Between September 1510 and December 1511, the friars had sent complaints about the treatment of the Indigenous people by the Spanish colonists to the governor of the island, Diego Columbus, the son of the Christopher Columbus, but with no result.[1] The friars then began a period of fasting, vigils, and prayers asking God to illuminate their path, deciding finally to preach a sermon to all the Spaniards in Santo Domingo on the fourth Sunday of Advent 1511 which would denounce Spanish practices as violations of the laws of God and nature. The sermon was prepared by all the friars, and Montesinos was chosen to deliver it because he was known to be the most efficient and forceful speaker.[2] We know most of the content of the sermon because it was written down by another Dominican friar, Bartolomé de Las Casas, who included it in his *History of the Indies*, from which the selection included here is taken. The original manuscript of the *History* is at the National Library of Spain in Madrid.[3] The Spanish colonists reacted to the sermon with anger and sent messages to the king, who recalled the friars to Spain in 1512 to defend themselves, which they did successfully.

After returning from Spain, Montesinos spent time in Puerto Rico, returning to Hispaniola in 1518. He later returned to Spain to work toward formally establishing the Dominican order in the New World. In 1525, he was sent to Puerto Rico with six other Dominicans. In 1526, Montesinos traveled with the expedition of Spanish explorer Lucas Vásquez de Ayllón to establish the colony of San Miguel de Guandape[4] in what is now either South Carolina or Georgia (both states claim the honor). While archaeologists may never be able to determine exactly where San Miguel de Guandape was located, what is certain is that it was the first Spanish settlement on the eastern seaboard of what would become the United States.[5] It lasted only a few months and, shortly after the death of Ayllón, the Spaniards returned to Santo Domingo. In 1529, Montesinos was sent to Venezuela as Dominican vicar there. He died in 1540 or 1545 (dates vary depending on the source).[6]

The fiery 1511 Advent sermon by Montesinos had enormous repercussions. Fr. Brian Pierce, himself a Dominican, states that, "There is probably no other preaching—in over five hundred years of Christian presence in the Americas—that has so impacted the history of the continent [as] this one."[7] When King Ferdinand received the letters from Diego Columbus and the other Spanish colonists, he was angry and wrote on March 20, 1512, a reply to Columbus saying that if the friars did not retract the sermon, he (Columbus) should put them on the first boat to Spain to receive their punishment from the Dominican superior.[8] The king added, "Every hour that they remain on the island holding this dangerous opinion will do much harm to all the affairs of that land."[9] In that same month, with political instability on the island and fear among the Spaniards of an Indian uprising, the Dominican Provincial Alonso de Loaysa wrote to Montesinos that "you gave, in your sermon, occasion for all this to be lost; everything might have been disturbed, and, on account of your sermon, all of India [the Indies] might have rebelled so that neither you nor any other Christian would have been able to remain there."[10]

Instead of recanting, Montesinos traveled to Spain to put his case before the king. In spite of efforts to stop him, Montesinos was finally able to see Ferdinand and convince him of the validity of the friars' denunciations of Spanish practices in the New World. The king called together a group of theologians and jurists known as the Junta of Burgos, which in 1512 released a statement of seven principles to govern Spanish rule over the Native peoples of the New World. According to Las Casas, the new rules mandated that the Indigenous people be treated as free people, that they be given Catholic instruction, and that their labor benefit them and the king and not prevent their religious instruction. They also mandated that the Indigenous people's labor be tolerable, that they be allowed to live in their own houses and be allowed to cultivate their own land, that communication between the Amerindians and

Spanish be mandatory, and that the Indigenous people be paid for their labor in clothing and household goods.[11] Spanish scholar Luciano Pereña states, however, that while the colonial authorities accepted the new laws, they did not follow them.[12]

These new regulations were a reaction to the rapidly deteriorating conditions of the natives on Hispaniola as denounced by the Dominican friars. According to historian Stafford Poole, "The real curse of the colonies was the encomienda." Under the encomienda system, a Spaniard was granted the right to the labor of a certain number of Indigenous people. Poole continues, "By 1511, this had deteriorated into wanton exploitation, with the Spaniards demanding higher tributes, more labor (especially in the gold and silver mines), with the result that the natives were being rapidly decimated."[13] Pereña says that the depopulation of the island of Hispaniola was, without a doubt, one of the most shameful pages of the conquest of America. He cites Las Casas as stating that by 1508, only 60,000 natives of the island remained from a possible preconquest population of six million.[14] By mid-century they were gone.

The new Laws of Burgos did not abolish the encomiendas and Pedro de Córdoba, who had sailed to Spain to convert his superiors in the Dominican Order to his ideas, did not accept them. Córdoba met with the king, who, as a result of their conversations, called for corrections, a call that resulted in the Laws of Valladolid of 1513. While an improvement on the Laws of Burgos, the Laws of Valladolid still did not abolish the encomienda system. Poole states that the laws were "an attempt to compromise two apparently irreconcilable principles: the freedom of the Indigenous and the need for some sort of compulsory labor system."[15] The sermon of Montesinos, according to some writers, also provided the stimulus for the so-called "*Requerimiento* (Requirement)," written by royal councilor Juan López de Palacios Rubios[16] as an attempt to establish the conditions for a just war. Conquistadors were mandated to read it (in Spanish) to New World Indigenous peoples, offering them the opportunity to accept the Catholic faith and avoid violent conquest. If they did not, then war against them would be considered just. Las Casas accused the conquerors of reading the document to the trees a league away from a village before attacking it and looking for gold "which was what they had come for."[17]

In the end, the king did allow Father Córdoba to return to Hispaniola and ordered Diego Columbus to "receive them [the friars] with love and treat them well and I hope in the Lord that their coming will bring much fruit based on the people that they are and the commitment that they bring with them."[18] Ferdinand's notable willingness to receive information, complaints, and suggestions from the New World dated back to August 14, 1509, when he ordered that "no official should prevent anyone from sending to the king or anyone else letters and other information which concerns the welfare of the Indies."[19]

In her last will and testament, written before her death in 1504, Queen Isabella had reminded her husband King Ferdinand and her daughter Juana, heir to the Kingdom of Castille, that Pope Alexander VI in 1493 had given them the "Islands and Lands of the Ocean Sea" with the clear goal of converting the Indigenous Amerindians "to our holy Catholic faith," and she also entreated her husband and daughter that the Indigenous people always "be well and justly treated."[20] The Montesinos sermon was a reflection of the queen's ideas and of the writings of the church fathers of earlier centuries. Historian Carl Watner says, "Unlike other European countries of that age, the Spaniards were vitally concerned with the moral problems of conquest, conversion, and the government of heathen peoples."[21] The desire to extract wealth from the western lands, however, always triumphed over any moral reservations about the conquest or oppression of the Indigenous population.

The questions that Montesino's sermon poses, "Tell me, what right have you to enslave them? What authority did you use to make war against them who lived at peace on their territories. . . . Are they not human beings? Have they no rational soul?" go to the heart of the questions of whether the people in the Indies were of the same nature as the Europeans and what their rights were under the laws of nature as laid out by Thomas Aquinas (1225–1274). Aquinas, in contrast with other medieval philosophers and Church authorities, ascribed to all humans, even pagans, the same capacity and the same rights as Christians. The Dominicans adopted the position that natural law must prevail over positive or statutory law.[22] Philosopher Ambrose Mary Little, himself a Dominican priest, states, "Montesinos and his Dominican brothers realized that there was something fundamentally immoral about enslaving another human being, one made in the image of God, who thus should enjoy an equality with all other human beings based upon a common or shared nature."[23] Writing about Montesino's sermon, philosopher Mauricio Beuchot, also a Dominican, notes that we can see others as similar or analogous (even while knowing that, in the similarity or analogy, difference predominates) and in this way respect as much as possible the differences of others without losing the awareness that they belong to the same human race, which makes them our brothers and sisters.[24]

But there is more. If the Indigenous people had the same natural rights as European Christians, then the latter had no right "to make war against them who lived in peace on their territories" as Montesinos put it. Pereña says, "The polemics about the legitimacy of the conquest of America had exploded."[25] Political scientist Anthony Pagden states that while Montesinos had denounced the colonists' treatment of the Indigenous people, the angry colonists interpreted him to be attacking the encomienda system and even the monarch's rights in the Indies and made it possible for critics to ask this fundamental question, "Did the crown in fact possess the right to colonise the Indies in the first place?"[26]

The argument supporting the rights of the Indigenous people and the questioning of the justice of the conquest would be carried forward in Spain by churchmen of the School of Salamanca dominated by Dominican friars, most especially Francisco de Vitoria and Domingo de Soto, but also including others such as Jesuit Francisco Suarez, and in the New World by Bishop of Chiapas Bartolomé de las Casas. Historian Juan Friede says, "So important was this debate that it helped make Spain pre-eminent in the juridical science of the period."[27] Francisco de Vitoria is often called the father of international law.[28]

It is notable that this examination at the highest levels of government and church in Spain and its colonies of the rights of the Indigenous inhabitants of the Americas did not happen in the other powers establishing settlements in the Western Hemisphere. But in the case of Spain, they began in Santo Domingo less than two decades after the arrival of Christopher Columbus with the voice of "one crying in the desert," that of Friar Antonio de Montesinos. The story of the Advent sermon, including much of the text of the sermon, is told here by Bartolomé de Las Casas, who was present to hear Montesinos preach.

THE 1511 SERMON OF ANTONIO DE MONTESINOS

[F]ull of compassion toward the Indians and zeal to defend the sullied honor of God, [the Dominican fathers] prayed, fasted, and kept vigils in order to receive enlightenment as to the best way to fight for a cause that had no other defendants. They knew how new and scandalous it would be to awaken people from such an abysmal slumber, and after mature reflection they decided to preach from the pulpit and in public that to oppress Indians was to go straight to Hell.

The most scholarly among them composed the first sermon on the subject by order of their superior, fray Pedro de Córdoba, and they all signed it to show that it represented common sentiment and not that of the preacher alone. They gave it to their most important preacher, fray Antón Montesinos, who was the second of three preachers the Order had sent here. Fray Antón Montesino's talent lay in a certain sternness when reproaching faults and a certain way of reading sermons both choleric and efficient, which was thought to reap great results. So then, as a very animated speaker, they gave him that first sermon on such a new theme: the novelty consisting in saying that killing a man is more serious than killing a beetle. They set aside the fourth week of Advent for the sermon, since the Gospel according to St. John that week is "The Pharisees asked St. John the Baptist who he was and he said: *"Ego vox clamantis in deserto* [I am the voice of one crying in the desert]."

The whole city of Santo Domingo was to be there, including the admiral Diego Columbus, and all the jurists and royal officials, who had been notified each and every one individually to come and hear a sermon of great importance. They accepted readily, some out of respect for the virtue of the friars; others, out of curiosity to hear what was to be said that concerned them so much, though had they known, they would have refused to come and would have censured the sermon as well.

At the appointed time fray Antón Montesino went to the pulpit and announced the theme of the sermon: *Ego vox clamantis in deserto*. After the introductory words on Advent, he compared the sterility of the desert to the conscience of the Spaniards who lived on Hispaniola in a state of blindness, a danger of damnation, sunk deep in the waters of insensitivity and drowning without being aware of it. Then he said: "I have come here in order to declare it unto you, I the voice of Christ in the desert of this island. Open your hearts and your senses, all of you, for this voice will speak new things harshly, and will be frightening." For a good while the voice spoke in such punitive terms that the congregation trembled as if facing Judgment Day. "This voice," he continued, "says that you are living in deadly sin for the atrocities you tyrannically impose on these innocent people. Tell me, what right have you to enslave them? What authority did you use to make war against them who lived at peace on their territories, killing them cruelly with methods never before heard of? How can you oppress them and not care to feed or cure them, and work them to death to satisfy your greed? And why don't you look after their spiritual health, so that they should come to know God, that they should be baptized, and that they should hear Mass and keep the holy days? Aren't they human beings? Have they no rational soul? Aren't you obliged to love them as you love yourselves? Don't you understand? How can you live in such a lethargical dream? You may rest assured that you are in no better state of salvation than the Moors or the Turks who reject the Christian Faith."

The voice had astounded them all; some reacted as if they had lost their senses, some were petrified and others showed signed of repentance, but not one was really convinced. After his sermon, he descended from the pulpit holding his head straight, as if unafraid—he wasn't the kind of man to show fear—for much was at stake in displeasing the audience by speaking what had to be said, and he went on to his thin cabbage soup and the straw house of his Order accompanied by a friend.

When he had left, the congregation began such whispering that I believe they could not finish the Mass. You can imagine they didn't sit around reading *Menosprecio del mundo* [a reference to the book *On the Imitation of Christ* by Thomas à Kempis, published in 1424] after dinner that day, and they can't have enjoyed the meal either since they all met at the admiral's house, that is, Diego Columbus, the discoverer's son. They decided to reprehend and frighten the preacher and his companions, to punish him as a scandalmaker and originator of a new doctrine that condemned them against the king's authority by stating they could not use the Indians the king had given them, which was a most serious and unpardonable matter. They called at the friar's house, the porter opened the door, they asked for the superior, and the venerable father fray Pedro de Córdoba came alone to meet them. Imperiously they demanded to see the preacher; he answered prudently saying that as prelate he could speak for all his friars. They insisted but he evaded the issue by using grave and modest words, as he was wont to do, with an air of prudence and authority. Finally, the reverence of his person prevailed upon the admiral and other royal officials to change their tone; they softened and begged him to please bring the friar to them because they wanted to question him about the basis of a sermon that had preached such new and prejudicial things in disservice of the king and damage to the residents of the island.

When the holy man saw that they showed a better disposition, he called fray Antón Montesino, who came with a great deal of fright. After all were seated, the admiral exposed their grievance, asking how he had dared say they couldn't use the Indians given them by the king and acquired at the cost of so much difficulty in wars against the infidel. And because the sermon had caused such a scandal, they demanded a revocation; otherwise they intended to resort to the necessary measures. Fray Antón Montesino answered that what he had preached was the result of mature deliberation and the common opinion of all: the need to save the souls of both Spaniards and Indians on the island had to be pointed out as gospel truth because they had noticed the extinction of the Indians, as well as the fact that they were left as uncared for as beasts in the fields. Therefore, as professed Christians and preachers of the Truth, their duty was to serve the king faithfully who had sent them to Santo Domingo to preach whatever was necessary for the salvation of souls; moreover, they were certain that once the king was informed of these happenings, he would thank them for the service. This justification of the sermon spoken to placate their anger fell on dead ears; to prohibit the tyrannization of Indians was hardly the way they could satiate their thirst for gold, since without Indians, they were defrauded of all their desires.

They decided then, each one for his own reasons, to demand a retraction on the following Sunday, and blindness drove them to the point of threatening to send the friars back to Spain if they should not comply. The superior answered that, "Surely, this [a return to Spain] could be easily done," and this was true, for, besides their habits of coarse frieze, they owned nothing but a rough blanket for the night. . . . [A]s for the articles of Mass and their scant library, that would easily fit in two trunks. When they realized that threats brought no results, they softened again and asked them to consider another sermon which in some way would satisfy a scandalized town. The friars, in order to put an end to their frivolous inportunities and get rid of them, conceded that the same fray Montesino would preach the following Sunday and do his best to satisfy them and elucidate things, and once this was agreed upon, they went home happily.

The news of the friar's recantation to be made the following Sunday spread so rapidly that, come Sunday, no invitation was needed to draw the whole town to church. Fray Antón Montesino went to the pulpit and read a theme from Job 36: "From the beginning I shall repeat my knowledge and my truth and I will show my words of last Sunday, that so embittered you, to be true." They were quick to sense the tenor of the sermon and sat there itching to restrain him. The friar backed up his sermon with supporting authorities and gave more reasons to condemn the tyranny of Spanish oppression as illegal, while stressing the point that in no way could a Spaniard save his soul if he persisted in that state. He asked them to mend their ways and said that his Order would refuse to confess anyone except those who moved from place to place. They could publicize this; they could write to anyone they pleased in Castile; for their part, the friars knew for certain this was the only way to serve both God and the king. After he left, they grumbled in indignation, frustrated in their hopes that the friar would deny what he had said, as if a disavowal could change the law of God which they violated by oppressing Indians.

NOTES

1. "Fr. Antón de Montesinos, O.P.," *Personajes Dominicanos*, accessed May 17, 2020, www.dominicos.org/grandes-figuras/personajes/anton-de-montesinos.

2. Dana E. Aspinall, "Introduction," in *Montesino's Legacy: Defining and Defending Human Rights for 500 Years*, ed. Edward C. Lorenz, Dana E. Aspinall, and J. Michael Raley (Lanham, MD: Lexington Books, 2014), 1.

3. The story of the friars and the sermon is in volume 3, chapter 3. It can be viewed here: http://bdh-rd.bne.es/viewer.vm?id=0000023195&page=1.

4. Henry Joseph Schroeder, "Antonio Montesino," in *The Catholic Encyclopedia* (New York: Robert Appleton Company: 1911), accessed May 20, 2020, www.newad vent.org/cathen/10534b.htm.

5. Douglas T. Peck, "Lucas Vásquez de Ayllón's Doomed Colony of San Miguel de Gualdape," *The Georgia Historical Quarterly* 8, no. 2 (Summer 2001): 193.

6. *Personajes Dominicanos.*

7. Brian Pierce, OP, "Seeing, Touching and Speaking the Truth: The First Dominicans in the Americas," *Spirituality* 13, no. 72–3 (2007): 2, https://www.domlife.org/2011Stories/files/anniv_brian_pierce.pdf.

8. "Carta de Fernando el Católico a Diego Colón, 20 marzo 1512," cited in Juan Manuel Perez, *Sermon de Antonio de Montesinos*, accessed May 17, 2020, http://jubileo.dominicos.org/kit_upload/file/Jubileo/materiales-2010/Sermon-de-Antonio-de-Montesinos-Esquema-3.pdf.

9. Lewis Hanke, "Free Speech in Sixteenth-Century Spanish America," *The Hispanic American Historical Review* 26, no. 2 (May 1946): 143.

10. Quoted in Anthony Pagden, *The Fall of Natural Man: The American Indian and the Origins of Comparative Ethnology* (Cambridge: Cambridge University Press, 1982), 31.

11. Bartolomé de las Casas, *History of the Indies*, translated and edited by Andreé Collard (New York: Harper & Row, 1971), 191.

12. Luciano Pereña, *La idea de la justicia en la conquista de America* (Madrid: Editorial MAPFRE: 1992), 19.

13. Stafford Poole, "Iberian Catholicism Comes to the Americas," in *Christianity Comes to the Americas—1492–1776*, ed. Charles H. Lippy, Robert Choquette and Stafford Poole (New York: Paragon House, 1992), 80.

14. Pereña, *La idea*, 15, 16.

15. Poole, "Iberian," 80.

16. Estrella Figueras Vallés "Las contradicciones de la conquista española en América: El Requerimiento y la evangelización en Castilla del Oro," *Orbis incognitvs: avisos y legajos del Nuevo Mundo: homenaje al profesor Luis Navarro Garcia* (Huelva: Universidad de Huelva, 2007), 376. However, other sources say the document was written in 1510, before Montesinos' sermon.

17. Quoted in Figueras Vallés, "Las contradicciones," 378.

18. "Carta de Fernando el Católico a Diego Colon, 18 septiembre 1512," cited in Perez, "Sermón."

19. Cited in Hanke, "Free," 142.

20. Isabel I de Castilla. *Testamento y Codicilo.* Medina del Campo: Villa de las Ferias, accessed May 17, 2020, www.delsolmedina.com/testamentoTexto-22.htm, 22. The original manuscript of this page of the will can be viewed by clicking on the manuscript icon in the upper left-hand corner.

21. Carl Watner, "'All Mankind Is One': The Libertarian Tradition in Sixteenth Century Spain," *The Journal of Libertarian Studies* 8, no. 2 (Summer 1987): 293.

22. Miguel Angel Medina Escudero, "¿Estos no son hombres? El profetismo de los primeros dominicos en América," accessed May 17, 2020, https://docplayer.es/406775–Estos-no-son-hombres-el-profetismo-de-los-primeros-dominicos-en-america.html, 6.

23. Ambrose Mary Little, "The Foundation of Human Rights in Natural Universals," in *Montesino's Legacy: Defining and Defending Human Rights for 500 Years*, ed. Edward C. Lorenz, Dana E. Aspinall, and J. Michael Raley (Lanham, MD: Lexington Books, 2014), 25.

24. Mauricio Beuchot, "Fray Antón de Montesino: Su novedad," *El grito y su eco: El sermón de Montesino*, ed. Ricardo de Luis Carballada (Salamanca: Editorial San Esteban, 2011), 91.

25. Pereña, "La idea," 31.

26. Pagden, "The Fall," 37.

27. Juan Friede, "Las Casas and Indigenism in the Sixteenth Century," in *Bartolome de Las Casas: Toward an Understanding of the Man and His Work*, ed. Juan Friede and Benjamin Keen (DeKalb: Northern Illinois University Press, 1971), 134.

28. One example: Charles H. McKenna, "Francisco de Vitoria: Father of International Law," *Studies: An Irish Quarterly Review* 21, no. 84 (Dec. 1932): 637.

Chapter Four

Bartolomé de Las Casas

"This Is against All Divine and Human Laws"

Bartolomé de Las Casas is a giant in Latin American history and thought. Known as the protector of the Indians, he became the conscience of the Spanish court, called on by Emperor Charles V to debate Juan Ginés de Sepúlveda about the rights of the Indigenous inhabitants of the New World at a famous debate in Valladolid, Spain, in 1550. Las Casas lived a long life and is estimated to have written 370 works, from letters to multivolume books. The number of written works about Las Casas is also overwhelming. In 1954, scholars Lewis Hanke and Manuel Giménez counted a total of 849 books and articles about him and his work and many hundreds have been written since,[1] especially in the years around 1992, the quincentennial of Columbus's arrival in America. Las Casas scholar Isacio Pérez estimated that in his lifetime Las Casas traveled some 22,442 leagues, or approximately 67,326 miles. Pérez calls him one of history's greatest travelers before motorized transportation.[2] Obviously, in this short essay we cannot begin to do justice to his life and contribution.

Biography

Las Casas was born in Seville in what scholars now agree was 1484, and not 1474 as some had believed. In 1502, when he was eighteen years old, he accompanied his father on Columbus's second voyage to Hispaniola, where he worked as a *doctrinero*, or lay teacher of religion, and was given an *encomienda*, a royal grant of land and Indigenous people in a system similar to serfdom and often likened to slavery. He took his final vows as a Catholic priest in Rome in 1507 and finished his bachelors of canon law at the University of Salamanca in Spain before returning to Hispaniola, where he celebrated his first mass in the New World in 1510.[3] Las Casas was present at and recorded the famous 1511 Advent sermon of Dominican Friar Antonio de Montesinos, but its denunciation of the treatment of the Indigenous Amerindians had limited effect on him at that time.

In 1512, he was sent to Cuba where he saw a destruction of the Taino Indian economy and civilization that was even worse than what had taken place on Hispaniola. Both men and women were dragged away to be worked to death in the mines and towns, leaving their children starving on the land. In August 1514, Las Casas announced in a Sunday sermon that he was renouncing his *encomienda* and condemned those who continued to hold Indigenous people enslaved.[4] In 1515, he obtained permission to leave his parish in Cuba and traveled to Spain with Friar Montesinos to plead the cause of the Indigenous people before the Spanish court. He won an audience with King Ferdinand, who promised reform but who died shortly thereafter. Las Casas presented his denunciations to Cardinal Cisneros, the regent of King Charles I (who would become also Emperor Charles V of the Holy Roman Empire), but the Cardinal passed off Las Casas's proposal for free Indian towns to a reform commission of three Hieronymite friars and gave Las Casas the title "Protector of the Indians" as a face-saver. The Hieronymite friars did little and were forgotten, but Las Casas would be known ever after as the Indigenous people's protector.[5]

In 1519, King Charles approved a plan by Las Casas to establish a colony on the mainland in what is now Venezuela made up of Amerindians and Spanish farmers. Las Casas set out in 1520 to the New World with a group of Spanish farm laborers. But the project failed because not enough farmers had been recruited and natives attacked the community after a Spanish slaving raid in the area.[6] Las Casas went into a profound depression and in 1522 entered a Dominican monastery in Santo Domingo to study to become a Dominican friar. He studied law and the writings of theologians Thomas Aquinas and Thomas Cajetan for four years, finding in them support for his views about the rights of the Indigenous people.[7] In 1526, he finished his preparations and was sent to the north coast of what is now Haiti to found a new Dominican house at Puerto de Plata. He sent letters to the Spanish court, denounced the *encomienda* system from the pulpit, and continued work on his prodigious and invaluable *History of the Indies*. He was able to cement a peace treaty with an Indian chief named Enriquillo, and, based on that experience, began a work titled *De Unico Vocationis Modo (The Only Way)* on the peaceful conversion of the Indigenous people to the Catholic faith.[8]

In 1534, Las Casas arranged to be sent as a missionary to Peru, leading a small band of Dominicans. But his vessel was becalmed, and he stopped in Nicaragua, where he joined Dominican Bishop Antonio Valdivieso in denouncing the enslaving of the Indigenous people there. He was made to leave Nicaragua by the same Governor Rodrigo Contreras whose sons would later murder Bishop Valdivieso.[9]

Las Casas's next efforts in peaceful evangelization were at Verapaz in what is now Guatemala. The Las Casas scholar Helen Rand Parish explains that, under the terms of Las Casas's contract, Spaniards would be forbidden to enter the territory for five years and all Indigenous people peacefully converted would never be subject to encomienda and would live as free Indigenous people in crown towns.[10] Opinions differ as to whether this experiment was a success or a failure, but scholar Benno Biermann notes that "to the end of his life [Las Casas] followed its development with the solicitous eye of a father and aided its progress in every possible way."[11]

In 1537 Las Casas was recalled to Mexico City, and in 1541, he was sent back to the Spanish court to recruit missionaries for New Spain. After successful completion of that task, Charles V ordered Las Casas to remain in Spain, and, for the next period, he was intimately involved in choosing the commission that would draft The New Laws for the governing of the Indies and the protection of the Indigenous people and wrote some of their provisions.[12] Anthony Pagden explains that the New Laws of 1542 freed all but a small number of Indigenous slaves and mandated that, as each holder of an *encomienda* died, his grant would revert to the Crown and the Indigenous people held would become full subjects of the king.[13] In America, while the Indigenous people celebrated the New Laws, the colonists who held encomiendas met them with disbelief, anger and, in some cases, open revolt.

Las Casas was offered the post of bishop of Cusco, Peru, one of the richest in the New World, but he declined, accepting instead the bishopric of Chiapas which included the region of his Verapaz experiment.[14] Arriving in his diocese in 1544, Las Casas began strict enforcement of the New Laws, but in 1546, he learned that the previous year the Emperor had revoked the key provision which freed the Indigenous people upon the death of the *encomendero*. The news caused a great celebration among Spaniards in Mexico City. Las Casas continued to enforce what remained of the Laws, expanding them with his own regulations: owners of encomiendas who had not sent out priests or catechists to teach the faith to the Indigenous people under their tutelage must make restitution; Amerindians were exempt from tithes; and other measures which included refusing absolution to Spaniards who kept Indigenous people in slavery. And then, in 1547 at the age of sixty-three, he prepared to return to Spain to resume his advocating for the Indigenous people at the Spanish court. He would not return to the New World.[15]

Las Casas became an influential figure at the Council of the Indies and at court, writing numerous petitions in support of the Indigenous people. This brought him into confrontation with historian and theologian Juan Gines de Sepulveda, who had written that war against the Native people of the New World was justified based on Aristotelian principles. The two debated each other in 1550 and 1551 at the Council of Valladolid and, although the theologians came to no final conclusion, the debate was of supreme importance. It was the only time an imperial government called for an official discussion of the morality and legality of its policies toward the native inhabitants of the Americas. Not the Portuguese, nor the British, nor the French, nor the Dutch would engage in any such debate.[16] After the debates, Las Casas began rewriting his *History of the Indies*, consulting other books and documents, and talking to participants in the conquest. The five-volume *History* was finally published in Madrid in 1875, its publication having been held up over the centuries because of its portrayal of the Spanish conquistadors.

Philip II came to the throne in 1556 with the empire in desperate financial straits. When owners of encomiendas in Peru offered to buy from the king the perpetual right to the lands and inhabitants of that vice-royalty, Philip seriously considered the proposal. Las Casas presented the king with twenty reasons why he should reject the proposal and return the lands of Peru to its native lords. Organized by Las Casas and other Dominicans, those Indigenous lords in 1560 proposed to buy their freedom with a larger sum than that offered by the Spanish conquistadors. But, in the end, Philip did not sell the encomiendas to the Spaniards in Peru nor did he accept the counteroffer of the native lords, rather he sold only a few minor posts.[17]

Bartolome de Las Casas died at age eighty-two in Madrid on June 18, 1566. Parish notes that "in his last words he professed that he had kept faith, for fifty years of untiring labor, with the charge that God had laid upon him to plead for the restoration of the Indians to their original lands, liberty, and freedom."[18]

Las Casas's Thought

Las Casas's thought evolved during his long lifetime from believing in peaceful conversion of the Indigenous people so that they could be profit-producing subjects of the king of Spain to supporting complete restoration of Indian lands under their own rulers and only nominally under the Spanish crown. His goals were to stop the evil being carried out against the Indigenous people and save Spain from God's justifiable wrath because of its sins in the New World. His beliefs originated in what historian David Orique call "late medieval and early modern legal, philosophical, and theological thought." Orique adds:

> Las Casas used the tripartite scheme of divine, natural, and human law as the specific analytical and juridical framework for his articulation and assessment

of the evils and harms done in the Indies. In this, he drew on the Thomistic intellectual paradigm of the hierarchy of law (eternal, divine, natural, and human) to make his judgments about what the Spaniards had been doing and were continuing to do in the Indies.[19]

Las Casas takes as the starting point of his arguments on behalf of the Indigenous people the modern scholastic discourse, logic, and philosophy of the School of Salamanca, the most important European university of the sixteenth century with its noted teachers Francisco de Vitoria, Domingo de Soto, and Francisco Suarez, but Las Casas had the advantage of a long military and political experience in the Indies on which to base his theories.[20]

Las Casas regarded the Indigenous people as rational creatures made in the image of God and thus as holders of rights under natural law. Theologian Gustavo Gutiérrez states that, with his first conversion in 1514, Las Casas realized that two fundamental human rights were being violated in the Indies—the right to life and the right to liberty. Gutiérrez adds that, "All of his work turns upon the defense of these two basic claims." Las Casas recognized the New World peoples as equal in human dignity to people of the Old World while also acknowledging them as culturally and religiously different.[21]

Las Casas's writings and advocacy before the Spanish crown, the Council of the Indies, and in ecclesiastical circles—in particular his *De Unico Vocationis Modo*—led to the issuing by Pope Paul III in 1537 of his encyclical *Sublimes Deus*. Paul III noted that, while the opinion had been presented to him that "the Indians of the West and the South . . . should be treated as dumb brutes created for our service," the Church declared that "the Indians are truly men" and "are by no means to be deprived of their liberty or the possession of their property nor should they be in any way enslaved."[22]

Las Casas also maintained that the Spanish wars of conquest were not legal under traditional principles of just war as set out by Thomas Aquinas, which required proper authority, just cause, and right intention. In fact, as Pagden explains, Las Casas went so far as to assert "in the *Short Account* and later and at greater length in *On Royal Power*, that the Indians now had sufficient cause, under natural, divine, and Roman law, for *them* to wage a 'just war' against the Spaniards."[23]

Political theorist Diego Von Vacano notes that in the *Short Account of the Destruction of the Indies*, Las Casas maintains that "the Spaniards do not understand that the inhabitants [of the New World] are members of the same species as the Europeans" and Von Vacano goes on to say, "Las Casas' task is to insist on the humanity of the natives in spite of external differences."[24] Las Casas portrays the Indigenous people as "unassuming, long-suffering, unassertive, and submissive" as well as less robust than Europeans[25] and Von Vacano asserts that "by setting the natives apart from the common understanding of normal human psychology, . . . Las Casas lays the basis of a human classificatory scheme, which we could call racial since it refers to large categories of people as distinguished from others along essential lines."[26] Las Casas, thus becomes "the first to recognize human variation while [at the same time] seeking to incorporate diverse groups into a unitary, non-hierarchical understanding of both the human species and a single political community." Von Vacano calls him "the first theorist to lay the grounds for a racial conception in politics."[27]

Valladolid Debate and the Apología

The selection from the Valladolid debate included here is from the 1992 English translation from the Latin by Stafford Poole of Las Casas's *Apologia fratris Bartholomaei a Casaus adversus Genesium Sepulvedam*, usually abbreviated as the *Apologia*. Scholars believe that Las Casas translated his original presentation at Valladolid against Sepúlveda into Latin from the Spanish between 1552 and 1553. There is no surviving manuscript of the Spanish version, and the only copy of the Latin resides at the National Library of France in Paris.[28]

In 1549, the Council of the Indies requested the suspension of conquests in the New World until it could be decided how they could be justly carried out and, early in 1550, Emperor Charles V sent instructions ordering such a cessation. Lewis Hanke states, "Probably never before, or since, has a mighty emperor—and in 1550 Charles V, Holy Roman Emperor, was the strongest ruler in Europe with a great overseas empire besides—ordered his conquests to cease until it was decided if they were just."[29] On July 7, 1550, letters were sent to fifteen prominent jurists, theologians and bishops asking them to be the judges of arguments on the future of royal policy. Fourteen were able to accept, among them theologians Domingo de Soto, Melchor Cano, and Bartolomé Carranza de Miranda, all Dominican friars like Las Casas.[30] The official mandate of the debate was "to inquire into and establish the manner and the laws by which our Holy Catholic faith can be preached and promulgated in that New World [and to examine] in what form those peoples may remain subject to His Majesty the Emperor without injury to his royal conscience, according to the bull of Pope Alexander"[31] (who in 1493 had assigned lands in the New World to Spain on the condition that Spain evangelize the native inhabitants).

Juan Ginés de Sepulveda was a royal historian and an authority on Aristotle, having published in 1548 a translation of the *Politics* from the original Greek into Latin which was recognized for centuries as an essential work. Hanke states that Sepúlveda "was completely saturated with the theory of 'The Philosopher,' including his much-discussed concept that certain men are slaves by nature."[32] Scholar Angel Losada describes him as "humanist, chronicler, confessor to the emperor, philosopher, theologian, one of the most lucid thinkers of the age, and an exponent of the use of force to overcome the opposition of the newly discovered peoples to the preaching of Christianity."[33] A member of the Council of the Indies had encouraged Sepúlveda to write a treatise on this subject, which he did, and although the treatise was not approved for publication, its author was chosen to defend at Valladolid the position of those who advocated war against the Indigenous people of the New World.

Las Casas engaged Sepúlveda's ancient Aristotelian arguments fully, and some scholars have wondered why. Hanke posits that it could have been merely because his opponent used them or possibly because he wanted to argue that Aristotle's ideas on barbarians and natural slavery were not relevant in the greatly expanded sixteenth-century world and he wished to establish "the Indians in the eyes of the Spanish community as human beings with a culture which it must respect."[34] Thomas Aquinas, whose ideas on natural law were the foundation of the philosophy of the School of Salamanca, had combined Aristotle's ideas with those of Christianity and thus it was logical for Las Casas to engage Aristotle.

At the debate, Sepúlveda spoke first, followed by Las Casas. Hanke describes the scene:

> On the first day Sepúlveda spoke for three hours, giving a resume of his treatise. On the second day Las Casas appeared, armed with his monumental manuscript, which, as he himself stated, he proceeded to read word for word. This verbal onslaught continued for five days, until the reading was completed—or until the members of the junta, as Sepúlveda suggested, could bear no more. The two opponents did not appear together before the Council; instead, the judges seem to have discussed the issues with them separately as they stated their positions.[35]

The judges requested that Domingo de Soto prepare a summary of each presentation. Sepúlveda then replied to the objections made by Las Casas to his arguments, and Las Casas replied to them at the second session scheduled for January 1551, which actually took place in April of that year. The judges reached no collective decision. In 1556, Emperor Charles V abdicated in favor of his son Philip II, and in that same year new instructions on how conquests were to be carried out were published.[36]

Las Casas's Impact through History

In spite of the ill-defined result of the Valladolid debate, Las Casas's impact on Spanish law and thought after that date and, indeed, after his death, was still substantial. In 1571, Juan de Ovando, president of the Council of the Indies, asked for Las Casas's manuscripts to be brought from Valladolid to the court in Madrid. In July of 1573, Philip issued a new ordinance designed to regulate future discoveries by Spain. The word "conquest" was replaced by "pacification" and, in a clear reference to Las Casas's arguments, the Indians' vices were to be addressed gently "so as not to scandalize them or prejudice them against Christianity," and if the natives did not accept Spanish settlement and Christianity, force could be used but in a way to do "as little harm as possible."[37] Enslaving captive Amerindians was prohibited. However, literary scholar David Solodkow says that, given the consequences for the Indigenous people on the ground in the New World, it would not be inaccurate to assert that it was Sepulveda's ideas which triumphed. He adds:

> During the century that saw the establishment of the legal bases for what subsequently evolved into "human rights" (Las Casas) and international law (Vitoria), one of history's greatest genocides occurred, a genocide which was to have extremely far-reaching political, economic, religious, and cultural consequences for the future history of humanity.[38]

Las Casas's best-known work was his *Short Account of the Destruction of the Indies*, in which he described the cruelties inflicted on the Indigenous people in all the colonies of the New World from Hispaniola to Nicaragua to Peru to Rio de La Plata. It was published in 1552 and arrived in New Spain shortly thereafter. The response was immediate. Franciscan Friar Toribio de Motolinía wrote a furious letter in 1555 to Charles V accusing Las Casas of defaming many good people for the actions of a few. Motolinía states:

> It should have been enough for Las Casas to give his vote and opinion on what he felt about giving *encomiendas* of Indians to Spaniards, and to put it down in writing, without printing so many insults, slanders and vituperation. It is well known what a sin it is to defame one person; more to defame many, and much more to defame a commonwealth and nation. If Las Casas called the Spanish residents of New Spain tyrants, thieves, robbers, murderers and cruel assailants only a hundred times, it might pass, but . . . he calls them that a hundred times a hundred.[39]

At this time, Spain had many enemies, based not entirely on its policies in the New World but in large part on conflicts within the Holy Roman Empire, of which Charles, as head of the Hapsburgs, was emperor. Translations of the *Short Account* were made in all of the Empire's restless subject provinces and in rival nations that opposed Spain on disparate issues that included the Protestant Reformation. By the end of the 1600s, many editions had been published, including twenty-nine in Dutch, thirteen in French, six in English, six in German, three in Italian, and three in Latin[40] giving rise to what was known as the Black Legend.

Only one edition of Las Casas work was published in Spain during the 1600s, and Las Casas acquired fame as someone who gave aid and comfort to the enemies of his country.[41] A prohibition on the publication of his works continued through the 1700s. But while his works may not have been published in Spain, Las Casas was a favorite of Enlightenment writers in the rest of Europe and inspired eighteenth- and nineteenth-century and nineteenth Latin American revolutionaries such as Simón Bolívar. Bolívar spoke of Las Casas as "that apostle of America," and he praised "the zeal, sincerity, and high character of that friend of humanity, who so fervently and so steadfastly denounced to his government and to his contemporaries the most horrible acts of sanguinary frenzy."[42] Fears of Indian revolts, even into the nineteenth century, limited enthusiasm for Las Casas's ideas within the Creole upper classes of Latin America, and, after 1850, racist and biological determinist theories such as those of Herbert Spencer influenced thought in the region. But Las Casas had his defenders, and, wherever the liberal-conservative divide was a real conflict of principles, as in Mexico after 1853, liberals invoked the name of Las Casas.[43]

Even in the twentieth century, conservative Spanish writers were critical of Las Casas for his role in the rise of the Black Legend. Ramón Menéndez Pidal (1869–1968), writing in 1963, took up the argument of Motolinía from 1555 and accused Las Casas of having a mental illness—an abnormal mania—in exaggerating the cruelties of the Spaniards and the goodness of the Indigenous people. Menéndez said that Columbus had found the Amerindians still in the Stone Age and that they needed to be brought into the more advanced Spanish life via the encomienda and not be allowed to preserve intact their political sovereignty as Las Casas had advocated. Menéndez Pidal insisted that "The Indians living under the Aztec and Inca empires were a minority and the jungle Indians were the greater number." He added: "What a beautiful fantasy is the absolute equality of all of the [world's] peoples, but also a deceptive fantasy that exaggerates the grave problems of the Indians. All peoples are equal in the sacred rights of their personal dignity but are very unequal in their mental capacity."[44]

Chilean historian Fernando Mires, writing in 1984, argues that Menéndez Pidal showed definite points of similarity with Juan Ginés de Sepúlveda, Las Casas's opponent at Valladolid. Mires notes that both represented the "so-called forces of progress" were "rationalists" and "modern," and accepted that it could be possible, even necessary, to sacrifice human dignity for a particular cause. Las Casas, in contrast, he said, showed a resistance to the new reality of world trade that began to measure everything by the criteria of profit. Mires says that, for Sepúlveda and Menéndez, those who fought for the survival of the Indigenous people were in favor of barbarism, while those who supported slavery and extermination were the defenders of civilization.[45] The clash between "civilization" and "barbarism" would be an enduring theme in Latin American thought.

Las Casas has been seen as the precursor of liberation theology, which grew to importance in Latin America beginning with the Conference of Catholic Bishops in Medellín, Colombia, in 1968. One of the founders of the movement, Peruvian theologian Gustavo Gutiérrez of Peru, author of a monumental biography of Las Casas, noted that the abuses Las Casas and others decried were not "the acts of individuals alone. They were rooted in the profound injustice of the economic and social system being implanted in the Indies at that time." Liberation theology identified similar structural injustice in the modern world, denouncing it and working to empower the oppressed to work for change. However, Gutierrez preferred not to call Las Casas a liberation theologian, saying, "We cannot ask him to speak after the fashion of a person of the twentieth century. The question we must ask when it comes to Las Casas is this one: How, in his time, was he able to proclaim the gospel of Jesus?"[46]

The controversies around Las Casas in the twenty-first century have been slightly different, and critiques have come from the political left rather than the right. Possibly most influential has been the 2007 biography of the friar by historian Daniel Castro in which he states that, while Las Casas differentiated his peaceful methods of conversion from the warlike methods of his opponents, he only "offered a different form of implementing the same goal of converting the natives to attain the ultimate objective of the colonization of consciousness." Castro goes on to say that while Las Casas and other religious "provided a humanitarian element absent among ordinary conquistadores . . . they could not escape their roles as advocates of the 'true' faith and as integral components of the vanguard of an imperialist church." He accuses Las Casas of an inability to grasp "the contradiction implied in the act of imposing an alien religious belief, like Christianity, on a people who already had well-defined theological beliefs and carefully constructed cosmogonies."[47]

Writer Agustín Yañez's 1942 biography of Las Casas was reissued in 2001 without doubt because its arguments corresponded with twenty-first century critiques. Yañez states that Las Casas's great love for the Indigenous people and his admiration for pre-Hispanic life were not enough to overcome his belief in the greater excellence of Christianity. And, surely, the greatest champion of Christianity was Catholic Spain. Yañez admits that Las Casas envisions a Spanish Empire as peaceful and pacifist and as an empire where national peculiarities and Indigenous rights are respected, but, Yañez emphasizes, only after the acceptance of baptism and assuming that their particular institutions do not violate the laws of the empire.[48]

According to philosopher Enrique Dussel, however, Las Casas maintained that the Indigenous people not only had the right to affirm all their beliefs as true but also had the obligation to comply with them. Dussel adds that Las Casas went so far as to show that the human sacrifice practiced by some Indigenous people could be considered to not be in violation of natural law and to correspond to a rational argument within their belief system. Dussel recognizes, however, that Las Casas at the same time firmly believed that the Spaniards had the obligation to preach the Christian Gospel to the Indigenous people even though he steadfastly maintained that they did not have the obligation to accept it.[49]

Writers have argued over whether Bartolomé de Las Casas was just a more benevolent type of imperialist,[50] over whether his advocacy was effective or ineffective,[51] and about his support during many years (from approximately 1516 to 1547) of bringing Black slaves from Africa to the Americas as a way to save the Native peoples. With relation to the last issue, Las Casas, writing about himself in the third person, said that

> [T]he permission the cleric Las Casas had gotten so the Spaniards could have help in working the land, so as to free their Indians, was turned into a profit-making scheme. . . . The cleric, many years later, regretted the advice he gave the King on this matter . . . when he saw proven that the enslavement of Blacks was every bit as unjust as that of the Indians. . . . [H]e was not certain that his ignorance and his good intentions would excuse him before the judgment of God.[52]

Las Casas biographer Lawrence Clayton notes that "slavery was a part of life in the early sixteenth century, an accepted form of servitude since ancient times, and unquestioned by anyone."[53] However, slavery has always been questioned, if only by the enslaved, and it was always considered a virtue to free one's slaves. Castro condemns Las Casas for his role in transferring slaves from the Old to the New World, but he admits that Las Casas "spoke of slaves in general, white and black, as they existed in Europe."[54] Slavery in Spain was strengthened after the 711 CE Moorish invasion by the almost continuous warfare between Muslim Moors and Christian Spaniards up until the defeat of Granada in 1492, during which period both sides captured their enemies and enslaved them.[55] It was after a trip in about 1547 to Lisbon where he read the reports of Portuguese historians about the beginnings of the African slave trade, that Las Casas changed his mind and became an opponent not just of Indian slavery but of all slavery.[56]

In summary, Clayton states:

> It is fashionable today to seek out the "other" voices in history, those voices of
> the downtrodden, the illiterate, men and women who left no written or docu-
> mentary record to remember them by. But, long before modern scholars, Las
> Casas discovered and advocated on behalf of the "other" voice in the Conquest
> of the Indies. . . . In doing so, he helped pioneer a new understanding of human
> rights, based on the discovery of an extraordinary world and people that chal-
> lenged Europeans to accommodate to a part of the universe they knew nothing
> of before Columbus returned to Spain in the winter of 1492–1493.[57]

Las Casas arrived in the New World with Columbus on his second voyage
and soon settled there as an *encomendero*. As he learned about the land and
its peoples, he went through at least three conversions that broadened his outlook and led him to articulate what would become known as universal human
rights, putting those thoughts into writings that combined ancient philosophy,
Christian teachings, and an openness to the beliefs of the New World's Indigenous peoples. And because of his long and active life and his monumental
written advocacy, Las Casas will continue to be the subject of discussion and
controversy for many more generations of thinkers, writers, and activists.

THE 1550 DEBATE OF BARTOLOMÉ DE LAS CASAS AGAINST JUAN GINÉS DE SEPÚLVEDA

Summary of Sepúlveda's Position by Fray Domingo de Soto

The work that [Juan Ginés de] Sepúlveda, the theologian and royal historian,
wrote against the Indians can be summarized in the following arguments by
which he defended armed expeditions against the Indians as justified so long
as the war is carried on lawfully and according to rules, as the Kings of Spain
have thus far commanded that it be waged.

He argues first that those people are barbaric, uninstructed in letters and
the art of government, and completely ignorant, unreasoning, and totally
incapable of learning anything but the mechanical arts; that they are sunk in
vice, are cruel, and are of such character that, as nature teaches, they are to
be governed by the will of others. . . . [F]or their own welfare, people of this
kind are held by natural law to submit to the control of those who are wiser
and superior in virtue and learning, as are the Spaniards. . . .

Therefore, if the Indians, once warned, refuse to obey this legitimate sovereignty, they can be forced to do so for their own welfare by recourse to the
terrors of war. And this war will be just both by civil and natural law, according to the second, third, and fifth chapters of the *Politics* of Aristotle. . . .

In the second place, Sepúlveda proves that the Indians, even though unwilling, must accept the Spanish yoke so that they may be corrected and be punished for the sins and crimes against the divine and natural laws by which they have been contaminated, especially their idolatry and the impious custom of human sacrifice. . . .

Thirdly, Sepúlveda argues that the injuries and extreme misery which the Indians used to inflict and which those who have not yet been subdued still inflict today on a great number of innocent persons, whom they used to sacrifice each year to the evil spirit, should be stopped. . . .

Fourthly, he advances the gain in bringing about the spread and growth of the Christian religion. This will be accomplished if, once those regions have been brought under control, the gospel of Christ can be preached by consecrated men safely and without any danger, so that they will not be massacred. . . . He supports this by the authority of Augustine, who writes that Christ wanted men to be drawn to the faith by meekness and gentleness during the first period of the infant Church. However, after the Church grew in power and numbers, Christ wanted men to be compelled, even when unwilling, to accept the Christian religion. . . .

Sepúlveda concludes his work by saying that it is totally just, as well as most beneficial to these barbarians, that they be conquered and brought under the rule of the Spaniards, who are worshipers of Christ. This is the easiest way for them to embrace the Christian religion, as experience has clearly taught. . . .

Furthermore, he asserts that the Roman Pontiff, Alexander VI, in a decree to the College of Cardinals declared armed expeditions against the Indians to be just. . . . Therefore, just as no one can deny that wars undertaken by God's command are just, no one will deny that a war is just that God's Vicar, after mature deliberation and in the exercise of his pontifical authority, declares to be justified. . . .

Preface to the Defense of the Most Reverend Fray Bartolomé de Las Casas, of the Order of Saint Dominic, Late Bishop of Chiapa, to Philip, Great Prince of Spain

Illustrious Prince:

It is right that matters which concern the safety and peace of the great empire placed in your keeping by the divine goodness be reported to you, for you rule Spain and that marvelous New World in the name of the great Charles, your father, and you strive for immortal glory, not just with the imperial power but especially with the generous spirit and with the wisdom implanted in you by Christ. Therefore I have thought it advisable to bring to the attention of Your Highness that there has come into my hands a certain brief synopsis in Spanish of a work that Ginés de Sepúlveda is reported to have written in Latin. In it he gives four reasons, each of which, in his opinion, proves beyond refutation that war against the Indians is justified. . . .

[W]hat will happen when evil men (for whom, according to the old proverb, nothing is wanting except the opportunity) read that a scholar, a doctor of theology, and the royal historian has published books approving those criminal wars and hellish campaigns and, by supporting arguments, confirms and defends the unheard-of crime whereby Christian men, forgetting Christian virtue, hold in slavery those people, the most unfortunate of all, who appear to have escaped the ferocity of that most cruel race by chance rather than by the mercy of the Spaniards? . . .

If, then, the Indians are being brought to the point of extermination, if as many peoples are being destroyed as widespread kingdoms are being overthrown, what sane man would doubt that the most flourishing empire of the New World, once its native inhabitants have been destroyed, will become a wilderness, and nothing but dominion over tigers, lions, and wild beasts for the Kings of Spain? . . .

Finally, it is intolerable that a man to whom has been entrusted the duty of writing the imperial history should publish a destructive error that is in total disagreement with the words of the gospel and the meekness and kindness of which all Christ's teaching is redolent and which the Church, imitating its master, exercises toward those who do not know Christ. For men of the future will, with good reason, decide that a man who has gone wrong so disgracefully in a matter so clear has taken no account of the truth when writing history, a fact that, no matter how learnedly and gracefully that history will have been written, will tarnish the most celebrated victories of the Emperor. . . .

I could not contain myself. Mindful that I am a Christian, a religious, a bishop, a Spaniard, and a subject of the King of Spain, I cannot but unsheathe the sword of my pen for the defense of the truth, the honor of God's house, and the spreading of the revered gospel of Our Lord Jesus Christ so that, according to the measure of the grace given to me, I might wipe the stain from the Christian name, take away the obstacles and stumbling blocks hindering the spread of belief in the gospel, and proclaim the truth which I have vowed in baptism, have learned in the religious life, and finally, however unworthy, have professed when consecrated bishop. . . .

Four things, therefore, that I must give a full account of are to be treated here.

First, I shall refute Sepúlveda's opinion claiming that war against the Indians is justified because they are barbarous, uncivilized, unteachable, and lacking in civil government.

Second, I shall show that, to the most definite ruin of his own soul, Sepúlveda is wrong when he teaches that war against the Indians is justified as punishment for their crimes against the natural law, especially the crimes of idolatry and human sacrifice.

Third, we shall attack his third argument, on the basis of which Sepulveda teaches that war can be waged unconditionally and indiscriminately against those people in order to free the innocent.

Fourth, I shall discuss how foreign to the teaching of the gospel and Christian mercy is his fourth proposition, maintaining that war against the Indians is justified as a means of extending the boundaries of the Christian religion and of opening the way for those who proclaim and preach the gospel. . . .

[Refutation of Sepúlveda's point that war against the Indians is justified because they are barbarous]

[A]s a sort of assault on the first argument for Sepúlveda's position, we should recognize that there are four kinds of barbarians, according to the Philosopher [Aristotle] in Books 1 and 3 of the *Politics* and in Book 7 of the *Ethics*, and according to Saint Thomas [Aquinas] and other doctors [of the Church] in various places.

First, barbarian in the loose and broad sense of the word means any cruel, inhuman, wild, and merciless man acting against human reason out of anger or native disposition, so that, putting aside decency, meekness, and humane moderation, he becomes hard, severe, quarrelsome, unbearable, cruel, and plunges blindly into crimes that only the wildest beasts of the forest would commit. Speaking of this kind of barbarian, the Philosopher says in the *Politics (Book 1, Chapt. 2)* that just as the man who obeys right reason and excellent laws is superior to all the animals, so too, if he leaves the path of right reason and law, he is the wickedest, worst, and most inhuman of all animals. . . .

The second kind of barbarian includes those who do not have a written language that corresponds to the spoken one, as the Latin language does with ours, and therefore they do not know how to express in it what they mean. For this reason they are considered to be uncultured and ignorant of letters and learning. . . . [I]t is obvious that a people can be called barbarians and still be wise, courageous, prudent, and lead a settled life. So, in ancient times, the Greeks called the Romans barbarians. . . .

The third kind of barbarian, in the proper and strict meaning of the word, are those who, either because of their evil and wicked character or the barrenness of the region in which they live, are cruel, savage, sottish, stupid, and strangers to reason. They are not governed by law or right, do not cultivate friendships, and have no state or politically organized community. . . . The Philosopher discusses these barbarians and calls them slaves by nature since they have no natural government, no political institutions (for there is no order among them), and they are not subject to anyone, nor do they have a ruler. . . . Therefore, this kind of barbarian is savage, imperfect, and the worst of men, and they are mistakes of nature or freaks in a rational nature as the Commentator [Thomas Aquinas] on *The Soul (Book 3)* says in the following words: "What intellectual error and false opinion are in relation to the thinking process, so is the freak to bodily nature." And since a rational nature is provided for and guided by divine providence for its own sake in a way superior to that of other creatures, not only in what concerns the species but also each individual, it evidently follows that it would be impossible to find in a rational nature such a freak or mistake of nature, that is, one that does not fit the common notion of man, except very rarely and in far fewer instances than in other creatures. . . .

Who, therefore, except one who is irreverent toward God and contemptuous of nature, has dared to write that countless numbers of natives across the ocean are barbarous, savage, uncivilized, and slow witted? . . . Again, if we believe that such a huge part of mankind is barbaric, it would follow that God's design has for the most part been ineffective, with so many thousands of men deprived of the natural light that is common to all peoples. And so there would be a great reduction in the perfection of the entire universe— something that is unacceptable and unthinkable for any Christian. . . .

The Philosopher adds that it is lawful to catch or hunt barbarians of this type like wild beasts so that they might be led to the right way of life. Two points must be noted here. First, to force barbarians to live in a civilized and human way is not lawful for anyone and everyone, but only for monarchs and the rulers of states. Second, it must be borne in mind that barbarians must not be compelled harshly in the manner described by the Philosopher, but are to be gently persuaded and lovingly drawn to accept the best way of life. For we are commanded by divine law to love our neighbor as ourselves, and since we want our own vices to be corrected and uprooted gently, we should do the same to our brothers, even if they are barbarians.

Again, if we want to be sons of Christ and followers of the truth of the gospel, we should consider that, even though these peoples may be completely barbaric, they are nevertheless created in God's image. They are not so forsaken by divine providence that they are incapable of attaining Christ's kingdom. They are our brothers, redeemed by Christ's most precious blood, no less than the wisest and most learned men in the whole world. . . .

Therefore, although the Philosopher, who was ignorant of Christian truth and love, writes that the wise may hunt down barbarians in the same way as they would wild animals, let no one conclude from this that barbarians are to be killed or loaded like beasts of burden with excessive, cruel, hard, and harsh labor and that, for this purpose, they can be hunted and captured by wiser men. Goodbye, Aristotle! From Christ, the eternal truth, we have the command "You must love your neighbor as yourself." (*Matthew 22:40*) And again Paul says, "Love is not selfish," but seeks the things of Jesus Christ (*1 Corinthians 13:5*). . . .

[Aristotle] admits, and proves, that the barbarians he deals with in the third book of the same work [the second kind of barbarian] have a lawful, just, and natural government. Even though they lack the art and use of writing, they are not wanting in the capacity and skill to rule and govern themselves, both publicly and privately. Thus they have kingdoms, communities, and cities that they govern wisely according to their laws and customs. Thus their government is legitimate and natural, even though it has some resemblance to tyranny. . . .

Now if we shall have shown that among our Indians of the western and southern shores (granting that we call them barbarians and that they are barbarians) there are important kingdoms, large numbers of people who live settled lives in a society, great cities, kings, judges and laws, persons who engage in commerce, buying, selling, lending, and the other contracts of the law of nations, will it not stand proved that the Reverend Doctor Sepúlveda has spoken wrongly and viciously against peoples like these, either out of malice or ignorance of Aristotle's teaching, and, therefore, has falsely and perhaps irreparably slandered them before the entire world? From the fact that the Indians are barbarians it does not necessarily follow that they are incapable of government and have to be ruled by others, except to be taught about the Catholic faith and to be admitted to the holy sacraments. . . .

Since, therefore, every nation by the eternal law has a ruler or prince, it is wrong for one nation to attack another under pretext of being superior in wisdom or to overthrow other kingdoms. For it acts contrary to the eternal law, as we read in Proverbs: "Do not displace the ancient landmark, set up by your ancestors" (*Proverbs 22:28*). This is not an act of wisdom but of great injustice and a lying excuse for plundering others. Hence every nation, no matter how barbaric, has the right to defend itself against a more civilized one that wants to conquer it and take away its freedom. And, moreover, it can lawfully punish with death the more civilized as a savage and cruel aggressor against the law of nature. And this war is certainly more just than the one that, under pretext of wisdom, is waged against them.

There is a fourth kind of barbarian, which includes all those who do not acknowledge Christ. For no matter how well governed a people may be or how philosophical a man, they are subject to complete barbarism, specifically, the barbarism of vice, if they are not imbued with the mysteries of Christian philosophy. . . . Now on Good Friday the Church prays against these barbarians, who are enemies of the Church, in these words: "Let us pray for the Most Christian Emperor, so that our God and Lord may make all barbarian peoples subject to him for our lasting peace," and later: "May all the barbarian peoples who put their trust in their fierceness be restrained by the right hand of your power." However, with regard to the barbarians who do not bother Christian people the Church does not pray that they be restrained but that iniquity be removed from their hearts so that they might abandon their idols and be converted to the one true God. . . .

Here there is a clear recognition of some distinction among barbarians, as the Church suggests in rather precise terms. Moreover, from everything that was brought forth above it is clear that there are four classes of barbarians and that the first, second, and fourth classes are based in some way on certain fierce practices and especially on their lack of faith. . . . Barbarians in the strict sense of the term, however, are those about whom we spoke in the third class. . . . And about such men the Philosopher speaks in a special way in the first book of the *Politics*. So let the ungodly men, and those who have enticed Sepúlveda to defend an evil cause by lies, stop citing the Philosopher in opposition to our position.

What has been said above is not contradicted in any way by the fact that the Church has the obligation of preaching the gospel to all nations and that, for this reason, we should be able to compel them to listen to the truth of the gospel. I readily grant that the Church is obliged to preach the gospel, as is said in the last chapters of Matthew and Mark, "Go out to the whole world; proclaim the Good News to all creation" (*Mark 16:15*). . . . These words are commands and indicate necessity. However, it does not follow from this that we can force unbelievers to hear the gospel. . . . [I]t is quite clear from the instructions with which Christ first sent his disciples to preach the gospel what should be done when unbelievers do not want to hear the gospel. For we read:

> As you enter his house, salute it, and if the house deserves it, let your peace descend upon it; if it does not let your peace come back to you. And if anyone does not welcome you or listen to what you have to say, as you walk out of the house or town shake the dust from your feet. I tell you solemnly, on the day of judgment, it will not go as hard with the land of Sodom and Gomorrah as with that town (*Matthew 10: 12–15*).

Note that Christ did not teach that those who refuse to hear the gospel must be forced or punished. . . .

Now, whoever, by preaching the gospel . . . seeks to impose the sweet yoke of Christ on peoples gently, rather than violently, satisfied Christ's command, for he has followed his instruction and example. But whoever preaches the gospel in the other way, that is, with arms, has already strayed from Christ's teaching, nor in his sight can he be excused in any way. For evils must not be committed "as a means to good," nor should impiety be committed under the pretext of piety. Saint Augustine very appropriately says: "Let a man also do what he can for the temporal welfare of men. When, however, it comes to the point that he cannot secure such welfare without sinning, he should then consider that he has no choice, since he has seen that what he may do rightly is beyond his reach" (*De Mendacio*).

From the foregoing it is evident that war must not be waged against the Indians under the pretext that they should hear the preaching of Christ's teaching, even if they may have killed preachers, since they do not kill the preachers as preachers or Christians as Christians, but as their most cruel public enemies, in order that they may not be oppressed or murdered by them. Therefore, let those who, under the pretext of spreading the faith, invade, steal, and keep the possessions of others by force of arms—let them fear God, who punishes such endeavors.

[Refutation of Sepúlveda's point that war against the Indians is justified as punishment for their crimes against the natural law, especially the crimes of idolatry and human sacrifice, and as a way to free the innocent]

There is another case . . . in which the Church can exercise actual coercive jurisdiction over any unbelievers; that is, if they are found to oppress and injure any innocent persons or to kill them in order to sacrifice them to their gods or in order to commit cannibalism. According to reports, some tribes in the Indian world do this. This is [another] argument or cause that Sepulveda introduces in order to justify those expeditions of his. His error in this, too, will be eliminated by the following explanations. . . . [S]ince the rescue of this kind of oppressed persons, who are killed as sacrifice or for purposes of cannibalism, cannot be accomplished (if it is a question of areas belonging to the oppressors) unless we take up arms, we should most carefully consider the tumult, sedition, killings, arson, devastation, and furor of the goddess of war that necessarily attend the prevention of this evil. Making its decision with prudence, the Church will at times take up arms, at other times it will overlook (such provocation). For circumstances sometimes make what is just in itself be unjust.

Therefore, when unbelievers are discovered to be committing a crime of this kind (that is, killing infants for sacrifice or cannibalism), they are not always to be attacked by war, although it may be the business of the Church to try to prevent it. But there must be lengthy consideration beforehand, so that in trying to prevent the death of a few innocent persons we should not move against an immense multitude of persons, including the innocent, and destroy whole kingdoms, and implant a hatred for the Christian religion in their souls, so that they will never want to hear the name or teaching of Christ for all eternity. All this is surely contrary to the purpose intended by God and our mother the Church. Instead, war must be avoided and that evil tolerated at least for a while. . . .

According to the rule of right reason when we are confronted by two choices that are evil both as to moral guilt and punishment and we cannot avoid both of them, we ought to choose the lesser evil. For in comparison with the greater evil, the choice of the lesser evil has the quality of a good. . . . Again, the death of the innocent is better or less evil than the complete destruction of entire kingdoms, cities, and strongholds. For not all of them eat the flesh of the innocent but only the rulers or priests, who do the sacrificing, whereas war brings the destruction of countless innocent persons who do not deserve any such thing. Therefore, if those evils cannot be removed in any other way than by waging war, one must refrain from it and evils of this kind must be tolerated.

[U]nless a war can prevent the evils of which the innocent are victims, the war should be brought to an end, and one should pay no attention to those who commit these wrongs. This is our position, for it is well-known that evidence, or even probability, that human sacrifice is at least contrary to reason cannot be easily imparted to unbelievers of this type, [who] believe that they and all their possessions are owed to God and that the idols they worship are the true God, a belief that is supported by a great many witnesses of the highest authority and superior to all others, such as kings, princes, high priests, theologians, prophets, or soothsayers. These latter are held in greatest reverence because the people think these men have frequent communications with the gods, from whom they receive secrets and the knowledge by which they predict future events. For these things they have approved custom, positive law, precept, and common error, and so they have a basis for a plausible argument in favor of human sacrifice.

[Refutation of Sepúlveda's point that, after the Church grew in power and numbers, Christ wanted men to be compelled, even when unwilling, to accept the Christian religion.]

At this point we shall refute Sepulveda's argument . . . in which he says that war can be waged against the Indians so that, once the path has been totally cleared for the preachers of the gospel, the Christian religion may be spread.

Indeed, I cannot cease being astonished by Sepúlveda. For what spirit leads a theologian, mature and well-versed in humane letters, to set these poisons before the world so that the far-flung Indian empires, contrary to the law of Christ, would be prey for most savage thieves? In the same way, and to this very moment, the greed of the Spanish people has led to such crimes among those peoples as—according to history—have never been committed by any other nation, no matter how fierce it may have been. In fact, Sepúlveda tries with all his might to increase these crimes, until the last nation in that world will finally be wiped out, when the just and upright God, provoked by these actions, will perhaps pour forth the fury of his anger and lay hold of all of Spain sooner than he had decreed.

And so Sepúlveda first cites what Augustine writes in his letter to the heretic Donatus. Sepúlveda claims that Augustine teaches that peoples during the first period of the nascent Church were to be led to the faith of Christ courteously and gently, whereas later, when the powers of the Church had increased, they could be forced to enter Christ's sheepfold, as in the parable of the wedding feast [Matthew 22:1–14]. Surely Sepúlveda speaks wickedly and commits many errors to the destruction of his soul. . . .

I would like Sepúlveda and his associates to produce some passage from sacred literature where the gospel parable is explained as he explains it; that is, that the gospel (which is the good and joyful news) and the forgiveness of sins should be proclaimed with arms and bombardments, by subjecting a nation with armed militia and pursuing it with the force of war. What do joyful tidings have to do with wounds, captivities, massacres, conflagrations, and the destruction of cities, and the common evils of war? They will go to hell rather than learn the advantages of the gospel. And what will be told by the fugitives who seek out the provinces of other peoples out of fear of the Spaniards, with their heads split, their hands amputated, their intestines torn open? What will they think about the God of the Christians?

Therefore, since the nature of men is the same and all are called by Christ in the same way and they would not want to be called in any other way, it should not be argued that Indians should be led to the Church in any way other than that by which other men are led.

[Refutation of Sepúlveda's point that the Roman Pontiff, Alexander VI, in a decree to the College of Cardinals declared armed expeditions against the Indians to be just.]

Finally, Sepúlveda claims that the Supreme Pontiff Alexander VI advised the kings of Castile to subjugate the Indians by war and that he condoned the war by which those peoples have been brought under our rule. This is absolutely false. The Pope granted the kings of Castile the right to set themselves over the Indian rulers whom they had converted to the faith of Christ and to keep them as subjects under their protection and jurisdiction. But the Pope never commanded or permitted them to subjugate these rulers by war. For how would he permit something that conflicts with Christ's precept and instruction and produced hatred of the name of Christ in the hearts of unbelievers, and is utterly irreligious? For the will of the ruler is always judged to be in conformity with the law.

Now it is unlawful to force the Indians to the faith by war, or by the misfortunes of war to make them hate the Christian religion, by whose preaching they see so many regrettable evils inflicted on them. It is beyond belief, then, that the Vicar of Christ permitted war to be waged against them, since this is against all divine and human laws, and especially as it is his concern to spread the faith. Therefore, we must believe that he wants what is just and in keeping with Christ's commands and example. . . .

That this was the Pope's intention is proved by the fact that in his bull of concession he cites the petition of the Catholic kings [Isabel and Ferdinand], which contains the statement that the Indians are a gentle people who have some knowledge of God and are such a people that if they were instructed in the faith, there would be hope that Christ's religion would be spread far and wide. Therefore, it is unthinkable that the Pope believed that a people whom the petitioners called gentle had to be overcome by war. And so Sepúlveda's assertion that Pope Alexander exhorted the kings to subjugate those peoples by war is not true.

[Conclusion]

I have preached these things, in keeping with the measure of grace granted me, in defense of this lengthy and holy cause, bound as it is by Christian piety. As for the rest, I exhort and advise by Jesus Christ, Sepúlveda, my brother and colleague in Christ, and the other enemies of the Indians to obey the words, to heed and respect the traditions of the holy Fathers, and to fear God, who punishes perverse undertakings.

The Indians are our brothers, and Christ has given his life for them. Why, then, do we persecute them with such inhuman savagery when they do not deserve such treatment? The past, because it cannot be undone, must be attributed to our weakness, provided that what has been taken unjustly be restored. . . . Let upright heralds be sent to proclaim Jesus Christ in their way of life and to convey the attitudes of Peter and Paul. . . .

Thanks be to God.

NOTES

1. Cited by Pedro Borges, *Quien era Bartolomé de Las Casas* (Madrid: Ediciones Rialp, S.A., 1990), 15, 20.

2. Isacio Pérez Fernández, *Bartolomé de Las Casas: Viajero por dos mundos* (Cuzco: Centro de Estudios Regionales Andinos Bartolomé de Las Casas: 1998), 162.

3. Helen Rand Parish, preface and introduction to Bartolomé de Las Casas, *The Only Way* (New York: Paulist Press, 1992), 15; Franklin W. Knight, introduction to Bartolomé de Las Casas, *An Account, Much Abbreviated, of the Destruction of the Indies* (Indianapolis: Hackett Publishing Company, 2003), xviii–xx.

4. Knight, introduction, xxii; Parish, preface, 19–20.

5. Parish, preface, 23.

6. Knight, introduction, xxiv; Anthony Pagden, introduction to Bartolomé de Las Casas, *A Short Account of the Destruction of the Indies*, ed. and trans. Nigel Griffin (London: Penguin Books, 1992), xv.

7. Parish, preface, 28–29.

8. Parish, preface, 34.

9. Parish, preface, 35–36.

10. Parish, preface, 37.

11. Benno M. Biermann, "Bartolomé de Las Casas and Verapaz," in *Bartolomé de Las Casas In History: Toward an Understanding of the Man and His Works,* ed. Juan Friede and Benjamin Keen (DeKalb, IL: Northern Illinois University Press, 1971), 443.

12. Parish, preface, 40.

13. Pagden, introduction, xxvii.

14. Parish, preface, 41.

15. Parish, preface, 43–46; Lewis Hanke, *All Mankind Is One: A Study of the Disputation Between Bartolomé de Las Casas and Juan Gines de Sepúlveda in 1550 on the Intellectual and Religious Capacity of the American Indians* (DeKalb: Northern Illinois University Press, 1974), 57–58.

16. Gustavo Gutiérrez, *Las Casas: In Search of the Poor of Jesus Christ*, trans. Robert R. Barr (Maryknoll, NY: Orbis Books, 1993), 3; Enrique Dussel, "The Discovery of an Invasion," trans. Gary McEoin, *CrossCurrents* 41, no. 4 (Winter 1991–1992): 445. However, in examining this question, Alicia Mayer highlights a fascinating debate between John Cotton and Roger Williams in the British colonies which, while it did not rise to the level of the Sepulveda-Las Casas debate, presents interesting similarities to that encounter. See Alicia Mayer, "El pensamiento de Bartolomé de las Casas en el discurso sobre el indígena. Una perspectiva comparada en las colonias americanas," *Historia Mexicana* 63, no. 3 (January–March 2014): 1145–165.

17. Rolena Adorno, *The Polemics of Possession in Spanish American Literature* (New Haven: Yale University Press, 2007), 85–86; Parish, preface, 50–52.

18. Parish, preface, 54.

19. David T. Orique, O.P., "Vox legis in Bartolomé de Las Casas' Brevísima relación de la destrucción de las Indias" in *Montesinos' Legacy: Defining and Defending*

Human Rights for 500 Years, ed. Edward C. Lorenz, Dana E. Aspinall, and J. Michael Raley (New York: Lexington Books: 2014), 28, 30.

20. Enrique Dussel, "Origen de la filosofía política moderna: Las Casas, Vitoria y Suarez," *Caribbean Studies* 33, no. 2 (Julio-Dic. 2005): 39–40.

21. Gutiérrez, *Las Casas,* 67, 272.

22. Cited in Hanke, *All Mankind*, 17, 21.

23. Pagden, introduction, xvii; Orique, *Vox,* 31.

24. Diego von Vacano, "Las Casas and the Birth of Race," *History of Political Thought* 33, no. 3 (Autumn 2012): 423.

25. Bartolomé de Las Casas, *A Short Account of the Destruction of the Indies*, trans. Nigel Griffin (London: Penguin Books, 1992), 9, 10.

26. Von Vacano, "Las Casas," 424.

27. Von Vacano, "Las Casas," 401.

28. Stafford Poole, preface to *Bartolomé de Las Casas, In Defense of the Indians: The Defense of the Most Reverend Lord Don Fray Bartolomé de Las Casas, of the Order of Preachers, Late Bishop of Chiapa, Against the Persecutors and Slanderers of the Peoples of the New World Discovered Across the Seas*, trans. and ed. Stafford Poole (DeKalb, IL: Northern Illinois University Press, 1992), xx. See also the new Spanish translation from the Latin with commentary: *Bartolomé de Las Casas, Apología o declaración y defensa universal de los derechos del hombre y de los pueblos*, trans. and ed. Vidal Abril Castelló, María Asunción Sánchez Manzano, Salvador Rus Rufino, Jesús Angel Barreda García, Isacio Pérez Fernández, and Miguel José Abril Stoffels (Salamanca: Junta de Castilla y León Consejería de Educación y Cultura, 2000). The Latin version is held at the National Library of France and can be viewed here: http://gallica.bnf.fr/ark:/12148/btv1b9080777g/f4.image and the sections included in this volume begin on this page: http://gallica.bnf.fr/ark:/12148/btv1b9080777g/f6.image.

29. Hanke, *All Mankind*, 67.

30. Adorno, *Polemics*, 82; Manuel Giménez Fernandez, "Fray Bartolomé de Las Casas: A Biographical Sketch," in *Bartolomé de Las Casas in History: Toward an Understanding of the Man and His Work,* ed. Juan Friede and Benjamin Keen (DeKalb, IL: Northern Illinois University Press, 1971), 109.

31. Quoted in Giménez, "Fray," 109.

32. Lewis Hanke, *Aristotle and the American Indians: A Study in Race Prejudice in the Modern World* (Bloomington: Indiana University Press, 1959), 31–32.

33. Angel Losada, "The Controversy between Sepúlveda and Las Casas in the Junta of Valladolid," in *Bartolomé de Las Casas in History: Toward an Understanding of the Man and His Work*, ed. Juan Friede and Benjamin Keen (DeKalb, IL, Northern Illinois University Press, 1971), 279.

34. Hanke, *Aristotle*, 55, 59.

35. Hanke, *All Mankind*, 68.

36. Adorno, *Polemics*, 83.

37. Quoted in Hanke, *All Mankind*, 121.

38. David Solodknow, "The Rhetoric of War and Justice in the Conquest of the Americas: Ethnography, Law, and Humanism in Juan Ginés de Sepúlveda and Bar-

tolomé de Las Casas," in *Coloniality, Religion, and the Law in the Early Iberian World*, ed. Santa Arias and Raul Marrero-Fente (Nashville: Vanderbilt University Press, 2014), 196.

39. Fray Toribio de Motolinía, "The Franciscan reply to the emperor, 1555," in *Letters and People of the Spanish Indies: Sixteenth Century*, trans. and ed. James Lockhart and Enrique Otte (Cambridge: Cambridge University Press, 1976), 237.

40. Adorno, *Polemics*, 78.

41. Benjamin Keen, "Introduction: Approaches to Las Casas, 1535–1970," in *Bartolomé de Las Casas in History: Toward an Understanding of the Man and His Work*, ed. Juan Friede and Benjamin Keen (DeKalb: Northern Illinois University Press, 1971), 12.

42. Simón Bolívar, "The Jamaica Letter," in *The Political Thought of Bolivar: Selected Writings*, ed. Gerald E. Fitzgerald (The Hague: Martinus Nijhoff, 1971), 28.

43. Keen, "Introduction," 31.

44. Ramón Menéndez Pidal, *El Padre Las Casas: Su Doble Personalidad* (Madrid: Espasa-Calpe, S.A., 1963), 107, 239, 320, 385. Translation by this author.

45. Fernando Mires, *En nombre de la cruz: discusiones teologícas y políticas frente al holocausto de los indios, período de conquista* (San Jose, Costa Rica: Editorial DEI, 1989, Segunda Edición), 177, 178, 179,180.

46. Gutiérrez, *Las Casas*, 8, 9.

47. Daniel Castro, *Another Face of Empire: Bartolomé de Las Casas, Indigenous Rights, and Ecclesiastical Imperialism* (Durham: Duke University Press, 2007), 8, 9.

48. Agustin Yañez, *Fray Bartolomé de Las Casas: El Conquistador conquistado* (Mexico: Editorial Planeta Mexicana, 2001), 58.

49. Dussel, "Origen," 43, 48.

50. For discussion of whether Las Casas was a benevolent imperialist, see Castro, *Another*, 70; Dussel; "Origen," 39; and José Cárdenas Bunsen, "Consent, Voluntary Jurisdiction and Native Political Agency in Bartolomé de Las Casas' Final Writings," *Bulletin of Spanish Studies* XCI, no. 6 (2014): 212–13.

51. For discussion of whether his advocacy was effective, see Castro, *Another*, 5–6; Borges, *Quien*, 288–289; and Juan Comas, "Historical Reality and the Detractors of Father Las Casas," *Bartolomé de Las Casas in History: Toward an Understanding of the Man and His Work*, ed. Juan Friede and Benjamin Keen (DeKalb: Northern Illinois University Press, 1971), 504.

52. Bartolomé de Las Casas, *The Only Way*, ed. Helen Rand Parish, trans. Frances Patrick Sullivan, S.J. (New York: Paulist Press, 1992), 160–61.

53. Lawrence A. Clayton, *Bartolomé de Las Casas: A Biography* (Cambridge: Cambridge University Press, 2012), 138.

54. Castro, *Another*, 505.

55. For a more detailed summary of slavery in this complex period, see Gwendolyn Midlo Hall, *Slavery and African Ethnicities in the Americas: Restoring the Links* (Chapel Hill: University of North Carolina, Press, 2005), 1–7.

56. Paul Vickery, *Bartolomé de Las Casas: Great Prophet of the Americas* (Mahwah, NJ: Paulist Press, 2006), 90; Clayton, 144.

57. Clayton, *Bartolomé*, 464.

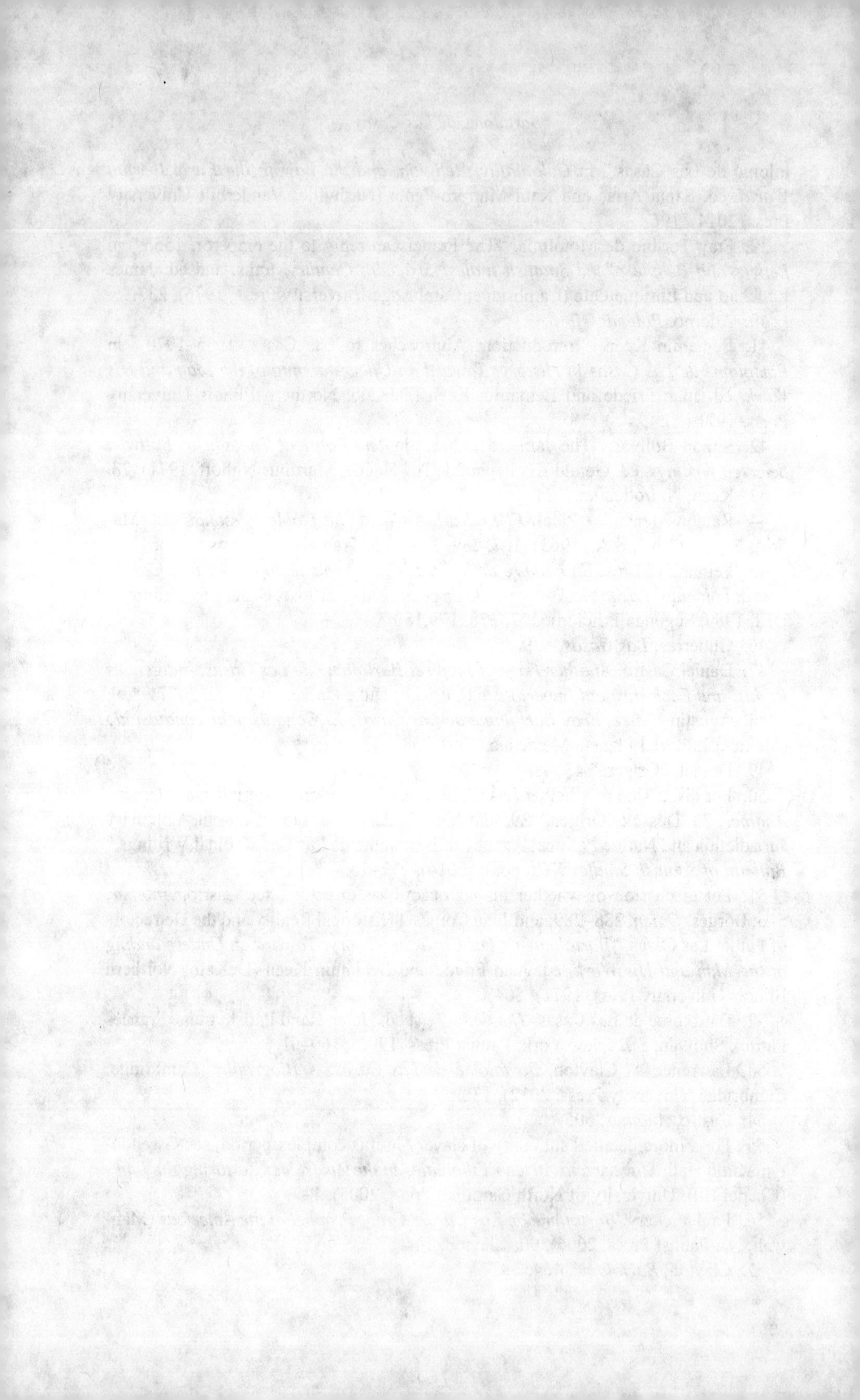

Chapter Five

Alonso de la Vera Cruz

"The Spaniards Cannot Have Just Dominion"

Alonso de la Vera Cruz, the first theology professor at the new University of Mexico when it was founded in 1553, was a member of that "golden age" of Spanish philosophy, led by his teacher Francisco de Vitoria of the University of Salamanca, which addressed the new issues arising from the discovery of the New World by Europeans. But, in contrast with Vitoria, who never left Europe, Vera Cruz had the experience of many years in New Spain. This experience is reflected in his work *De dominio infidelium et iusto bello* (On the Dominion of the Infidels and Just War) which defended the rights of the Indigenous people to their lands. At the same time, Vera Cruz was not as polemical in his condemnation of Spain as his friend Bartolomé de las Casas. And, after Vera Cruz took legitimate authority away from the Spanish crown, he confronted reality and found ways to legitimize the Spanish presence and the limited exercise of its power in the new lands.[1] Vera Cruz also discussed practical issues in his writings such as tributes, land expropriation, and distribution of wealth, all from the viewpoint of the natural rights of the Indigenous people.

Born Alonso Gutiérrez in 1507 to moderately wealthy parents in the town of Capueñas, near Toledo, he attended first the University of Alcalá de Henares and then the University of Salamanca where he studied under Vitoria and Domingo de Soto. He was ordained to the priesthood, awarded a master's degree in theology, and accepted a position as a lecturer in philosophy at Salamanca. Then, his life took a turn from what might have been expected to be his career. Francisco de la Cruz, one of the first Augustinian missionaries in New Spain, who was visiting Salamanca to recruit priests to teach seminarians in that land, persuaded the young Alonso to sail with him for the New World. On the voyage, Alonso decided that he wished to join the Augustinian

Order and, upon arrival at the port of Veracruz in June of 1536, he took the name Alonso de la Vera Cruz.[2]

The Augustinians had joined the two other mendicant orders, the Franciscans and the Dominicans, in New Spain in 1533 (the others having arrived in 1523 and 1526 respectively) and immediately began to establish monasteries and schools in the regions assigned to them from which they worked to convert and teach the Indigenous people. After spending a few years as master of novices, Vera Cruz was sent to Tiripetío in Michoacán, where a monastery and church had already been built, to found a school of higher studies for seminarians and lay students, both Spanish and Indigenous. There he would teach the first courses in European philosophy and Catholic theology in the New World.[3] One of the goals of the Augustinian schools was the teaching of the Amerindian languages to the Spanish seminarians and Vera Cruz himself learned to speak Tarascan well enough to preach in that language.[4] One of his most prominent students was Antonio Huitziméngari Mendoza y Caltzontzín, the son of the last king of Michoacán,[5] with whom he established a close relationship. Vera Cruz donated his books to form at Tiripetío the first library of European books in the New World.[6] As part of his missionary work, Friar Alonso was firm in his insistence that the newly converted Indigenous people should receive all the sacraments, overcoming the resistance of many theologians to their receiving communion.[7] After Tiripetío, he was sent to found seminaries and teach philosophy at Tacámbaro and Atotonilco. He was elected to serve a term as head of the Augustinian Order in New Spain from 1548 to 1551 and served another term from 1557 to 1560.[8]

While teaching and carrying out administrative duties for the Augustinians, Vera Cruz was appointed Bishop of Leon, Nicaragua, upon the death of Bishop Antonio Valdivieso in 1550. He refused this honor, stating that he wished to remain a teacher. Legend has it that, when he first read the letter of appointment, he reacted with a pun, "*Ab ore Leonis, libera me, Domine!*" or "From the mouth of the Lion, free me, Lord!"[9] He would later refuse other appointments to bishoprics.

In 1551, royal decrees were signed establishing the University of Mexico, the first university in the Western Hemisphere, to be modeled on the University of Salamanca and teach the sons of natives and of Spaniards. The university was inaugurated on January 25, 1553. Friar Alonso was fully involved in the organizing of the university and was named to occupy chairs of Scholastic Theology and of Holy Scripture.[10]

Vera Cruz began his first theology course, following the custom of Vitoria, with a public lecture called a *relectio* which dealt with an important moral issue. Vera Cruz, in fact, chose possibly the most controversial issue of the day, the rights of the Indigenous peoples. The previous few years had seen a series of important developments: the passage of the New Laws for the protection of the Indigenous people in 1542, the repeal of some of those laws in 1546, the suspension of further conquests in 1549–50, and the debate on the justice of the conquest at Valladolid in 1550–51.[11] Vera Cruz's polemical lecture dealt with the dominion of the Indigenous people over their land and the practical implications of that recognition of dominion. It became the first part of his treatise *De dominio infidelium et iusto bello* and over the next few years he added further chapters containing commentary on the justice of the conquest itself. Selections from this work are included below. Vera Cruz also published two other philosophical texts while teaching at the University.

In 1556, Vera Cruz published an important work that was more like a practical manual that a philosophical treatise entitled *Speculum coniugiorum* in which he examined the complicated problems related to the marriages of the newly converted Amerindians. Vera Cruz, following Thomas Aquinas, distinguishes between first and second natural law principles. The first, he says, include the Golden Rule and similar precepts which are the same for all peoples. But the secondary natural law principles could vary, as Vera Cruz says, among different nations or different times.[12] Philosopher Virginia Aspe states that this openness allows him to understand key variations in natural law based on cultural plurality and makes *Speculum coniugiorum* a contribution to the theory of human rights and multiculturalism.[13]

At this time, a conflict was ongoing in New Spain between the secular clergy (parish priests) and diocesan bishops on the one side and the friars of the religious orders on the other over a number of issues, including who would administer the sacraments of baptism and matrimony to the Indigenous people and most controversially the payment of tithes to the Church by the Amerindians, which the bishops were mandating and the friars opposing.[14] The Crown had given the religious orders the dominant role in converting the Indigenous people to Christianity in the early Spanish colonies, but as time went on and bishops began to set up dioceses and form parishes, the bishops began to assert their religious authority over the entire population of Spanish and Indigenous people.

Vera Cruz was at the center of the controversies because of his leadership position with the Augustinians and because his treatise *De decimas* (On Tithes), which came out strongly against the payment of tithes by the Indigenous people, was considered heretical by the bishops. The archbishop of Mexico, Alonso de Montufar, sent a copy of Vera Cruz's treatise to the Inquisition in Madrid noting eighty-four propositions which he deemed heretical.[15] The archbishop also wrote King Philip asking him not to allow publication of any book by Vera Cruz, in particular *De decimas*.[16] In 1562, King Philip called Vera Cruz and the leaders of the religious orders to Spain to sort things out. During the years that Vera Cruz was in Spain, King Philip gained a high respect for him. Through the king's influence, Friar Alonso was able to achieve from the Pope the rescinding of the mandates of the recent Church Council of Trent that had limited the privileges of the religious orders in their ministry to the Indigenous people in the New World. And from the king and the Council of the Indies he obtained an exemption for the Indigenous people from paying tithes to the Church.[17]

Friar Alonso returned to New Spain in late 1573, bringing with him authorization for a new college, the College of San Pablo in Mexico City, and sixty boxes of books, maps, globes and scientific instruments for its library, which would become famous as one of the best in the Spanish colonies. In 1575, he was elected to serve still another three-year term as head of his order and after his term was finished he became rector of San Pablo.[18] Alonso de la Vera Cruz died in July 1584 at the age of seventy-seven.

Vera Cruz was one of the philosophers of the school of thought known as Second Scholasticism. Scholasticism was a method of reasoning in dialectic form closely associated in the Catholic Church with the ideas of St. Thomas Aquinas (1225–1274) who worked to reconcile the ideas of Aristotle with Christian revelation. Second Scholasticism arose in Europe in the sixteenth and seventeenth centuries and among its most noted practitioners were scholars at the Spanish universities. One of the few theses of Aristotelian philosophy that Vera Cruz and the Second Scholastic writers rejected was his division of men into those who were by nature free and those who were by nature slaves.[19] (Aristotle put women, children, and beasts together with slaves in the lower category.) While recognizing that there were differences among human beings, Vera Cruz felt that they all had the same rights under natural law. The philosophers of Second Scholasticism also expanded on and modified in various ways Aquinas ideas on natural law.[20]

As part of a debate that had been going on since the 1400s between the rhetoric of humanists and the dialectic of scholastics, philosopher Ambrosio Velasco states that Vera Cruz developed a humanistic orientation for the scholastic dialectic. Humanists were inspired by the art and philosophy of the ancient Greeks and Romans and looked to them for enlightenment. Velasco describes two kinds of humanists. The first is exemplified by Juan Ginés de Sepúlveda, who justified Spain's imperial project as a way to rescue the Amerindians from their barbarism. The second is exemplified by writers including Vera Cruz, who rejected the characterization of the Indigenous people as barbarians and maintained that they were as rational and civilized as the Spaniards.[21]

Vera Cruz was also influenced by the nominalism of such philosophers as William of Okham. Nominalism maintains that everything that exists is individual and that universals only exist as concepts in the mind. Velasco states that we could call Vera Cruz's nominalist ideas multiculturalist since he accepts a diversity of nations with different ideas about such things as justice, kindness, and beauty.[22] Vera Cruz's humanism leads him to denounce the injustices of the oppressors and defend the oppressed Indigenous people while his nominalism leads him to appreciate the value of each culture and oppose the imposition of false universal concepts by the Europeans.[23]

The School of Salamanca was the leading philosophical movement espousing these ideas. Political scientist Anthony Pagden describes the School in these terms:

> The years around 1520–1530 mark the beginning of a major change in direction in the intellectual life of Spain. For these were the early years of a new movement in theology, logic and the law, whose creators have come to be known as the 'School of Salamanca.' The members of this 'School' from the generation of the Dominicans Francisco de Vitoria (c. 1492–1546), Domingo de Soto (1494–1560) and Melchor Cano (1509–1560) to that of the Jesuits Francisco Suárez (1548–1617) and Luis de Molina (1535–1600) were to influence, and in many areas substantially restructure, the theological thinking of Catholic Europe. . . . The 'School' also had a single master, for all its members had been either pupils, or pupils of pupils, of Francisco de Vitoria.[24]

While there were commonalities between Vitoria and Vera Cruz, there were also differences. Political theorist Monica Quijada explains that "Vitoria affirmed that the people elect the prince and grant him authority to make decisions with respect to the republic, thus situating the origin of political power in the consent of the people." She goes on to say, "But he also added that the king's power does not come from the community but from God." Vera Cruz would rather have agreed with Francisco Suarez that power comes from the people and the community.[25] On other questions such as whether the Indigenous people were true lords and possessed true dominion over their persons and property, there was full agreement between them that they were, in fact, true lords and did have true dominion.

Like *De decimus,* the treatise on tithes, Vera Cruz's work *De dominio infidelium* was not published during his lifetime. In fact, *De dominio infidelium* disappeared, its existence only assumed because of references to it in *Speculum coniugiorum,* the treatise on Indigenous marriages. However, we should remember that it was common practice in the sixteenth century to circulate manuscripts among colleagues and we should not discount the possibility that the work was known during Friar Alonso's life. He would also have expressed the ideas included in *De dominium* in his classes at the university and at the other schools of higher learning where he taught.[26] But, for over three hundred years the work itself was lost. We shall let E. J. Burrus, S.J., the Jesuit historian who found the manuscript in 1958, tell the story.

> In the course of time, all first-hand acquaintance with the treatise was lost. Then, about a century ago [Burris writes in 1963], the original manuscript somehow got into the hands of José Fernando Ramirez, Mexican collector and historian. . . .[His] almost entirely inaccurate outline along with a brief description of the manuscript was first published in 1898. Ramirez's [outline] has been all that scholars have had to go by in order to form an idea of Veracruz's treatise. . . . The reader will understand that it was with no little satisfaction that the present writer succeeded in identifying several years ago Veracruz's supposedly lost treatise carefully preserved in a private collection. It is now hoped that the Latin text with an English translation and commentary will appear before long.[27]

Burris was allowed to transcribe and translate the work from Latin into English on the condition that he not reveal the name of the owner of the manuscript.[28] The treatise was published in 1968 as Volume II of a five-volume set of Vera Cruz's works. In 2004, a translation of *De dominio* into Spanish by Roberto Heredia, Antonio Gómez, and Paula López was published, followed in 2007 by Heredia's translation of the entire work. Heredia gives us the names of some of the owners of the manuscript after it left the hands of Ramirez, including that of the noted Mexican historian Francisco del Paso y Troncoso.[29] He does not explain why Paso y Troncoso did not publish the manuscript or at least make it known to the world.

Vera Cruz's treatise can be divided into two parts with the first section being, in general, the more practical and the second more theoretical. He begins by saying, "We shall discuss some doubts which arise in the New World" and he follows with eleven "doubts" or "questions" which he argues back and forth in the scholastic style.

The first doubt asks whether those Spaniards who hold the Indigenous people in encomienda without just title may receive their tribute justly or if they must free the natives and return any tribute they have received. In this first doubt, Vera Cruz lays out several basic principles that will recur again and again in the text. All power or dominion comes from the community itself. The community can transfer dominion to several people as in an aristocracy or a democracy or to one person as in a monarchy, but that power will extend only to those spheres which the people mandate. The ruler and those he appoints under him are entitled to tribute in order to carry out their duties, but the ruler and those he appoints must rule in the benefit of the people (the common good) or their rule is not valid. If the people object to the person a king puts over them because of tyrannical rule or unjust tribute, then that appointment is not valid. Friar Alonso goes on to say that the natives had a ruler before the conquest who was dethroned in an unjust war "and from an unjust cause of war dominion cannot originate." And "consequently, no one who holds any community without title, is in just possession of it."

Vera Cruz then discusses land, defending Indigenous dominion over all types of property. Burris explains that, according to Vera Cruz, no Spaniard "may take over cultivated lands belonging either to individuals or to communities. Even if the emperor himself made a grant of such property, the Spaniards cannot in conscience retain it, since the emperor would be giving away what is not his."[30] A Spaniard cannot in good conscience purchase communal land from the Indigenous lord or governor without the permission of the community as the governor is not the true owner.[31] Unused and unoccupied land can be taken only if it is not claimed by any native community. There is one case where land may be taken from the natives. If one group in a commonwealth has a superabundance and another suffers want, the ruler may take away, even against the will of the citizens, what was superfluous and give it to those who lack it.[32] Legal scholar Jesús De la Torre states that Vera Cruz lays out here the social function of property, positing that what is unneeded by those with abundance in justice belongs to those with little or nothing.[33]

In his discussion of excessive tribute, Friar Alonso repeats again and again that the Indigenous people should not be obliged to pay more in tribute than they paid to their lords prior to the Spanish conquest. He also states that it is unjust for officials to require from the natives what their region does not produce, saying, "where grain is harvested, the tribute is to be grain, where cotton is picked, the tribute is to be cotton. Consequently, no other tribute may be imposed."[34]

In Doubt V, Friar Alonso asks whether the Indigenous people were really their own masters; and, consequently, whether they might be deprived of their dominion. He argues that the infidel rulers in the New World were true lords of their lands because "true dominion does not depend on faith," noting that pagan kings in the Bible were recognized as legitimate. Those appointed by the Indigenous rulers also had true dominion over the regions assigned to them and, if the tribute paid to them was transferred to a Spanish official, it was done unjustly and restitution must be made. In Doubt VI, Vera Cruz continues his discussion of land acquisition by the Spaniards.

Vera Cruz then asks whether the Holy Roman Emperor Charles V (who ruled most of continental Europe) was lord of the whole world. Friar Alonso cites the many writers who maintained that he was indeed lord of the world and goes into great detail in challenging them, saying finally that "there never was one who could be termed lord of all and the universal emperor ruling over the entire world."[35] He goes on to say that "the emperor is not allowed, merely because he is emperor, to take over the property of the various people who are not subject to him either *de iure* [jure] or *de facto* and, consequently, he may not, on his own authority, claim them for himself or give them to others."[36] Doubt VIII asks whether the emperor is the owner of all things possessed by those currently under his rule, and Vera Cruz answers by saying that "he is by no means the owner of the things possessed by his subjects nor has he any more dominion over them than over an object of a person not his subject."[37]

In the final Doubts, numbers X and XI, Vera Cruz examines first the reasons that would not justify war against the Indigenous people and finally the reasons for which war might be justified. Philosopher Mauricio Beuchot explains the justifications for war that the Friar considers illegitimate: Nonbelief on the part of the Indigenous people could not be a legitimate reason because they were in ignorance of the faith. War could not be justified by saying that the New World was by law part of the ancient Roman Empire because the Romans knew nothing of the New World. Neither is it legitimate to justify war by saying that the Native peoples had gravely injured Spaniards when the Indigenous people were only defending themselves against unjust aggression. One could not say that the Indigenous people rejected the preaching of the Gospel because the majority accepted the faith. And their sins against nature such as human sacrifice and cannibalism would not be enough to deprive them of dominion over their lands.[38]

Vera Cruz, while he never justifies for any reason the wars of conquest and overthrow of the Indigenous governments, ends up accepting the legitimacy of the dominion of Charles V over the Indies.[39] He states:

> It is possible that those who began the war acted unjustly; but that later with victory secured, the retention of the territory is just. . . . Hence it could be that, in the beginning, the emperor was forbidden to start the war; but later, with the *fait accompli*, the step is validated, with the consequence that he is now in legitimate possession.

Vera Cruz considers the conquest and the encomienda irreversible and so what he feels must be done is to examine how the damage to the rights of the Indigenous people by the conquest might be minimized. Here as in other places he shows he is more practical than other theologians of the Salamanca School.[40]

After rejecting a number of possible reasons for overthrowing the Indigenous rulers as invalid, Vera Cruz accepts that the Spanish Crown could remove an Indigenous ruler if his Christian subjects were in danger of returning to their old gods under his rule. He states: "If the unbelievers accepted the faith of Christ and if there were any well-founded fear of their apostatizing should their otherwise legitimate masters retain their jurisdiction in governing, the latter might be deprived of such jurisdiction, if there were no other way to prevent their apostasy."

Vera Cruz also says that unbelievers "may be coerced into accepting baptism and the faith, not so that they pretend to believe but that they will want to believe with all their heart what they formerly rejected. This is termed indirect coercion." Writer and translator Antonio Gómez considers that there is no way that our modern minds can understand the radical contradiction involved in employing coercion for the exercise of freedom. He adds that the only explanation he can see is that Vera Cruz believed that it was possible for grace to move the will of persons while they remained free.[41]

Another valid reason for war, that of the right to trade freely, is in agreement with Vitoria for whom it was the basis of international law. Vera Cruz always qualifies his statements by acknowledging that the Spaniards did not arrive in the New World peacefully to evangelize or trade. But here he appears to provide a justification for his countrymen's unrelenting search for gold and silver:

> If the inhabitants of the New World . . . forbade the Spanish travelers or dwellers from enjoying a peaceful abode for trade or extraction of metals, to the extent that the Spaniards could not defend themselves from injury except by waging war to the point of depriving them of their dominion, the Spaniards would be justified in taking such action.[42]

Gómez also points out that Vera Cruz provides for what today we would call humanitarian intervention by saying that another country can assist an oppressed people in throwing off a tyrant. For Vera Cruz this intervention would only be allowed in extreme cases as in human sacrifice. And, when the barbarities were ended, dominion should be restored to the community. Vera Cruz admits, however, that even if these customs had not existed among the Indigenous people, the Spaniards would have continued with their conquest which had not been based on humanitarian instincts.[43]

Did the ideas of the philosophers of the School of Salamanca influence Enlightenment writers such as Locke and Rousseau one hundred years later in England and France, or did they form a separate and more radical current of humanitarian thought? Philosopher Jorge Gracia states that "their views formed the basis for the kind of humane and liberal thinking that was to become mainstream in European philosophy."[44] Monica Quijada adds: "These were the political principles that, incorporated in the Western European imaginaire, came to influence the radical thinking of the modern era by providing the principal tools with which to oppose the growing absolutism of monarchies."[45]

However, other scholars highlight the differences between the two streams of thought. Velasco notes that the ideas of Las Casas and his fellow friars preceded in time and in their radical nature the republican thought of the English and French.[46] Liberation theologian Gustavo Gutiérrez notes that both promoted natural law and human rights but that the human rights of the School of Salamanca should not be seen "in a laissez-faire, liberal, merely formally equalitarian perspective; rather, along the lines of the rights of the poor who are condemned to death and destruction by the oppressor whose quest is for gold."[47] De la Torre states that both Enlightenment thought and the earlier Spanish thought emphasize natural law, but Enlightenment thought is eminently rationalist and puts the emphasis on individual rights, while the Spaniards refer back to Christian thought on the liberation of the oppressed and the treatment of the poor.[48]

The distinction between these two streams of thought about rights has lasted through history and was brought to the fore after 1948 when the Universal Declaration of Human Rights was being transformed into legally binding obligations. Scholar Elif Gözler Çamur states, "While the Western states aimed to reduce human rights to the traditional concept of civil and political rights, socialist states defended the dominance of economic, social and cultural rights." They were finally divided into two separate covenants that went into effect in 1976.[49] Liberation theology took up the call of the rights of the poor in the 1960s and 1970s in a way that echoed the writings of the sixteenth century friars. And the distinction marks the division between political parties in many countries today with one party emphasizing the rights to freedom of speech and worship while another party maintains that people also have the right to adequate shelter, food, and health care.

In conclusion, we can say that Vera Cruz found the conquest of the Indigenous people of the New World impossible to justify but, recognizing its reality, he laid out concrete measures for its present and future legitimacy in practical areas such as tribute, dominion over common and individual Indigenous property, restitution of property or tribute unjustly taken, dominion of Indigenous lords over Indian towns, encomiendas and Indian labor, evangelization, and tithes. All his conclusions were carefully argued in the Scholastic dialectic common among Catholic philosophers at the time and based on the ideas of his contemporaries of the School of Salamanca on natural law and the right to justice applied to all equally.

DEFENSE OF THE INDIANS: THEIR RIGHTS, A DISCUSSION BY THE REVEREND FATHER ALONSO DE LA VERA CRUZ (1553)

Give unto Caesar the things that are Caesar's and unto God the things that are God's.

Matthew XXII.

We shall discuss some doubts which arise in the New World.

Doubt I

The first doubt is whether those who hold natives without any title to them may justly receive tribute or whether they are bound to restore the tribute and free the natives from bondage.

To solve the problem, one should first of all keep in mind that dominion possessed by a community resides primarily and principally in the community itself. For neither natural nor divine law appoints any one as a true temporal ruler to whom others owe tribute.

Even though some men are said to be naturally free and others in the same way bondsmen, according to Aristotle, yet this is true only in the sense that some are outstanding for their ability and prudence and thus deservedly direct and command, whereas others are naturally bondsmen; that is, they are of such inferior character that they must rather obey others and be governed by them than command or direct them. Such, however, who are naturally freemen, do not possess, merely because they are more capable, actual dominion over others regardless of how servile character the latter may be.

Consequently, if one is to have just dominion, it must come from the will of the community itself which transfers its dominion to others, as happens in an aristocracy or democracy; or to one only, as is the case in a monarchy. Or the divine will—since God is the Lord of heaven and earth—can confer this dominion on one or on many, as is evident from the appointment of kings in the persons of Saul and David and others.

But when there is no such divine indication, recourse must be made to the community itself which can transfer its power of ruling and, accordingly, may choose one or several from among many to rule; such will then possess so much power and in those spheres as the community confers it on the one or several rulers for the good of its people.

And since such a ruler is to govern for the common good and should direct all his efforts to that end, he is to receive a salary in keeping with his position; for Scripture has it: "Who serveth as a soldier at any time at his own charges?" Nor "Shall thou muzzle the ox that treadeth out the corn."

From this concession of the community the emperor rules in his empire and a king in his kingdom. Likewise through imperial or regal power, dominion is conferred on inferiors; or the community itself chooses some to be dukes, marquises, counts, and others to whom is entrusted the authority and power to receive from the people such tribute as would be due to the king or emperor.

In such a concession it is necessary that the explicit or implicit will of the community intervene. It is said to be implicit when the king or emperor, keeping before him the common good, confers rewards in accordance with merit, and creates dukes, marquises [and other dignitaries in keeping with this same principle]; for it is to the advantage of the entire kingdom that there be nobles and that they be rewarded from the possessions of the kingdom according to their deeds. For as the entire kingdom serves the king in matters temporal because he looks out for the good of the kingdom, so it seems just that a part of the kingdom serve with the explicit will of the king and with the implicit will of the community.

The implicit will of the community is that through which the king bestows a gift for the good of the community; should the gift prove to be detrimental to it, then such a gift would not constitute a sufficient title, especially if the people should object. For example, if the emperor or king gave away a city or town to some duke, and it were probable that for such a city to be under the latter's dominion were detrimental to the same city because the one to whom it was given and entrusted governed it like a tyrant or acted impiously by demanding excessive tribute; in such a case the king or emperor would exceed his power, and, should the people protest or not give its consent, such a donation would not be valid. All this is recognized by the natural light of reason.

The second point to be considered is that those who now have under them a group of people and receive tribute from them, have a title to them either through the gift of the emperor or through the governor who held the place of the ruler entrusting them, or through the concession of some one who had no authority to entrust the people, or they have this group because they were the first to take them into their possession and now hold them without contradiction, and so on. With these facts in mind [let us consider the following propositions].

The first proposition. The one who has this people through the emperor entrusting them or through the consignment of one who held the place of the emperor to effect the handing over of the people (supposing the emperor is their true lord) such a one has these people in good conscience and lawfully receives from them a moderate tribute. . . .

[I]f the tribute exceeds the ability of payment by the subjects, then it would be unlawfully demanded and received. The reason is evident: those to whom a people has been entrusted do not possess a greater right to exact excessive tribute than does the emperor himself. Therefore the one to whom a community has been entrusted—termed in the New World—*encomendero*—may neither demand nor receive exorbitant tribute.

The second proposition. If a group of people has been entrusted either by the emperor or by one who has been specifically empowered to do so by the emperor to some one against the just will of the group itself because it is burdened in many respects when it is under another, whereas under the emperor it would not be so burdened, then in probability the one to whom the group has been entrusted may not in safe conscience exact more than the emperor would demand.

For the reason why he might is because the emperor gave the people as a donation. But the emperor has no other dominion than that given him by the community itself, so much so that should he rule tyrannically, the community could depose and deprive him of his kingdom. But the community is opposed to such a donation conferred by the emperor. Therefore, he who received the donation may not accept what the emperor would not be allowed to accept. . . .

If one holds a group of people not through a bestowal of the ruler nor of the governor nor of the commonwealth, but only because he seized them by force or on his own authority without any violence, he is not their true lord and is bound to make restitution of all the tribute gathered.

This is obvious, since, if such a one had just ownership and could justly receive tribute, it would be because he was the first to occupy the towns. But such is not our present case, as is evident, because both by natural and human law only those things are given over to the first occupant which either never belonged to anyone or were considered abandoned.

But such is not the case with the dominion of peoples, since such dominion always and from the beginning resided in the community itself and was never abandoned. And if they had a ruler, as these natives had as their king and superior and subalterns, there could be no justice in the seizure, for the added reason that it took place during a war. And, consequently, the war would have to be just; and this is impossible on the part of a private person who makes a seizure. And from an unjust cause of war dominion cannot originate, since it is characteristic of tyranny to exert unjust oppression. But if he comes into possession not through violence but peacefully, then it must be by the will of the ruler or of the commonwealth. But no such will has authorized his action, rather the contrary. Consequently, no one who holds any community without title, is in just possession of it. . . .

Doubt V

The fifth doubt: whether the Indians were really their own masters: and, consequently, whether they might be deprived of their dominion.

We are thus inquiring whether the natives who ruled in the New World prior to the coming of the Spaniards were true lords; and, if they were, whether they might justly be deprived of their dominion and whether they are now actually so deprived.

First, it would seem that they were not true lords. They were unbelievers, idolaters, homicides, tyrants. But where such a condition prevails, there is no true dominion. Therefore [they were not true lords].

Secondly, the contention is proved by the fact that although they might be true lords, they were justly deprived of their dominion for whoever rules to the detriment of his subjects, is justly to be deprived of his dominion. But these native rulers at the time of their unbelief, even if they had been true lords, ruled to the detriment of the community.

This is obvious since the people remained in their idolatry, and this is the greatest detriment to a community. There were also other unspeakable sins, and these were vices common to the rulers and others imitating their example. It follows, then, that they might be justly deprived of their dominion.

Refutation. The refutation is founded on the principle that true dominion does not depend on faith. Therefore, an unbeliever may possess dominion.

To solve the problem it is necessary to realize first, that dominion among these natives can be taken in two ways: either such dominion as resided in one single person, as was the case with the monarch Montezuma in the Mexican province or with Caltzontzin in the province of Michoacán, or such as resided in other subordinate lords who lived in various towns and were subject to the one king: as in Spain there are dukes, counts, marquises, and others possessing towns; those who are lords in this way are under the king who rules over the entire kingdom so that he is obeyed in the country even against the will of the count.

Secondly, one must realize that dominion can be taken in two ways: first by succession, thus a son succeeds a father as in Spain, and so in practically all regions; another way is by election, and this in turn takes place in two ways: either by choice on the part of the community or province over which he is being put in charge, or through appointment by the ruling monarch himself. . . .

The first conclusion. He who was monarch among these Indians, regardless how much of an unbeliever or idolater he was, was a true lord. Here is the proof: first, because among the pagans, as is evident from Scripture, there was true dominion; secondly, dominion, as we stated above, results from divine choice or the will of the commonwealth publicly transferring its authority. But this will could be and actually seems to have been to transfer the authority to one ruler. Therefore, for this reason, there was true dominion even at the time of their unbelief because the faith, which is of divine right, neither confers nor takes away dominion, which is of the right of nations.

Corollary. From this it follows that one who was a monarch in a kingdom, because he was an unbeliever or idolater, might not be deprived of his kingdom. For if he might justly be deprived for such a reason, it would follow that unbelief would exclude true dominion. But this is false and evident from Scripture; for it calls Pharao king, likewise Nabuchodonosor and Sennacherib are so styled; and in Genesis XLVII, we read that Joseph subdued the entire land of Egypt to Pharao; and Paul [in his letter] to the Romans XIII orders princes, who at the time were unbelievers, to be obeyed; and with him agrees Peter in his first Epistle, chapter II.

Nor is one to be deprived of dominion because of idolatry; because all infidel idolaters would for this reason be deprived of their dominion, which is absolutely false. . . .

The second conclusion. At the time of their unbelief there was just and legitimate dominion among these natives who designated some according to villages either as rulers by hereditary succession or by appointment of the king or by a group of his councilors deputed for this purpose.

This is proved in the same way as the first conclusion; namely, dominion derives either from natural right or from human will; but, whether derived from one or the other source, unbelief does not keep the Indians from being able to enjoy true dominion and, as the dominion could be valid through the entire commonwealth choosing one monarch, so, to, could it be valid through one nation choosing a leader for only this one nation.

And likewise, it would be valid dominion through the monarch himself or the king choosing such a one, as the emperor designates a duke or a count, and so on. For as the governing of the kingdom pertains to the king, if it is conducive for the good of his kingdom that there would be such officials appointed from the villages, he may choose them, even if the commonwealth does not appoint them and, the more so, if it does not oppose such an action but rather approves of it. All this is evident to anyone who reflects on the subject.

Corollary. It follows from this conclusion that those who were deputed officials by their tribes, might not be deprived by the Spaniards of their true dominion, even had they remained in their unbelief, and much less after their conversion to Christ. And, thus, the Spaniards could not have true dominion even through grant of the emperor, because not even the emperor himself might take away dominion from the true lords and give it to others.

Even if we conceded that the emperor is the true lord of the entire world—which we deny, as we shall discuss later—because, granting that he is the lord of the universe, it would not follow that he was the proprietor; and thus he might not remove against the will of the commonwealth the official whom it itself had appointed, nor might he in this country remove against the will of the king the official whom the latter appointed by virtue of the authority vested in him by the commonwealth.

The third conclusion. As the officials among the Indians prior to the advent of the Spaniards might not be deprived of their true dominion, so likewise they might not be deprived of the lawful and moderate tribute they were receiving from their subjects. This conclusion is proved in the following way: true and just dominion consists in the lord being able to receive from his subjects moderate tribute. But as we indicated above, they might not be deprived justly of their dominion; therefore in the same way they might not be deprived of their just tribute.

The first corollary. From this it follows that whoever he be who took away the tribute due Caltzontzin or Montezuma who were kings and, as we suppose, true lords even though unbelievers and idolaters, is bound to make restitution to them, and that he committed theft and rapine; and, consequently, as long as he remains in possession of another's goods, he is in a state of sin.

The second corollary. It follows secondly that also all those who deprived of tribute the officials of the villages deputed throughout the villages either by choice of the people or will of the prince, as was their wont, and appropriated the tribute, are in sin and are bound to make restitution of all they stole from them; nor may they make the tribute their own. The reason is evident, since it does not become theirs by will of the emperor (who may not have the tribute taken away from one and given to another, either by his own will or that of the king of these natives whether Caltzontzin or Montezuma). First, because this would not be done freely but by force, as is evident. Secondly, even granting that he would be acting freely, he might not do so against the official himself who had been chosen, nor against the will of the commonwealth by will of the officials set up throughout the towns, because they never had any such will but rather the opposite.

Even granting that they wished to hand over this power to the Spaniards, they might not do so against the will of the people nor against the will of the king. Nor could the Spaniards be true lords even by will of the people because such a will never existed; and it would not suffice even if it alone came into question, because the people might not without the consent of their lords admit a ruler without a reasonable cause.

The fourth conclusion. For the emperor to be true lord of the tribute in all of the New World and the Spaniard in the community entrusted to him, it does not suffice for [native] governors or *caciques* to be appointed for the various towns. . . .

It follows that the Spaniards cannot have just dominion since they have despoiled the true owners of their tribute. The second owner (who is the Spaniard) either has the right to the tribute or not. If not, then, he has no claim to the tribute. If he has the right, he is rightly paid the tribute, nonetheless the real lord ought to retain the right to the entire tribute. But it is contrary for a commonwealth to have two lords to whom it pays double tribute. Therefore, it follows that, since there are *caciques* and governors in the villages, such dominion [of the Spaniards] is unjust.

The fifth conclusion. In truth, as things are in the New World, all true lords constituted either by succession or appointment may be said to be deprived of their true dominion.

Here is the proof: if they were not deprived, their lord would be he who rules over the monarchy; but there is no proof of such, since this is neither Montezuma nor his successor, unless we hold that his son Don Pedro is such because he receives from the royal tribute five hundred *pesos de minas* yearly and that the Caltzontzin is still ruling because his only son Don Antonio has a pension of three hundred *pesos de tepuzque*. No other *caciques* or governors are lords. This is obvious. If they were, it would be especially because the natives consider them such and maintain them from the community property, planting their fields and serving them. But this does not suffice.

First, because these *caciques* are not lords but rather like wretched slaves do they help in exacting tribute for the Spaniards themselves; they are insulted, they are flung into prison, they "bear the day's burden and heat," a condition proper not to lords but rather to servants.

Secondly, because the tribute is not given to them as belonging to them of old; and if it were given to them and is paid also to the Spaniards, a double tribute would result.

Thirdly, because if they have any Indians from their patrimony, such are taken away from them and they are called thieves, as I have stated.

So much so that as I once heard one of the *oidores* speaking on the subject who could not control his anger saying: "You who rule the world call him who is a true lord a thief who has fifty or a hundred men to serve him and pay him tribute but you do not call the Spaniard a thief who has an entire native population even if it add up to thirty thousand and they all pay him tribute; I am at a loss to know whence such abysmal ignorance." They all kept silent.

And so I hold that this conclusion is true that, as things now are, these *caciques* or governors are not true lords except in name only, and yet they were true lords before the arrival of the Spaniards, as we proved. . . .

[I]t is perfectly clear that among the natives there existed a government for the good of the commonwealth, that there were true lords and whosoever took things into his own hands was immediately removed by the king or put to death. Therefore, the assigned tribute that had been levied was given to the ruler of the people and further another [portion] was assigned to the king from the tribute gathered from among the people, much as in Spain such revenue is given to a count or duke. And the king also receives his sales tax. . . .

In answer to the first argument we reply that idolatry does not hinder true dominion; for, as is evident from Scripture, there were many unbelievers who nonetheless were true kings and true lords, as has been proved. But if the lords were homicides so that they ruled to the detriment of the people, then in such a case such princes should be removed and suspended. For if the believing rulers who commit such crimes are to be punished and despoiled, a fortiori should unbelievers be treated in the same way if they are guilty of such; but nonetheless they are not to be deprived of their dominion solely because of their unbelief. . . .

In answer to the second argument it is to be noted that he who rules badly is to be corrected, to be punished, but not for that reason is he to be despoiled. If the true lord does not direct his subjects to their end, he is to be admonished by the one who is aware of it; and if he does not listen, and the people persist in their error because their lord does not consent to their conversion or does not wish it, then in that case he is to be removed because he does not govern for the good of the commonwealth; but if the people do not wish to be converted and their conversion does not depend on him, then he should not be deprived of his kingdom.

Doubt XI

Whether there is any motive to justify war against the inhabitants of the New World.

It is commonly asked whether . . . there is some just cause for war which can be found on the part of the emperor either through his own authority or that of the pope.

First. It seems that there can be no such justifying cause; for if there were any it would be especially the propagation of the Christian faith and the preaching of the gospel. But this does not suffice.

Evidently, for Christ our Redeemer who sent his disciples to evangelize the entire world, forbade war when he said, "Remember, I am sending you out to be like sheep among wolves; you must be wary as serpents, and yet innocent as doves," and so on. Elsewhere he said: "When you enter the house, you are to wish it well;" and, again: "Whenever you enter a city or village, make your lodging there—and if they will not receive you, shake off the dust from your feet as you leave;" and finally: "You are not to carry purse, or wallet, or staff," and so on. From all these texts we conclude that in order to disseminate the gospel and to convert unbelievers to the faith, it is not allowed to begin a war nor to wage a war, since Christ not only did not teach those first leaders, the very foundations of the faith, that war was permissible, but he positively deterred them, instructing them how the world is to be conquered and converted to the worship of the true God.

Secondly, if there were any just cause of waging war against these natives, it would be especially because they were ruled tyrannically, and were held in oppression by their evil and unbelieving king and by other subordinate officials. But this was not a just cause for war. The right to slay a tyrant does not reside in a private person but rather in the commonwealth from whom the ruler is authorized to govern in matters temporal, or it is vested in some power higher than the king. But the emperor or leader who first declared war was neither a private person of the tyrannically-ruled community nor was the army the oppressed commonwealth nor was the emperor their superior, since, as has been stated, the unbelievers of the New World neither *de jure* nor *de facto* had been subjected to the emperor. It follows, accordingly, that this was not a just cause for waging war.

Thirdly, if any just cause for war could be alleged it would be especially because they are cannibals who devour human flesh, considering this one of their supreme delights, as is stated about the inhabitants of this New World. But this does not justify warring on them.

This is evident, since they devoured the flesh of those taken in war and offered in sacrifice. But this took place without wronging anyone; for such [prisoners] were slaves and lost their rights to their captors. Consequently, they might, without inflicting wrong on anyone, eat human flesh since they might throw it to the dogs or burn it. Therefore, on this score there is no just cause for war.

Fourthly, if there were any cause for just warfare it would be especially because of the alliance through which the Tlascalan commonwealth suffered injustice from the Mexicans, and, being unable to get the better of them or to avenge themselves, called on the Spaniards to assist them against the Mexicans. And thus it was at least an act of justice for the Spaniards to attack and defeat the Mexicans; as Cajetan[50] teaches . . . such action may be undertaken for reasons of alliance. But this does not suffice: first [in order to justify such an alliance, those who assist] must be invited; but the Spaniards were not first invited by the Tlascalans, inasmuch as there were already armed [Spanish] soldiers in the land who were the terror and nightmare to all the inhabitants. Secondly, because it is not evident that justice was on the side of the Tlascalans and injustice on that of the Mexicans. From this it follows, accordingly, that this [alliance with the Tlascalans] was not a just cause [of war].

Fifthly, if there were any just cause for waging war, it seems that it would be the free will of both the ruler and the entire people which wished to submit to the emperor and his leaders acting in his name, as though the ruler and his people were choosing the emperor for their king. But this does not suffice. First, because there always remains the doubt whether the first entrance into the New World by armed soldiers took place lawfully. Secondly, because, granting that the subjection was lawful, it does not seem to have been free, but rather effected under compulsion. For it was not out of love but out of fear, knowing as they did the ability of the armed Spaniards, yes, and their ferocity. One must also keep in mind the unfavorable conditions and faint-heartedness of these inhabitants. Consequently, the concession was not free and does not hold; especially since it was not made by the entire people but either by some ruler alone or by some ruler and a few of the leading citizens of the community.

Sixthly, if there was any just cause for war, it would have been especially because, while the Spaniards were hunting among these people for their treasures, such as gold, silver, and precious stones, which are commonly found and belong to the first one to claim them, they were not allowed by the natives to do so nor were they permitted to move about at will in this New World, nor could they carry on trade or conduct business; all of which forms a part of the "law of nations." Yet this does not furnish a just cause for war. First, because [the Spaniards] never attempted any such moving about among the natives. Secondly when the Spaniards began to carry on trade and business, they were not satisfied to limit themselves to such activity but claimed that they were bringing about the subjection [of the natives] to the emperor. Thirdly, to effect the carrying on of business, they came not unarmed but armed terrifying the inhabitants and oppressing them in many ways.

Seventhly, if any just cause of war existed, it would be especially because these natives are naturally slaves and the Spaniards naturally free and, thus, the former should deservedly be subjected, and so on. But this is not a sufficient cause, since the natives, too, had their form of government, and so on.

To decide the problem one must keep in mind that, in speaking about the justice of war, it is necessary to distinguish between beginning a war for the sake of securing possession and the holding on to territory acquired through war. Thus, it is possible that those who began the war acted unjustly; but that later with victory secured, the retention of the territory is just. As we are wont to say, many things that were forbidden, on coming to pass, are valid. Hence it could be that, in the beginning, the emperor was forbidden to start the war; but later, with the *fait accompli*, the step is validated, with the consequence that he is now in legitimate possession.

The first conclusion. If these primitive natives of the New World had the faith sufficiently explained to them so that they were bound to believe, they might, strictly speaking, be forced by their ruler by means of war to accept the faith if there were no fear of apostasy.

What I want to say in this conclusion is that if any nation of unbelievers which never heard about Christ has the faith sufficiently proposed and preached to it so that those who listen to the explanation of the faith would sin in not assenting to it who earlier were excused through invincible ignorance from believing, since its tenets were either not explained at all or were not sufficiently explained so that they were bound to believe; such persons—strictly speaking, and precluding scandal and apostasy—may be coerced into accepting baptism and the faith, not so that they pretend to believe but that they will want to believe with all their heart what they formerly rejected. This is termed indirect coercion. I will use as an example to clarify it: the emperor has under his sway Moors and Jews in Spain, Italy or elsewhere, or some other nation of unbelievers who are really subject to him; he may so govern such a nation, supposing that it has the faith sufficiently preached to it, that it embrace the faith; and refusing to accept it, he may coerce it, even waging war against the inhabitants if they are stubborn. . . .

[S]upposing that the emperor has legitimate dominion over the provinces of this New World, if there is any province where unbelief still prevails, he may at will either empower his ministers and governors or other officials to destroy their temples and idols and abolish every rite and sort of sacrifice. And, hence, he may enact laws so that they come to the faith and be baptized and induce them in every way for them to do so; not so that they feign belief or that they be forced into believing, because, although one can do all things even against one's will, he cannot believe unless he wishes to do so; but they should be induced to freely wish what is so vitally necessary for them. . . .

[S]ince the aborigines themselves accepted the faith without reluctance and were baptized even without sufficient preaching, their real rulers, as is obvious, might not be deprived of their legitimate dominion, since there was no just cause, unless perchance it be alleged that there was danger of their probably apostatizing. Hence, follows: . . . If the unbelievers accepted the faith of Christ and if there were any well-founded fear of their apostatizing should their otherwise legitimate masters retain their jurisdiction in governing, the latter might be deprived of such jurisdiction, if there were no other way to prevent their apostasy. What I want to say . . . is that should it happen that after some of the aborigines accepted the faith they would run the risk of abandoning the faith if they remained under the same government as before their conversion and should this risk have its source in the governor or in the subjects and no other remedy for the evil could be found, then in such an instance the person entrusted with their spiritual welfare might do away with such dominion, however legitimate it might otherwise be, and hand it over to one who could assist them along the path of the faith that they had embraced.

NOTES

1. Jesús de la Torre Rangel, *Alonso de la Veracruz: amparo de los indios. Su teoría y práctica jurídica* (Aguascalientes: Universidad Autónoma de Aguascalientes, 1998), 217.

2. Arthur Ennis, "Fray Alonso de la Vera Cruz, O.S.A. (1507–1584): A Study of His Life and His Contribution to the Religious and Intellectual Affairs of Early Mexico," *Augustiniana* 5, no. 1/2 (April 1955): 64–67.

3. John F. Blethen, "The Educational Activities of Fray Alonso de la Vera Cruz in Sixteenth Century Mexico," *The Americas* 5, no. 1 (July 1948): 34.

4. Ennis, "Fray Alonso," (April 1955): 71, 91–93.

5. Ennis, "Fray Alonso," (April 1955): 93.

6. E. J. Burrus, "Alonso de la Veracruz's Defence of the American Indians (1553–1554)," *The Heythorp Journal* 4, Issue 3 (July 1963): 226; and Ennis "Fray Alonso," (April 1955): 108.

7. Antonio Gómez Robledo, "Alonso de la Veracruz: Vida y Muerte," in *Homenaje a fray Alonso de la Veracruz en el cuarto centenario de su muerte (1584–1984)* (México: Instituto de Investigaciones Jurídicas, 1986), 46; and Carlos E. Castañeda, "The Coming of the Augustinians to the New World," *Records of the American Catholic Historical Society of Philadelphia* 6, no. 4 (Dec. 1949): 195.

8. Arthur Ennis, "Fray Alonso de la Vera Cruz, O.S.A. (1507–1584): A Study of His Life and His Contribution to the Religious and Intellectual Affairs of Early Mexico, Chapt. IV." *Augustiniana* 5, no. 3 (August 1955): 261; Arthur Ennis, "Fray Alonso de la Vera Cruz, O.S.A. (1507–1584): A Study of His Life and His Contribution to the Religious and Intellectual Affairs of Early Mexico, Chapt. VI and VII." *Augustiniana* 7 (1957): 149–150.

9. Ennis, "Fray Alonso," (April 1955), 96. There may be more to the story than just a humble man refusing an honor. Bishop Valdivieso, another friend of Bartolomé de las Casas, was murdered by the sons of Rodrigo Contreras, the Nicaraguan governor, because of his defense of the rights of the Indians and opposition to the encomiendas. None of the biographers of Vera Cruz seemed to know how Valdivieso died or suspect that there might be more to Vera Cruz's unwillingness, as another defender of the Indians, to literally go into the mouth of the lion in León, Nicaragua.

10. Ernest J. Burrus, "Alonso de la Vera Cruz (d. 1584), Pioneer Defender of the American Indians," *The Catholic Historical Review* 70, no. 4 (Oct. 1984): 531; Ennis, "Fray Alonso," (April 1955): 98, 99, 100; Blethen, "Educational," 36–37, 41.

11. Roberto Heredia Correa, introducción, to Alonso de la Vera Cruz, *Sobre el dominio de los indios y la guerra justa*, trans. from the Latin by Roberto Heredia, Antonio Gómez, and Paula López (México: Facultad de Filosofía y Letras UNAM, 2004), 40–41.

12. Quijano, "Las repúblicas," 144–45.

13. Virginia Aspe Armello, "El viejo al nuevo mundo: El tránsito de la noción de dominio y derecho natural de Francisco de Vitoria y Alonso de la Veracruz," *Revista Española de Filosofía Medieval* 17 (2010): 152.

14. Antonio Rubial García, "Fray Alonso de la Veracruz, agustino. Individualidad y corporativismo en la Nueva España del siglo XVI," *Innovación y tradición en Alonso de la Veracruz*, ed. Carolina Ponce Hernández (México: Facultad de Filosofía y Letras, 2007), 90.

15. Burrus, "Alonso," (1984): 538.

16. Rubial, "Fray Alonso," 93.

17. Gómez Robledo, "Alonso," (1986), 51–52; Heredia, introducción, 27; Burrus, "Alonso," (1984): 539; Rubial, "Fray Alonso," 93; Ennis, "Fray Alonso," (April 1955): 176, 177–178; Burrus, "Alonso," (1963): 229.

18. Carlos E. Castañeda, "The Coming of the Augustinians to the New World," *Records of the American Catholic Historical Society of Philadelphia* 6, no. 4 (Dec. 1949), 195; Ennis, "Fray Alonso," (1957), 185–186; Heredia, "Introduccion, 28.

19. Francisco Quijano Velasco, *Las repúblicas de la Monarquía: Pensamiento constitucionalista y republicano en Nueva España, 1550–1610* (México: Instituto de Investigaciones Históricas UNAM, 2017), 139.

20. For further discussion of the ideas on natural law of the Spanish philosophers, see Chapter 5 in Quentin Skinner, "The Revival of Thomism," in *The Foundations of Modern Political Thought, Volume Two: The Age of Reformation* (Cambridge: Cambridge University Press, 1978), 135–73.

21. Ambrosio Velasco Gómez, "La filosofía de Alonso de la Veracruz a 500 años de la conquista," *Revista Portuguesa de Filosofía* 75, no. 2 (2019): 1030, 1024.

22. Velasco, "La filosofía," 1030–33. See also Mauricio Beuchot, "Escolástica, humanismo y derechos humanos en la conquista según Fray Alonso de la Vera Cruz," *Revista de Filosofía* 21 (1995): 90–91.

23. Velasco, "La filosofía," 1042.

24. Anthony Pagden, *The Fall of Natural Man: The American Indian and the Origins of Comparative Ethnology* (Cambridge: Cambridge University Press, 1982), 60.

25. Monica Quijada, "From Spain to New Spain: Revisiting the Potestas Populi in Hispanic Political Thought," *Mexican Studies/Estudios Mexicanos* 24, no. 2 (Summer 2008): 196–197.

26. Quijano, "Las repúblicas," 119–20.

27. Burrus, "Alonso," (1963): 253.

28. Roberto Heredia Correa, "Breve historia del texto" in introducción to Fray Alonso de la Vera Cruz, *De dominio infidelium et iusto bello, Sobre el dominio de los infieles y la guerra justa,* trans. from the Latin and notes Roberto Heredia Correa (Mexico: Universidad Nacional Autónoma de México, 2007), xxxvi.

29. Heredia, introduccion, 42.

30. Burrus, "Alonso," (1963): 235.

31. Alonso de la Vera Cruz, *The Writings of Alonso de la Vera Cruz: Vol. II. Defense of the Indians: Their Rights.* The original Latin texts with English translation, edited by Ernest J. Burrus. (St. Louis: Jesuit Historical Institute, 1968), 141. Only quotations not included in the Vera Cruz selection in this volume are cited.

32. Heredia's Spanish translation is clearer than Burris' here. See Fray Alonso de la Vera Cruz, *De dominio infidelium et iusto bello, Sobre el dominio de los infieles y*

la guerra justa, trans. and notes Roberto Heredia Correa (Mexico: Universidad Nacional Autónoma de México, 2007), 30. See also Quijano, "Las repúblicas," 131–132.

33. De la Torre, "Alonso," 130, 134.

34. Vera Cruz, *The Writings*, 181.

35. Vera Cruz, *The Writings*, 247.

36. Vera Cruz, *The Writings*, 249.

37. Vera Cruz, *The Writings*, 269

38. Beuchot, "Escolástica," 85–86.

39. Quijano, "Las repúblicas," 153.

40. De la Torre, "Alonso,"122–123; Gómez, "El Problema," 406.

41. Gomez, "El Problema," 399.

42. Vera Cruz, *The Writings*, 459.

43. Gómez, "El Problema," 403–404; Vera Cruz, *The Writings*, 418–421.

44. Jorge J. E. Gracia, "Hispanic Philosophy: Its Beginning and Golden Age," in *Hispanic Philosophy in the Age of Discovery*, ed. Kevin White (Washington, DC: Catholic University of America Press, 1997), 25.

45. Quijada, "From Spain," 202–3.

46. Velasco, "La filosofía,"1042–43.

47. Gustavo Gutiérrez, *Las Casas: In Search of the Poor of Jesus Christ*, trans. Robert R. Barr (Maryknoll, NY: Orbis Books, 1993), 44.

48. De la Torre, "Alonso," 93.

49. Elif Gözler Çamur, "Civil and Political Rights vs. Social and Economic Rights: A Brief Overview," *Journal of Bitlis Eren University Institute of Social Sciences* 6, no. 1 (June 2017): 206.

50. Thomas Cajetan was an Italian Catholic philosopher who died in 1534.

Chapter Six

Isabel de Guevara
"This Was Men's Work"

In 1556, Isabel de Guevara wrote a letter to Princess Juana, Governor of the Provinces of Spain, asking for compensation for herself and her husband for the role she had played in the first, failed, settlement of Buenos Aires and the subsequent, and successful, founding of Asunción. It is one of only a few published letters to describe the contribution of women to the Spanish colonization of the Americas and in it Guevara dramatically challenges assumptions about the capabilities and proper role of women.

Isabel de Guevara sailed from Spain to South America in 1534 with the massive expedition of the Spanish nobleman Pedro de Mendoza. The expedition was composed of eleven ships, 1,500 men (according to Guevara, although another source says 1,200, and still another two thousand), one hundred horses, and an unknown number of women that could have been as few as ten or twenty but were probably more. The fleet ran out of water during the long voyage and when they arrived at the mouth of the Rio de la Plata, they found, not another Peru with rich settlements of Indigenous inhabitants and fertile fields as they had expected, but a dismal landscape populated by a few hostile Amerindians and little game, which they soon exhausted. Historian Lucía Gálvez notes that there were noblemen and high-ranking military officers among the expedition members along with foreigners including Germans, Englishmen, and Italians. She says, "None of them came with the work history of a laborer: they had come to take charge of rich lands in the name of the king and not to found industrious colonies. Their disenchantment could not have been greater."[1] The supplies of food that they had brought with them were soon consumed and, while at first some of the nearby Indigenous people brought them food, when hostilities broke out between them, that link was broken. Hunger set in and expedition members were reduced to eating rats and snakes and even dead comrades.[2] As many as one thousand were reported to have died. In Isabel de Guevara's retelling of the troubles they suffered, the women were essential in keeping a core number of the men alive.

When the simple settlement dedicated to Our Lady of Buen Ayre at the mouth of the Platte River was built, Mendoza sent his lieutenants Juan de Ayolas and Domingo Martinez de Irala upriver in search of more favorable site for a permanent colony. In June of 1537, Pedro de Mendoza died. His last orders had been to abandon Buenos Aires. Irala (who had taken command of the recently founded settlement of Asunción after Ayolas was killed by some Native people) ordered that the settlers comply with those last wishes and move the colony.[3] The second founding of Buenos Aires would not take place until another forty years had passed.

During the trip upriver to Asunción and during the first period after their arrival, the travelers did not fare any better. Expedition member Francisco de Villalta said that 100 men died of "pure hunger" on the river voyage. The men were still weak when they got to the new colony and Isabel de Guevara says that the women needed to help with the work of building and planting although the accounts by members of the expedition, including Villalta, give the credit to the men.[4]

Eighteen years later, in 1555, Martinez de Irala was named governor of all the territories of Rio de la Plata with the power to assign allotments of the services of Indigenous people, called *encomiendas* or the later *repartimientos*, to the settlers. On May 14 of the next year he allotted 20,000 Indigenous people to three hundred colonists. Isabel de Guevara was not among them. On July 2, Guevara wrote (or had a scribe write) her letter to Princess Juana which was a challenge to the governor, a legal document asking for justice in the form of compensation for services rendered by her and the other women, and which is, as historian Raul Marrero says, "above all a demand for women's rights."[5] Marrero goes on to say that Irala's ordinances had not recognized the rights of women to encomiendas and that the question was a subject of great controversy during the colonial period. He notes that Emperor Carlos V had annulled several allotments given to women but the tendency in general was to give women encomiendas.[6]

It is uncertain who Isabel de Guevara was. Spanish legal scholar Enrique Peña records a possibly relevant entry from passenger lists of the Mendoza expedition: "Domingo de Guevara . . . (erasure) and Don Vitor de Guevara, sons of Don Carlos de Guevara and Doña Isabel de Laserna, a native of Toledo, stayed on this armada."[7] While it is clear that the sons took part in the expedition, it is not at all certain that the parents did also.[8] If Isabel de Guevara was indeed Doña Isabel, native of Toledo, then she was a lady of some social standing rather than a servant, a supposition supported by the tone of her letter.

Guevara's letter, as one notes at first glance, is unusual in that both the writer, Isabel, and the addressee, Juana, are women. The letter has two parts. In the first, Guevara narrates the participation of the women in the preservation of the expedition at the time of the famine suffered at Buenos Aires, during the journey up the Paraná River, and finally their work in Asunción in the early life of that colony. The second part of the letter, much shorter in length, lays out her claim for compensation based on her contribution to Spanish colonization, a contribution that she maintains was equal to that of the men.

Was Guevara's letter unique? Spanish literature scholar Nina Scott says that "The letter that Isabel de Guevara wrote to Princess Juana, asking to be rewarded for services rendered, is one of the only published documents to record the participation of Spanish women in the settlement of the Americas."[9] Linguist Gladys Lopreto explains that the cultural and ideological context of the conquest, which the women internalized, led them to relegate themselves to anonymity. "The motive of the Spanish in these lands in the first twenty years was to discover in order to later despoil. . . Here women did not fit," she writes.[10] But, literary scholar Rocío Quispe-Agnoli insists that Isabel de Guevara's letter is not an isolated document among sixteenth-century letters. She notes that women wrote "to ask for land, encomiendas, recognition of privileges, scholarships for their children, positions for their husbands, and stipends, among other things." The Guevara letter, she insists, is rather one of many documents dominated by the feminine voice that exist in the Spanish archives waiting for a researcher to give them the place they merit in the history of the founding of the American colonies.[11] Writing a decade later, the same scholar reports she has found a similar letter to the king from Inés Muñoz, the wife of conquistador Francisco Pizarro's half-brother, who wrote in 1543 telling of her service to the Crown and asking for restitution of one of her grants of Indian labor.[12]

There are a number of other controversies around the letter. The first is easy to resolve. For some reason, many writers misidentify the "Juana" to whom Guevara was writing, believing that it was Queen Juana I, known as "Juana La Loca" or Joan the Mad, daughter of Isabel and Ferdinand, even though Guevara identifies her quite clearly as Princess Juana, Governor of the Provinces of Spain. Argentine historian Paul Groussac, writing in 1916, besides calling Guevara's letter "a mess of commonplaces and exaggerations," says that Isabel was so behind in the news that she wrote her letter to Juana in July of 1556, more than a year after the queen's death.[13] However, he should have known that Princess Juana, also known as Juana of Austria, was the granddaughter of the deceased Queen Juana. She was appointed by her father Carlos I (Carlos V of the Holy Roman Empire) who was about to abdicate in favor of her brother, who became King Philip II, to govern in Philip's stead when he went to England to marry Queen Mary Tudor. She held that post from 1554 to 1559. Groussac was the uninformed party. Other scholars have continued to make that same error through the years[14] in spite of the fact that, as Langa Pizarro notes, no one who is writing a letter to a queen asking for a favor would lower her to the rank of princess.[15]

But Groussac challenges the letter in a more fundamental way. He says, "Not enough women travelled with Mendoza for them to have played the absurd male role that is described [in the letter]" and he suggests that "the 'noble lady' may have come on one of the later expeditions."[16] In other words, he challenges the basic truth of the letter. Lopreto points out that the Emperor Carlos V had ordered some expeditions to carry no women at all, but she says that the presence of women has been proven, albeit in a way that is implicit in the text, between the lines. And to indicate that women were present in the colony and performed male roles, she cites a 1545 letter by Father Francisco González Paniagua which tells of a battle with the Amerindians on the Paraná River in which there was a "*capitana*" (female captain) of a vessel and that "from this disaster we ended up with eleven men and three women fewer."[17] The number of women remains unclear. Enrique Larreta, who wrote in the first half of the twentieth century about the settlement of Buenos Aires, said, "As a great exception, many women came in the expedition of Mendoza although it was forbidden. Some were dressed as men and in the hardest moments carried dagger and sword."[18] Langa Pizarro states that Groussac's use of quotation marks around the term "noble lady" harkens back to the image that all the women who traveled with the ships were prostitutes, and she remarks, "What a fantastic country Spain would have been if its prostitutes wrote like Isabel de Guevara!"[19]

Isabel de Guevara's letter gives what Marrero calls "a distinct version of history" from the one that "ascribed subordinate roles to women or simply erased them." He notes that Guevara's letter challenges the "chivalrous values of the conquerors: honor, bravery and tenacity, among others."[20] Not only that, but she holds herself in check from saying more that would discredit the men. The women efforts included roles traditionally assigned to women including caring for the sick men, cleaning them and washing their clothes, cooking what food they had and feeding it to the sick men. But the women did much beyond that, including numerous activities normally performed only by men such as performing guard duty, sounding alarms, drilling the men, arming the crossbows, and even firing the cannons. Quispe-Agnoli describes the women's actions as belonging to two spheres, the domestic sphere and the public sphere of war and government.[21] Lopreto notes that the women "carried out the traditional masculine tasks without help while not abandoning the food and care of the wounded and the dying,"[22] the traditional work of women. As Guevara ascribes attributes normally associated with men such as bravery and strength to the women, she tells how the men were brought low by hunger and illness and had to be carried by the women as if they were children. Literary scholar Monica Szurmuk calls the image of a woman carrying a conquistador "absolutely subversive."[23] While Guevara definitely portrays a role reversal, she also says that the women took on their unusual role out of charity, an acceptable, traditional motivation and that they were able to do so because the "women could get by with less food and had not fallen into such a state of weakness as the men."

Isabel de Guevara told Princess Juana that her services to the Crown merited compensation similar to that received by the men who had participated in the discovery and conquest of the Rio de la Plata region. She seems to have expected a *repartimiento* when Governor Irala began his distribution of allotments of Indian services to the colonists and laments the "ingratitude that has been shown to me" when she received nothing. She realized that the work of the women in the founding of the colony had been ignored, pushed underground, and her goals therefore became both to revive that history and to present her petition for compensation. Lopreto remarks, "It is undeniable that by putting herself at a level of equal rights with the men conquerors, she surpasses her cultural competence, or at least advances beyond the ideology of the epoch."[24]

However, in advancing her claim of rights for women, Guevara put herself at what Szurmuk calls "the center of the contradiction" between her subaltern position as a woman and her hegemonic position as a white European participating in the Spanish imperial project.[25] Szurmuk goes on to say, "Guevara performs a subversive act supported by a highly reactionary ideology and includes women in the masculine enterprise of the colonization, which at the same time involved them in genocide."[26] While the word genocide was not used at the time, the treatment of the native inhabitants of the New World had been a major controversy within the Spanish empire for decades with the major debate on the issue called by Emperor Carlos V at Valladolid having taken place a few years before Guevara's letter.

Is Isabel's letter an example of political theory? Or is it simply a document of social history describing unusual life experiences and requesting compensation for services rendered? Szurmuk states, "If women have not been able to be philosophers, one has to look for ways that they have practiced philosophy outside of the traditional fields of philosophy."[27] And, if a definition of normative political philosophy is that it lays out how the author believes a polity's political or social life should be structured, often by contrasting it with current injustices, Guevara's letter meets that definition in demanding recognition of the forgotten participation of women in the founding of the Rio de la Plata colonies, in challenging the stereotypes that caused that history to be forgotten, and in demanding equal compensation based on a contribution equal to that of the men of the Pedro de Mendoza expedition of which she was a part.

LETTER OF ISABEL DE GUEVARA TO THE PRINCESS JUANA

Very High and Very Powerful Lady:

To this province of the River Plate, with Don Pedro de Mendoza being the first governor thereof, there came certain women, of whom my destiny willed it that I should be one, and as the fleet arrived at the port of Buenos Aires with fifteen hundred men and they were in need of food, the starvation was so great that after three months a thousand of them died. So great was the famine that not even in Jerusalem[28] could it have been worse, nor can it be compared to any other. The men became so weak that all the work fell on the poor women: from washing their clothes to caring for the sick, making them eat the little they had, cleaning them, standing guard, tending the watch-fires, arming the crossbows when sometimes there were Indian attacks and even firing the culverins [a type of cannon]; we would sound the alarm to the soldiers with loud voices, we drilled them and put them in order, for at that time we women could get by with less food and had not fallen into such a state of weakness as the men. Your highness will understand that had it not been for the care and concern we had for them, all of them would have been finished, and were it not for the honor of the men, I might truly write a great deal more and offer the (men) as witnesses. I am sure they will write this report to Your Highness in greater detail, and for that reason I will desist.

When this terrible time was over the few who remained alive determined to go upriver in two brigantines, as weak as they were and with winter about to begin. And the exhausted women cared for them and watched over them and cooked their food, lugging firewood onto the ships on their backs, and encouraging them with manly words not to let themselves die, that soon they would get to lands where there would be food, and carrying them aboard the brigantines on their backs with as much love as if they had been their own children. And when we came to a tribe of Indians called Timbues, lords of good places to fish, again we served the men by thinking up different ways of preparing the fish so that it would not disgust them, for they had to eat it without bread and were very feeble.

After that they decided to go up the Paraná River in search of food, on which journey the unfortunate women underwent such hardships that God determined that they should survive miraculously because He saw that the men's lives were in their hands, for the women took all the labors on board so to heart that one would feel affronted if she did less than another, so they all worked at handling the sails and steering the ship, taking soundings at the bow and taking over the oar from a soldier unable to row, and bailing the ship and encouraging the soldiers not to lose heart; this was men's work, and in truth the women were not rewarded for it, nor did it out of obligation, but only out of love. So they got to this city of Asunción which, although now it produces a great deal of food, was then very much in need of it, and thus it was necessary for the women to set to work again, clearing the land with their own hands, digging, weeding, sowing, and harvesting the food with no help from anyone until the soldiers had recovered from their weakness and began to govern the land and acquire Indian men and women as their servants, until the land came to be in the state it is now.

I have wanted to write and bring this to Your Highness's attention, to let you know the ingratitude that has been shown me in this country, because by now the greater part of it has been granted to those who reside here, the old colonists as well as the new, without any acknowledgment whatsoever of me and of my work, and I was left out, not having been given an Indian or any other kind of reward. I would dearly love to be free to go and appear before Your Highness, and tell you about the many services I have rendered His Majesty and the injuries now being done to me, but this is not in my power because I am married to a gentleman of Seville named Pedro d'Esquivel, whose services to His Majesty have caused mine to be quite forgotten, and they should be told again, because thrice I have saved his life when he had a knife at his throat, as Your Highness over there must know. And so I beg you to order that my *repartimiento* [allotment of Indians] be given me in perpetuity and that in appreciation of my services my husband be assigned a position worthy of his person, as he for his services also merits this. May Our Lord God increase your royal life and state for many years. From this city of Asunción and on July 2, 1556.

Your Highness's servant who kisses your royal hands
Doña Ysabel de Guevara

(Seal) Envelope—To the very high and very powerful lady the Princess Doña Juana, Governor of the kingdoms of Spain, etc.—at her Council of the Indies

NOTES

1. Lucía Galvez, *Mujeres de la Conquista* (Buenos Aires: Editorial Planeta Argentina, 1990), 64. Translation by the author.

2. Nina M. Scott, *Madres del Verbo/Mothers of the Word: Early Spanish-American Women Writers, a Bilingual Anthology* (Albuquerque: University of New Mexico Press, 1999), 4.

3. Galvez, *Mujeres*, 68.

4. Mar Langa Pizarro, "Mujeres en la expedición de Pedro de Mendoza: Cartas, crónicas y novelas; verdades, mentiras, ficciones y silencios," *América sin nombre* no. 15 (2010), 22.

5. Raul Marrero Fente, "De retórica y derechos: estrategias de la reclamación en la carta de Isabel de Guevara," *Hispania* 79, no. 1 (Mar. 1996), 4–5.

6. Marerro, "De retórica," 5.

7. Enrique Peña, *Documentos relativos a la expedición de don Pedro de Mendoza y acontecimientos ocurridos en Buenos Aires desde 1536 a 1541* (Buenos Aires: Imprenta Angel Curtolo, 1936), 27.

8. Gladys Lopreto, "La Carta de Isabel de Guevara (Siglo XVI): La mujer y la conquista," *Páginas de Estudio* (blog), written 1996, posted Feb. 28, 2011, http://pginasdeestudio.blogspot.com/2011/02/carta-de-isabel-de-guevara-siglo-xvi.html.

9. Scott, *Madres*, 3. The original document is in the State Archives of Spain and can be viewed here: http://pares.mcu.es/ParesBusquedas20/catalogo/description/1339358.

10. Lopreto, "La carta."

11. Rocio Quispe-Agnoli, "Discursos coloniales escritos y agencia femenina: La 'Carta a la Princesa Juana,'" *Cuaderno Internacional de Estudios Humanísticos y Literatura, Edición Especial Monográfica: Más allá del Convento* 5 (2005–6), 83, 88.

12. Rocio Quispe-Agnoli, "Secular Women Writers in the New World," *The Routledge Research Companion to Early Modern Spanish Women Writers*, ed. Nieves Baranda and Anne J. Cruz (London: Routledge, 2017), 329.

13. Paul Groussac, *Mendoza y Garay: Las Dos Fundaciones de Buenos Aires* (Buenos Aires: Casa Editora de Coni Hermanos, 1916), 73.

14. Among the misinformed writers are Galvez, *Mujeres,* 67, 70; Luis Martin, *Daughters of the Conquistadores: Women of the Viceroyalty of Peru* (Dallas: Southern Methodist University Press, 1989), 28, 29; and Monica Szurmuk, "Gesto autobiográfico: Historia y narrative de viajes de Isabel de Guevara," in *Modalidades de representación del sujeto auto/biográfico feminino*, ed. Magdalena Maiz and Luis H. Pena (Mexico: Grafo Print Editores, SA, 1997), 93.

15. Langa Pizarro, "Mujeres," 23. Other scholars besides Langa Pizarro who "get it right" include Scott and Quispe-Agnoli.

16. Groussac, *Mendoza*, 73–74.

17. Lopreto, "La carta."

18. Enrique Larreta, *Tenía que suceder: Las dos fundaciones de Buenos Aires* (Buenos Aires: Espasa-Calpe, S.A., 1944), 152.

19. Langa Pizarro, "Mujeres," 23.

20. Marrero, "De retórica," 3, 4.

21. Quispe-Agnoli, "Discursos," 87.

22. Lopreto, "La carta," 13.

23. Szurmuk, "Gesto," 92.

24. Lopreto, "La carta," 16.

25. Szurmuk, "Gesto," 95.

26. Szurmuk, "Gesto," 90.

27. Szurmuk, "Gesto," 89.

28. She could be referring to a first-century CE famine that is mentioned in the New Testament in the letters of Paul.

Chapter Seven

Council of Huejotzingo
"Our Fathers Knew No Tribute"

In the year 1560, the Indigenous officials of the city of Huejotzingo wrote to King Philip II of Spain asking for a reduction in their recently assigned tribute which was much higher than what they had previously been paying. But there is more to the letter than a simple petition. As a way of justifying their request, the letter recounts to the king the city's collaboration with Spanish conquistador Hernán Cortés in his war against their enemies (the Mexica of Tenochtitlan), their acceptance of the first Franciscan friars, and their joyful conversion to Christianity. The letter is written, as anthropologist Arthur Anderson and his colleagues note, with "the structure, syntax, and rhetoric [that] belong to the well-developed art of central Mexican public discourse in pre-conquest times."[1] Historians James Lockhart and Enrique Otte call the letter "a magnificent fabric" and "a verbal tapestry."[2]

The letter was written in Nahuatl and translated into Spanish before being sent to King Philip. It is not clear where the Nahuatl letter and its translation are currently located but, in 1877, the Spanish Ministry of Development published a facsimile of the Nahuatl original in the book *Cartas de Indias*.[3]

Before talking about the history of this town, it is necessary to address the issue of the spelling of its name. This has varied from Huexotzinco, Guaxocingo and Huexotzingo (colonial) to the modern Huejotzingo. Except when quoting an author who uses a different spelling, the modern spelling will be used here.

At the time of the arrival of the Spaniards, the Indigenous territory of Huejotzingo included an extensive Nahuatl-speaking area located just to the east of the Popocatépetl and Iztaccíhuatl volcanoes. Huexotzingo was probably founded in the twelfth century as a Chichimeca settlement.[4] During the last decades of the fourteenth century, it was the most powerful city-state in the region of Atoyac. But, in succeeding years, it had to deal with the rising power of its neighbors Tlaxcala and Tenochtitlan and over time more and more cities fell under the yoke of the Mexica of Tenochtitlan.[5] [Here again, we have controversies about names. Anthropologist Nigel Davies proposes using the name Tenochtitlan when referring only to the capital of the growing empire; Mexica when referring to Tenochtitlan and Tlatelolco; and Aztec when referring to the Triple Alliance of Tenochtitlan (with Tlatelolco), Tetzcoco, and Tlacopan].[6]

During this period the city-states engaged in what were known as "Flower Wars," ritual conflicts that showed off the prowess of the fighters and enabled the capture of prisoners for religious sacrifice. These battles often took place in Huejotzingo territory as the city's warriors fought those of Tlaxcala and Tenochtitlan. Some sources say that the Aztecs chose not to conquer Tlaxcala and Huejotzingo in order to continue to fight them in the Flower Wars.[7]

Around 1513, Huejotzingo found itself in such dire straits from warfare over boundaries with Tlaxcala that its citizens were forced to take refuge in the city of Tenochtitlan, capital of their enemy, the Aztec empire. There they remained for over three years until overcrowding and religious conflict caused them to return to their lands where, a few years later, anthropologist Robert Barlow notes that Hernán Cortés found them "defeated and bitter." [8] Davies says, however, that there had been a genuine reconciliation between Huexotzingo and Tlaxcala, which explains Huexotzingo's lack of hostility toward Tlaxcala when the Spanish arrived.[9] The cities of Tlaxcala, Huejotzingo, and Cholula, all of which were traditional opponents of the Mexica in the Flower Wars, joined Cortés as allies.[10] Evidently, Cortés himself interceded so that Tlaxcala would return to Huejotzingo certain lands that Tlaxcala had won from its neighbor in battle. Troops from Texcoco and Cholula fought the Aztecs in the final siege of Tenochtitlan, along with those from Tlaxcala and Huejotzingo, providing possibly as many as 100,000 allied troops to Cortés's relatively meager army of about 1,500 men. Historian Stuart B. Schwartz says that "in terms of scale, the battle for Tenochtitlan was a major military effort, equal to the great contemporaneous battles of the Old World."[11]

In 1524, after the victory of the Spanish and their allies, Cortés took control of Huejotzingo and set up farms there, worked by the Indigenous inhabitants, which produced substantial earnings for him. However, with the establishment of the First *Audiencia* (or royal court) in New Spain in 1527, things became complicated. The Audiencia officials came determined to limit the power of Cortés, and they also demanded high tribute from Huejotzingo. Cortés departed for Spain to make counterclaims and New Spain officials called Huejotzingo leaders before them to announce that they no longer belonged to Cortés but rather to the king. Then, Audiencia members exploited

Huejotzingo for their own personal benefit demanding tribute in corn, farm animals, gold and labor.[12]

However, Huejotzingo was under the protection of the Franciscan friars with one of the earliest Franciscan monasteries in New Spain having been built there in 1525. Juan de Zumárraga, first bishop of Mexico and himself a Franciscan, in 1529 took up the cause of the Huejotzingo Indigenous people in a battle with the Audiencia that came to excommunication and violence, including capture and torture of Indigenous people and the upsetting of a pulpit with the priest still preaching inside.[13] Upon returning from Spain, Cortés filed a claim against the First Audiencia in 1530 that was heard by the Second Audiencia which took office in 1531. Part of the evidence presented at that trial were the eight pages that are now known as the Huexotzinco Codex,[14] one of four illustrated sixteenth-century manuscripts produced by Indigenous scribes in Huexotzinco.[15] Cortés won his claim in the first instance but First Audiencia members appealed to a higher court in Spain. (Eventually, in 1543, that court ruled that two-thirds of the tribute paid by Huejotzingo should be returned to Cortés and to Huejotzingo.[16] However, by that time, Huejotzingo had been given to the conquistador Diego de Ordaz).

The arrival of the first royal viceroy, Antonio de Mendoza, in New Spain in 1535 brought several major changes. First of all, Huejotzingo passed again under direct control of the king. Also, a new system of government of the Indigenous cities was established which, as Mesoamerica scholar Baltazar Brito notes, took as a model the Spanish form while conserving the pre-conquest social order and respecting the rights of the Indigenous nobility who were named to the leadership posts and exempted from tribute. Huejotzingo, beginning in the 1540s, was governed by a *Corregidor* (royal district official) who had to be a Spaniard, an Indigenous *Gobernador* (governor), several Indigenous *alcaldes* (mayors) who represented each of the sections of the city, and a number of other officials. All except the Corregidor were known as the Republic of Indians.[17] In the elections, normally held every year, only nobles had the right to vote. The results had to be approved by the viceroy, who could refuse to approve them if the chosen candidates were not, according to Brito, cooperative, obedient and without vices.[18]

The Spaniards made few changes from the Aztec tribute system although, in the case of Huejotzingo, the change from not paying tribute to the Aztec Empire to paying tribute to the Spanish King was substantial. Historian B. H. Slicher van Bath explains how the tribute changed through time:

> After the Conquest, the Spaniards simply took over the system, making a few small changes. More payments were to be made in gold; on the other hand, the new masters were less interested in the feathers and warriors' costumes. Maize was partly replaced by wheat, which the Spanish had introduced in America.

The exemptions for individuals working for the temples and priests were eliminated. In their place, new exemptions were created for Indians who worked for
the Christian churches and priests. . . . Fundamental changes in the tribute system only took place gradually. Payments in goods and services were replaced
by money payments, and personal assessments—equal tribute requirements per
individual, household or family—came to replace the original assessment per
community. The number of exemptions was drastically reduced. The Spanish
were forced into making such reforms by the effects of the massive decline in
Indian population.[19]

On top of the decline in population, Spain was experiencing difficulties in
financing its expenditures for maintaining military superiority in Europe,
especially as the Protestant Reformation spread. Historian Carlos Assadourian states that by 1555 there was consensus in the Spanish court that the
only way to balance the budget was by increasing revenues from the New
World colonies.[20] However, conflict continued between the Spaniards, who
had received large grants of land and Indigenous labor, and the members of
the religious orders, who were attempting to protect the Indigenous people
from exploitation, and between these two factions and the king. At the same
time, visiting investigators sent by the crown reported that the Indigenous
nobles took a substantial share of the tribute paid by their subjects for the
support of local government functions and for their own maintenance in the
style to which they were accustomed. In the decade following the writing of
the letter by the council members of Huejotzingo, changes were made in the
tribute system which would increase royal revenues to the detriment of the
traditional Indigenous nobility.[21]

Slicher Van Bath explains that by adding previously exempt groups to the
tribute-paying population, the Spaniards were able to make up for the continuing decline in the Indigenous population. He states that, "As a result of
the reform of the tribute system, the number of tributaries in the highlands increased by a factor of 2.5. . . . In Huejotzingo, for instance, the tributary population quadrupled after 1557: from 2,000 or 2,500 to 10,000 or 11,000."[22] The
recurring increases through the years in tribute amounts and in particular the
extraordinary increase in 1558 motivated the Indigenous leaders of Huejotzingo to protest. In answer, the Audiencia ordered a new census carried out by
Judge Diego de Madrid, with the help of the Indian inhabitants of the town.[23]
The census, both the part done by the Indigenous people with words and
pictures and the part done by the Spaniards under Diego de Madrid, has been
preserved as the 1,000-folio (2,000-page) Matricula de Huexotzingo and is
in the collections of the National Library of France in Paris.[24] Even after the
new census, however, the tribute assigned in 1560 to Huejotzingo was placed
at 11,308 pesos and 5,654 bushels of corn, a substantial increase from the

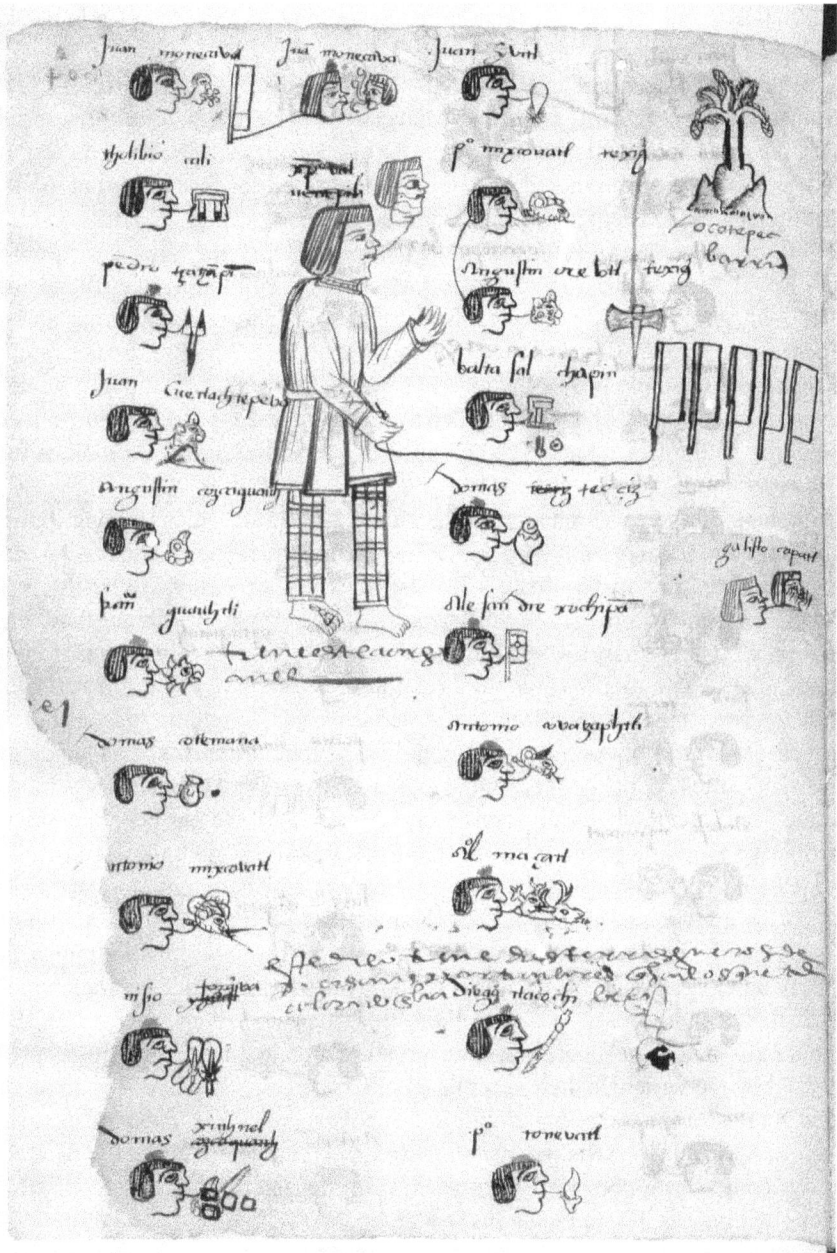

Figure 7.1. One of the census pages of the 1560 Matrícula de Huexotzingo (Folio 604V)

Courtesy of the Bibliotheque Nacionale de France in Paris.

2,000 pesos and 2,200 bushels of corn assessed in 1552 and even an increase from the 1558 amount.[25]

Huejotzingo continued to battle for its rights before the courts of New Spain, and the Spaniards continued to accept as evidence in court the written and pictorial documents submitted by the Indigenous people. The Guillermo Tovar Codex was completed in 1570 and submitted for the determination of tribute amounts. Then, in 1578, another census, now called the Chavero Codex[26] was submitted as evidence by the people of Huejotzingo in a case before the Royal Audiencia in which they accused their own Indigenous officials of bad management and overcharging of tributes.[27] Brito says, speaking about the Chavero Codex (but in a way that could apply to all the four codices) that it is a clear example of the tensions felt by the Indigenous community under their own officials who often took advantage of their positions and under Spanish authorities who never achieved a just and clear tribute policy for Huexotzingo.[28]

Notable in the 1560 letter from the Huejotzingo authorities to King Philip are a respect for hierarchy, a belief in benevolent rule, and in adequate compensation for rulers. The writers say that they are unworthy to kiss the feet of the king their lord, and say also that, with the new high tribute, they, the nobles who have charge of the king's subjects, are now so very poor that they resemble the commoners ("as they eat and dress, so do we") and that this is not the way things should be in an ordered world. They note that, in olden times, Huejotzingo was independent and paid tribute to no one. Conquistador Hernán Cortés cherished them and while he charged them tribute, it was moderate. But now, the letter goes on to say, the city's tribute has been increased from two thousand pesos to seven times that per year which they are unable to pay and which they beg the king to reduce to a just amount.

In their favor and in support of their petition, the writers describe their assistance to Cortés in the conquest of Tenochtitlan, noting that, along with many other contributions, "it was we who worked so that they could conquer the Mexica with boats; we gave them the wood and pitch with which the Spaniards made the boats." Another justification for better treatment presented by the writers is their acceptance of Christianity "with very good will" and their prompt compliance with the Spaniards' demand that they destroy "the stones and wood that we worshiped as gods" and burn their temples. Precious codices were certainly burned as well, limiting our knowledge of their lives and beliefs before the arrival of the Spaniards.

The letter reflects the leaders' belief in elite rule and that the king of Spain should recognize them as his representatives and not deprive them of the means to live in a way that is appropriate to their positions and obligations. Indigenous leaders for generations sought royal favors by telling how their ancestors became Christians and allied themselves with the Spaniards to help conquer New Spain for the king, which historian Peter Villella says demonstrates "the relevance of pre-Hispanic memories to postconquest legal and political negotiations."[29]

Even as conquered people, the Amerindians of New Spain and of Peru maintained their Indian identity. Indigenous nobles kept their special position within Indian society and functioned as intermediaries between the Spanish and the conquered Indigenous people. Anthropologist Ronald Spores states that the commonly held idea that the Indigenous people after the conquest existed "as a dominated, subjugated and seamless underclass with little or no power over their own lives or their relationships with the colonials" is a myth. Rather, he states, "They were part of a stratified colonial-Indigenous social system in which some Indians ranked above other Indians, some Spaniards ranked above other Spaniards, and Indians ranked both below and above Spaniards. Most ranked at the lower end of the social hierarchy, but clearly not all."[30]

Would the writings of the Huejotzingo leaders be considered subaltern expressions, expressions of people who are outside the power structures of a colony? According to literary theorist Gayatri Spivak, the subaltern do not include dominant foreign groups or dominant Indigenous groups on the national level, regional level, or local level.[31] Mónica Díaz says that definition of subaltern "would easily annul many of the Indigenous subjects who have left a written record in Latin America" because Spivak would consider the Huejotzingo nobles and others like them to be members of a privileged elite rather than of a subaltern group.[32] Historian Florencia Mallon, however, states that "no subaltern identity can be pure and transparent; most subalterns are both dominated and dominating subjects, depending on the circumstances of location in which we encounter them."[33] This certainly applies to the Huejotzingo mayor and council members, dominated as they are by the Spanish authorities while endeavoring to maintain their positions of leadership among their people. Their letter provides us with a valuable historical record of those efforts.

LETTER FROM THE COUNCIL
OF HUEJOTZINGO TO KING PHILIP II, 1560

Catholic Royal Majesty:

Our lord sovereign, you the king don Felipe our lord, we bow low in great reverence to your high dignity, we prostrate and humble ourselves before you, very high and feared king through omnipotent God, giver of life. We have not deserved to kiss your feet, only from afar we bow down to you, you who are most high and Christian and very pleasing to God our lord, for you are his true representative here on earth, you who govern us and lead us in things of Christianity. All of us creatures and subjects of the life-giving God, we poor vassals and servants of your majesty, we people here, we who dwell here in New Spain, all together we look to you, our spirits go out toward you; we have complete confidence in you in the eyes of our lord God, for he put us in your hands to guard us, and he assigned us to you for us to be your servants and your helpers. By our lord God and by your very honored and very high majesty, remember us, have compassion with us, for very great is the poverty and concern visited on us who dwell here in New Spain.

Our lord sovereign, King don Felipe our lord, through our words we appear and rise before you, we of Huejotzingo who guard for you your city—we citizens, I the governor and we the alcaldes and regidores and we the lords and nobles, your men and your servants. Very humbly we address ourselves to you: Oh unfortunate are we, very great and heavy sadness and concern lie upon us, nowhere do your pity and compassion come to us and reach us, we do not deserve, we do not attain your rulership. And ever since your subjects the Spaniards arrived among us, we have been looking toward you, we have been confidently expecting that sometime your pity would reach us, as we also had confidence in and were awaiting the mercy of your very revered dear father the ruler of the world, don Carlos the late emperor. Therefore now, our lord sovereign, we bow humbly before you; may we deserve your pity, may the very greatly compassionate and merciful God inspire you so that your pity is exercised on us, for we hear, and so it is said to us, that you are very merciful and humane toward all your vassals, and when a vassal of yours appears before you in affliction, so it is said, then you have pity on him with your very revered majesty, and by the grace of omnipotent God you help him. May we now also deserve and attain the same, for every day such poverty and afflic-tion reaches us and is visited on us that we weep and mourn. Oh unfortunate are we, what is to become of us, we your poor vassals of Huejotzingo, we who live in your city? If you were not so far away, many times we would ap-pear before you. Though we greatly wish and desire to reach you and appear before you, we are unable because we are very poor and do not have what is needed for the journey, things to eat on the boat nor the means to pay people for things in order to be able to reach you. Therefore now we appear before you only through our words, we set before you our poor commoners' words. May you only in your very great Christianity and very revered high majesty attend well to this our prayer.

Our lord sovereign, before anyone told us of or made us acquainted with your fame and your story, most high and feared universal king who rules all, and before we were told or taught the glory and name of our lord God, before the faith reached us, and before we were Christians, when your servants the Spaniards reached us and your captain-general don Hernando Cortés arrived, although we were not yet acquainted with the omnipotent, very compassionate holy Trinity, our lord God the master of heaven and earth caused us to deserve that in his mercy he inspired us so that we took you as our king to belong to you and become your people and your subjects; not a single altepetl [city-state] surpassed us here in New Spain in that first and earliest we threw ourselves toward you, we gave ourselves to you, and furthermore no one intimidated us, no one forced us into it, but truly God caused us to deserve that voluntarily we adhered to you so that we gladly received the newly arrived Spaniards who reached us here in New Spain, for we left our homes behind to go a great distance to meet them; we went twenty leagues to greet captain-general don Hernando Cortés and the others whom he led. We received them very gladly, we embraced them, we saluted them with many tears, though we were not acquainted with them, nor did our fathers and grandfathers know them; but by the mercy of our lord God we truly recognized them as our neighbors, so that we loved them; nowhere did we attack them. We began to feed them and serve them; some arrived sick, so that we carried them in our arms and on our backs, and we served them in many other ways, which we are not able to say here. Although the people who are called and named Tlaxcalans indeed helped, yet we strongly pressed them to give aid, and we admonished them not to make war; but although we so admonished them, they made war and fought for fifteen days. But we, when even one Spaniard was afflicted, then we managed to reach him; (there was no one else). We do not lie in this, for all the conquerors know it well, those who have died and some now living.

And when they began their conquest and war making, then also we prepared ourselves well to aid them, for out came all of our arms and insignia, our provisions and all our equipment, and we not merely named someone, we went in person, we who rule, and we took all our nobles and all of our vassals to aid the Spaniards. We helped them not only in warfare, but also we gave them everything they needed; we fed and clothed them, we would go carrying in our arms and on our backs those whom they wounded in war or who were simply very ill, and we did all the tasks in preparing for war. And it was we who worked so that they could conquer the Mexica with boats; we gave them the wood and pitch with which the Spaniards made the boats. And when they conquered the Mexica and all belonging to them, we never abandoned them or left them behind in it. And when they went to conquer Michoacan, Jalisco, and Colhuacan, and at Pánuco and Oaxaca, Tehuantepec, and Guatemala, and all over New Spain here where they conquered and made war until they finished their conquests, we never abandoned them, nor did we do anything detracting from their war making, though some of us were destroyed in it, (though not a single one of our subjects was left), for we truly performed our duty properly. But as to those Tlaxcalans, several of their nobles were hanged for making war poorly; in many places they ran away, and often they did badly in the war. In this we do not lie, for the conquerors themselves know it.

Our lord sovereign, we also declare and manifest before you that your fathers the twelve children of Saint Francis [the first Franciscan missionaries who arrived in New Spain in 1524] came to us, whom the very high priestly ruler the Holy Father sent and whom you sent, both granting us the favor that they came to teach us the gospel, to teach us the holy Catholic faith, the belief, to make us acquainted with the single deity God our Lord, and likewise God favored and inspired us, us of Huejotzingo, who dwell in your city, so that we gladly received them. When they entered the altepetl of Huejotzingo, of our own free will we honored them and showed them esteem. When they embraced us so that we would abandon the wicked belief in many gods, we forthwith voluntarily relinquished it; likewise they did us the good deed (of telling us) to despise, destroy, and burn the stones and wood that we worshiped as gods, and we did it; very willingly we destroyed, demolished, and burned the temples. Also when they gave us the holy gospel, the holy Catholic faith, with very good will and desire we received and grasped it; no one intimidated us into it, no one forced us, but very willingly we seized it, and we quietly and peacefully arranged and ordered among ourselves all the sacraments they gave us. Not once was anyone, whether nobleman or commoner, ever tortured or burned over this, as was done on every hand here in New Spain. People of many altepetl were forced and tortured, were hanged or burned because they did not want to relinquish idolatry, and unwillingly they received the gospel and faith. Especially those Tlaxcalans pushed out and rejected the fathers, and would not receive the faith, for many of the high nobles were burned, and some hanged, for combating the advocacy and service of our lord God. But we of Huejotzingo, we your poor vassals, we never did anything in your harm, always we served you in every command you sent and what at your command we were ordered. Quietly and peacefully we accept and take absolutely all of it, though only through the mercy of God do we do so, for it is not within our personal power. Hence now, by and through God, may you hear these our words, all that we declare and manifest before you, so that you will do us the favor of exercising on us your rulership to console us and aid us in (this trouble) with which we daily weep and sorrow. We are afflicted and sore pressed, and your altepetl and city of Huejotzingo is as if it is about to crumble and disappear. Here is what is happening to us: now your stewards the royal officials and the prosecuting attorney Dr. Maldonado are assessing us a very great tribute to belong to you. The tribute we are to give is 14,800 pesos in money, and an equal number of fanegas [bushels] of maize.

Our lord sovereign, never has such happened to us in the whole time since your servants and vassals the Spaniards came to us, for your servant don Hernando Cortés, former captain-general, the Marqués del Valle, as long as he lived here among us always greatly cherished us and kept us happy; he never disturbed or agitated us. Although we gave him tribute, he assigned it to us only with moderation; even though we gave him gold, it was only very little; no matter how much, no matter in what way, or if not very pure, he just received it gladly. He never reprimanded us or gave us concern, because it was evident to him and he understood well how very greatly we served and aided him. Also he told us many times that he would speak in our favor before you, that he would help us and inform you of all the ways in which we have aided and served you. And when he went before you, then you confirmed him and were merciful to him, you honored and rewarded him for the way he had served you here in New Spain. But perhaps before you he forgot us. What are we to say? We did not reach you, we were not given audience before you. Who then will speak for us? Unfortunate are we. Therefore now we place ourselves entirely before you, our sovereign lord. And when you sent your representatives, the President and Bishop don Sebastián Ramírez, and the Audiencia judges, Licentiate Salmerón, Licentiates Ceinos, Quiroga, and Maldonado, they themselves realized and confirmed the orders you gave for us people here, us who live in New Spain. In many things they aided us and lightened the very great tributes we had, and with many things that were our tasks they delivered us from and pardoned us all of it. And we your poor vassals, we of Huejotzingo who dwell in your city, when Licentiate Salmerón came to us and entered the altepetl of Huejotzingo, he saw how troubled the altepetl was with our tribute in gold, sixty pieces that we gave each year. The reason it troubled us is that gold is not gathered here and is not to be found here in our altepetl, though we searched for it everywhere. Then at once Licentiate Salmerón abolished it on your behalf and substituted and exchanged money for it; he set our tribute in money at 2,050 pesos. And ever since he assigned it to us, we have kept doing it; we hasten to give it to you, for we are your subjects and belong to you. We have never neglected it, we have never done it badly, we have given the full amount. But now we are greatly taken aback and very afraid and we ask, have we done something wrong, have we behaved badly and ill toward you, our lord sovereign, or have we committed some sin against almighty God? Perhaps you have heard something of our wickedness and for that reason now this very great tribute has fallen upon us, seven times exceeding all we had gone along paying before, the 2,000 pesos. And we declare to you that it will not be long before your city of Huejotzingo completely disappears and crumbles, because our fathers, grandfathers, and great-grandfathers knew no tribute and gave tribute to no one, but were independent. We nobles who have charge of your subjects are now truly very poor. Nobility is seen among us no longer. Now we resemble the commoners; as they eat and dress, so do we. We have been very greatly afflicted, and our poverty has reached its culmination. Of the way in which our fathers and grandfathers and great-grandfathers were rich and honored, there is no longer the slightest trace among us.

O our lord sovereign king, we rely on you as on God the one deity who dwells in heaven, we consider you our very father. Take pity on us, have compassion with us. May you especially remember those who subsist and live in the wilds, those who move us to tears and pity. Their poverty is before our eyes, we are gazing directly at it, wherefore we speak out before you so that afterward you will not become angry with us when your subjects have disappeared or dispersed. There ends this our humble supplication.

We cannot write here for you the very many ways in which your city of Huejotzingo is poor and stricken; we are leaving that to our dear father fray Alonso de Buendía, child of Saint Francis, if God the one deity should will that he arrive safely before you. He himself will be able to tell you many more things about our anguish and poverty, because he learned and saw it well while he was father guardian (of the Franciscan monastery) here in the city of Huejotzingo for two years. We hope that he will tell and relate it to you, for we have much confidence in him and have placed ourselves completely in his hands. This is all with which we come and appear before you.

This letter was done in the city of Huejotzingo on the thirtieth day of the month of July, in the year of the birth of our lord Jesus Christ 1560.

Your poor vassals who bow down humbly to you from very far,

Don Leonardo Ramírez, governor. Don Mateo de la Corona, alcalde. Diego Alameda, alcalde. Don Felipe de Mendoza, alcalde. Hernando de Meneses. Miguel de Alvarado. Alonso Pimentel. Agustín Osorio. Don Francisco Vásquez. Don Diego de Chaves. Juan de Almo[. . .]. Diego de Niza. Agustín de Santo Tomás. Diego Juárez. Toribio de San Cristóbal Motolinia.

NOTES

1. Arthur J. O. Anderson, Frances Berdan, and James Lockhart, "The Historical-Anthropological Potential of Nahuatl Documentation," in *Beyond the Codices: The Nahua View of Colonial Mexico*, trans. and ed. Arthur J. O. Anderson, Frances Berdan, and James Lockhart (Berkeley: University of California Press, 1976), 10.

2. James Lockhart and Enrique Otte, "Petitions, Correspondence, and Other Formal Statements," in *Letters and People of the Spanish Indies, Sixteenth Century*,

trans., ed., and commentary by James Lockhart and Enrique Otte (Cambridge: Cambridge University Press, 1976), 164.

3. "Carta del Cabildo de Huejotzingo, 1560," in *Cartas de Indias* (Madrid: Ministerio de Fomento, 1877) 1006; The letter has been scanned by the Virtual Library of Andalucía and can be viewed on-line at http://www.bibliotecavirtualdeandalucia .es/catalogo/consulta/registro.cmd?id=1039364. Click on "copia digital" and scroll to page 1006. In 2008, a new edition of *Cartas de Indias* was published in Mexico that includes the 1560 Huejotzingo letter which is identified only as "Facsimile U."

4. Baltazar Brito Guadarrama, *Códice Chavero de Huexotzingo: Proceso a sus oficiales de república* (México: Instituto Nacional de Antropología e Historia, 2008 [1578]), 21.

5. Brito, *Códice Chavero*, 22.

6. Nigel Davies, *Los Señores Independientes del Imperio Azteca* (Mexico: Instituto Nacional de Antropología e Historia, 1968), 19

7. For example, Xavier Noguez, introduction to *Huexotzinco Codex*, Facsimile of the 1531 Huexotzinco Codex in the Harkness Collection of the Library of Congress, Washington, DC (Mexico, DF: Ediciones Multiarte, SA de CV, 1995), 98–99; https:// babel.hathitrust.org/cgi/pt?id=uc1.31210010190401;view=1up;seq=89.

8. Robert Barlow, "El Derrumbe de Huexotzinco," *Cuadernos Americanos* 7, número 3 (mayo-junio 1948): 155, 157.

9. Davies, *Los Señores,* 139. See also Brito, *Códice Chavero*, 25.

10. Stuart B. Schwartz, *Victors and Vanquished: Spanish and Nahua Views of the Conquest of Mexico* (Boston: Bedford/St. Martin, 2000), 12.

11. Schwartz, *Victors,* 14–15. For a first-person account of the battle from the Spanish viewpoint, read Bernal Díaz del Castillo, *The History of the Conquest of New Spain* (Albuquerque: University of New Mexico Press, 2008) and for the story from the point of view of the Aztecs, see Book Twelve of the *General History of the Things of New Spain: Florentine Codex* compiled by Bernardino de Sahagún (Salt Lake City: University of Utah Press, 1982).

12. Rafael García Granados and Luis MacGregor, *Huejotzingo: La ciudad y el convento franciscano* (México: Secretaría de Educación, 1934), 83.

13. Noguez, introduction, 100; Garciá and MacGregor, *Huejotzingo,* 84–86.

14. Baltazar Brito Guadarrama, *Códice Guillermo Tovar de Huejotzingo, Libro I: Estudio introductorio* (Puebla: Gobierno del Estado de Puebla/Secretaría de Cultura, 2011 [1566]), 15.

15. *Huexotzinco Codex*, Facsimile of the 1531 Huexotzinco Codex in the Harkness Collection of the Library of Congress, Washington, DC (Mexico, DF: Ediciones Multiarte, SA de CV, 1995), https://babel.hathitrust.org/cgi/pt?id=uc1.31210010190 401;view=1up;seq=2.

16. John R. Hébert and Barbara M. Loste, introduction to *Huexotzinco Codex* (Mexico: Ediciones Multiarte, SA de CV, 1995), XVI; María del Carmen Herrera M. and Marc Thouvenot, "Tributarios en la escritura indígena de la Matrícula de Huexotzinco," *Dimensión Antropológica* 22, Vol. 65 (Septiembre/Diciembre 2015): 126–127.

17. Brito, *Códice Chavero*, 30.

18. Brito, *Códice Guillermo*, 31.

19. B. H. Slicher van Bath, "The calculation of the population of New Spain, especially for the period before 1570," *Boletín de Estudios Latinoamericanos y del Caribe* 24 (junio 1978): 69.

20. Carlos Sempat Assadourian, "The Colonial Economy: The Transfer of the European System of Production to New Spain and Peru," *Journal of Latin American Studies* 24 (1992, Quincentenary Supplement): 56.

21. For further information, see Charles Gibson, *The Aztecs under Spanish Rule: A History of the Indians of the Valley of Mexico, 1519–1810* (Stanford: Stanford University Press, 1964), 202; Margarita Menegus Bornemann, "Encomienda, tributos y señores naturales," in *Historia colonial de México: Instauración y desarrollo del sistema de encomiendas,* ed. Isabel Fernández Tejado (México, DF: Universidad Iberamericana, 1995), 125–126.

22. Slicher van Bath, "The Calculation," 75.

23. Hans Prem, *Matricula de Huexotzinco*, MS. Mex. 385, Bibliotheque Nationale, Paris (Graz, Austria, 1974), 708.

24. *Matrícula de Huexotzingo 1560*, Bibliotheque Nacionale de France, Mexicain 387, https://gallica.bnf.fr/ark:/12148/btv1b7200005f/f7.image The first drawings of the Indigenous census begin here: https://gallica.bnf.fr/ark:/12148/btv1b7200005f/ f283.image. See also Herrera and Thouvenot, "Tributarios," 125–161; and Carmen Aguilera, "The Matrícula de Huexotzinco: A Pictorial Census from New Spain," *Huntington Library Quarterly* 59, no. 4 (1996): 529–41.

25. María Justina Sarabia Viejo, *Don Luis de Velasco, virrey de Nueva España, 1550–1564* (Sevilla: Escuela de Estudios Hispano-Americanos, 1978), 337–38.

26. This codex is located at the National Museum of Anthropology and History of Mexico and can be viewed online at the World Digital Library at https://www.wdl .org/en/item/3246/view/1/1/ (Vol 1) and https://www.wdl.org/en/item/3246/view/2/1/ (Vol. 2).

27. Brito, *Códice Guillermo*, 16.

28. Brito, *Códice Chavero*, 170.

29. Peter Villella, *Indigenous Elites and Creole Identity in Colonial Mexico, 1500–1800* (Cambridge: Cambridge University Press, 2016), 20–21.

30. Ronald Spores, "Mixteca *Cacicas*" in *Indian Women of Early Mexico*, ed. Susan Schroeder, Stephanie Wood, and Robert Haskett (Norman: University of Oklahoma Press, 1997), 195.

31. Gayatri Chakravorty Spivak, "Can the Subaltern Speak?" *Marxism and the Interpretation of Culture*, ed. Cary Nelson and Lawrence Grossberg (Urbana and Chicago: University of Illinois Press, 1988), 284.

32. Mónica Díaz, *Indigenous Writings from the Convent: Negotiating Ethnic Autonomy in Colonial Mexico* (Tucson, University of Arizona Press, 2010), 17.

33. Florencia E. Mallon, "The Promise and Dilemma of Subaltern Studies: Perspectives from Latin American History," *The American Historical Review* 99, no. 5 (Dec. 1994): 1482.

Chapter Eight

Bernardino de Sahagún
"I Assembled All the Leaders"

Friar Bernardino de Sahagún, a Franciscan priest who was born in Spain but who lived most of his long life in Mexico, compiled information about things "divine, human, and natural" from the Indigenous Nahua people of central Mexico into the twelve books known as the *General History of the Things of New Spain* or the *Florentine Codex*. While authorship of the work is usually attributed to Sahagún, a number of scholars, including anthropologist/historian Miguel Leon-Portilla, have spoken of it as the "texts of Sahagún's native informants."[1] Linguist Angel M. Garibay writes that in their language they said it, with their manner of thinking they expressed it, and by means of these writings, which fortunately we conserve, we can see their own conception and composition.[2] Literary scholar Sara Castro-Klaren states that, from the beginning, the work suggests, not one individual author, but rather a network [of authors] who worked with their specific assignments in the construction of a project that took more than forty years.[3] It was Sahagún who brought the knowledgeable elders together, supervised the compilation of their testimony in Nahuatl, translated much of it into Spanish, and wrote extensive commentaries. Therefore, the compilations, several versions of which have survived in European libraries, can legitimately be considered the work of Bernardino de Sahagún AND his Indigenous informants.

Friar Bernardino was born in Sahagún in the Spanish province of León in the year 1499. He studied and took his religious vows at the University of Salamanca which, at the time, was over three hundred years old and one of the principal centers of learning in Europe. He very possibly studied under the noted philosopher Francisco de Vitoria, who had arrived to teach there in 1526.[4]

Friar Bernardino left Cádiz, Spain, for the New World in 1529 as a member of a group of religious led by Friar Antonio de Ciudad Rodrigo. Upon arrival in New Spain, he immediately began his study of Nahuatl in order to be able to preach to the Indigenous people, making use of the work of earlier Franciscans who had converted the Native people's spoken language into written form using the Spanish alphabet. Those first Franciscans greeted the new arrivals from Spain with the news that the Amerindians had been converted and almost all had been baptized. Sahagun soon found, however, that the "miracle" of the massive conversion of the Indigenous people was not true and that they accepted Jesus Christ only as one of their many gods as was their tradition when they came in contact with foreign peoples.[5] Thus, Sahagún believed, much further education of the Native people using their own Nahuatl language would be necessary.

In 1536, Sahagún helped found the Royal College of Santa Cruz at Tlatelolco and taught there until 1540. He and Friar Arnald de Bassacio taught Latin, history, and other classes in the humanities to promising young men from the Mexican elite.[6] This was a period of discord in New Spain, between Hernán Cortés and his opponents, between civil and religious authorities, among the different religious orders, and even between factions within the religious orders.[7]

From 1540 until 1545, it is assumed that Friar Bernardino worked as a missionary in the Valley of Puebla, during which time he climbed the Popocatepetl Volcano. He returned to the College of Santa Cruz in time for the epidemic of 1545 when he said he buried 10,000 and in 1546 nearly died of the disease himself. As a result of the loss of students in the epidemic, Santa Cruz was opened to students from any social rank who had the intellectual ability to succeed and its staff was made up of Indigenous Mexicans under the supervision of the friars.

Sahagún had already begun collecting materials on Mexican culture with the help of his students at the College of Santa Cruz when, in 1558, he was transferred to Tepepulco and, in that same year, the newly appointed Franciscan provincial Friar Francisco de Toral ordered him to write down in the native language those things that he believed would be useful for the evangelization of the Indigenous people and helpful to the Christian preachers. In 1561, Sahagún returned to Tlatelolco, but to the Monastery of Santiago not the College, where he continued his compilations.

Sahagún is usually described as having two principal motives for compiling twelve books of information about the Mexican people. Anthropologist Arthur Anderson, who along with linguist Charles Dibble, worked on the English translation of the Codex over a period of forty years, states that Sahagún and some of his colleagues had become convinced that the project of converting the Indigenous population was failing and "that idolatry persisted unchecked because it went undetected, and that it must be recognized before it could be combatted." If they knew what to look for, the missionaries would know what to combat. Thus the work had as its first motivation evangelization.[8] Scholar Walden Browne adds that "Sahagún was faced with a vast array of Indigenous cultural information that did not easily fit into a preexisting Western schema. Once [he] noticed what lay beneath the superficial compatibility of a few Christian and Indigenous practices, *everything* was subject to reinterpretation." His research then reflected his desire to understand "the entirety of Nahua culture."[9]

But much of the detailed compilation appears to have little relation to a pastoral purpose and it becomes obvious that a second motivation for Sahagún was concern for the well-being of the Indigenous people and a growing respect for their preconquest culture. Anthropologist Jorge Klor de Alva observes that "Sahagún sought to create a credible record of the Nahuas' past and present that would highlight the positive aspects of the culture, thereby protecting the natives from unwarranted charges of incompetence or cultural inferiority."[10] Sahagún often compared the Aztecs to the ancient Greeks and Romans, and scholar John Keber notes that, "While the Fathers of the Church were one in rejecting the Greek gods as false, some accepted Greek philosophy, properly adjusted, as good and useful." He goes on to say that Sahagún saw the connections between the Indigenous religion, morality and the administration of government and felt that all were related to the proper education of the young. He adds, "By calling attention to such Aztec moral achievements as the rearing of children to be responsible citizens . . . he could interpret the Aztecs in categories applicable in principle to all humans, Christian or not."[11]

By 1569, Sahagún noted that he had completed "a clean copy of the twelve books" and a Franciscan Chapter meeting the next year judged them of great value and urged their completion in three columns—Nahuatl, Spanish, and an explanatory column. However, the fathers voted against allocating funds for Friar Bernardino to hire scribes, thus limiting the amount of work he could do on the manuscripts. When he appealed, those who opposed the recording of Aztec customs and idolatries convinced the father provincial to collect all the writings and disburse them around the province, depriving Sahagún of access to them. But, a few years later, two successive commissioners general who favored Sahagún's project returned his writings to him and by 1575 he was able to resume work.[12]

With the help of native scribes, Sahagún began the translation of the greater portion of his compilations into Spanish. Linguist Munro Edmunson says that a Spanish version of the work "was suddenly necessary in order to defend not only Sahagún but the whole thrust of the Franciscan missionary effort from the Inquisition."[13] Possibly Sahagún's enemies had written the

King saying that the preservation in the Nahuatl language of ancient superstitions could allow the Indigenous people to revive their old religion.[14] In
1577, King Philip II ordered that all texts in Nahuatl and Spanish prepared
by Sahagún be sent to the Council of the Indies in Seville and in compliance
Sahagún sent a complete manuscript to the government in Spain.[15] Father
Rodrigo de Sequera, head of the Franciscans in New Spain and a principal
supporter of Sahagún, took another copy with him to Spain in 1580 and this
is the one that most scholars believe is the one we know today as the Florentine Codex,[16] located in the Medicea Laurenziana Library in Florence, Italy.
What happened to the copy that was sent to Spanish crown is the subject of
some controversy. But, it is probable that the Madrid Codex located at the
old Royal Palace is the manuscript sent to the Spanish court in 1577 and the
one at the Royal Academy of History, also in Madrid, is a copy (without the
drawings) that was previously housed at the Franciscan Convent at Tolosa.[17]

Describing Sahagún's later years, anthropologist Georges Baudot writes
that, "Even up to the last days of his life, Fray Bernardino tried to change
the ideology of the Indian by using the Indian's own cultural and subjective
reality and originality."[18] He worked to prohibit customs that he felt were
part of the old religion, most notably the flying pole dance (*palo volador*).
On the other hand Sahagun would have liked to infuse the Spanish system, as
Keber says, "with Aztec moral wisdom so that something new would result in
this new land. Why this new thing did not appear must have deeply troubled
Sahagún. One cannot miss the sadness and disappointment in his last writings."[19] Friar Bernardino died on October 28, 1590, at the Convent of Saint
Francis in Mexico City at the age of 90 or 91.[20]

Many scholars believe that in arranging the material from his informants
into the twelve books Sahagún used *Natural History* by the Roman Pliny the
Elder as a model. Pliny begins his work with astronomy and ends with miner-
alogy while Sahagún begins with the Mexican gods, proceeds through moral
philosophy, heavenly bodies, and government, ending with plants, animals
and minerals. Leon-Portilla states that the format harkens back to Sahagún's
education at the University of Salamanca, where "the interest was palpable in
a universal approach to the knowledge of the cultural and natural realities of
the peoples of classical antiquity and those of modern times."[21]

Some of the materials in the *Codex* were the answers by Sahagún's native
collaborators to his prepared questionnaires; others were spontaneously offered by the collaborators based on drawings in native books, many of which
Sahagún includes in his *History*. Sahagún also includes in the *Codex* a collection of traditional Indigenous speeches, orations, and exhortations, known
as *huehuetlahtolli*, and, in the last of the twelve books, a narration from the
point of view of the Indigenous people of the conquest of the Aztec capital of
Tenochtitlan by the Spanish.

Figure 8.1. Men keeping watch over their town, an illustration from volume 2, book 8 of the Florentine Codex with Nahuatl text

"Florence, Biblioteca Medicea Laurenziana, Ms. Med. Palat. 219, f. 291r By permission of MiBACT"

Sahagún does not give us the names of all of the elders who served as his informants signaling out only Don Diego de Mendoza of Tepepulco, "an old man of great distinction and talent, very expert in all things courtly, military, governmental, and even idolatrous." Along with Don Diego, Sahagún worked with "ten or twelve leading elders" of the town of Tepepulco. With the assistants, known as trilinguals (having knowledge of Nahuatl, Spanish and Latin), who helped him organize the volumes he is more generous with names. He lists Antonio Valeriano of Azcaputzalco, "foremost and most learned," who became dean of the College of Santa Cruz; Martin de Jacobita of Santa Ana in Tlatilulco, who also served as dean of the College; Alonso Vegerano of Quauhtitlan; and Pedro de San Buenaventura also of Quauhtitlan. The scribes who, Sahagún said, "copied all the works in a good hand," were Diego de Grado, Bonifacio Maximiliano, and Mateo Severino. Castro-Klaren says that, from the beginning, Sahagún's work was a collaboration among a number of people, under the eye and with the encouragement of the friar, but with the intellectual and physical labor of the Indigenous collaborators and that exclusive authorship should not be attributed to Sahagún since it hides the multiplicity of persons, cultures, and ways of knowing that emerge in the Nahuatl texts and in their Spanish translations.[22] One can add that hopefully they emerge in the English translations as well!

Sahagún's work, based as it is on information from elders "of great distinction," reflects the social bias of the native upper classes, certainly a small minority of the population. Anderson notes that "there is no evaluation by the commoner of himself or of his betters."[23] Anthropologist Edward Calnek states that informant bias "accounts at least in part for systematic omissions and for the lack of interest in large groups not represented among Sahagún's informants" but he adds that "none of this detracts from the authenticity of the material presented."[24]

Sahagún called book 6, the collection of traditional sermons, prayers, and orations, "the greatest of them all."[25] These *huehuetlahtolli* mark, among other things, the important stages of family life, the end of the reign of an old ruler and the beginning of the reign of a new one, prayers to the gods, and advice to children. Linguist Thelma Sullivan states, "Of all the material gathered by Sahagún, none is as rich in language or as revealing of the pre-Hispanic Indian mind and thought as the rhetorical orations."[26] In the advice to children, we can view the roles assigned to members of the noble class and what Sullivan calls "an emphasis on abstemiousness, austerity, proper conduct, and a regard for the opinions of others that bespeaks a rigidly controlled society."[27]

Sahagún, while condemning the Aztec religion, held the values expressed in the *Huehuetlatolli* in high esteem and could not understand how the Indigenous society, under idolatry, produced virtue, while the same people, living under Christianity, were reduced to vice. He developed the idea that the climate corrupted both the Mexicans and the Spanish and he admired the wise elder teachers who were able to educate the youth in a way that protected them from corruption.

The *General History of the Things of New Spain* was probably purchased by Ferdinand I de' Medici of Florence prior to 1588, a mere eight years after Fr. Sequera took it to Spain, but its date of acquisition by the Medicea-Laurenziana Library is uncertain. Bibliographer Angelo Maria Bandini discovered it there in 1793[28] but scholars took little note of it until the 1800s when interest in Sahagun blossomed as part of efforts to bring together foundational writings for the Mexican nation. Browne says that Sahagún's works offered an example for Mexican historians who were grappling with how to reconcile the Indigenous and Spanish aspects of Mexico's colonial past.[29] In the 1980s historians Alfredo López Austin and Josefina Garcia Quintana published Sahagún's complete Spanish text and in 1990 Juan Carlos Temprano edited a new edition of the Spanish text. However, no Spanish translation of the complete Nahuatl text has yet been completed and published. Between 1950 and 1982, Arthur Anderson and Charles Dibble published their translation into English of Sahagún's prologues and commentaries and the entire Nahuatl text. It is that version that is used here. In October of 2012, the Medicea-Laurenziana Library announced that the Florentine Codex was available online as part of the World Digital Library.[30]

One of the principal controversies around the compilations of Sahagún is whether he should be referred to as an anthropologist and ethnographer, even as the founder of anthropology. Leon-Portilla famously called him "First Anthropologist" in his book by the same name. But Browne maintains that Sahagún "was a man of his time and could not have been the inventor of an academic discipline that emerged in the nineteenth century in a context quite alien from his world."[31] Anderson says that Sahagún was the first researcher to use ethnographers' methods as they are conceived today, developing them centuries before their time.[32]

Another controversy arises out of postmodern scholarship. Klor de Alva, admittedly not a friend of that philosophical trend, summarizes post-modernism as maintaining that "fully objective descriptions or 'translations' of cultural reality" where the observed and the observer are separated by time or culture "are either fundamentally problematic or not possible at all."[33] Which presents us with two separate but related problems—the difficulty for the modern reader of fully understanding the sixteenth century friar and the even greater difficulty for the Spaniard Sahagún of comprehending the Nahuatl culture. Post-modernist Browne states, "I treat Sahagún, the Nahuas, and myself as three interfaces that brush up against each other but never really coalesce. This is not . . . about recuperating lost authenticities because, in this historical moment, I question whether there are any lost authenticities available for recuperation."[34] It is obviously up to each reader of the translations of Sahagún's compilations to decide whether they can derive valid meaning from them.

In the case of Sahagún, as is the case for many other early Latin American writers, the problem of Christian bias arises. Sahagún biographer Luis Nicolau D'Olwer notes that one should not conclude from Sahagún's harsh criticism of the Spanish "that he condemned the Conquest as a historian; for despite its violence and excesses, it had served as God's instrument, so that the natives of these lands 'could be converted and would be able to reach the Kingdom of Heaven.'"[35] However, Nicolau adds that Sahagún appears to feel that the Christian faith was the only gain for the native inhabitants of New Spain, adding "for the rest, the autochthonous culture had been in no way inferior to the imported one, and in some ways had surpassed it."[36] And Keber asks: "By praising the virtues of the Aztecs, did Sahagún set up the possibility of an ethical critique of Christian theology, as if he were to say that human virtue may owe little to Christian belief?"[37]

The selections chosen for this volume include four introductions or insertions by Sahagún in which he describes his methodology, expresses his attitude toward the conquest, his views about how the Aztec nation had been governed, and his pessimistic predictions of the future of the Nahuatl people. Then, in the selection from book 8, "Kings and Lords," elders tell how young boys of the Mexican nobility were raised to be future rulers of the empire, reflecting how their society was structured to assure the best governors. In the next two selections, first a noble father and then his wife speak to their daughter about how she should behave as a young woman, wife, and mother, revealing to us the ideas of the Nahuatl elites about the proper role of women in society. These writings give us a brief view of how elders of the Mexican elite believed young people should be raised in order to preserve both order and virtue in their nation. In total, what began as a compilation of customs and beliefs designed to be used to convert the Mexica people to Christianity turned out to be priceless compendium of knowledge about them based on valid methodology and that was respectful and even portrayed their culture as laudable.

GENERAL HISTORY OF THE THINGS OF NEW SPAIN: FLORENTINE CODEX

Sahagún's "Prologue" to Book 1: The Gods

The physician cannot advisedly administer medicines to the patient without first knowing of which humour or from which source the ailment derives. Wherefore it is desirable that the good physician be expert in the knowledge of medicines and ailments to adequately administer the cure for each ailment. The preachers and confessors are physicians of the souls for the curing of spiritual ailments. . . .The sins of idolatry, idolatrous rituals, idolatrous superstitions, auguries, abuses, and idolatrous ceremonies are not yet completely lost.

To preach against these matters, and even to know if they exist, it is needful to know how they practiced them in the times of their idolatry, for, through [our] lack of knowledge of this, they perform many idolatrous things in our presence without our understanding it. . . .

In order that the ministers of the Gospel, who will follow those who have come first in the cultivation of this new vineyard of the Lord, may not have reason to complain of the first ones for having left the facts about these natives of this New Spain undivulged, I, Fray Bernardino de Sahagún, a professed monk of the Order of Our Seraphical Father San Francisco de la Observancia, a native of the town of Sahagún en Campos, by order of the very Reverend Father, Father Fray Francisco Toral, Provincial of this Province of the Holy Gospel, and later Bishop of Campeche and Yucatán, wrote twelve Books of the divine, or rather idolatrous, human, and natural things of this New Spain. . . .

All this work will be very useful to learn the degree of perfection of this Mexican people, which has not yet been known, because there came over them that curse which Jeremiah, in the name of God, thundered upon Judea and Jerusalem in the fifth chapter, saying: "I will cause to come upon you, I will bring against you a people from afar, a very vigorous and brave people, a very ancient people skillful in battle, a people whose language ye will not understand, nor hast thou ever heard their manner of speech, all powerful and courageous people, lusting to kill. This people will destroy you and your women and children and everything ye possess, and will destroy all your villages and buildings."

This has literally happened to these Indians by way of the Spaniards. They and all their possessions were so trampled underfoot and destroyed that no vestige remained of what they were before. Thus they are considered as barbarians, as a people at the lowest level of perfection, when in reality (excluding some injustices their mode of governance contained) in matters of good conduct they surpass many other nations which have great confidence in their administrations.

Sahagún's "Prologue" to Book 2: The Ceremonies

I was ordered, by the holy command of my highest prelate, to write in the Mexican language that which seemed to me useful for the indoctrination, the propagation and perpetuation of the Christianization of these natives of this New Spain, and as a help to the workers and ministers who indoctrinate them. Having received this command I made an outline or summary in Spanish of all the topics to be considered. . . .

In [Tepepulco] village I assembled all the leaders with the lord of the village, named Don Diego de Mendoza, an old man of great distinction and talent, very expert in all things courtly, military, governmental, and even idolatrous. Having assembled them, I presented that which I intended to do and requested that they afford me capable and experienced persons with whom I could confer and who would know how to give me the information regarding that which I should ask of them. They replied that they would consult one another regarding the proposition and that they would answer me the next day. And thus they took their leave of me. The next day the lord came with the leaders. And having made a very solemn speech, as they were wont to do at that time, they assigned me as many as ten or twelve leading elders. They told me I could communicate with them, and they would give me answers to all that I should ask them. As many as four Latinists, whom I had taught grammar a few years earlier in the College of Santa Cruz in Tlatilulco, were also there.

With these leaders and grammarians, who were also leaders, I conferred many days. Close to two years, following the sequence of the outline which I had prepared. They gave me all the matters we discussed in pictures, for that was the writing they employed in ancient times. And the grammarians explained them in their language, writing the explanation at the bottom of the painting. I still have these originals.

Sahagún's "Author's Account Worthy of Being Noted" in Book 10: The People

With regard to what they were most capable of in times past in the administration of the state as well as in the service of the gods, it is the reason why they held the affairs of their administration in accordance with the need of the people. And, therefore, they reared the boys and girls with great sternness until they were adults. And this was not in the home of their parents, because, each one in his home, they were not effective at rearing them as was fitting. Therefore, they reared them conjointly under very careful and stern teachers, the men by themselves and the women by themselves. There they taught them how they were to honor their gods and how they were to revere and obey the state and its rulers. They had heavy punishments to punish those who were disobedient and irreverent, especially to their teachers. They took great care that they not drink pulque. . . .

Those who lived in the temples had so many labors by night and day and were so abstinent that sensual things did not occur to them. As for those who were of the military calling, the wars they had one with another were so continuous that there was little time that they ceased war and its works.

This manner of governing was much in conformity with natural and moral philosophy, because the mildness and abundance of this land and the climates which prevail in it considerably aided human nature to be licentious and idle and much given to sensual vices. And moral philosophy taught these natives through experience that, to live morally and virtuously, rigor, austerity, and continuous concern for things beneficial to the state was necessary.

Since this ceased with the coming of the Spaniards, and since these put down and destroyed all the ways of governing these natives had, and tried to convert them to the ways of living of Spain in things divine as well as human, understanding that they were idolaters and barbarians, all the government which they possessed was lost.

Sahagún's Insertion into "Eighth Paragraph: Of the Varieties and Kinds of Roads" in Book 11: Earthly Things

It seems to me the Catholic Faith can endure little time in these parts. One thing is that the people are becoming extinct with great rapidity, not so much from the bad treatment accorded them as from the plagues God sends them. Since this land was discovered there have been three very general and extensive plagues in addition to others not so extensive nor general. The first was the year 1520 when, in warfare, they drove the Spaniards from Mexico and [the Spaniards] withdrew to Tlaxcala. There was a plague of smallpox wherein a nearly countless number of people died. After this the Spaniards having conquered this New Spain, and maintained it in peace, and the preaching of the Gospel being practiced very successfully, in the year 1545, there was a very great and general plague in which the major portion of the people living in all this New Spain died. And at the time of this plague I resided in this city of Mexico, in the district of Tlatilulco. And I buried more than ten thousand bodies. And at the conclusion of the plague I contracted the sickness and was near death.

After this the matters of the Faith proceeding peacefully for more or less thirty years, the people recovered. Now, in this year of 1576, in the month of August a general and great plague began, which already continues for three months. Many people have died, die, and every day more are dying. I do not know how long it will last nor how much illness there will be.

Book 8: Kings and Lords

Twentieth Chapter, in which is told how they reared the sons of lords and noblemen.

And here is described the rearing of the sons of those who were lords, and of all the princes, who were the sons of lords and noblemen.

Their mothers and fathers nourished and raised them, or nursemaids raised them while they were still small children.

And when they could run, when they were perhaps six years old, thereupon [the boys] went [forth] to play. Their pages—perhaps two, or three—accompanied them that they might amuse them. [The child's] father or mother charged these [pages] that [the boy] not behave ill, that he not taint himself with vice, as he went along the streets.

And also they took great care that he should converse fittingly with others—that his conversation should be proper; that he should respect and show reverence to others—[when] perchance he somewhere might chance to meet a judge, or a leading militia officer, or a seasoned, warrior, or someone of lesser rank; or a revered old man, or a respected old woman; or someone who was poor. He should greet him and bow humbly. He said: "Come hither, my beloved grandfather; let me bow before thee." And the old one who had been greeted then said: "O my beloved grandson, O precious necklace, O precious feather, thou hast shown me favor. May it go well with thee."

And when the young boy thus saluted others, they praised him highly for it. They rejoiced greatly over it; they were joyful because of it. They said: "How will this beloved child be, if he shall live? He will in sooth be a nobleman. Mayhap his reward will be something [great]."

And when he was already maybe ten, twelve, or thirteen years old, they placed him in the priests' house; they delivered him into the hands of the fire priests and [other] priests, that he might be reared there, corrected, and instructed; that he might live an upright life. They constrained him to do the penances, setting fir branches [on the city altars] at night, or there where they went to place the fir branches on mountain tops—there where sacrifices were made at midnight. Or else he entered the song house; they left him in the hands of the masters of the youths. They charged him with the sweeping or with dancing and song—with all which was concerned with the performance of penances.

And when he was already fifteen years old, then he took up arms; or, reaching twenty years of age, then he went forth to war. First [his parents] summoned those who were seasoned warriors. They gave them to eat and to drink, and they gave gifts to all the seasoned warriors. They gave them large, cotton capes, or carmine colored breech clouts, or capes painted with designs. And then they besought the seasoned warriors; in just the same way as hath been told above, so they entreated them. [This reference appears to be a passage found in the manuscript at the Academy of History in Madrid but omitted from the Florentine Codex in Italy.]

And then they took him to the wars. The seasoned warriors went taking great care of him, lest somewhere he might be lost. And they taught him well how to guard himself with a shield; how one fought; how a spear was fended off with a shield. And when a battle was joined, when already there was fighting and perhaps already captives were being taken, they taught him well and made him see how he might take a captive. Perhaps then he took a captive with the aid of others, or he [alone] could take one. For truly it was well seen to that many men became brave warriors.

And when captives were being taken, then at once couriers, of marriageable age, quickly went forth, called victory messengers, who speedily went to inform Moctezuma. And when the victory messengers had come to arrive, then they quickly entered into the presence of Moctezuma and said to him: "O our lord, O my youth, pay thy debt and thy service [to the god]; for the omen of evil, Uitzilopochtli, hath shown favor and been gracious. For they have pierced the rampart of men dexterous in arms of the city against which they have gone. Into it have marched the Mexicans of Tenochtitlan, the Mexicans of Tlatilulco, the Tepaneca, the Acolhua, the Otomí, the Matlatzinca, and finally all the people of the uplands and those of the swamplands. . . .

And if war should be proclaimed against Atlixco, or Uexotzinco [Huejotzingo], and if there . . . they took captives, they won much glory thereby; Moctezuma accorded them great honor for it. For his noblemen had taken captives, and had gained repute, and had reached the station of nobility—the estate of the eagle and the ocelot warriors. From there they came to rule, to govern cities; and at that time they seated them with [the nobility], and they might eat with Moctezuma.

Then [he gave them] headbands with two quetzal feather tassels [intertwined] with flint knives [fashioned] of gold and with golden pendants; . . . and costly capes—the one [known as] the lord's cape, with the obsidian serpent design; or the ashen grey one with the red eyes on the border; . . . or the golden conical cap; or the quetzal feather banner; or the obsidian butterfly with quetzal feathers and eyes of gold; and costly shields—perhaps [the one of] the skin [and feathers] of the blue cotinga; or of the yellow parrot feathers—verily, all the costly shields. And he gave them stewardships; possibly in two places or in three he gave them [such offices]. For truly they had taken [captives].

And if the ruler should die, from these one was chosen to govern the city. And likewise from these some were placed in the Tlacxitlan, where they pronounced judgments and meted out death sentences. [These were] the Tlacochcalcatl tecutli, or the Ticociauacatl tecutli, or the Cioacoatl tecutli, or the Tlillancalqui tecutli.

Book 6: Rhetoric and Moral Philosophy

Eighteenth Chapter. Here it is related how the rulers admonished their daughters when they had already reached the age of discretion. Thus they urged them to prudence [and] virtue, public [and] private. They placed before them, revealed to them, the nobility, the government, the honor, that they should in no way blacken, dirty, discredit the lineage. Very good were the words with which they admonished them.

"Here art thou, thou who art my child, thou who art my precious necklace, thou who art my precious feather, thou who art my creation, my offspring, my blood, my color, my image. Now grasp, hear that thou hast come to life, thou wert born; that our lord of the near, of the nigh, the maker, the creator, hath sent thee to earth. . . .

"Hear well, O my daughter, O my child, the earth is not a good place. It is not a place of joy, it is not a place of contentment. It is merely said it is a place of joy with fatigue, of joy with pain on earth; so the old men went saying. In order that we may not go weeping forever, may not die of sorrow, it is our merit that our lord gave us laughter, sleep, and our sustenance, our strength, our force, and also carnal knowledge in order that there be peopling. . . .

"And now, O my daughter, hear it well, look at it deliberately; for behold, here is thy mother, thy noble one. From her womb, from her breast thou wert chipped, thou wert flaked. It is as if thou wert an herb, a plant which hath propagated, sprouted, blossomed. It is also as if thou hadst been asleep and hadst awakened. . . .

"Know that thou comest from someone, thou art descended from someone; that thou wert born by someone's grace; that thou art the spine, the thorn, of our lords who went leaving us, the lords, the rulers who already have gone to reside beyond, those who came guarding the realm, and who came giving fame, who came giving renown to nobility.

"Hear this. Especially do I declare unto thee that thou art a noblewoman. If thou wert only to esteem thyself as a precious person!—This, even though thou art a woman. Thou art a precious green stone, thou art a precious turquoise. . . . Do not, just of thy own accord, bring dishonor upon thyself. Do not in something cause embarrassment to our lords, the lords, the rulers who have gone leaving us. Do not be a commoner; do not lower thyself.

"Thus art thou to conduct thyself on earth among others, for verily thou art a little woman. Here is thy task which thou art to do: be devout night and day. . . . What wilt thou seize upon as thy womanly labors? Is it perhaps the drink, the grinding stone? Is it perhaps the spindle whorl, the weaving stick? Look well to the drink, to the food: how it is prepared, how it is made, how it is improved; the art of good drink, the art of good food, which is called one's birthright. This is the property of—it belongeth to—the lords, the rulers. . . .

"Open thine eyes well as to how to be an artisan, how to be a feather worker; the manner of making designs by embroidering; how to judge colors; how to apply colors [to please] thy sister, thy ladies, our honored ones, the noblewomen. . . .

"Now is the opportune time, and it is yet a good time. Thy heart is yet a precious green stone, yet a precious turquoise. It is still keen; nothing defileth it; it is still untouched, nowhere twisted, still virgin, pure, undefiled.

"And we are still here, we who have had great regard for thee. Wilt thou perchance say, thou who art our child, 'I make myself, I form myself'? It was our affair; we have suffered for thee; but thus the world endureth. Was it perhaps so ordained? For our lord declared, determined the propagation, the multiplication [of man] on earth.

"We are still here; it is still our time. The club, the rock of our lord fall not yet. And not yet do we die, not yet do we perish. Take heed, O my youngest, O dove, O little one. When our lord hath hidden us, thou wilt live by the grace of others. . . .

"Someone will select thee, will speak for thee. If [thou art] unable in anything, how will it be? It will not for this reason be thrown in our faces. And if our lord hath hidden us, there will be no murmuring against us therefor in our absence; we will not be chidden therefor in the land of the dead. And thou wilt not move, thou wilt not separate condemnation from thyself.

"But if already thou payest attention to the same, wherefrom cometh the reprehension? To a purpose thou wilt glorify thyself by one's grace, thou wilt esteem thyself, thou wilt be proud. It is as if thou wert to be of the order of eagles, of the order of ocelots. . . . Also there, because of thee we will raise up our heads; thou wilt render us honor. . . .

"Especially note that which I say to thee, that which I cry out to thee. Thou art my creation, thou art my child. Take special care that thou not dishonor our lords from whom thou art descended. Cast not dust, filth upon their memory. May thou not dishonor the nobility with something.

"May thou not covet carnal things. May thou not wish for experience, as it is said, in the excrement, in the refuse. And if truly thou art to change thyself wilt thou become as a goddess? May thou not have quickly destroyed thyself. Yet calmly, with special care, present thyself well.

"If it so please our lord, if someone so will demand, will speak for thee, thou art not to reject, to kick away the spirit of our lord. Take him. Thou art not to refuse; thou art not to retreat twice, not to retreat thrice; thou art not to resist. . . .

"Give thyself not to the wanderer, to the restless one who is given to pleasure, to the evil youth. Nor are two, three to know thy face, thy head. When thou hast seen the one who, together with thee, will endure to the end, do not abandon him. Seize him, hang on to him even though he be a poor person, even though he be a poor eagle warrior, a poor ocelot warrior, even though he be a poor warrior, or a poor son, or one who struggleth for existence. Do not detest him therefor. Our lord, the wise one, the maker, the creator will dispose for you, will array you.

"This is all I give thee of my word to comply with my duty unto, before our lord. Perhaps somewhere thou wilt reject it. Thou knowest it. Meanwhile, I do my duty. O my daughter, O my child, O dove, O little one, pay close heed. May our lord rest thee in peace."

Nineteenth Chapter. Here it is told how, when the father had spoken, the mother then replied. And with very tender words she told her daughter to guard well, to place well within her, the words of her father; to consider them as precious, as costly. . . .

"O dove, little one, child, my daughter. . . . Nowhere reject the spirit, the words of thy lord, for they are precious, wonderful; for only as precious things do the spirit, the words of our lords come forth. For they are the words of rulers; for they are considered as precious green stones, as round, reed-like precious turquoises.

"Take them, guard them, place them by thy heart, inscribe them on thy heart. If thou art to live, with them thou wilt instruct, thou wilt indoctrinate [thy] children. Thou wilt give them to others; thou wilt tell them to others.

"And behold a second word which I give thee, which I say to thee, my child, little one. Look to me, for I am thy mother. I carried thee for so many months. And when they were ended I was lulling [thee] to sleep. I was laying thee in the cradle; I was placing thee on my thigh. And certainly with my milk I gave thee strength.

"Thus I say this, for we are thy mothers, we are thy fathers who speak to thee, who cry out to thee. Take our words; grasp them, guard them. In order that thou wilt live prudently, thou art not to clothe thyself [excessively]. Thou art not to place on thyself finely worked clothing, replete with design, for it achieveth gaudiness. Nor art thou to take rags; thou art not to place on thyself the goods, the property of the vassals, for it achieveth ridicule. In moderation art thou to clothe thyself, not in gaudiness, in vanity.

"And thy speech is not to come forth hurriedly. As thou art to speak, thou art not to be brutish, not to rush, not to disquiet. Thy speech is to come forth in tranquility and with gentleness. Thou art not to lift up nor to lower much [thy voice]. . . .

"And next behold, in truth thou art of the nobility. As thou art to go, thou art not to look here and there, not to look from side to side, not constantly to look upward, nor art thou to be a hypocrite. Nor art thou to put hatred in thine eyes; thou art not put hatred in thy face. Look joyously at everyone. And also, that no one will have occasion to despise thee, put anger in the spirit at the proper time. And behold never concern thyself with words; let what is said be said. Do not speak with others; pretend that thou dost not hear it. With thee will the words end.

"And never long for, never desire the color, the cosmetics, the darkening of the teeth, the coloring of the teeth, the coloring of the mouth; for they denote perverseness, they mean drunkenness. That is the property of the restless ones, the dissolute ones, the evil women; that is the domain of those who have become drunk, those who have wasted the earth; that is the work of those who go drinking, who go eating jimson weed; that is the way of life of those who go drinking crude pulque. These are the ones called harlots.

"But in order that thy helpmate will not hate thee, pay attention to thyself, bathe thyself, wash thyself. . . .

"Behold the road thou art to follow. In such a manner thou art to live. Thy lords, our lords, the noble women, the old women, the white-haired ones, the white-headed ones reared us in such a manner as this. Did they perhaps leave so very much? . . . Behold the word: heed and guard it, and with it take your way of life, your works. On earth we live, we travel along a mountain peak. Over here there is an abyss, over there is an abyss. If thou goest over here, or if thou goest over there, thou wilt fall in. Only in the middle doth one go, doth one live.

"Place this word, my daughter, dove, little one, well within the chambers of thy heart. Guard it well. Do not forget it; for it will become thy torch, thy light, all the time thou art to live on earth. . . . Never at any time abuse thy helpmate, thy husband. Never at any time, never ever betray him; as the saying is said, do not commit adultery.

"This, my youngest, my daughter, is the endless, the bottomless [pit] on earth; there is no more a return, there is no more a cure. If it becometh discovered of thee, if it becometh known of thee, thou wilt be cast on the road, thou wilt be dragged on the road, thy head will be crushed with a stone, thy head will be fractured. It is said thou wilt test the stone; thou wilt be dragged. . . .

"Thou wilt go dishonoring our lords, the lords, the rulers by whom thou art of noble birth, through whom thou art descended. Thou wilt cast dust, refuse upon their memory. Thou wilt disgrace them. . . .

"And this, my youngest one, my daughter, child, little one: live in calm, in peace on earth, if thou art to continue for a while. Do not with anything dishonor thyself. And do not with anything raise up the heads of thy lords, the rulers from whom thou art descended. And as for us, may we through thee gain glory; may we gain renown.

"Pay heed, my youngest one, my daughter, little one. Enter with our lord, the lord of the near, of the nigh."

NOTES

1. Miguel Leon-Portilla, "The Problematics of Sahagún: Certain Topics Needing Investigation," in *Sixteenth-Century Mexico: The Work of Sahagún*, ed. Munro S. Edmonson (Albuquerque: University of New Mexico Press, 1974), 244–45.

2. Angel María Garibay K., *Historia de la Literatura Nahuatl, Segunda Parte: El trauma de la conquista (1521–1750) Segunda Edición* (México, D.F.: Editorial Porrua, S.A: 1971), 77.

3. Sara Castro-Klaren, "Produciendo a Sahagún: El problema de la autoría en Sahagún, Pablo de San Buena Ventura, Antonio Valeriano, Alonso Vegerano, Martín Jacobita y otros o, Sahagún y los neo-Tlacuilos," *Revista de Crítica Literaria Latino-america* 43, no. 86 (2do semestre de 2017): 91.

4. Leon-Portilla, "The Problematics," 37–38; Luis Nicolau D'Olwer, *Fray Bernardino de Sahagún (1499–1590)*, trans. Mauricio J. Mixco, (Salt Lake City: University of Utah Press, 1987), 1.

5. Nicolau, *Fray Bernardino*, 2, 4–5.

6. Miguel Leon-Portilla, *Bernardino de Sahagún: First Anthropologist*, trans. Mauricio J. Mixco (Norman: University of Oklahoma Press: 2002), 96.

7. Juan Carlos Temprano, introducción, to *Historia General de las Cosas de Nueva España* by Bernardino de Sahagún (Madrid: Editorial Historia 16, 1990), xii.

8. Arthur J. O. Anderson, "Sahagún: Career and Character," in *Florentine Codex: General History of the Things of New Spain In Thirteen Parts, Part I, Introductions and Indices* by Bernardino de Sahagún (Salt Lake City: University of Utah Press, 1982), 35.

9. Walden Browne, *Sahagun and the Transition to Modernity* (Norman: University of Oklahoma Press, 2000), 109–110.

10. J. Jorge Klor de Alva, "Sahagún and the Birth of Modern Ethnography: Representing, confessing, and inscribing the native other," in *The Work of Bernardino de Sahagún: Pioneer Ethnographer of Sixteenth Century Aztec Mexico*, ed. J. Jorge Klor de Alva, H.B. Nicholson, and Eloise Quiñones Keber (Austin: University of Texas Press, 1988), 39.

11. John Keber, "Sahagún and Hermeneutics: A Christian Ethnographer's Understanding of Aztec Culture," in *The Work of Bernardino de Sahagún: Pioneer Ethnographer of Sixteenth Century Aztec Mexico*, ed. J. Jorge Klor de Alva, H. B. Nicholson, and Eloise Quiñones Keber (Austin: University of Texas Press, 1988), 59.

12. Leon-Portilla, *Bernardino*, 204–5.

13. Munro S. Edmonson, introduction to *Sixteenth-Century Mexico: The Work of Sahagún*, ed. Munro S. Edmonson (Alburquerque: University of New Mexico Press, 1974), 9.

14. Nicolau, *Fray Bernardino*, 72.

15. Lopez-Portilla, *Bernardino*, 211–12.

16. Anderson, "Sahagún," (1982), 37.

17. Nicolau, *Fray Bernardino,* 145–6; Browne, *Sahagún,* 34.

18. Georges Baudot, "The Last Years of Fray Bernardino de Sahagún (1585–90): The Rescue of the Confiscated Work and the Seraphic Conflicts. New Unpublished Documents," in *Sixteenth-Century Mexico: The Work of Sahagún*, ed. Munro S. Edmonson (Albuquerque: University of New Mexico Press, 1974), 185.

19. Keber, "Sahagún," 61.

20. Edmonson, introduction, 9.

21. Leon Portilla, *Bernardino*, 139–40.

22. Castro-Klaren, "Produciendo," 91, 95.

23. Anderson, "Sahagún," 40.

24. Edward E. Calnek, "The Sahagún Texts as a Source of Sociological Information" in *Sixteenth-Century Mexico: The Work of Sahagún*, ed. Munro S. Edmonson (Albuquerque: University of New Mexico Press, 1974), 189–90.

25. Quoted in Leon-Portilla, *Bernardino*, 223.

26. Thelma D. Sullivan, "The Rhetorical Orations or *Huehuetlatolli* Collected by Sahagún," in *Sixteenth-Century Mexico: The Work of Sahagún,* ed. Munro S. Edmonson (Albuquerque: University of New Mexico Press, 1974), 79.

27. Sullivan, "The Rhetorical," 92.

28. Charles E. Dibble, "Sahagún's *Historia*," in *Florentine Codex: General History of the Things of New Spain In Thirteen Parts, Part I, Introductions and Indices*, by Bernardino de Sahagún (Salt Lake City: University of Utah Press, 1982), 16.

29. Browne, *Sahagún*, 38.

30. It can be viewed at http://mss.bmlonline.it/?search=Bernardino%20de%20 Sahag%C3%BAn. The *huehuetlahtolli* are found at the beginning of Vol. 2.

31. Browne, *Sahagún*, 9.

32. Anderson, "Sahagún," 40.

33. Klor de Alva, "Sahagún," 31–32.

34. Browne, *Sahagún*, 11.

35. Nicolau, *Fray Bernardino*, 123.

36. Nicolau, *Fray Bernardino*, 139.

37. Keber, "Sahagún," 62.

Chapter Nine

The Inca Titu Cusi Yupanqui
"The Natural Lords That Used to Rule Peru"

While students of Latin American history are familiar with the accounts of the conquerors, few have read the writings of the people they conquered. Titu Cusi Yupanqui was the second to the last Inca and his writing was the first to document the forty-year resistance to the Spanish invaders of the people of the Andes. The full Spanish title of this account is *Ynstrucción del Ynga Don Diego de Castro Titu Cussi Yupangui para el muy ilustre señor el licenciado Lope García de Castro, governador que fue destos reynos del Piru.* But, it is usually called the *Instrucción* or *Relación del Inca Titu Cusi.* The word *Instrucción* refers to the instructions to the governor, Lope de Castro, which are followed by the lengthy section where Titu Cusi relates his story of the conquest.

The 1570 work has been called "a rare legacy from the Inca world."[1] It is an account of the conquest from the point of view of the vanquished, where, in what reads like a dramatic performance, Titu Cusi presents speeches by his father and others that question the nature of the invaders from across the sea and whether they are gods or men. Other speeches lament the evils and injustice being committed by the invaders against the inhabitants. Titu Cusi begins by saying that his ancestors were "natural lords" of the "kingdoms and provinces of Peru," a statement similar to those of Spanish philosophers and theologians of the period asserting the legitimacy of Inca rule and the rights of the Indigenous kingdoms of the New World to govern themselves. But, there are controversies around authorship of this work given that Titu Cusi was assisted in its writing by his Mestizo secretary and a Spanish friar.

Titu Cusi was the grandson of Huayna Capac who had at his prime ruled a vast empire that extended from what is now Ecuador to central Chile. That empire, called Tawantinsuyo and centered on the highland city of Cusco,

Figure 9.1. Viracocha Inca, who ruled from 1410 to 1438, was an ancestor of Titu Cusi

Unknown artist, 1616. Courtesy of the J. Paul Getty Museum in Los Angeles, California

had grown in the 1400s with the conquests of the ninth Inca, Pachacuti Inca Yupanqui, and his son and successor Tupac Inca.

The Inca Empire, however, had no established policy of succession, only the custom that the Inca's most able son would inherit the title of Inca. At the death of Huayna Capac in 1525 (from smallpox brought by the Spaniards who had landed in South America the year before), a conflict arose between two of his sons, Huascar and Atahualpa, over who would take the throne. Atahualpa with his generals controlled the north while, in Cusco, his brother Huascar and his allies controlled the state apparatus and the rest of the empire.[2] In the end Atahualpa defeated his brother Huascar and ordered the killing of Huascar's family, generals, and supporters in 1532 and finally of Huascar himself in 1533. However, in November of 1532, Atahualpa was captured by the Spanish under Francisco Pizarro in the town of Cajamarca when he agreed to a meeting with the strange new men who had arrived in his land. He was killed by the Spanish only a few months after the death of his brother Huascar. The Spanish proclaimed Tupac Huallpa, a younger brother of Atahualpa and Huascar, as Inca and, when he died suddenly, they chose another brother, Manco Inca Yupanqui, Titu Cusi's father, as their puppet ruler.

Manco Inca initially collaborated with the Spaniards but, in 1536, as their treatment of him worsened, he turned against them, calling together an army of 100,000 warriors and attacking Cusco and Lima. His army laid siege to Cusco for more than a year but that effort eventually failed and, in 1537, Manco abandoned the highlands for the eastern slopes of the Andes, establishing his capital at Vilcabamba.[3] From there, his forces were able to harass the Spaniards, their towns, their crops, and the travelers on their roads, until his death in 1545. In his jungle hideaway, Manco Inca made the mistake of giving refuge to six Spaniards, followers of Diego de Almagro, fleeing punishment for the assassination of Francisco Pizarro. However, after a time, Spanish officials offered the murderers clemency if they would kill Manco Inca. This they did while playing *herron*, a type of ball game, with him. The murderers were then themselves killed while trying to escape.[4]

Sayri Tupac succeeded his father Manco Inca while his brother Titu Cusi Yupanqui was named high priest of the Sun. But, in 1556, emissaries from the Spanish viceroy convinced Sayri Tupac to leave Vilcabamba to live in Cusco with the grant of substantial lands and tax income plus the threat of military attack if he did not agree. Sayri Tupac died unexpectedly in 1560 or 1561[5] and Titu Cusi then succeeded to the throne.

Titu Cusi was born around 1530 in Cusco. The name of his mother is not known but she was referred to as a wife of Manco Inca and an important woman from the town of Anta.[6] Titu Cusi and his mother and sisters were taken by Manco Inca to Vilcabamba in 1537 but shortly thereafter the children and their mother were captured during a Spanish raid and taken to Cusco where they spent about five years in the home of a Spanish official. In about 1542, Manco Inca succeeded in abducting his son and returning him to Vilcabamba[7] where he would remain for the rest of his life.

The territory controlled by the rebellious Inca was an enormous expanse on the eastern tropical side of the Andes in the area known by the Incas as Antisuyo. All of the inhabitants of those provinces paid him tribute.[8] Titu Cusi, like his father before him, harassed the Spanish settlements and commerce while engaging in sporadic diplomatic negotiations with the apparent goal of establishing a recognized neo-Inca state.

In 1565 a messianic religious rebellion called the *Takiy Unquy* arose in which leaders said the old gods would be revived and the Spanish defeated. The hope was that Indigenous people from Quito in the north to the land of the Araucanians in the south would rise up. The plot was betrayed and was crushed by the Spanish.[9] In the wake of the foiled plot, Titu Cusi negotiated favorable terms with Governor Lope García de Castro, signing the Treaty (or Capitulations) of Acobamba in 1566 or 1567, depending on the source.[10] The negotiations had been initiated by King Philip II himself in a 1563 letter to Governor García in which Philip notes that "mistreatment by the Spanish" had made the native Indigenous people flee into the Andes. He authorizes the governor to negotiate with Titu Cusi for him to become a Christian and be given lands from which to make a living.[11] In the treaty, Titu Cusi agreed to end the fighting and accept Christianity, taking the Christian name of Diego de Castro. He would be a vassal prince of the king of Spain. In turn, he achieved agreement on the marriage of his son to the daughter of Sayri Tupac and the promise of lands that had previously been under control of the Inca, plus tax revenues. Following this agreement, Augustinian friars were allowed to enter the Inca kingdom to evangelize the Indigenous people but Titu Cusi, in this as in every aspect of his relations with the Spanish, ceded only the minimum necessary. It is likely that he never intended to leave Vilcabamba as the Spanish hoped.[12] Historian Catherine Julien says that the Capitulations did not mention Titu Cusi leaving Vilcabamba, adding that they were rather "about Titu Cusi's acceptance of vassalage to the King of Spain and about the peaceful incorporation of the province of Vilcabamba into Spanish Peru, agreed to by both sides."[13]

In 1570, Titu Cusi finished his missive to the governor with a message for the king of Spain that we examine here. But before he could even know whether his message was delivered, Titu Cusi died, from pneumonia or, according to some historians, including Edmundo Guillén Guillén, poisoned,[14] in 1571. He was succeeded by his half-brother Tupac Amaru.

At this time, although a war against the Vilcabamba Incas had not been authorized by King Philip,[15] Viceroy Francisco de Toledo realized, according to literary historian Raquel Chang-Rodríguez, that

Spanish hegemony in the region would always be challenged as long as Vilcabamba remained in the hands of the rebels; thus he ordered the military campaign that destroyed that last bastion of Andean resistance. The capture of Tupac Amaru I, and of the statue of the god Punchao belonging to the Cusco temple of Coricancha, put an end to a struggle which had lasted more than forty years.[16]

Viceroy Toledo held a three-day trial after which a Spanish judge ordered the beheading of Tupac. The execution took place on the plaza of Cusco on September 24, 1572,[17] before a crowd of his mourning subjects. Sayri Tupac's daughter Beatriz (who had been betrothed to Titu Cusi's son) was then married to the Spaniard who had led the expedition that captured Tupac Amaru, her uncle.

Andean resistance against the Spanish invaders continued. While the execution of Tupac Amaru marked the end of the paternal line of the Incas, descendants of the maternal line, including Tupac Amaru II, leader of the resistance in the 1780s, claimed the mantle of the royal house.[18]

As for Vilcabamba, the Spanish founded a town with the same name some distance away and, as time passed, the site of the Inca city was lost to the memory of even the local people. Scholar-explorer Hiram Bingham was actually at the site (called Espiritu Pampa) in his 1911 search for the "lost city of the Incas" and wrote an article about the area for the *American Anthropologist* in 1914 in which he stated "There appears to be no reason why the ruins of Espiritu Pampa are not those of the residence of the Inca Titu Cusi Yupanqui in 1565."[19] That same year, he was taken to the spectacular ruins of Machu Pichu, which he speculated could be what he called "the cradle of the later Inca race," the original location from whence the Incas set out to found Cusco, the capital of their empire.[20] Espíritu Pampa, was explored in the 1960s and 1970s but it would not be until 1976 that Peruvian scholar Edmundo Guillén Guillén claimed credit for finally proving that it was the actual "lost city of the Incas"—Vilcabamba.[21]

There is general agreement that Titu Cusi's manuscript was completed in February of 1570 and taken to Spain by Lope García de Castro who was just then completing a term as governor of Peru. In 1574, it was copied and the original returned to García de Castro with the copy given to King Philip II.[22] The copy resides in the Royal Library of the Monastery of El Escorial, the royal residence, chapel, library, and mausoleum built by Philip outside Madrid.[23] The work was rediscovered and a few fragments published in 1877 by Marcos Jiménez de la Espada but it was not published in its entirety until 1916 by Horacio H. Urteaga and Carlos A. Romero.[24] Further Spanish editions were released in 1973, 1985, 1988, 1992 and 2001, while translations were made into German (1984) and Japanese (1987) and finally, in 2005 and 2006, three English translations appeared all at once.[25] It is the first English translation, that of Ralph Bauer, that is used here. Digital versions of the Spanish text are also available on several web sites.

Titu Cusi's work is composed of three parts—1) a few introductory paragraphs addressed to Governor García de Castro with the request that, "upon safe arrival in Spain," he present Titu Cusi's case for compensation to King Philip; 2) the long historical "*relación*" or relating of the conquest and Incan resistance; and 3) a power of attorney for the former governor to represent his interests in Spain.[26]

Although Titu Cusi had spent part of his boyhood among the Spanish in Cusco, he was probably not fluent in the Spanish language so the production of the document was complicated: Titu Cusi told his story aloud in Quechua; his Mestizo secretary Martin de Pando translated it into Spanish and finally Friar Marcos García put it in proper order in cultured 16th century Spanish.[27] A lengthy document, its writing probably took at least two years.[28] The long section in which Titu Cusi related the resistance struggle of his father was witnessed by Pando and García and also by three of Titu Cusi's captains, Suya Yupanqui, Rimache Yupanqui, and Sullca Varac. Chang-Rodríguez states that it was important to show that the narrated story was an accurate account of what had occurred.[29]

How important was the involvement of Pando and García in the final product of Titu Cusi's account? To what degree is it a hybrid work? Historian Liliana Regalado de Hurtado states that, given what we know about the manner in which the document was written, we cannot deny the difficulties for the modern reader in distinguishing in every case between what are Titu Cusi's ideas and what might have been the ideas of Pando or García.[30] Titu Cusi recognized the importance of the written word. Chang-Rodríguez says that he and other Indigenous writers accepted those important European symbols in order to describe their history and personal merits and make demands while, at the same time, they were rejecting European institutions.[31] Literature scholar Ben Post notes that the text tries, at the same time, to accommodate to the colonial world and resist it.[32]

Some Indigenous scribes appropriated the Spanish alphabet to write in their Indigenous languages, including the collaborators of Friar Bernardino de Sahagún and the writers of the *Annals of the Cakchiquel Maya*. Guaman Poma de Ayala was able to write in Spanish and, like Sahagún, made extensive use of drawings. Titu Cusi chose to work with a scribe and a translator, and literature scholar Susana Jákfalvi-Leiva says that, in her view, all three must share credit for authorship.[33] Ralph Bauer, however, gives more credit to Titu Cusi and says that, in his account, Titu Cusi made "calculated use of everything he had learned about Spanish culture without becoming unfaithful to his own culture."[34]

Titu Cusi's writing can be classified as what is known as a *relación de méritos*. Nicole Delia Legnani, one of the translators of Titu Cusi's work, states, "The *instrucción* or *relación* had a specific function within the legal framework of the Spanish conquest: often addressed to the king, it requested immediate gratification or relief for the services that the author or the petitioner had rendered to the Crown."[35] Titu Cusi's account tells a story of injustice and then asks for redress. It is similar to the letter from Isabel de Guevara to Princess Juana of Spain elsewhere in this volume. Jákfalvi-Leiva adds, however, that what is new here is that an Indigenous leader demands the return of his own lands and the recognition of his authority as Inca.[36] In that sense, it might better be likened to the letter from the Council of Huejotzingo to the king in which Indigenous nobles ask for a reduction in tribute.

Titu Cusi's narration is different from the *relaciones de méritos* sent by colonial Spaniards in another way also: its oral nature. In the first place, it was designed by Titu Cusi to serve as a memory aide for Governor García de Castro (much as the knotted strings known as *quipus* served as memory aides for the Incas) when he presented the petition verbally to King Philip, rather than to be delivered to the king for him to read. Oral presentations by claimants were not unheard of in the Spanish court but, in this case, there is no evidence that the document was read to the king.[37]

Secondly, Titu Cusi's account is full of speeches in the voices of Manco Inca and his captains and dialogue from the Pizarro brothers to the degree that it reads like a dramatic performance. Julien speculates that the speeches were based on the memories of Manco's comrades and "may have been truer to the emotions of the speakers . . . than to the words themselves." She adds that in combining the Spanish informational *relación* with Indigenous oral discourse, "Titu Cusi created an entirely new and original literary genre."[38]

"Are they gods or men?" is what the Incas asked themselves when they saw the first Spaniards mounted on giant beasts and carrying sticks which emitted deadly fire. Titu Cusi reports that a group of Manco Inca's subjects brought news of the arrival in his land of "a race of people that has never been heard or seen before by our nations and that without doubt appears to be that of the Viracochas (which means 'gods')." The Spaniards seventy years earlier had also asked themselves what kind of beings they had found on this new continent. Less than two decades after Columbus's arrival on the island of Hispaniola, it fell to Dominican Friar Antonio de Montesinos to chastise the Spanish colonizers for their treatment of the Indigenous people. He attacked them in an Advent sermon asking about the Amerindians, "Are they not human beings? Have they no rational soul?"[39] While this question was debated at the highest levels of the Spanish government for decades, the nature of the Spaniards was also a subject for debate in the courts of Montezuma in Mexico and Atahualpa and Manco Inca in Peru. Historian Nathan Wachtel states, "The whole of Indian mythology implied the *possibility* that the white men might be gods and everywhere this was a source of doubt and anguish."[40]

The Indigenous people of Peru soon decided that, based on their behavior, the Spaniards were not, in fact, gods but rather demons. Titu Cusi has Manco Inca explain to his people that "they are the sons not of Viracocha but of the Devil as they have proven to me." Historian Hélene Roy states that Titu Cusi sets up a contrast in which the Indigenous people exhibit virtues such as generosity and loyalty and the Spanish exhibit contrasting negative values such as greed and cruelty. Roy postulates that this use of dualities, contrasting of good and evil, by Titu Cusi reflects the influence of Christianity.[41]

Julien makes the point that most historians have accepted the version that control of Peru passed to the Spanish with the capture of Atahualpa in 1532 and that what followed were merely operations to put down various rebellions. But, she notes, "As Titu Cusi's *History* makes clear, there are other ways to tell the story."[42] Chang-Rodríguez says that it "is not a simple tale, but rather history recorded from the point of view of the vanquished. The events narrated thus acquire a unique poignancy because the writer uses them to defy Spanish rule."[43] She adds that Titu Cusi's is the first Indigenous chronicle to narrate the resistance of the Incas to the conquest and that it is saturated with the nostalgia of one who contemplates the disappearance of a way of life, of a world that is disappearing.[44] Regalado de Hurtado states that, until the capture of the Inca Tupac Amaru, Vilcabamba constituted for the Andean people the tangible expression of an ideological position, of a hope for the reconstruction of a lost world.[45]

Titu Cusi states at the very beginning of his narrative that his ancestors were "natural lords" of the "kingdoms and provinces of Peru." This term was also used by Spanish theologians such as Francisco de Vitoria at the University of Salamanca and the activist Bishop of Chiapas, Bartolomé de Las Casas, to indicate rulers of ordered societies whose subjects accepted their rule. Vitoria maintained that it was not legitimate to attack these societies except in the case of tyranny, protection of innocent people, or self-defense.[46] Las Casas wrote in his late work *Doce Dudas* that the Catholic King of Castille, in order to save his soul, was obligated to return the kingdom of Peru to the king, Titu, because the Spanish had established a tyranny over that kingdom that in the past had belonged to his grandfather and which had been taken from him against all justice.[47]

Titu Cusi makes a special point of tracing his ancestry as son of Manco Inca and grandson of Huayna Capac in order to establish his legitimacy as the natural lord of his land of Peru. And Ralph Bauer also notes that

> [T]he emphasis on the uncompromising loyalty of the various local leaders to Titu Cusi's father as well as his own conversion to Christianity, reinforces the political ideal of him as a natural Christian prince *voluntarily* placing himself under the imperial protection of the king. . . . [H]e requires legal assurances from the monarch that his status as the legitimate Christian prince of Peru will be respected before he can reasonably be expected to consider giving up his refuge at Vilcabamba.[48]

Jákfalvi-Leiva adds that Titu Cusi uses a series of dichotomies (again dualities) of good versus evil, order versus chaos, virtue versus vice in an effort to convince the king that the native government has the moral and political right to exercise power.[49]

Las Casas speaks of Titu Cusi Yupanqui as the Inca ruler in *Doce Dudas* in 1564 but, after the fall of Vilcabamba in 1572, Titu Cusi was largely forgotten, most remarkably by the important Indigenous historians Guamán Poma de Ayala and El Inca Garcílaso de la Vega. Both writers tell the stories of Manco Inca and of Tupac Amaru while omitting reference to Inca Titu Cusi. (Spanish historian Andrés González de Barcía added information about the life of Titu Cusi to the 1723 edition of Garcilaso's *Royal Commentaries of the Incas*.[50]) No one has a satisfactory answer to the question of why Poma de Ayala and Inca Garcilaso did not include Titu Cusi. Some writers, Spanish and Indian, rejected Titu Cusi's legitimate right to the Inca throne although Garcilaso refers to him as of legitimate birth and royal blood and also as an army commander.[51] Scholar Moisés Castillo discusses the question of whether Titu Cusi was involved in the *Takiy Unquy* religious rebellion as a possible reason (Poma and Garcilaso were Catholics) and suggests, as an alternative explanation, the Inca custom to eliminate all reference to rulers who were judged inadequate, possibly because of Titu Cusi's negotiations with the Spanish.[52]

Are the ideas of the *Takiy Unquy* movement reflected in Titu Cusi's writing? Legnani states that independent of whether there was "military and ideological coordination between the Takiy Unquy and Vilcabamba movements, some of the phrases in the *Instrucción* seem to echo Takiy Unquy precepts."[53] She notes as an example that Titu Cusi has his father tell his people as he prepares to withdraw to Vilcabamba that, although the Spaniards may order them to worship "mere rags," they should not obey and should instead "keep what we have . . . as we can see the sun and the moon with our own eyes."

Spanish language scholar Michael J. Horswell notes that "missionaries and early extirpators of idolatry . . . attempted to tie a localized millennialist movement known as *Takiy Unquy* to the Inca priests of Vilcabamba." Spanish missionaries called Vilcabamba a "university of idolatry" led by Titu Cusi Yupanqui and Túpac Amaru.[54] Horswell adds that Titu Cusi's writing "marks the beginning of a new culture of Inca accommodation and resistance in the colonial Andes [that] will give way to a later, new Inca elite's negotiations with the subsequent viceroyal and Republican societies of the Andes."[55]

What has been the influence of Titu Cusi's account in recent times? The publication in 1916 of the work edited by Urteaga with Romero's biography of Titu Cusi was intended, according to Legnani, to raise the Peruvian national consciousness with a text "that seems to embody for the editors the promise of a new 'mestizo' morality." She notes that liberal Peruvians of that period were turning to their pre-Hispanic roots in their search for a national identity.[56] Guillén Guillén puts the resistance at Vilcabamba at the center of what he calls a three century history of struggle for reconquest from Spanish domination that was not achieved until the Battle of Ayacucho in 1824 which assured independence. However, the struggle continued, Guillén says, because the new leaders of the republic disdained ancestral values and it was not until the early twentieth century that anthropologist Luis Valcarcel and archaeologist Julio Tello rescued the early social principles of the Andean world.[57] Chang-Rodríguez adds that Titu Cusi's 1570 account shows the duality of the Peruvian history and soul [between Spanish and Indigenous] described by philosopher José Carlos Mariátegui and Peru's destiny of division into two universes as described by novelist José María Arguedas.[58] Legnani adds that in modern times, "Tawantinsuyu has been characterized as a primitive communist society, a socialist empire or a totalitarian theocracy, the dictatorship of one ethnic group over many. Increasingly, it has become the salient symbol for unity and cooperation among the Indigenous peoples of the Andean region."[59]

Titu Cusi's narration is an example of a voice from among the vanquished, a voice that is rarely heard in history. His speeches and dialogues present a vivid story of Spanish injustice, back up his claims for compensation in accord with his status and make demands for recognition as a natural lord and legitimate prince of Peru under the Spanish king.

TITU CUSI YUPANQUI'S
ACCOUNT OF THE CONQUEST OF PERU

[Addressed to Lope García de Castro, former governor of Peru]

As I, Diego de Castro Titu Cusi Yupanqui, grandson of Huayna Capac and son of Manco Inca Yupanqui, the natural lords that used to rule these kingdoms and provinces of Peru, have received many graces and favors from the very illustrious Señor licentiate Lope García de Castro, formerly governor of these kingdoms by the grace of his Majesty, King Don Philip, our lord; and as Your Excellency are a person of great valor and piety who are about to leave these kingdoms for those of Spain, it seems to me that I couldn't have a person with better credentials and disposition to serve as an advocate on my behalf before His Majesty regarding certain affairs of utmost importance to me and my sons and descendants. . . . First, that Your Excellency, upon your safe arrival in Spain, may do me the favor of enlightening His Majesty the King, our lord Don Philip under whose protection I have placed myself about my identity and the hardships I suffer in these jungles as a result of His Majesty's and His vassals' having taken possession of this land, which belonged to my ancestors. Perhaps His Excellency could begin by giving a testimony about who and whose son I am, so that His Majesty is entirely clear on the reasons why I am entitled to compensation.

At the time when the Spaniards first landed in this country of Peru and when they arrived at the city of Cajamarca, which is about 190 leagues from here, my father Manco Inca was residing in the city of Cusco. . . .

[M]y uncle Atahuallpa was engaged in war and altercations with one of his brothers, Huascar Inca, over the question of who was the rightful king of this land. In truth, neither one of them was the legitimate heir, for they had only usurped the power from my father, who was still a boy then. . . . [W]hile these two brothers—sons of different mothers—were caught up in these said altercations, it was reported that forty or fifty Spaniards had arrived at Cajamarca, the town mentioned above, on their well-equipped horses. . . . When my uncle [Atahuallpa] was approaching Cajamarca with all of his people, the Spaniards met them at the springs of Conoc, one and a half leagues from Cajamarca. . . .The Spaniards were on the lookout and took possession of the four gates of the plaza where they were, which was enclosed on all its sides. The Indians were thus penned up like sheep in this enclosed plaza. . . . [The Spaniards] started killing them with the horses, the swords or guns [and] when all were dead, they took my uncle to a jail.

When the Spaniards saw that my uncle Atahuallpa procrastinated in informing my father of their arrival, they agreed among themselves to send their own messengers. Meanwhile. . . . The Talana people on the coast found out about the whole thing and . . . decided to bring the news themselves to my father. . . . Thus, they left for Cusco and, upon their arrival, addressed my father with these words: "Sapai Inca" (which means "you, our sole lord"), "we have come to tell you that a new sort of people [*género de gente*] has arrived in your land, a race that has never been heard or seen before by our nations and that without doubt appears to be that of the Viracochas" (which means "gods").

When my father heard this, he was beside himself and said, "How dare those people intrude into my country without my authorization and permission? Who are those people and what are their ways?" The messengers answered, "Lord, these people cannot but be Viracochas, for they claim to have come by the wind. They are bearded people, very beautiful and white. They eat out of silver plates. Even their sheep, who carry them are large and wear silver shoes. . . . From this you may yourself conclude that people like this, who live and behave in such a manner, must be Viracochas." . . . [My father] believed them and said, "If you are so eager to testify to the arrival of these people, why don't you go and bring one of them to me, so I can see them and thereby be persuaded." Thus, the messengers carried out what my father had ordered, returning to Cajamarca accompanied by a great number of Indians. . . . Upon their arrival, they were received very well by the Marquis Don Francisco Pizarro, who was most pleased about the news from my father. . . . The messengers conveyed to the Spaniards my father's request that some of them might come to see him. The Spaniards accepted the invitation and decided to send two of them in order to kiss his hands. . . . Once they had arrived in Cusco, they were introduced to my father who received them very respectfully and supplied them with shelter and everything they needed.

The next day, he invited them to his residence and hosted a great celebration with many people and much display of gold and silver dishes, among them innumerable pitchers, cups, bowls, and pots from the same material. When the Spaniards caught a glimpse of so much gold and silver, they told him to let them have some of it, so that they could show it to the marquis and his companions in order to demonstrate to them the greatness of his power. My father agreed. . . .

While these two Spaniards had been on their way to kiss my father's hands and to meet with him in Cusco, my uncle Atahuallpa gave the Spaniards a huge amount of gold and silver [and] he sent out several messengers with the mission to instigate a conspiracy among [his brother] Huascar's people in order to kill him. . . . When Atahuallpa found out about the death of Huascar Inca, he was exceedingly pleased, for he thought that he no longer had anyone to fear. On the one hand, he had destroyed and killed his main antagonist and, on the other, he had bribed the Spaniards. Thus, he thought he was safe. However, he was mistaken. . . .

When the Spanish messengers who had been at my father's court and the Indians whom my father had sent returned with the aforesaid treasure of gold and silver, . . . they presented it to the governor. . . . They said that Manco Inca Yupanqui was very glad about the arrival of so many good people in his land and requested that they come to his residence in Cusco, if they pleased. . . . He further wanted to inform them that . . . they should not recognize

[Atahuallpa] because he [Manco Inca Yupanqui] alone was the legitimate ruler of the land, having been appointed as such by his father Huayna Capac in his last days.

[Titu Cusi tells how Atahuallpa roused the Indians to rebellion against the Spaniards but Pizarro found out about the plot and had Atahuallpa garroted "on a pole in the middle of the square." Atahuallpa's generals, Quisquis and Challcochima, escaped and continued to launch attacks against the Spaniards. Manco Inca "departed from Cusco with more than 100,000 people" to meet with Pizarro and make an alliance. Quisquis was defeated in battle and eventually killed.]

How the Spaniards Took Manco Inca Prisoner

[The Spaniards] spent many days in Cusco in my father's company and enjoyed themselves thoroughly. But greed, so powerful in all men, overcame them so completely that they were seduced by the Devil, always a friend of all evil and enemy of virtue, to conspire and plot in secrecy how and by what means they would torment my father and extort a greater amount of silver and gold than what they had already extorted from him. When my unsuspecting father, a few days after this plot had been forged, was serenely staying in his house, more than a hundred Spaniards came with treacherous intentions under the pretext of paying him a visit. When my father saw them coming, he received them happily and gladly, for he was under the assumption that they had come to visit him, as they had many times before. But then, they executed their treason and arrested him saying, "We have found out, Manco Inca, that you are planning to rise up against us just like your brother Atahuallpa in order to destroy us. Be informed, however, that the governor has ordered us to arrest you and to put you in chains, so that you will be unable to harm us."

When my father saw them so determined, he was very upset and exclaimed, "What have I done to you that you should treat me in this manner and chain me like a dog? Is this how you reciprocate the favors I have done by guiding you through my land and by making you many loving presents of things that I owned here? You are doing me very wrong. Are you not those who claimed to be Viracochas and emissaries of Tecsi Viracocha? But it is not possible that you really are his sons, for you want to do evil onto those who have done you so much good. Have I not sent you a large amount of gold and silver to Cajamarca? . . . Have I not given servants to you and your subordinates and ordered the entire country to pay tribute to you?"

. . . The Spaniards, as though they were blinded by their evil greed, replied, "Whatever, *Sapai* Inca, don't waste your breath by making excuses, for we have proof that you are intending to start an uprising in the entire land. Listen, men bring some shackles." These were brought without delay and put on my father's feet without any respect to his august person or to all the good things he had done for them. . . .

Finally, after some days—I don't know how many—Hernando Pizarro, Juan Pizarro, and Gonzalo Pizarro returned with many others and said to my father, "Señor Inca, are you still plotting an uprising throughout the land?" And my father said, "I am suspected of plotting an uprising throughout the land? What are you talking about?" . . . [The Spaniards replied], "If it is not true that you were plotting an uprising, it would be well if you redeemed yourself by giving us some gold and silver, for this is what we have come to seek. If you give it to us, we will set you free." . . . When my father saw them so determined in their bad intentions, he said, "So that's what Viracocha commands you to do: to rob another man of his possessions and wives? With us, on the other hand, this is not customary behavior and I assert that you are not sons of Viracocha but of supai—which is to say the Devil in our language. But so be it! I will try to find the things that you require." . . . Still half dubious whether their design would work out, the Spaniards left. The next day, my father made an announcement throughout the land that the population was to gather and bring treasures in such amounts as the Spaniards demanded from him so insistently. When they had all gathered, he made the following speech.

Manco Inca Yupanqui's Speech to His People about the Raising of the Treasure which He Handed Over to the Spaniards during his first Imprisonment

"My brothers and sisters, a few days ago I had already had you gather in this way in order to introduce to you a new race [*género*] of people, which landed in our country. I am referring to those bearded ones who are now staying in this city. I did so because they claimed to be Viracochas and because their clothes appeared to corroborate their claim. Then I commanded you to serve and venerate them as you would do for me personally and to pay tribute to them with whatever your region has to offer for I presumed that they were a grateful people and that they were emissaries of Him that, according to their words, appeared to be Teqsi Viracocha" (meaning "God"). "However, I now believe that I was mistaken in my assumptions. For you must know, my brothers, that they are the sons not of Viracocha but of the Devil [*demonio*], as they have proven to me time and again since they first arrived in this country. What they have done to me since their arrival, and are still doing to me, is evil, as you can see with your very own eyes. If you truly love me, you must feel great pain and sorrow when seeing your lord in chains and, without any wrongdoing on his part, so maltreated; only because I admitted such people to this county and, thus, put the noose around my own neck. If you want to do something for me, attempt, by your lives, to find a reasonable amount of gold and silver—for that is what they covet—so that I can redeem myself from this pain and this captivity in which you see me now."

How the Indians Responded to Manco Inca's Call to Gather a Treasure while He Was in Captivity

Thus, a multitude gathered from the four parts of the land, which is more than 1,200 leagues long and almost 300 leagues wide and according to cosmography divided up into east, west, north, and south. We name these parts in circular order Antisuyu, Chinchaysuyu, Contisuyu, and Collasuyo, for Antisuyu refers to the east, Chinchaysuyu to the north, Cuntisuyu to the west, and Collasuyo to the south. This way of dividing up the land originated in Cusco, the center and capital of the entire land. . . . When they were thus gathered before my father and saw him in such a miserable condition, they exclaimed with great sorrow, "Sapai Inca! Which heart in this world would not break and melt in lamentation at the sight of our king suffering from such oppression and pain? To be sure, Sapai Inca, by admitting such people into the country, you have made a grave mistake. But since what happened has happened and cannot be changed now, we your subjects, are prepared to do everything that you command us to do."

The Speech of the Imprisoned Inca to the Spaniards as He Handed Over the first Treasure to Them

"Gentlemen, for many days now you have been doing me great injustice by treating me the way you do, despite the fact that I did not give you any reason whatsoever, especially considering that I admitted you into my country, that I have received you with great honors and pomp in my city and my house, and that I have willingly let you have everything that I owned in my land and my house, which was, you may remember, not insignificant: more than two million in gold and silver; more, as I know than everything your king owns taken together. You know very well that it was in my hands whether or not to admit you into my country; for had I not wished it, you would not have been able to enter, even if there had been ten times as many of you as you are. You don't know how powerful the people of this country are and how many fortresses and troops there are. You would do well to remember my benevolence in inviting you, without you having to ask for it, and how I sent you everything I could as a token of friendship, because I had been informed

that you were Viracochas, emissaries of Tecsi Viracocha. You would do well
to remember that immediately after your arrival I provided you with servants
and summoned the entire population of the land in order to call on them to
pay tribute to you. And in gratitude for this, as well as for the devotion and
benevolence I have shown you, you have imprisoned me and brought me into
this situation, all on the pretext that I wanted to rise up against and kill you,
although I never thought of anything like this. I know well that greed has
blinded you and seduced you to commit such foolishness; that is the reason
why you have mistreated me like this. I never would have thought that people
who initially appeared in such positive light, and who even claimed to be
sons of Viracocha, would become guilty of such acts. On your lives, release
me and understand that I wish you no evil but only to please you. In order
to satisfy your greed and the great hunger that you have for silver, you shall
be given what you request. But beware that you receive it under the obligation not to torment and maltreat me and the entire population of this country.
Don't think that I am handing these things over to you out of fear, for I am
doing it voluntarily. Why should I be afraid? After all, the entire country is
under my power and command. If it were my wish, my people could chase
you out of the land in a very short time. And don't think that I am worried
about the fetters with which you have kept me imprisoned. Had I wanted to,
it would have been very easy for me to rid myself of them. But I didn't do it
in order to make you understand that my conduct is inspired by love, not fear.
That's why I have been dealing with you like this and will continue to deal
with you as I have been. Let us keep the peace from now on and live in love
and friendship. For you should know that it would greatly upset Viracocha
(which is to say God) and your king if it were to be any different. And I, too,
wouldn't want it any differently."

When my father was finished with his speech, the Spaniards who had come
with Hernando Pizarro, Gonzalo Pizarro, and Juan Pizarro thanked him for
his words and even more for the gifts, namely the treasure and other pieces
of jewelry.

Manco Inca's Second Imprisonment by Gonzalo Pizarro

[Three months later, Gonzalo Pizarro accused Manco Inca again of plotting to
rise up and kill the Spaniards and he ordered him imprisoned and demanded
that the Incas bring more treasure to achieve his freedom. Manco Inca was
angry and spoke to Pizarro.]

"What sort of game are you playing with me? Are you mocking me at every
turn? Do you not know that I am a son of the sun and a son of Viracocha, as
you claimed to be? Do you think that I am just any person or some Indian of

the common sort? Do you want to scandalize the entire country and be hacked to pieces? Do not mistreat me, for I have not given you any reason." . . .

When Gonzalo Pizarro and his lieutenants saw my father so furious, they all threw themselves upon him in order to put the chain around his neck. They said, "Don't try to resist us, Manco Inca. Rest assured that we will tie your hands and feet so well that all the people of the world will not be able to free you. We are arresting you in the name and on behalf of the emperor, not on our own behalf. But were it on our own behalf, now you will hand over much more gold and silver than last time; also, you will give me the señora coya Cura Oclo, who is your sister, as my wife."

In great alarm, the principal leaders of the entire country made their way to the interior of the house to ascertain what was happening and to see about my father. . . .Vila Oma, who governed the entire land as the supreme commander on behalf of my father, spoke in a loud voice to all who were present and then, trying to control himself, turned to my father.

"Sapai Inca, what are these Viracochas designing to do? Today they take you prisoner, tomorrow they release you. They seem to be playing a silly game with you. However, I am not surprised that they treat you in this manner. You have brought it upon yourself by allowing such insidious people into the country without first asking our opinion. I tell you, if you had left me to deal with them when they first arrived at Cajamarca, they would have never made it to where you are now, for I and Challcochima, with the help of our faithful troops, would have prevented them from entering the country, regardless of what they wanted to do. . . .We are losing our possessions, our women, our sons and daughters, our fields; we are becoming the subjects of people we don't even know. We are being so oppressed and tormented that we are even forced to clean the dirt of their horses with our capes." . . . .

[When he had accumulated the demanded treasure, Manco Inca again spoke to the Spaniards.]

"For more than two months now, I have been chained here like a dog—I can't help but say this: not only have you not acted like Christians and sons of Viracocha, from whom you claim descent; rather, you have acted like servants of supai. . . . But, I tell you that it is my sense that you will not reap glory from the fact that you took, without right and reason, what those poor Indians have gathered with great toil. But be that as it may, take these things and finally set me free to leave this prison." . . .

But when they seemed to be about to release him, which was only a trick, Gonzalo Pizarro suddenly appeared and said, "Not so fast! Don't set him free! First he has to give us the lady coya, his sister, whom we saw the other day. Why do you rush to set him free without ordering him to do so? Let's go, Señor Inca, let's have the lady coya! As for the silver is concerned, you're fine, because that's what we primarily wanted."

When my father saw the importunity with which they demanded the coya and realized that he would not be able to get around this matter, he had a very beautifully dressed and adorned Indian woman presented to be turned over in place of the coya whom they were demanding. When the Spaniards saw her but did not recognize her as the coya, they said that this woman did not seem to them to be the coya but some other Indian woman, that he had better turn over the coya and stop this sort of trickery. . . . [Manco Inca then had a number of Inca women parade before Pizarro but none of them satisfied him until finally he brought out Ynguill, the companion of his sister who was also very beautiful, and the Spaniards accepted that she was the coya.] Gonzalo Pizarro, who desired her more than the others and had pursued her with particular persistence, said the following words to my father: "Sir Inca, if she is for me, let me have her now because I cannot wait any longer." And my father who had initiated her well, said, "Very well then do what you desire." And so, before everyone's eyes and without seeing anything else, he went up to her in order to kiss and embrace her as though she were his legitimate wife. . . . As she saw herself being grabbed by a man whom she did not even know, she began screaming like a mad person, saying that she did not want to give herself to such people, that she would rather run away, and that on no account would she have them. Although my father saw how recalcitrant she was and how much she resisted going with the Spaniards, he knew that his redemption depended on her so he furiously ordered her that she should go with them. And when she saw my father so upset, she did what she was ordered to do and went with them, more out of fear than anything else. . . .

[Manco Inca was then released from this second imprisonment. But Juan Pizarro, angry that his brothers had received more treasure than he had, sent his men to capture Manco Inca yet again. When the Inca heard of this, he gave a speech to his people.]

The Inca's Speech to His Chiefs

"My much beloved sons and brothers, I never thought that I would find myself compelled to require of you what I am about to; for I thought and always took for granted that these bearded people whom you call Viracochas would never deceive or harm me, for I used to think and say that they had indeed come on orders of Viracocha. Now, however, I look back on my experiences with them and discover—as you have seen—how badly they have treated me and how poorly they have thanked me for all that I have done for them. They have disrespected me a thousand times; they have taken me prisoner and chained my hands and feet like you would a dog; and, not enough, after they have promised me that they would from now on respect our compact of mutual love and friendship, they are now engaged in a plot to capture and kill me. So now I will ask you, like one asks one's sons, to remember what you have so often urged me to do, which is precisely what I want to do now: you said that I should rise up against them and you asked why I tolerated them in my country. So far, I have been reluctant to do so because I deemed it impossible that the things would happen that I now see happening. But because this is the way it is and because they insist on vexing me, I find myself compelled to do them likewise. I will not tolerate any more of their chicaneries. On your lives, you have always shown me much love; and you did your best in fulfilling my wishes. Now, fulfill only this one and gather all that are here. Get ready to send your messengers all over the land, so that in twenty days' time all are united here in this city but without the knowledge of those bearded ones. Meanwhile, I will send messengers to Lima, to Quiso Yupanqui, my captain who governs that region, in order to inform him that on the day that we attack these Spaniards who are here, he is also to attack those Spaniards who are there. Thus, if he acts there at the same time as we act here, we will finish them off without any of them staying alive; and we will rid ourselves of this nightmare and will be happy thereafter." After he had finished explaining his plan to his captains about how to get their men ready for the impending battle with the Spaniards, they all replied in unison and with one voice that they were very glad, willing, and ready to carry out what my father had ordered them to do.

[The Indians laid siege to the Spaniards inside the city of Cusco but, in a series of battles, the Spaniards were able to break out of the siege and take the fortress of Cusco, called Saczahuaman, in which battle Juan Pizarro was killed. There were some other battles that were won by the Indians and others where neither side could claim victory. Manco Inca said that he would go to spend some time in the land of Antisuyo and he left the following advice to his people.]

"From now on until I return or until I send word through a messenger, you shall do the following, which shall be your way of life. First, you are not to believe anything that these bearded ones, who have mocked me because of my good faith, may say for they lie a lot, as they have lied to me in all their dealings with me. . . . [T]hese people are so crude and so different from us. . . . Second, you are to keep yourself ready for the time when I send for you or when I send word about what is to be done with these people. In the case that they attack you or try to take your land from you, always defend yourself, even though you might lose your life in the attempt. . . . Further, they may order you to worship what they themselves worship, namely some sort of painted rags that they claim to be Viracocha. Even though they are just mere rags, they will demand that you pray to these rags as you would pray to our huacas. Don't do it but keep with what we have, for, as you can see, the *villcas* speak to us; we can see the sun and the moon with our own eyes, but we can't see whatever it is that they are talking about. Now and then, I suppose, they will get you to worship what they worship through force and deceit. By all means, go through with it while they are present if you can't help it. But never forget our own ceremonies. If they were to order you to bring forth your huacas in order to have them destroyed, show them only what you have to but hide the rest."

[Manco Inca traveled with his family and supporters to Vitcos, 30 leagues from Cusco where they were attacked by Spaniards who took both living captives, including author Tito Cusi and his mother, and the mummies of former Inca rulers. Tito Cusi was put into the care of a Spanish official. Manco Inca and his followers fought many more battles with the Spaniards, finally retiring to the Inca stronghold of Vilcabamba. A messenger from Manco Inca was able to kidnap Titu Cusi and take him to his father at Vilcabamba. It was some years later, at Vitcos (located in the same district as Vilcabamba), that seven Spanish deserters who had been granted refuge for several years with Manco Inca fell upon the Inca and fatally wounded him with daggers and knives. Before he died, he spoke to his son.]

"My beloved son, you can see well what's happening to me, so I don't need to express in words my pain, which is obvious in the facts. Do not weep, for if there is anyone who has reason to weep, it is me, provided I still could. For I have myself brought about this situation in which I now find myself by trusting people of that sort. . . . But listen to what I have to say: I order you never to deal with people like these, so you won't end up like me. Don't allow them to enter into your lands, regardless of how much they try to persuade you with words. . . .

I entrust to you your brothers and sisters, as well as your mother. Look after them, help and support them, as I have done for you. . . . I also entrust these poor Indians to you. Take care of them as you are supposed to and remember how they gave up their lands and their homes out of love for me and how they have accompanied, guarded, and protected me in the course of all my trials. Don't work them too hard and don't harass them; don't scold or punish them without cause, for this would bring forth the wrath of Viracocha." . . .

After these words, he expired and left me in the town of Vitcos. From there I moved to Vilcabamba, where I remained for more than twenty years. . . .

Verification

I, Don Diego de Castro Titu Cusi Yupanqui, son of Manco Inca Yupanqui, formerly legitimate ruler of this kingdom of Peru, affirm that I—because it was necessary for me to give an account to our lord, King Don Philip, about the things that concern me and my descendants but since I am unfamiliar with the phrases and modes of expression used by the Spaniards in such writings—have asked the reverend fray Don Marcos García and the secretary Martín de Pando to arrange and compose the said account in their customary ways of expression so that it be sent to the illustrious licentiate Don Lope García de Castro in the kingdoms of Spain and with my explicit authorization be presented and related to His Majesty, our lord and king Don Philip. May His Majesty honor me, my sons, and descendants with royal favors commensurate with my rights to compensation.

NOTES

1. Frank Salomon, preface to *Titu Cusi: A 16th Century Account of the Conquest*, by Titu Cusi Yupanqui, trans. and ed. by Nicole Delia Legnani (Cambridge: Harvard University Press, 2005), v.

2. Kenneth J. Andrien, *Andean Worlds: Indigenous History, Culture, and Consciousness under Spanish Rule, 1532–1825* (Albuquerque: University of New Mexico Press, 2001), 37.

3. The Incas "had already constructed four major installations (Machu Pichu, Choquequirao, Vitcos, and Vilcabamba) and dozens of smaller settlements within the [Vilcabamba] region." Brian Bauer, Madeleine Halac-Higashimori, and Gabriel E. Cantarutti, *Voices from Vilcabamba: Accounts Chronicling the Fall of the Inca Empire* (Louisville, CO: University Press of Colorado, 2016), 4.

4. For more information about the killing of Manco Inca, see Edmundo Guillen Guillen, *Visión peruana de la Conquista: La Resistencia Incaica a la invasion española* (Lima: Editorial Milla Batres, 1979), pp. 102–5; and George Kubler, "A Peruvian Chief of State: Manco Inca (1515–1545)," *The Hispanic American Historical Review* 24, no. 2 (May 1944), 271–74.

5. Raquel Chang-Rodríguez, "Writing as Resistance: Peruvian History and the *Relación* of Titu Cusi Yupanqui," in *From Oral to Written Expression: Native Andean Chronicles of the Early Colonial Period*, ed. Rolena Adorno (Syracuse: Maxwell School, 1982), 46–48; Guillen, *Visión,* 107; Andrien, *Andean,* 197–98.

6. Ralph Bauer, introduction to *An Inca Account of the Conquest of Peru*, by Titu Cusi Yupanqui, trans., intro., and annotated by Ralph Bauer (Boulder: University of Colorado Press, 2005), 37.

7. Ralph Bauer, introduction, 14.

8. Nathan Wachtel, *The Vision of the Vanquished: The Spanish Conquest of Peru through Indian Eyes: 1530–1570*, trans. Ben and Sian Reynolds (New York: Harper & Row Publishers, 1977), 174–75.

9. Chang-Rodríguez "Writing," 50; Wachtel, *The Vision,* 176.

10. Legnani gives the date as 1566 while Andrien says 1567. Andrien, *Andean,* 198; Nicole Delia Legnani, introduction to *Titu Cusi: A 16th Century Account of the*

Conquest, by Titu Cusi Yupanqui, trans. and ed. Nicole Delia Legnani (Cambridge: Harvard University Press, 2005), 33.

11. Quoted in Alejandro Herrera Villagra, "Titu Cusi Yupanqui: diálogo, comunicación y traducción en la redacción de epístolas entre la mascapaicha quechua y la corona española. Vilcabamba, 1560–1570. Revisitado," in *Yuyay Taqe: Los Incas en su tiempo y en el nuestro,* ed. Roberto Ojeda Escalante and Alejandro Herrera Villagra (Cusco: Universidad Andina del Cusco, 2019), 82.

12. Ralph Bauer, introduction, 26.

13. Catherine Julien, "Francisco de Toledo and His Campaign against the Incas," *Colonial Latin American Review* 16, no. 2 (Dec. 2007), 250.

14. Guillen, *Visión,* 114.

15. Julien, "Francisco," 257–58.

16. Chang-Rodríguez, "Writing," 52–54.

17. Andrien, *Andean,* 193. For a detailed description of the capture of Tupac Amaru, see Guillen, *Visión,* 131–41.

18. Bauer, Ralph, introduction, 11.

19. Hiram Bingham, "The Ruins of Espiritu Pampa, Peru," *American Anthropologist* 16, no. 2 (Apr.–Jun., 1914), 199.

20. Hiram Bingham, "In the wonderland of Peru—rediscovering Machu Picchu: The work accomplished by the Peruvian Expedition of 1912, under the auspices of Yale University and the National Geographic Society," *National Geographic,* March 31, 2013—reprinted from the April 1913 edition, https://www.nationalgeographic .com/magazine/article/machu-picchu-peru-inca-hiram-bingham-discovery. Scholars agree that Machu Pichu was built in the 15th century.

21. Edmundo Guillén Guillén, *La Guerra de Reconquista Inca: Historia épica de como los Incas lucharon en defensa de la soberanía del Perú o Tawantinsuyo de 1536–1572* (Lima: R.A. Ediciones e.i.r.l., 1994), 225. See also Brian S. Bauer, Javier Fonseca Santa Cruz, and Mirian Araóz Silva, *Vilcabamba and the Archaeology of Inca Resistance* (Los Angeles: Cotsen Institute of Archaeology, 2015) and Laurence Blair, "Peru's last Inca city reveals its secrets: 'It's genuinely a marvel,'" *The Guardian,* Sept. 28, 2015, https://www.theguardian.com/world/2018/sep/28/perus-last -incan-city-reveals-its-secrets-its-genuinely-a-marvel.

22. Catherine Julien, introduction to *History of How the Spaniards Arrived in Peru* by Titu Cusi Yupanqui. Dual-Language Edition (Indianapolis: Hackett Publishing Company, Inc. 2006), xxviii.

23. It has been digitized but not yet posted on the internet; however, scholars can request a digitized copy. José Luis del Valle Merino, Real Biblioteca del Monasterio del Escorial, email note to author, March 6, 2018.

24. Diego de Castro Titu Cussi Yupangui, *Relación de la conquista del Perú y hechos del Inca Manco II,* ed. Horacio H. Urteaga and bio. Carlos A. Romero (Lima: Imprenta SanMarti y Ca., 1916). A copy of this publication at the Yale University Library has been digitized and can be viewed at hathitrust.org.

25. Ralph Bauer's and Nicole Delia Legnani's books were published in 2005, and Catherine Julien's in 2006.

26. Ralph Bauer, introduction, 22.

27. Song No, "La heterogeneidad suterada: Titu Cusi Yupangui, *Revista de Crítica Literaria Latinoamericana* 31, no. 62 (2005), 88–89.

28. Herrera, "Titu Cusi," 19.

29. Raquel Chang-Rodríguez, "Rebelión y religión en dos crónicas del Perú de ayer," *Revista de Crítica Literaria Latinoamericana* 14, no. 28 (1988), 177.

30. Liliana Regalado de Hurtado, estudio preliminar to *Instrucción al Licenciado Don Lope García de Castro (1570)* by Inca Titu Cusi Yupanqui. (Lima: Fondo Editorial de la Pontifica Universidad Católica del Perú, 1992), xxxii.

31. Raquel Chang-Rodríguez, *La apropiación del signo: Tres cronistas indígenas del Perú* (Tempe: Center for Latin American Studies, Arizona State University, 1988), 40.

32. Ben Post, "Titu Cusi Yupanqui (ca. 1526–1570)," in *Narradores Indígenas y mestizos de la época colonial (siglos XVI–XVII)*, ed. Rocío Cortés and Margarita Zamora (Lima: Centro de Estudios Literarios Antonio Cornejo Polar, 2016), 180.

33. Susana Jákfalvi-Leiva, "De la voz a la escritura: La Relación de Titu Cusi (1570)," *Revista de Crítica Literaria Latinoamericana* 19, no. 37 (1993), 266.

34. Ralph Bauer, introduction, 18.

35. Nicole Delia Legnani, A Necessary Contextualization to *Titu Cusi: Account of the Conquest*, by Titu Cusi Yupanqui, tran. and ed. Nicole Delia Legnani (Cambridge: Harvard University Press), xvi.

36. Jákfalvi-Leiva, "De la voz," 274.

37. Legnani, introduction, 49.

38. Julien, introduction, (2006), xxi.

39. Bartolome de las Casas, *History of the Indies*. Translated by Andrée M. Collard (New York: Harper & Row, 1971) 184.

40. Wachtel, *The Vision,* 24. Camilla Townsend has a different analysis, at least for Mexico, saying, "Available evidence indicates that the Aztecs responded to their situation with clear-sighted analysis of the technological differential, rather than by prostrating themselves before the 'white gods.'" Camilla Townsend, "Burying the White Gods: New Perspectives on the Conquest of Mexico," *The American Historical Review* 108, no. 3 (June 2003), 680.

41. Hélene Roy, "El discurso neo-inca y su significado político: Vilcabamba entre sumisión, sincretismo y resistencia," *Revista de Crítica Literaria Latinoamericana* 40, no. 80 (2014), 95.

42. Julien, introduction, viii.

43. Chang-Rodríguez, "Writing," (1982) 55.

44. Raquel Chang-Rodríguez, *Violencia y subversión en la prosa colonial hispanoamericana, siglos XVI y XVII* (Madrid: José Porrúa Turanzas, S.A., 1982).

45. Regalado de Hurtado, estudio preliminar, xxi.

46. Karen Spalding, "Notes on the Formation of the Andean Colonial State," in *State Theory and Andean Politics: New Approaches to the Study of Rule*, ed. Christopher Krupa and David Nugent (Philadelphia: University of Pennsylvania Press, 2015), 221.

47. Bartolomé de Las Casas, *Obras completas 11.2 Doce dudas* (Madrid: Alianza, 1992 [1564]), 194–95.

48. Ralph Bauer, introduction, 25–26.

49. Jákfalvi-Leiva, "De la voz," 276.

50. Julien, introduction, xxvii.

51. Moisés R. Castillo, "Estrategias de Resistencia y de crítica en el Perú colonial: La 'Relación de Titu Cusi Yupanqui y los 'Coloquios de la verdad' de Pedro de Quiroga," *Latin American Literary Review* 40, no. 80 (July–Dec. 2012), 143.

52. Castillo, "Estrategias," 135 and 143.

53. Legnani, introduction, 42.

54. Michael J. Horswell, "Negotiating Apostasy in Vilcabamba: Titu Cusi Yupanqui Writes from the Chaupi," *The Romanic Review* 103, no. 1–2 (2012), 82. The missionaries were Cristóbal de Molina, Cristóbal de Albornoz and Antonio de la Calancha.

55. Horswell, "Negotiating," 83.

56. Legnani, introduction, 1–2.

57. Guillén Guillén, *Visión* (1979), 141–42.

58. Chang-Rodríguez, *Violencia y subversión* (1982), 18.

59. Legnani, "A Necessary," x.

Chapter Ten

Pedro Sarmiento de Gamboa
"The Horrible Tyranny of the Incas"

Pedro Sarmiento de Gamboa was born in Alcalá de Henares, Spain, to a Galician father and a Basque mother in about the year 1532[1] and was well educated in languages and the sciences which proved useful in his varied life as navigator, explorer, writer, and conquistador. *The History of the Incas*, which he completed in Cuzco, Peru, in 1572, was written at the direction of Viceroy Francisco Toledo in an attempt to prove that the Incas were not natural lords in their lands because their rule was tyrannical, and their customs violated natural law. The work is considered by historians to be one of the most important surviving manuscripts from the period of the Spanish conquest of Peru and most particularly from the works associated with the administration of Toledo, the preeminent viceroy of that time.[2]

Sarmiento's *History* was sent to King Philip II of Spain in 1572 as part of the effort to prove the justice of the Spanish conquest of Peru. Two hundred years later in 1772, it was to be found in the library of Abraham Gronovius in the Netherlands. In 1785 it was sold to the University of Göttingen in Germany[3] but was not revealed to scholars until 1893.[4] Historian Richard Pietschmann published the first transcription of the manuscript as *Geschichte des Inkareiches* with an introduction in German in 1906 and geographer Sir Clements Markham published an English translation in 1907, which is the version used here. It is a very good translation that is in the public domain and can thus be used freely by scholars and students. The first edition published in a Spanish speaking country was released in Buenos Aires in 1942. A new English translation by Brian S. Bauer and Vania Smith was published in 2007.

It is not known where Sarmiento studied to acquire his knowledge of mathematics, languages, history, astronomy and navigation but he was probably in his early twenties when he first traveled to the New World in 1555. In Puebla,

Mexico, he was brought before the Inquisition (something to do with magic
and what he claimed was a joke) and was punished with a public lashing.[5]
After a similar encounter with the Inquisition in Lima, Sarmiento served six
months imprisonment. He was freed in order to serve as pilot with a fleet
of ships under the command of Alvaro Mendaña that set out to explore the
Pacific Ocean, "discovering" the Solomon Islands in 1567.[6]

Returning to Peru, Sarmiento was taken into the service of Francisco de
Toledo, who was to serve as viceroy from 1569 to 1581. Toledo had been
charged by King Philip with several tasks, among them ending the tradition of
the encomienda in Peru, thus centralizing authority in the hands of the viceroy
and the crown; ending the war with the Inca royalty exiled in the jungle fast-
ness of Vilcabamba;[7] and bringing the scattered Andean Indigenous people
together in villages so that they could be taught Christian doctrine.[8]

Another of Toledo's principal goals was to prove to the satisfaction of the
Crown that the Incas had not been natural lords in their lands by showing that
their rule was tyrannical and that their customs violated natural law. In this
way he could establish that the Spanish conquest was justified and that Friar
Bartolomé de Las Casas's insistence that the Andean lands be returned to the
Inca was unfounded.[9] The arguments supporting a return to Inca rule could
still be heard and Viceroy Toledo believed that they could best be countered
not by again asserting the Spanish right to rule but rather by proving that
Inca rule had been illegitimate.[10] In 1570, Toledo began inspections of his
viceroyalty in order to send reports to the king and charged Pedro Sarmiento
de Gamboa with the writing of a history of the Incas. Sarmiento interviewed
Inca elders to compile his *History,* and comparative literature scholar Ralph
Bauer and anthropologist Jean-Jacques Decoster praise his collection methods saying that the history was largely based on material compiled in the
Cuzco region where Sarmiento had access to the highest Inca nobility. They
add that he "went to extremes to collect and compare separate versions of
the Inca past."[11] Sarmiento intended to write three works: a geography of the
region of Peru, a history of the Incas, and a history of the conquest of Peru
by the Spaniards. While he completed and sent to Spain only the second one,
the history of the Incas, he wrote to King Philip II assuring him that he was
working on the geography as well.[12]

Upon completion of the *History*, Sarmiento called together senior representatives of the Inca dynastic groups of Cuzco and had the entire work read
to them in Quechua asking them to suggest any corrections, of which reportedly there were few. These representatives could not know that, in only a few
months, the last outpost of the Incas in rebellion would be conquered and the
last Inca monarch, Tupac Amaru, would be captured, tried, and beheaded in
the plaza of Cusco.[13] Sarmiento's manuscript, "bound in green leather and

lined with red silk,"[14] along with four painted cloths depicting the origin myth of the Incas and their history, were sent to King Philip in March of 1572. The cloths were put on public display by the king, but Sarmiento's book was never mentioned in court documents.[15]

On April 14, 1572, less than two months after sending the *History* and the painted cloths to Spain, Viceroy Toledo declared war on the Inca Titu Cusi Yupanqui in the mountain refuge of Vilcabamba, supposedly in retaliation for the killing of an emissary of the viceroy near the refuge. Sarmiento was named royal ensign of the party of some 250 Spaniards and five hundred Amerindians who were sent to capture this last safe haven of the Incas, task which they accomplished on June 24.[16] In the Vilcabamba plaza, Sarmiento planted the Spanish flag and said the words that normally accompanied Spanish conquest upon taking "possession" of newly conquered territory for the king, words that were similar to those Columbus had used on the first islands he found in the Western Atlantic in 1492: "I, Capitan Pedro Sarmiento de Gamboa, Royal Ensign of this field, by order of the illustrious Martín Hurtado de Arbieto, General, take possession of this town of Vilcabamba and all its provinces and jurisdictions." Then he said three times, "Vilcabamba, for Philip, King of Castile and Leon."[17]

By this time the Spaniards had learned that Titu Cusi had died and had been succeeded by his brother Tupac Amaru. Tupac Amaru escaped during the attack and but was later captured and taken to Cuzco. There he was tried and, on Sept. 24, 1572, executed by decapitation in front of thousands of mourning countrymen and women in spite of pleas by religious authorities that, because of his rank, he be sent to Spain for the king to decide his fate.[18]

Sarmiento declared that the capture of Vilcabamba and of Tupac Amaru was one of the most important services for God and the king since the beginning of the conquest because it had punished rebels against His Majesty's rule and totally extirpated the idolatries and sins against nature and God committed by the Incas. He later wrote the king that "these kingdoms were not truly conquered until the final conclusion of this campaign."[19] Toledo's position was the same. But, according to historians, Toledo had not had authorization from the king to go to war against Vilcabamba; in fact just the opposite. In a 1567 treaty, Titu Cusi had agreed to be a vassal prince of the Spanish crown.[20] The King eventually wanted to bring him down from Vilcabamba and give him land from which to make a living. However, Toledo's actions were in accord with a current in Spanish policy promoted by Royal Council President Cardinal Diego de Espinoza who favored policies of repression against dissident populations whether in Europe or the New World.[21]

The last twenty years of Sarmiento's life were marked by one adventure after another. After British privateer Francis Drake attacked Spanish ships off Peru's coast, Sarmiento was sent on an unsuccessful voyage to capture him, after which he made a proposal for colonizing and fortifying the Straits of Magellan to prevent the passage of British ships around the southern tip of South America. After a 1579 exploratory voyage,[22] he convinced King Philip to support his plan and in Dec. 1581 set off from Spain with twenty-three ships holding three thousand persons and with the title of governor of the new province. Off Brazil, the admiral of the fleet deserted, leaving Sarmiento to lead the ships to the Straits, where he founded two settlements. Numerous calamities befell the colonists, including hunger and desertions, prompting Sarmiento to decide to return to Spain for supplies and reinforcements. But on this return trip he was captured by Sir Walter Raleigh and taken to England as a prisoner with valuable navigational knowledge. All sources state that he spoke with Queen Elizabeth I for a half hour in Latin, their only common language.[23] After a year, Sarmiento was released by the English with peace proposals for King Philip but, on his journey through France in Dec. 1586, he was captured and held for ransom by the Protestant Huguenots, fierce foes of Catholic Spain. The Spanish court finally ordered payment of the 15,000 escudos demanded by the Huguenots, and Sarmiento was freed in 1590. However, the Spanish Armada had been defeated in 1588 and the peace proposals he carried were no longer relevant. In 1591, King Philip named Sarmiento admiral of a fleet charged with protecting Spanish ships bringing gold and silver from the Americas. The fleet left Cádiz in May of 1592, but Sarmiento fell ill off the coast of Portugal and was taken to Lisbon, where he died between the July 15 and July 18. He was probably sixty years old. [24]

Sarmiento's goal in his *History of the Incas* was to disprove the theories of a number of Spanish clergymen and philosophers about the right of the Spaniards to conquer and hold in subjugation the lands of the Indies. For example, Bartolomé de Las Casas had argued forcefully in his Treatise of Twelve Doubts (1564) that the Spanish had no right to take Inca land which he declared should be returned to Titu Cusi Yupanqui, self-exiled at Vilcabamba.[25] So, Sarmiento frames his history of the Incas in a way that reinforces one of the few justifications for conquest as laid down by Spanish philosopher Francisco de Vitoria in his *Relectio de Indis* (1539). Vitoria rejected most justifications for violent conquest but argued that it could be justified to end tyranny or harm to innocent people.[26] Historian Karen Spalding states that, "Vitoria insisted conversion to Christianity was not a justification for war and conquest; it was not legitimate to attack or plunder people who lived in ordered societies subject to rulers they accepted, unless those rulers systematically oppressed their subjects."[27] To prove that all the Incas were unfit to rule, Sarmiento set out to show that each Inca had committed crimes against natural law.[28]

An old controversy related to Sarmiento is whether his *History of the Incas* or El Inca Garcilaso's *Royal Commentaries of the Incas* gives the more accurate picture of the Inca reign. Historian Soledad González Díaz says that scholars in the first half of the twentieth century (after Sarmiento's history was published in Spanish in 1906 and in English in 1907) were divided between those who ascribed to the vision of the Incas as a civilizing force as portrayed by Garcilaso and those who chose to defend the more warlike version of Sarmiento. She states that the academic conflict, which lasted until the last quarter of the century, held back the emergence of new levels of interpretation.[29] On the one side, historian Raul Porras Barrenechea (1897–1960) wrote that Sarmiento's vision of the Inca Empire was full of power and strength as opposed to that of Garcilaso who portrayed a tame, idyllic empire led by Incas who were able to conquer all of South America without breaking a single plate. He added that Sarmiento's version was more virile and more real.[30] Anthropologist Philip A. Means, writing in 1932, on the other hand, stated that Toledo and Sarmiento "made it their business to anathematize the Inca dynasty in such a way that their fair name would perish and that it would become clear to everyone that the King of Castile is legitimate Lord of these realms."[31] In contrast, he notes that El Inca Gacilaso was one of those chroniclers who produced "saner, sounder . . . pictures of Peru and its grandeurs."[32]

Many writers have questioned the validity of Sarmiento's verification of his history. Forty-two representatives of the Inca royal kin groups had been

Figure 10.1. A sketch made by Clements Markham of a 1570 painting in the Church of Santa Ana in Cuzco and used as an illustration in his 1907 translation of Sarmiento's History of the Incas

called together to listen to the translated reading of the work. After each chapter, they were asked if they had any corrections. Historian Roberto Levillier, writing in 1935, insisted that the information given to the viceroy and his cosmographer, Sarmiento, was among the most trustworthy in existence with which to reconstruct the events and to appreciate the spirit of the Inca republic.[33]

However, his contemporary Means differed, saying that the witnesses "were cowed by the martial strength of the Viceroy's government and by the new spiritual terrorism which Catholic Christianity had put in place of the old cults."[34] Writing eighty years later, anthropologist R. Alan Covey appears to side with Means, adding that "most witnesses relying on their own memories or what they had heard from their parents could only reproduce hazy recollections of the pre-Conquest period, which by then was forty years past."[35]

However, there is also controversy over whether Sarmiento actually portrayed the Incas as the tyrants that he announced them to be at the beginning of his work. Historian Sabine MacCormack believes that he did. She states that "the Incas emerged not as legitimate rulers but as war-leaders . . . who differed little from other leaders of the region except that they were more aggressive and successful." Citing crimes by each ruler, Sarmiento "condemned the Incas as tyrants who maintained their imperial power only in the face of persistent opposition and rebellion by their subjects."[36] Historian Jeremy Ravi Mumford says, however, that Sarmiento "sometimes seemed to forget which side he was on. Of Topa Inca, he wrote: 'He was liberal, forgiving in peace and cruel in war and punishment, a favorer of the poor, spirited and a man of much industry, a builder. He was the greatest tyrant of all the Incas.' The tyrant had become, it appears, a model for kings."[37]

González points out another problem with Sarmiento's account. By extending the life spans of the twelve Inca rulers, Sarmiento describes an Inca state that lasted a thousand years, challenging another of Toledo's principal objectives, which was to show that the Incas were a recent or modern tyranny with little right to be considered legitimate lords of Peru.[38] González suggests that the reason Sarmiento's *History* was not published for three hundred years was because it did not satisfy the expectations of Viceroy Toledo and the king.[39]

MacCormack warns that "the Spanish, when translating and ordering the narratives that they collected from their Inca and Andean informants, inevitably viewed Inca history self-referentially." She notes that while the Incas historical recitations highlighted glorious deeds and skipped shameful ones, the Spanish in their writings about the Incas also emphasized in Inca history and customs what they found useful for their own ends and she adds, "In light of all these difficulties, modern historians of the Incas view these Spanish accounts with some distrust."[40]

Sarmiento's *History* has been caught up in the long-standing controversy about the historicity or historical validity of narratives of the Inca past. In her 2000 book, Anthropologist Catherine Julien wants to establish that the Incas did have a knowable history and she sets her arguments up in opposition, first, to writers who "doubted the capacity of Spaniards to interpret a fundamentally foreign world" in a foreign language (the postmodern argument) and, second, to others who would deny the existence of an Andean history saying that history only arrived with the Spaniards and the tales told by the locals were myths. In answer to the first question, Julien notes that, while recognizing the language and cultural difficulties, "the Spanish historical narratives offer a perspective on Inca history that must be considered." [41]

Among those in the second group is anthropologist R. Tom Zuidema, whose view that the Incas had no history comes from structural anthropology and the analysis of small-scale societies elsewhere in the world. He says:

> Every one of the preceding rulers were said [by chroniclers of Andean history] to have founded his own panaca, a social group consisting of all his descendants with the exception of his heir. These panaca had an important function in the organization of Cuzco. . . . As I hope to demonstrate, the panaca were never formed in the manner described by the chroniclers. Moreover, their interpretations of the exploits ascribed to the imperial dynasty cannot as such be used as the basis of a description of the history and culture of the Inca.[42]

He subscribes instead to a theory "of a simultaneous origin of all the *panaca*" that included a "fabricated presentation of the dynasty" in the case of each Inca ruler. He chides modern scholars for assuming that the facts of Inca history described by the Spanish chroniclers were "real historical facts"[43] when in fact they were myths created to give prestige to their clan groups. Writing some years later in the same vein, historian Franklin Pease maintained that many of the stories told by the Spanish chroniclers, but not all, were myths converted into history.[44] Pease maintained that Inca history as recounted by the elders had not passed through the secularization caused by humanism's development in Europe which had removed most of the religious and miraculous elements from European history.[45]

To disprove such writers as Zuidema and Pease, Julien dives into what she calls "a kind of archeology of the source materials" by such methods as comparing "two manuscripts dependent on the same source" and finding inexplicable passages in a chronicle, as she did in Sarmiento's history, showing where he "gives voice to an overarching narrative about the Inca expansion that he does not seem to understand."[46] She states that she benefited from the 1985 publication of the transcription of a 1569 reading, as part of a legal petition, of a *quipu* (the knotted-string record keeping of the Incas) which narrates the conquests of the tenth Inca ruler and from the concordance done by archaeologist John Rowe between this transcription and the writings of Sarmiento and other Spanish chroniclers.[47] She summarizes by saying, "The Incas had developed their own forms of recording and transmitting representations of their past, forms that responded to a native historical consciousness. There is an Incan history."[48]

Pedro Sarmiento de Gamboa, the navigator, explorer, conquistador, and faithful servant of the Spanish king, will continue to be controversial as long as his writings about the history of the Incas and defense of the Spanish right to rule them are studied. His obvious admiration for the achievements of the Inca rulers and their empire could not overcome his commitment to support King Philip's domination over their land and riches. In order to justify Spanish rule under the religious and philosophical principles that dominated Spain at the time, he set out to prove that the Incas were cruel tyrants and thus not natural lords of their lands. Whether he achieved that goal will likely continue to be subject to dispute.

PEDRO SARMIENTO DE GAMBOA'S *HISTORY OF THE INCAS*

To His Sacred Caesarian Majesty the King, Don Felipe, Our Lord

Among the excellencies, O sovereign and catholic Philip, that are the glorious decorations of princes, placing them on the highest pinnacle of estimation, are, according to the father of Latin eloquence, generosity, kindness, and liberality. . . . [F]or a king who complies so well with the obligation of liberality, and who gives so much, it is necessary that he should possess much; for nothing is so suitable for a prince as possessions and riches for his gifts and liberalities, as Tully[49] says, as well as to acquire glory. For it is certain, as we read in Sallust[50] that "in a vast empire there is great glory"; and in how much it is greater, in so much it treats of great things. Hence the glory of a king consists in his possessing many vassals, and the abatement of his glory is caused by the diminution of the number of his subjects.

Of this glory, most Christian king, God Almighty gives you so large a share in this life that all the enemies of the holy catholic church of Christ our Lord tremble at your exalted name; whence you most justly deserve to be named the strength of the church. As the treasure which God granted that your ancestors should spend, with such holy magnanimity, on worthy and holy deeds, in the extirpation of heretics, in driving the accursed Saracens out of Spain, in building churches, hospitals and monasteries, . . . the most merciful and almighty God, whom they served with all their hearts, saw fit to commence repayment with temporal goods, in the present age. This was the grant to them of the evangelical office, choosing them from among all the kings of this world as the evangelizers of his divine word in the most remote and unknown lands of those blind and barbarous gentiles. We now call those lands the Indies of Castille, because through the ministry of that kingdom they will be put in the way of salvation. . . . The Indies are also most abundant in all kinds of inestimable treasures, with which the heavy expenses were repaid to them [your ancestors] and, yet remained the richest princes in the world, and thus continued to exercise their holy and Christian liberality until death.

. . . [Pope] Alexander VI, the Vicar of Jesus Christ . . . gave [to Spain] and conceded forever, the islands and main lands which were then discovered and which might hereafter be discovered within the limits and demarcation of 180° of longitude, which is half the world. . . .

But as the devil saw that this door was shut, which he had begun to open to introduce by it dissensions and disturbances, he tried to make war by means of the very soldiers who resisted him, who were the same preachers. They began to make a difficulty about the right and title which the kings of Castille had over these lands. As your invincible father [Emperor Carlos V] was very jealous in matters touching his conscience, he ordered this point to be examined, as closely as possible, by very learned doctors [in Valladolid in 1550] who, according to the report which was given out, were indirect and doubtful in their conclusions. They [the friars] gave it as their opinion that these Incas, who ruled in these kingdoms of Peru, were and are the true and natural lords of that land. This gave a handle to foreigners, as well catholics as heretics and other infidels, for throwing doubt on the right which the kings of Spain claim and have claimed to the Indies. Owing to this the Emperor Don Carlos of glorious memory was on the point of abandoning them, which was what the enemy of the faith of Christ wanted, that he might regain the possession of the souls which he had kept in blindness for so many ages.

All this arose owing to want of curiosity on the part of the governors in those lands, at that time, who did not use the diligence necessary for ascertaining the truth, and also owing to certain reports of the Bishop of Chiapa [Bartolomé de las Casas] who was moved to passion against certain conquerors in his bishoprick with whom he had persistent disputes, as I knew when I passed through Chiapa and Guatemala. Though his zeal appears holy and estimable, he said things on the right to this country gained by the conquerors of it, which differ from the evidence and judicial proofs which have been seen and taken down by us, and from what we, who have travelled over the Indies enquiring about these things, leisurely and without war, know to be the facts.

This chaos and confusion of ignorance on the subject being so spread over the world and rooted in the opinions of the best-informed literary men in Christendom, God put it into the ear of your Majesty to send Don Francisco de Toledo, Mayor-domo of your household, as Viceroy of these kingdoms. When he arrived, he found many things to do, and many things to amend. Without resting after the dangers and long voyages in two seas which he had suffered, he put the needful order into all the things that were necessary. He amended the errors of former times, and laid a sure foundation for the future in such a way that the fruits of his measures will be lasting, because they rest on solid and reasoned foundations. . . .

His determination was to travel over this most rugged country himself, to make a general visitation of it, during which, though it is not finished, it is certain that he has remedied many and very great faults and abuses in the teaching and ministry of the Christian doctrine, giving holy and wise advice to its ministers that they should perform their offices as becomes the service of God, and the discharge of your royal conscience, reducing the people to congregations of villages formed on suitable and healthy sites which had formerly been on crags and rocks where they were neither taught nor received spiritual instruction. In such places they lived and died like wild savages, worshipping idols as in the time of their Inca tyrants and of their blind heathenism. Orders were given to stop their public drinking bouts, their concubinage and worship of their idols and devils, emancipating and freeing them from the tyrannies of their *curacas* [traditional magistrates], and finally giving them a rational life. . . .

Among Christians, it is not right to take anything without a good title, yet that which your Majesty has to these parts, though more holy and more honourable than that which any other kings in the world have for any of their possessions, has suffered detriment, as I have said before, in the consciences of many learned men and others, for want of correct information. The Viceroy proposes to do your Majesty a most signal service in this matter, besides the performance of all the other duties of which he has charge. This is to give a secure and quiet harbor to your royal conscience against the tempests raised even by your own natural subjects, theologians and other literary men, who have expressed serious opinions on the subject, based on incorrect information. Accordingly, in his general visitation, which he is making personally throughout the kingdom, he has verified from the root and established by a host of witnesses examined with the greatest diligence and care, taken from among the principal old men of the greatest ability and authority in the kingdom, and even those who pretend to have an interest in it from being relations and descendants of the Incas, the terrible, inveterate and horrible tyranny of the Incas, being the tyrants who ruled in these kingdoms of Peru, and the *curacas* who governed the districts. This will undeceive all those in the world who think that the Incas were legitimate sovereigns, and that the *curacas* were natural lords of the land. In order that your Majesty may, with the least trouble and the most pleasure, be informed, and the rest, who are of a contrary opinion, be undeceived, I was ordered by the Viceroy Don Francisco de Toledo, whom I follow and serve in this general visitation, to take this business in hand, and write a history of the deeds of the twelve Incas of this land, and of the origin of the people, continuing the narrative to the end. This I have done with all the research and diligence that was required, as your Majesty will see in the course of the perusal and by the ratification of witnesses. It will certify to the truth of the worst and most inhuman tyranny of these Incas and of their *curacas* who are not and never were original lords of the soil, but were placed there by Tupac Inca Yupanqui, the greatest, the most atrocious and harmful tyrant of them all. The *curacas* were and still are great tyrants appointed by other great and violent tyrants, as will clearly and certainly appear in the history; so that the tyranny is proved, as well as that the Incas were strangers in Cuzco, and that they seized the valley of Cuzco, and all the rest of their territory from Quito to Chile by force of arms, making themselves Incas without the consent or election of the natives.

Besides this, there are their tyrannical laws and customs. It will be understood that your Majesty has a specially true and holy title to these kingdoms of Peru, because your Majesty and your most sacred ancestors stopped the sacrifices of innocent men, the eating of human flesh, the accursed sin, the promiscuous concubinage with sisters and mothers, the abominable use of beasts, and their wicked and accursed customs. For from each one God demands an account of his neighbor, and this duty specially appertains to princes, and above all to your Majesty. Only for this may war be made and prosecuted by the right to put a stop to the deeds of tyrants. Even if they had been true and natural lords of the soil, it would be lawful to remove them and introduce a new government, because man may rightly be punished for these sins against nature, though the native community has not been opposed to such practices nor desires to be avenged, as innocent, by the Spaniards. For in this case they have no right to deliver themselves and their children over to death, and they should be forced to observe natural laws, as we are taught by the Archbishop of Florence, Innocent, supported by Fray Francisco de Vitoria in his work on the title to the Indies. So that by this title alone, without counting many others, your Majesty has the most sufficient and legitimate right to the Indies, better than any other prince in the world has to any lordship whatever. For, whether more or less concealed or made known, in all the lands that have been discovered in the two seas of your Majesty, north and south, this general breaking of the law of nature has been found. . . .

May your Majesty receive my work with the greatest and most favourable attention, as treating of things that will be of service to God and to your Majesty and of great profit to my nation; and may our Lord preserve the sacred catholic and royal person of your Majesty, for the repair and increase of the catholic Church of Jesus Christ.

From Cuzco.

The 4th of March, 1572.

Your catholic royal Majesty from the least vassal of your Majesty,

The Captain Pedro Sarmiento de Gamboa.

Chapter 10: How the Incas Began to Tyrannize over the Lands and Inheritances

Having explained that, in ancient times, all this land was owned by the people, it is necessary to state how the Incas began their tyranny. Although the tribes all lived in simple liberty without recognizing any lord, there were always some ambitious men among them, aspiring for mastery. They committed violence among their countrymen and among strangers to subject them and bring them to obedience under their command, so that they might serve them and pay tribute. Thus bands of men belonging to one region went to others to make war and to rob and kill, usurping the lands of others.

As these movements took place in many parts by many tribes, each one trying to subjugate his neighbor, it happened that six leagues from the valley of Cuzco, at a place called Paccari-tampu, there were four men with their four sisters, of fierce courage and evil intentions, although with lofty aims. These being more able than the others, understood the pusillanimity of the natives of those districts and the ease with which they could be made to believe anything that was propounded with authority or with any force. So they conceived among themselves the idea of being able to subjugate many lands by force and deception. Thus all the eight brethren, four men and four women, consulted together how they could tyrannize over other tribes beyond the place where they lived, and they proposed to do this by violence. Considering that most of the natives were ignorant and could easily be made to believe what was said to them, particularly if they were addressed with some roughness, rigour and authority, against which they could make neither reply nor resistance, because they are timid by nature, they sent abroad certain fables respecting their origin, that they might be respected and feared. They said that they were the sons of Viracocha Pachayachachi, the Creator, and that they had come forth out of certain windows to rule the rest of the people. As they were fierce, they made the people believe and fear them, and hold them to be more than men, even worshipping them as gods. Thus they introduced the religion that suited them.

Chapter 34: The Nations which Pachacuti Inca Subjugated and the Towns He Took

Near Cuzco there is a nation of Indians called Ayamarcas who had a proud and wealthy Sinchi [chief] named Tocay Ccapac. Neither he nor his people wished to come and do reverence to the Inca. On the contrary, he mustered his forces to attack the Inca if his country was invaded. This being known to Inca Yupanqui, he assembled his *ayllus* and other troops. He formed them into two parties, afterwards called Hanan-cuzcos and Hurin-cuzcos, forming them into a corps that, united, no one might be able to prevail against them. This done he consulted over what should be undertaken. It was resolved that all should unite for the conquest of all neighbouring nations. Those who would not submit were to be utterly destroyed; and first Tocay Ccapac, chief of the Ayamarcas, was to be dealt with, being powerful and not having come to do homage at Cuzco. Having united his forces, the Inca marched against the Ayamarcas and their Sinchi, and there was a battle at Huanancancha. Inca Yupanqui was victorious, assaulting the villages and killing nearly all the Ayamarcas. He took Tocay Ccapac as a prisoner to Cuzco, where he remained in prison until his death.

After this Inca Yupanqui took to wife a native of Choco named Mama Aahuarqui. For greater pleasure and enjoyment, away from business, he went to the town of the Cuyos, chief place of the province of Cuyo-suyo. Being one day at a great entertainment, a potter, servant of the Sinchi, without apparent reason, threw a stone or, as some say, one of the jars which they call *ulti*, at the Inca's head and wounded him. The delinquent, who was a stranger to the district, was seized and tortured to confess who had ordered him to do it. He stated that all the Sinchis of Cuyo-suyo, who were Cuyo Ccapac, Ayanquilalama, and Apu Cunaraqui, had conspired to kill the Inca and rebel. This was false, for it had been extorted from fear of the torture, or, as some say, he said it because he belonged to a hostile tribe and wished to do them harm. But the Inca, having heard what the potter said, ordered all the Sinchis to be killed with great cruelty. After their deaths he slaughtered the people, leaving none alive except some children and old women. Thus was that nation destroyed, and its towns are desolate to this day.

Chapter 49: Tupac Inca Yupanqui Conquers the Province of the Antis

Pachacuti Inca Yupanqui being dead, and Tupac Inca ruling alone, he caused all the Sinchis and principal men of the conquered provinces to be summoned. Those came who feared the fury of the Inca, and with them the Indians of the province of Anti-suyu, who are the dwellers in the forests to the eastward of Cuzco, who had been conquered in the time of Pachacuti his father.

Tupac Inca ordered them all to do homage, adore, and offer sacrifices. The Antis were ordered to bring from their country several loads of lances of palm wood for the service of the House of the Sun. The Antis, who did not serve voluntarily, looked upon this demand as a mark of servitude. They fled from Cuzco, returned to their country, and raised the land of the Antis in the name of freedom.

Tupac Inca was indignant, and raised a powerful army which he divided into three parts. . . . [T]he three divisions formed a junction three leagues within the forest, at a place called Opatari, whence they commenced operations against the settlements of the Antis. The inhabitants of this region were Antis, called Opataris, and were the first to be conquered. Chalco Yupanqui carried an image of the Sun.

The forests were very dense and full of evil places; so that they could not force their way through, nor did they know what direction to take in order to reach the settlements of the natives, which were well concealed in the thick vegetation. To find them the explorers climbed up the highest trees, and pointed out the places where they could see smoke rising. So they worked away at road making through the undergrowth until they lost that sign of inhabitants and found another. In this way the Inca made a road where it seemed impossible to make one. . . .

Tupac Inca and his captains penetrated into this region of the Antis, which consists of the most terrible and fearful forests, with many rivers, where they endured immense toil, and the people who came from Peru suffered from the change of climate, for Peru is cold and dry, while the forests of Anti-suyu are warm and humid. The soldiers of Tupac Inca became sick, and many died. Tupac Inca himself, with a third of his men who came with him to conquer, were lost in the forests, and wandered for a long time, without knowing whether to go in one direction or another until he fell in with Uturuncu Achachi who put him on the route.

On this occasion Tupac Inca and his captains conquered four great tribes. The first was that of the Indians called Opataris. The next was the Mano-suyu. The third tribe was called Mañaris or Yanasimis, which means those of the black mouth: and the province of Rio, and the province of the Chunchos. . . .

Chapter 52: Tupac Inca Yupanqui Orders a Second Visitation of the Land, and Does Other Things

Apu Achachi set out and made his general visitation, reducing many of the Indians to live in villages and houses who had previously lived in caves and hills and on the banks of rivers, each one by himself. He sent those in strong fastnesses into plains, that they might have no site for a fortress, on the strength of which they might rebel. He reduced them into provinces, giving them their Curacas. . . . In each province all those of the province made a great sowing of every kind of edible vegetable for the Inca, his overseers coming to the harvest. Above all there was a *Tucurico Apu*, who was the governor-lieutenant of the Inca in that province. It is true that the first Inca who obliged the Indians of this land to pay tribute of everything, and in quantity, was Inca Yupanqui. But Tupac Inca imposed rules and fixed the tribute they must pay, and divided it according to what each province was to contribute as well for the general tax as those for *Huacas*, and Houses of the Sun. . . .

He divided the months of the year, with reference to labour in the fields, as follows. Three months in the year were allotted to the Indians for the work of their own fields, and the rest must be given up to the work of the Sun, of *huacas*, and of the Inca. In the three months that were given to themselves, one was for ploughing and sowing, one for reaping, and another in the summer for festivals, and for make and mend clothes days. The rest of their time was demanded for the service of the Sun and the Incas.

Chapter 54: Death of Tupac Inca Yupanqui

Having visited and divided the lands, and built the fortress of Cuzco, besides edifices and houses without number, Tupac Inca Yupanqui went to Chinchero, a town near Cuzco, where he had very rich things for his recreation; and there he ordered extensive gardens to be constructed to supply his household. When the work was completed he fell ill of a grave infirmity, and did not wish to be visited by anyone. But as he became worse and felt the approach of death, he sent for the *orejones* [Inca nobles] of Cuzco, his relations, and when they had assembled in his presence he said: "My relations and friends! I would have you to know that the Sun my Father desires to take me to himself, and I wish to go and rest with him. I have called you to let you know who it is that I desire to succeed me as lord and sovereign, and who is to rule and govern you." They answered that they grieved much at his illness, that as the Sun his father had so willed it so must it be, that his will must be done, and they besought the Inca to nominate him who was to be sovereign in his place. Tupac Inca then replied: "I nominate for my successor my son Titu Cusi Hualpa, son of my sister and wife, Mama Ocllo." For this they offered many thanks, and afterwards the Inca sank down on his pillow and died, having lived 85 years. . . .

The deceased Inca was frank, merciful in peace, cruel in war and punishments, a friend to the poor, a great man of indefatigable industry and a notable builder. He was the greatest tyrant of all the Incas. He died in the year 1528.

Chapter 70: It Is Noteworthy How These Incas Were Tyrants Against Themselves

It is a thing worthy to be noted for the fact that besides being a thing certain and evident the general tyranny of these cruel and tyrannical Incas of Peru against the natives of the land, may be easily gathered from history, and any one who reads and considers with attention the order and mode of their procedure will see, that their violent Incaship was established without the will and election of the natives who always rose with arms in their hands on each occasion that offered for rising against their Inca tyrants who oppressed them, to get back their liberty. Each one of the Incas not only followed the tyranny of his father, but also began afresh the same tyranny by force, with deaths, robberies and rapine. Hence none of them could pretend, in good faith, to give a beginning to time of prescription[51], nor did any of them hold in peaceful possession, there being always some one to dispute and take up arms against them and their tyranny. Moreover, and this is above all to be noted, to understand the worst aims of these tyrants and their horrid avarice and oppression, they were not satisfied with being evil tyrants to the natives, but also to their own proper sons, brothers and relations, in defiance of their own laws and statutes, they were the worst and most pertinacious tyrants with an unheard-of inhumanity. For it was enacted among themselves and by their customs and laws that the eldest legitimate son should succeed, yet almost always they broke the law, as appears by the Incas who are here referred to. . . . Turning their arms against their own entrails, robbing, and with inhuman intestine wars they came to a final end. Thus as they commenced by their own authority, so they destroyed all by their own proper hands.

It may be that Almighty God permits that one shall be the executioner of the other for his evil deeds, that both may give place to his most holy gospel which, by the hands of the Spaniards, and by order of the most happy, catholic, and unconquered Emperor and King of Spain, Carlos V of glorious memory, father of your Majesty, was sent to these blind and barbarous gentiles. Yet against the force and power of the Incas on foot and united, it appeared that it would be impossible for human force to do what a few Spaniards did, numbering only 180, who at first entered with the Governor Don Francisco Pizarro.

. . . For the above reasons it will be right to say to those whose duty it may be to decide, that on such clear evidence is based the most just and legitimate title that your Majesty and your successors have to these parts of the Indies, proved by the actual facts that are here written, more especially as regards these kingdoms of Peru, without a point to raise against the said titles by which the crown of Spain holds them. Respecting which your Viceroy of these kingdoms, Don Francisco Toledo, has been a careful and most curious enquirer, as zealous for the clearing of the conscience of your Majesty, and for the salvation of your soul, as he has shown and now shows himself in the general visitation which he is making by order of your Majesty, in his own person, not avoiding the very great labours and dangers which he is suffering in these journeys, so long as they result in so great a service to God and your Majesty.

NOTES

1. Clements R. Markham, introduction to *Narratives of the Voyages of Pedro Sarmiento de Gamboa to the Straits of Magellan*, by Pedro Sarmiento de Gamboa, trans. Clements R. Markham (New York: Burt Franklin, Publisher, 1895), x.

2. Brian S. Bauer and Jean-Jacques Decoster, introduction to *The History of the Incas*, by Pedro Sarmiento de Gamboa, trans. and ed. by Brian S. Bauer and Vania Smith Austin (Austin: University of Texas Press, 2007), 1; and Soledad González Díaz, "Del Génesis a los Andes: la cronología del incario en la *Historia de los Incas* de Pedro Sarmiento de Gamboa," *Estudios Atacameños* 51 (2015): 153.

3. The original manuscript has been scanned by the Göttingen Library, but it is not yet available to view online. Dietlind Willer, University Library, Göttingen University, e-mail message to author, Feb. 26, 2019.

4. Raúl Porras Barrenechea, "Pedro Sarmiento de Gamboa [1532–1592?]," *Los Cronistas del Peru (1528–1650) y Otros Ensayos*, ed. Franklin Pease (Lima: Biblioteca Clásicos del Péru, 1986 [1962]), 366. See also: Soledad González Díaz, "A Three-Century Journey: The Lost Manuscript of the History of the Incas by Pedro Sarmiento De Gamboa," *The Americas* 78, no. 3 (2021): 467–91.

5. Francisco Carrillo, *Cronistas del Peru Antiguo: Encyclopedia Histórica de la Literatura Peruana, Vol. 4* (Lima: Editorial Horizonte, 1989), 103.

6. Porras, "Pedro," 363.

7. Bauer and Decoster, introduction, 2.

8. Stephen Clissold, *Conquistador: The Life of Don Pedro Sarmiento de Gamboa* (London: Derek Verschoyle, 1954), 67.

9. Lewis Hanke, "Viceroy Francisco de Toledo and the Just Titles of Spain to the Inca Empire: The Defense of the Spanish Title to Peru," *The Americas* 3, no. 1 (July 1946): 3–5.

10. Rolena Adorno, *The Polemics of Possession in Spanish American Narrative* (New Haven: Yale University Press, 2007), 51–52.

11. Bauer and Decoster, introduction, 14, 18–20.

12. José Miguel Barros Franco, "Los últimos años de Pedro Sarmiento de Gamboa," *Boletín de la Academia Chilena de la Historia* 90 (1997/1998): 55.

13. Bauer and Decoster, introduction, 18.

14. Catherine Julien, *Reading Inca History* (Iowa City: University of Iowa Press, 2000), 56.

15. Bauer and Decoster, introduction, 18.

16. Barros, "Los últimos," 60–62.

17. Barros, "Los últimos," 60–62. Translation by this author.

18. Barros, "Los últimos," 63–64.

19. Barros, "Los últimos," 65. Translation by this author.

20. Ralph Bauer, introduction to *An Inca Account of the Conquest of Peru,* by Titu Cusi Yupanqui, translated, introduced and annotated by Ralph Bauer (Bolder: University of Colorado Press, 2005), 26.

21. Catherine Julien, "Francisco Toledo and His Campaign against the Incas," *Colonial Latin American Review* 16, no. 2 (Dec. 2007): 251–52.

22. Sarmiento kept a log about the voyage which was published in 1768 with the title *Viage al Estrecho de Magallanes por el Capitan Pedro Sarmiento de Gamboa en los Años 1579 y 1580* and which can be viewed online at: http://www.cervantesvirtual. com/obra-visor/viage-al-estrecho-de-magallanes-por-el-capitan-pedro-sarmiento-de -gamboa-en-los-anos-de-1579-y-1580-y-noticia-de-la-expedicion-que-despues-hizo -para-poblarle--0/html/. It was translated into English by Clements Markham in 1895.

23. For example, Carrillo, *Cronistas,* 104.

24. Porras, "Pedro," 364–365; Barros, "Los últimos," 12–27; Carrillo, *Cronistas,* 104.

25. Bartolomé de Las Casas, *Obras completas 11.2 Doce dudas* (Madrid: Alianza, 1992 [1564]), 194–195.

26. Luis Millones Figueroa, "Colonial Andean Texts in English Translation," *Latin American Research Review* 44, no. 2 (2009): 187.

27. Karen Spalding, "Notes on the Formation of the Andean Colonial State," in *State Theory and Andean Politics: New Approaches to the Study of Rule*, ed. Christopher Krupa and David Nugent (Philadelphia: University of Pennsylvania Press, 2015), 220–21.

28. Bauer and Decoster, introduction, 15.

29. González Díaz, "Del génesis," 154.

30. Porras, 366.

31. Philip Ainsworth Means, *Fall of the Inca Empire and the Spanish Rule in Peru: 1530–1780* (New York: Charles Scribner's Sons, 1932), 124.

32. Means, *Fall,* 229.

33. Roberto Levillier, *Don Francisco de Toledo, Supremo Organizador del Perú: su vida, su obra (1515–1582, Tomo I: Años de andanzas y de guerras (1515–1572)* (Madrid: Espasa-Calpe, 1935), 297.

34. Philip A. Means, "Sarmiento de Gamboa, Captain Pedro," *Biblioteca Andina, Part I*, (New Haven: Transactions of the Connecticut Academy of Arts and Sciences, 1928), 496–7. https://archive.org/details/b29827322/page/496 Posted Oct. 19, 2017.

35. R. Alan Covey, "Chronology, Succession, and Sovereignty: The Politics of Inka Historiography and Its Modern Interpretation," *Comparative Studies in Society and History* 48, no. 1 (Jan. 2006): 184.

36. Sabine MacCormack, "History, Historical Record, and Ceremonial Action: Incas and Spaniards in Cuzco," *Comparative Studies in Society and History* 43, no. 2 (April 2001): 348.

37. Jeremy Ravi Mumford, *Vertical Empire: The General Resettlement of Indians in the Colonial Andes* (Durham: Duke University Press, 2012), 105.

38. It is generally believed that the Incas established themselves at Cuzco in about 1100 CE and began to build their empire in about 1425. See Mark Cartwright, "Inca Civilization," *Ancient History Encyclopedia* (Sept. 2014) https://www.ancient.eu/Inca_Civilization/.

39. González, "Del genesis," 173.

40. MacCormack, "History," 331.

41. Julien *Reading*, 6–7.

42. R. T. Zuidema, *The Ceque System of Cuzco: The Social Organization of the Capital of the Inca* (Leiden: E.J. Brill, 1964), 12.

43. Zuidema, *Ceque System*, 13, 15–16.

44. Franklin Pease G. Y. *Las Crónicas y Los Andes* (Mexico: Fondo de Cultura Económica, 2010 [1995]), 86.

45. Pease, *Las Crónicas*, 107.

46. Julien, *Reading*, 12, 234.

47. Julien, *Reading*, 15.

48. Julien, *Reading*, 302.

49. Tully is an archaic Anglicized version of the name of Roman philosopher and politician Marcus Tullius Cicero.

50. Sallust was a Roman historian and politician.

51. Brian S. Bauer and Vania Smith translate this phrase as, "none of them could therefore claim to have begun [their rule] in good faith." Pedro Sarmiento de Gamboa, *The History of the Incas*, ed. and trans. Brian S. Bauer and Vania Smith with intro Brian S. Bauer and Jean-Jacques Decoster (Austin: University of Texas Press, 2007), 203.

Chapter Eleven

Alonso de Illescas

"Suspend the Expedition"

In February of 1586, in the Province of Esmeraldas, in what is now Ecuador, a fugitive enslaved African named Alonso de Illescas wrote a letter to King Philip II of Spain. In that letter he promised to bring his rebellious Maroon community under the King's rule and pacify the nearby native Campaces if the king would refrain from sending a military expedition into the area to dominate it and set up Spanish settlements. Illescas and a few other enslaved men and women had been shipwrecked on the coast of Esmeraldas in 1553 and within a few years Illescas rose to a position of leadership of his mixed community of Africans and Native Americans. Born in Cabo Verde off the African coast, he was enslaved by a prominent Spanish merchant family, the Illescas, and had spent twelve years of his childhood and youth in Seville. He was thus fluent in Spanish and familiar with Spanish customs. The Maroon community he led was one of many that were formed in the New World from the earliest days of European colonization by escaped enslaved Africans. This essay will look at the history of slavery in Spain and its empire and of Maroonage in the New World before examining in more detail what we know about the life of Alonso de Illescas and about his letter to the king.

The history of slavery in Spain goes back to ancient times when Spain was part of the Roman Empire and members of the nations defeated by the Roman Army were enslaved, among them people of many ethnicities and occupations.[1] Slavery in Spain was strengthened after the 711 CE Moorish invasion by the almost continuous warfare between Muslims from North Africa and Christian Spaniards during which both sides captured their enemies and enslaved them. The Almoravids, who ruled much of Spain in the eleventh and twelfth centuries, established a kingdom that reached from Zaragoza in Spain to the Senegal and Gambia Rivers in Africa. Historian Gwendolyn Midlo Hall notes that as a result, "Many dark-skinned peoples appeared [in the

Iberian Peninsula] in the late eleventh century not as slaves but as warriors, conquerors, rulers, bards, and musicians." She adds that many paintings of meetings between Christians and Muslims in that period portrayed Muslim negotiators and generals as Black people.[2]

Meanwhile, in the 1460s, the Portuguese were exploring along the coast of Africa and bringing back enslaved Africans to Lisbon. Spanish merchants soon followed and by the end of the fifteenth century, Africa, which had been only one source of slaves among many had become the only remaining source of servile labor.[3] In this period, Seville and Lisbon had the biggest slave markets in Western Europe and enslaved Africans began to outnumber white slaves on the Iberian Peninsula.[4]

The first Spaniards and Portuguese in the New World enslaved many of the Indigenous people that they conquered, but the government of Spain decided, after high-level debates on the issue, not to allow permanent enslavement of Native Americans and, between 1526 and 1548, Emperor Carlos V issued several decrees prohibiting Spaniards from enslaving the Indigenous people.[5] Queen Isabella and King Ferdinand had, however, authorized the importation of slaves to the Americas in 1501 while prohibiting the entry of Jews, Muslims, or new converts unless they were Black Africans enslaved by Christians.[6] Introduction of slaves from Africa was seen very early as a way to replace laborers as millions of the Native inhabitants of the Western Hemisphere died of disease, war, and overwork. Friar Bartolomé de Las Casas himself suggested it as a way to protect the Indigenous people although he later came to regret this early view.[7]

Enslavement was used in Africa at the time as a punishment for persons convicted of serious crimes or captured in war. The trade goods carried by the traffickers tempted African leaders to enslave those convicted of lesser crimes and to wage war for the express purpose of capturing men, women, and children to sell into slavery. The Spanish monarchy earned a vast income from the licensing fees paid by Atlantic slave traders and from a tax on each enslaved person sold.[8]

Recent compilations of the records of transatlantic slaving voyages between 1501 and 1866 estimate that 12,521,337 persons embarked on slaving ships while 10,702,656 persons disembarked. The years of highest numbers were between 1676 and 1850 with by far the greatest number of slaves going to Brazil.[9] Historian James Ferguson King states that, in the sixteenth century, Mexico City and Lima probably had more Africans than Europeans while what later became the Viceroyalty of New Granada (and even later, Colombia) also had a large population of Africans.[10] Historian David Wheat's figures, based on previously unexamined port entry records, show "a minimum of 487 slave ships known to have arrived in Cartagena, a leading transfer point, between 1573 and 1640, disembarking at least 78,453 enslaved Africans in the city and neighboring ports."[11] During those years, 132 ships came from Upper Guinea and 218 from Angola.[12] In the sixteenth and seventeenth centuries, before the plantation economy took off in the 1700s, Africans in Spanish America worked in the mines, in construction as skilled and unskilled laborers, as servants, gardeners, and also as overseers and supervisors. Free Africans owned property and served in the military and in the professions.[13]

Spanish law dating from the 1200s, known as the *Siete Partidas*, recognized slaves as human beings with certain rights and protections. In contrast, in countries such as England, where slavery had not existed for centuries, there were no laws establishing the rights of slaves, and slaves were considered mere property. Under Spanish law, slaves could marry in the church, sue their owners for mistreatment in courts of law, and purchase their freedom. Enslaved men sometimes married Native American women so that their children would be born free.[14]

In 1685, as the result of an international dispute, King Carlos II summoned a council to rule on the slave trade. The ideas discussed ranged from those of Aristotle to those of Alonso de Sandoval. The council ultimately ruled that the traffic in enslaved people from Africa to America was legal, principally because it was viewed as economically necessary. From then on, discussions dealt only with the conduct of the trade or the harsh treatment of the enslaved.[15]

From the beginning, enslaved people rebelled. Rebellious movements and independent African communities that were called *palenques* in Colombia, *cumbes* in Venezuela, *quilombos* in Brazil, and Maroons in Jamaica and Guyana arose throughout the hemisphere over the years. One of the first uprising was in 1522 on the island of Hispaniola on the sugar plantation of one of the sons of Christopher Columbus. Others followed in what is now Colombia, Panama, and Mexico.[16] Writer Alberto Angulo states that the rebellion of Bioho in 1599 in Colombia became a symbol of freedom for all the Black people of the colony who rejected slavery.[17] Although Bioho was captured and hanged in 1619, the *palenque* he established remained independent for almost two hundred years.[18]

The province of Esmeraldas on the north coast of what is now Ecuador was home to a substantial Indigenous population with complex cultures that had remained unconquered by the Inca Empire but that suffered a disastrous population decline from Spanish raiding and disease. By the time of the wreck of Alonso de Illesca's ship in 1553, the Indigenous communities on the coast were gone and only small chieftaincies were left in the interior.[19] The Spaniards made more than fifty religious, military, and diplomatic expeditions to subjugate the region between 1526 and 1603 without success. In contrast, historian Charles Beatty-Medina notes that "Illescas and his small band of African renegades established a community that would thrive for generations; their survival resulted from factors that included the region's remote geography and its prolonged Indigenous resistance to Spanish rule."[20]

Alonso de Illescas was born on the Cape Verde Islands in the 1530s. When he was eight or ten years old, he was sent to Seville. As a child he had been called Enrique, but at his confirmation he took the name of his owner, Alonso de Illescas, the wealthy head of one of the major Spanish trading companies which sent both goods and enslaved Africans to the Indies. Alonso was likely a personal servant, and it is believed that he knew formal Spanish, played the guitar, and knew the Catholic prayers and sacraments. He may have assisted in the protection and safety of his owner.[21]

Alonso was sent to work for the Illescas firm first to Panama and, in 1553, to Peru. While sailing from Panama to the Peruvian port of Callao, he and twenty-two other enslaved Africans were able to take advantage of the wrecking of their ship on the coast of Esmeraldas Province to escape to freedom into the tropical forest. A man named Anton, the first leader of the fugitives, led the seventeen men and six women into an alliance with the local Indigenous people after defeating them in battle.[22] Africans and Amerindians intermarried and gave rise to a new ethnic group which at the time was called *mulatos* although the term used by the later *casta* system was *zambos*.

When Anton died or was killed, leadership passed to Alonso de Illescas. Fr. Miguel Cabello de Balboa, in the chronicle of his 1577 religious-diplomatic expedition to Esmeraldas, tells us that the Niguas Indigenous people

> began to be friends with one of these blacks called Alonso. Several groups in the region began to respect him as well because, though he was young, he was brave, a connoisseur of the Spanish customs, industrious in the art of war, and already fluent in the language of the region. . . . Therefore, these Indigenous people began to love him honestly and they gave him a beautiful Indigenous woman as his partner. She was the daughter of an important person with powerful relatives, who, as part of their strategy to maintain their power, helped him to acquire power and dominion over black and Indigenous people.[23]

The community led by Alonso de Illescas was not the only Maroon settlement in Esmeraldas. Andrés Mangache led a group of formerly enslaved people who had escaped a shipwreck around 1540–1542 and, after his death, leadership was taken up by his son Juan Mangache. The Maroon bands became sometime allies even though Alonso Illescas was suspected of being involved in Andres Mangache's death.[24] The isolated coast of Esmeraldas, according to anthropologist José Alcino Franch, is one of the few sites where the first contact between Old World and New was of Amerindians with Africans rather than with Europeans.[25]

While the Spanish officials at the *Real Audiencia* (crown court) in Quito[26] may have wanted the emeralds and gold of Esmeraldas, their main desire was to build a road that would connect the capital with the Pacific by the shortest possible route, which happened to be through Esmeraldas. And for that they needed to pacify the Maroons and their Native allies who could serve as a labor force and establish a settlement on the coast. The first expedition with which Alonso Illescas made contact was Captain Andrés Contero's failed mission of 1568. Contero did not see his mission as one of peaceful negotiations and, in 1570, imprisoned Illescas and his family. They were helped to escape by one of Contero's soldiers, Gonzalo de Avila. Avila then joined the Maroons and became Illescas's son-in-law.[27]

Illescas and his Maroons made a point of saving and assisting shipwrecked passengers along the Esmeraldas coast as a way of gaining favor with the Spanish authorities. In 1577, Illescas sent a letter to the authorities in Quito with a survivor of a 1576 shipwreck, a Catholic deacon named Juan de Reina.[28] In it Illescas offered to make peace with the Spanish Crown in exchange for recognition of his free status and that of his people. Beatty-Medina speculates: "If the *audiencia* had simply granted Illescas' request, an immediate peace would have resulted. Instead, in 1577 the judges set forth a grander scheme. They proposed to raise Alonso de Illescas, Maroon leader, to the post of *gobernador* [governor] of the region"[29] along with pardoning his offenses against the Crown and those of his followers. While treaties had been negotiated with Maroons before, never had a Maroon leader been named governor of a province.[30] But, along with the title of governor for Illescas, the Maroons would have to commit to pacify the Amerindians in the province, move the Maroon settlement from its hidden forest site to the coast, and establish a port town on the Bay of San Mateo.

The emissary sent to present the offer to Illescas was the above-mentioned Miguel Cabello de Balboa, a priest with military experience and a talent for writing. His report on the expedition, entitled the *Verdadera descripción de la provincia de Esmeraldas,* is one of the only eyewitness descriptions of a Maroon community in Spanish America.[31] Cabello de Balboa spent a month and a half on the coast of Esmeraldas, meeting with Illescas twice. The second meeting included the sons of Andres Mangache, Juan and Francisco, because Illescas wanted them to join the agreement and submit to the Crown and his governorship. When Illescas and the Mangache brothers left Cabello de Balboa to begin to gather their people to move to the coast, it appeared that the agreement was made. But they did not return. Cabello and a small expedition rowed upriver, where they found destroyed canoes and damaged orchards that led them to believe that there had been fighting among the local groups.[32] Alarmed, the Spanish prepared to leave.

In an attempt to understand Illescas's failure to return, Cabello de Balboa imagines a dialogue between Illescas and the people, particularly the Amerindians, under his rule. Illescas's subjects say to him:

> Leave aside the idea of surrender to your enemies, and you will not have any regret. Otherwise, regret will come and you will not be able to do anything but cry. If you do not want to do that for you, do it for us, because you are our father, we obey you and love you. Do not pay us back by putting our women and children in the hands of these bearded ones. They will punish you and your son-in-law as malefactors, your children will become slaves, and we never will be free again.[33]

Whatever the reasons, and Cabello Balboa's scenario seems possible, the Maroons in the end had rejected the proposal.

Between 1583 and 1585, Captain Diego López de Zuñiga, who had now been named governor of the province, carried out a number of unsuccessful expeditions in an attempt to "punish the blacks" and find the legendary gold and emeralds of Esmeraldas.[34] When Zuñiga's wife in Quito heard that the men were suffering and dying, she sent a young friar named Alonso de Espinoza and a few soldiers to assist her husband. Friar Espinoza, however, found that the Spanish fighters were returning to Quito, and he stayed on to assist the Maroons. Over the next years he became their advocate, pleading their cause with letters to the *Audiencia* in Quito in which he asserted that the Maroons had the right to reject conquest by the Spanish and that they were the ones best suited to pacify the Indigenous people of the region.[35]

In August of 1585, the rich merchant Rodrigo de Ribadeneira was working to be named governor of Esmeraldas. His plan was to shower the Maroons and their Indigenous allies with gifts and encourage Friar Espinoza to convince them to become vassals of the king and help in a project to bring Spanish colonizers to the region.[36] But, while Ribadeneira was maneuvering to receive his appointment and his brother, a military man, was assembling troops, Espinoza was writing to the king. The friar called Illescas the "key to the province" and wrote further: "The blacks and mulattos asked Your Majesty to grant them and concede to them a general pardon for all and sundry crimes committed against your Royal Crown as subjects and vassals and along with this letter of liberty as much for them as for their children. . . ."[37] The favors Espinoza asked for the Maroons and their Indian allies were similar to what Cabello Balboa had offered eight years earlier but Espinoza also urged autonomy for their territory. The King received the letter in early 1586 but merely asked for more information on the matter from the president of the *Audiencia*.

On February 24, 1586, Friar Espinoza was at the home of Juan Mangache when Alonso de Illescas arrived, an unusual occurrence as the two Maroon leaders had not spoken for eight years since their meeting with Cabello de Balboa. When Espinoza informed them of the appointment of Ribadeneira as governor and of his plans for colonization, Illescas indicated his obedience but that same day dictated to the friar a letter for the king (which is the letter we include here) asking him to modify his orders and not send Ribadeneira and the colonizers to Esmeraldas.[38] Illescas said that he and his people could bring the Indigenous Campaces under the king by peaceful means and settle them on the coast. Therefore, it was not necessary to bring in a military mission and cause more loss of life. In short, the Maroons would not assist Ribadeneira, and without their help the colonizing mission would fail.

Juan Mangache and fourteen Amerindians took Illescas's letter to the *Audiencia* in Quito, where, as historian Kris Lane notes, on April 14, 1586, "they ceremoniously rendered fealty, symbolized by a bow and quiver of arrows. The items were handed back to them with equal pomp, reluctant recognition of their continued, de facto autonomy."[39] Ribadeneira himself entertained the ambassadors and gave them gifts. However, on the return, Friar Espinoza (who had traveled with them) and Mangache were captured and, while Mangache was released, the friar was put in chains and sent back to Spain. However, he was rumored to have escaped and returned to Esmeraldas where he never interacted with the Spaniards again.[40]

Sometime between 1587 and 1596, Alonso de Illescas died in Esmeraldas. Beatty-Medina notes that he spent more than thirty years in freedom in the homeland he had created there and adds that just as important was the fact that he "passed this freedom on to his children and followers."[41]

In 1599, Francisco Adobe, Juan Mangache's brother, and Adobe's two sons made peace with the *Audiencia* in Quito and were baptized. They also had their portrait painted by Ecuadoran painter Andrés Sánchez Galque, dressed in fine garments and wearing the traditional gold ornaments of the Indigenous people of Esmeraldas. The painting was sent as a coronation present to King Philip III and is in the collection of the Prado Museum in Madrid.[42]

And, finally, in July of 1600, Sebastian and Antonio Illescas, sons of Alonso, traveled to Quito to swear fealty to the king of Spain. They were granted freedom, pardon for themselves and their subjects, and exoneration from tribute to the Crown in exchange for vigilance of the coasts for shipwrecks and pirates. They were confirmed by the bishop in a magnificent ceremony at the church of St. Blas, Sebastian taking name of his father Alonso and Antonio taking the name of Balthazar, traditionally the Black Wise Man.[43]

In the letter dictated by Alonso de Illescas and written down by Friar Espinoza in 1586, we have one of the few early examples of a document composed by an African person in rebellion. Most of the surviving early texts about Maroon communities were not produced by the members of those communities "or even from a point of view that recognized the value of their resilience and organization" as Spanish language scholar Ruben A. Sanchez-Godoy notes.[44] They are rather, for the most part, written by those who were trying to subdue them. Beatty-Medina states that, "Although Espinosa may have been the one to put pen to paper, much of the letter's contents reflects the experience and knowledge gained by Illescas from years steeped in Hispanic culture."[45]

Illescas insists that his desire is to serve the Spanish crown, and he expresses this in the way that he believes the crown wants to hear it. He states that he will do all in his power to "pacify all the natives of this province" and he will settle them close to the sea as the Audiencia desires. Sanchez-Godoy notes that the "narrative frame imposed by the dominant group reduces, without eliminating, the possibility of expression of the oppressed group."[46] And Martin Lienhard adds that texts (such as the Illescas letter), if properly read, are a priceless source that enable us to capture the discourse of the rebels.[47]

Illescas makes full use of religion in his letter, reminding the king in the first sentence of his previously expressed "desire to submit to God Our Father and to Your Royal Crown" and of his request for a priest to preach the Holy Gospel. He goes on to say that it would "be of disservice to God" and result in a loss of many souls to send Rodrigo de Ribadeneyra to dominate the Compaces by force of arms when he, Illescas, could bring them peacefully to know God. Beatty-Medina explains that the Esmeraldas Maroons "utilized religion for their own ends: the maintenance of their autonomy and authority in the region."[48] He goes on to say: "The Esmeraldeños were not only subjected to Christian conversion, they used agents of the church and religious rhetoric and symbols in their efforts to consolidate their position and power."[49]

Illescas immediately recognizes that Ribadeneyra's plan to pacify the Indigenous people by force and bring in Spanish settlers would mean loss of his territory, his leadership, and his freedom. But, as Sanchez-Godoy points out, Illescas is not seeking the same independence that South Americans wanted two centuries later. He is offering to submit to the king while conserving "an emancipatory space . . . designed to protect the fugitive Africans and their descendants rather than to constitute an independent territory that would guarantee absolute freedom for everyone."[50] But Illescas writes from a position of strength. He beseeches the king not to form another government in the areas that he offers to settle and predicts chaos if the king sends an expedition of soldiers to pacify the region. In the end, both the troops and the settlers failed, and Maroon autonomy was preserved.

The sixteenth-century Maroon heritage of Esmeraldas has lived on even to the present day. Historian Leslie Rout notes that the province has been "a preeminent center" of Black settlement since that time and it "has long possessed a tradition of Afro-Ecuadorean literary protest uniquely its own," the best-known example being the poet-novelist Adalberto Ortiz.[51] Maroon communities served as historical examples of struggle for the Black Power movements of the 1970s in Latin America and the Caribbean. Anthropologist Peter Wade states that the movement of Cimarronismo "took the cimarrón and the palenque as symbols of resistance to oppression and the continuity of African traditions," with Brazil, Colombia, and Jamaica particularly noteworthy in this regard.[52]

Alonso de Illescas's success in defending his Maroon community has been credited to his many special qualities and skills. Historian Rafael Savoia states that his success was based on his abilities as a strategist[53] while Lane says that he applied

> a confusing blend of tactics: now prodigious generosity, now shrewd negotiation, here offers of future assistance, there hints of unexploited treasure, and constant promises of submission—always followed by an unexpected, unannounced retreat to the interior. . . . Alonso de Yllescas seems to have preferred classic Renaissance dissimulation to the cruder and more risky practice of traditional guerrilla rebellion. Though shared with the Mangache-Arobe clan and several independent Indigenous bands, the Province of Esmeraldas was unequivocally his.[54]

Illescas's letter to King Philip, although mediated through the pen of Friar Espinoza, gives us a window into the thoughts on strategies and tactics of this sixteenth century leader of a rebellious African and Indigenous community in the forested coastal Ecuadoran province of Esmeraldas.

ALONSO DE ILLESCAS TO THE CROWN, 24 FEBRUARY 1586

Most powerful sir:

Having the devout Fray Alonso de Espinosa of the Holy Order of Trinitarians, by me and on my behalf, in a letter that he carried from me to your *Real Audiencia*, requested that I desire to submit to God Our Father and to Your Royal Crown and that on your part I be sent a general pardon and remission, because I have not been in your service, and that you send a priest to preach to us the Holy Gospel and teach our women and children, I will do everything in my power and I will try to pacify all the natives of this province.

And Your Highness having conceded what I have requested and entreated, I give thanks to God Our Father for the many mercies I have received from His most liberal hands and from Your Lordship.

And so Father Espinosa brought me news that Your Royal Highness in Spain has granted the government of this land to Rodrigo de Ribadeneyra, who will bring many people to pacify and populate this land. And so I ordered that we should all gather to discuss and communicate [to His Royal Highness] what will best serve your royal interest.

And if Your Royal Highness granted Rodrigo de Ribadeneyra this government, it was before, without our report expressing our desire and willingness to join in union with the Church and Your Royal Crown.

And so what can be conquered with the indoctrination of the Holy Gospel would only be of disservice to God and Your Majesty to conquer by force of arms and at the cost of many souls on the one hand, and on the other in order to dominate the Campaces and have them recognize and know of my God.

Therefore, because I have not been in your service, I will encourage the people under my command, and receiving your license to enter the territory of the Campaces and require them to surrender peacefully to your service. And I will settle them near to the sea in the best place possible. And in time I will ask your *Real Audiencia* for aid in order to form two towns in another province for Your Royal Crown that will be in the service of Our Lord.

Thus I beseech and supplicate Your Highness: do not form another government of the areas I offer to settle. Likewise, I ask Your Highness to suspend the expedition of soldiers; it will only bring chaos to the peace the devoted father [Espinoza] has brought with the Holy Gospel.

If you must allow a [Spanish] settlement, let it be in the Valle Vicioso and Barbacoas,[55] as I am truly afraid because your captains have always broken their promises given in Your Majesty's name. The devoted father [Espinoza] has gained our confidence, and we know it is from his heart that he comes to bring us into union with the Church and Your Royal Crown.

To prove and make credible what is contained herein, I am sending Juan Mangacho with the said father to the *Real Audiencia* [in Quito] to kiss the feet of Your Highness. And with the same trust as a most Christian king in all things, Your Highness will give us mercies, and [we desire] that Our Lord provide Your Highness with long life and the growth of many kingdoms and lands.

From the Province of Esmeraldas, the twenty-fourth of February [15]86, most powerful Lord, your humble vassal, Don Alonso de Illescas, kisses the feet of Your Highness.

And the letterhead of this letter says, "To the most powerful Lord, King Don Felipe, our Lord and his royal agreement in the *Real Audiencia* of Quito."

NOTES

1. Robin Blackburn, *The Making of New World Slavery: From the Baroque to the Modern, 1492–1800* (London and New York: Verso, 2010), 3.

2. Gwendolyn Midlo Hall, *Slavery and African Ethnicities in the Americas: Restoring the Links* (Chapel Hill: University of North Carolina, Press, 2005), 4.

3. Frederick P. Bowser, *The African Slave in Colonial Peru, 1524–1650* (Stanford, CA: Stanford University Press, 1974), 2.

4. Ann M. Pescatello, "The *Leyenda Negra* and the African in Sixteenth and Seventeenth Century Iberian Thought," *The Catholic Historical Review* 66, no. 2 (April 1980): 172. See also Leo Garofalo, "The Shape of a Diaspora: The Movement of Afro-Iberians to Colonial Spanish America," in *Africans to Spanish America: Expanding the Diaspora*, ed. Sherwin K. Bryant, Rachel Sarah O'Toole, and Ben Vinson III (Urbana: University of Illinois Press, 2012), 30.

5. Enriqueta Vila Vilar, introducción to Alonso de Sandoval, *Un tratado sobre la esclavitud* (Madrid: Alianza Editorial, 1987), 17.

6. Herbert S. Klein and Ben Vinson III, *African Slavery in Latin America and the Caribbean* (New York and Oxford: Oxford University Press, 2007 second edition), 22–23.

7. Bartolomé de Las Casas, *The Only Way*, ed. Helen Rand Parish, trans. Frances Patrick Sullivan, S.J. (New York: Paulist Press, 1992), 160–61.

8. Hall, *Slavery*, 20.

9. *Voyages: The Trans-Atlantic Slave Trade Database*. Voyages Database. 2009. Emory University. https://slavevoyages.org/assessment/estimates.

10. James Ferguson King, "Negro History in Continental Spanish America," *The Journal of Negro History* 29, no. 1 (Jan. 1944): 12, 14.

11. David Wheat, "The First Great Waves: African Provenance Zones for the Transatlantic Slave Trade to Cartagena de Indias, 1570–1640," *The Journal of African History* 52, no. 1 (2011): 2.

12. Wheat, "The First," 22.

13. Blackburn, 143,144; Nicole Von Germeten, introduction to *Treatise on Slavery: Selections from De instauranda Aethiopum salute* by Alonso de Sandoval, S.J., ed. and trans. Nicole von Germeten (Indianapolis: Hackett Publishing Company, 2008), xi.

14. Frank Tannenbaum, *Slave and Citizen: The Negro in the Americas* (New York: Vintage Books, 1946), 42, 48; David M. Davidson, "Negro Slave Control and Resistance in Colonial Mexico, 1519–1650," in *Maroon Societies: Rebel Slave Communities in the Americas*, ed. Richard Price (Baltimore: Johns Hopkins University Press, 1979), 85–87.

15. Vincent P. Franklin, "Alonso de Sandoval and the Jesuit Conception of the Negro," *The Journal of Negro History* 58, no. 3 (July 1973), 359.

16. José L. Franco, "Maroons and Slave Rebellions in the Spanish Territories," in *Maroon Societies: Rebel Slave Communities in the Americas*, ed. Richard Price (Baltimore: Johns Hopkins University Press, 1979), 35.

17. Alberto Angulo, *Moros en la costa: Vivencia afrocolombiana en la cultura colectiva* (Bogotá: Docentes Editores, 1999), 47.

18. Leslie B. Rout, Jr. *The African Experience in Spanish America* (Princeton: Markus Wiener Publishers, 2003), 110.

19. Charles Beatty-Medina, "Alonso de Illescas (1530s–1590s): African, Ladino, and Maroon Leader in Colonial Ecuador" in *The Human Tradition in the Black Atlantic,* ed. Beatriz Gallotti Mamigonian and Karen Racine (Lanham, MD: Rowman & Littlefield, 2010), 15.

20. Charles Beatty-Medina, "Maroon Chief Alonso de Illescas' Letter to the Crown, 1586," in *Afro-Latino Voices: Narratives from the early modern Ibero-Atlantic world, 1550–1812,* ed. Kathryn Joy McKnight and Leo J. Garofalo (Indianapolis: Hackett Publishing Company, 2009), 30–31.

21. Beatty-Medina "Alonso," 9–11, 13.

22. Jane Landers, "Maroon Women in Colonial Spanish America: Case Studies in the Circum-Caribbean from the Sixteenth through the Eighteenth Centuries," in *Beyond Bondage: Free Women of Color in the Americas*, ed. David Barry Gaspar and Darlene Clark Hine (Champaign: University of Illinois Press, 2004), 7.

23. Miguel Cabello Balboa, "Verdadera Descripción de la Provincia de Esmeraldas [1583]," in *Descripción de la Provincia de Esmeraldas*, ed. with notes and intro. by José Alcino Franch (Madrid: Consejo Superior de Investigaciones Científicas, 2001), 50–51, quotation translated by Rubén A. Sánchez-Godoy, "We Never Could Understand Why the Black Man Did Not Come to Us': Early African-Amerindian Subjectivities in Miguel Cabello Balboa's Verdadera Descripción de la Provincia de Esmeraldas (1583)," *Comparative Literature Studies* 49, no. 2, Special Issue: Comparative Perspectives on the Black Atlantic (2012): 175–176.

24. Sanchez-Godoy, "We Never Could," 179.

25. José Alcino Franch, introducción to *Descripción de la Provincia de Esmeraldas*, ed. with notes and intro. José Alcino Franch (Madrid: Consejo Superior de Investigaciones Científicas, 2001), 20.

26. The *Real Audiencia* or royal court of Quito was formed in 1563 under the Viceroyality of Peru. It had a president, judges, and other officials.

27. Rocio Rueda Novoa, *Zambaje y Autonomía: Historia de la gente negra de la provincia de Esmeraldas Siglos XVI–XVIII* (Esmeraldas, Ecuador: Municipalidad de Esmeraldas, Taller de Estudios Historicos, 2001), 54–56; Charles Beatty-Medina, "Caught between Rivals: The Spanish African Maroon Competition for Captive Indian Labor in the Region of Esmeraldas during the Late Sixteenth and Early Seventeenth Centuries," *The Americas* 63, no. 1 (July 2006, The African Diaspora in the Colonial Andes): 118.

28. Rueda, *Zambaje*, 57; Charles Beatty-Medina, "Between the Cross and the Sword: Religious Conquest and Maroon Legitimacy in Colonial Esmeraldas," *Africans to Spanish America: Expanding the Diaspora*, ed. Sherwin K. Bryant, Rachel Sarah O'Toole, and Ben Vinson (Urbana, IL: University of Illinois Press, 2012), 101.

29. Beatty-Medina, "Caught," 119.

30. Beatty-Medina, "Alonso," 17.

31. Beatty-Medina, "Between," 101.

32. Cabello Balboa, *Verdadera*, 74, 81. See also Beatty-Medina, "Alonso," 17–18; Beatty-Medina, "Between," 103; and Rafael Savoia, "El Negro Alonso de Illescas y sus descendientes (entre 1553–1867) *Actas del Primer Congreso de Historia del Negro en el Ecuador y sur de Colombia*, Edited by Rafael Savoia (Quito: Centro Cultural Afro-Ecuatoriàno, 1988) 38.

33. Cabello Balboa, *Verdadera*, 84–85; quoted and translated by Sanchez-Godoy, "We Never Could," 182.

34. Kris Lane, *Quito 1599: City and Colony in Transition* (Albuquerque: University of New Mexico Press, 2002), 33; Beatty-Medina "Between," 103.

35. Beatty-Medina, "Alonso," 18; Beatty-Medina, "Caught," 124.

36. Lane, *Quito,* 41; Beatty-Medina, "Alonso, 18.

37. "Alonso de Espinoza a la Audiencia de Quito, 22 mayo 1585," *Colección de documentos para la historia de la Audiencia de Quito*, ed. José Rumazo Gonzalez, 4:11–12; quoted and translated by Lane, *Quito,* 37.

38. Adam Szazdi, "El trasfondo de un cuadro: 'Los Mulatos de Esmeraldas' de Andrés Sánchez Galque," *Cuadernos Prehispánicos* 12 (1986–1987): 119. The original letter is titled *Alonso de Illescas a la Corona, 24 febrero 1586* and is in the Archivo General de Indias in Seville, Spain, Escribania 922b, folio 11.

39. Lane, *Quito*, 41; see also Szazdi, "El trasfondo," 119.

40. Beatty-Medina, "Alonso," 19–20; Lane, *Quito*, 42–43.

41. Beatty-Medina, "Alonso," 20.

42. Lane, *Quito*, 27, 50–51; Painting "Los tres mulatos de Esmeraldas" de Andrés Sánchez Galque, Museo del Prado. The painting can be viewed at https://www.museodelprado.es/coleccion/obra-de-arte/los-tres-mulatos-de-esmeraldas/1224cef3–e625–4ea6–9c27–2ae81d789e14.

43. Rueda, *Zambaje*, 71–72; Savoia, "El Negro Alonso," 44–45.

44. Sánchez-Godoy, "We never," 170.

45. Beatty-Medina, "Maroon," (2009), 32.

46. Sánchez-Godoy, "We Never," 171.

47. Martin Lienhard, *Disidentes, rebeldes, insurgentes: Resistencia indígena y negra en América Latina, Ensayos de historia testimonial* (Madrid: Iberoamérica, 2008), 17.

48. Beatty-Medina, "Between," 110.

49. Beatty-Medina, "Between," 100.

50. Sanchez-Godoy, "We Never," 177.

51. Rout, *The African*, 233–234.

52. Peter Wade, "The Cultural Politics of Blackness in Colombia," *American Ethnologist* 22, no. 2 (May 1995): 344. See also Anthony Ratcliff, "'Black Writers of the World, Unite!' Negotiating Pan-African Politics of Cultural Struggle in Afro-Latin America," *The Black Scholar* 37, no. 4 (Rethinking Pan-Africanism for the 21st Century, Winter 2008): 27.

53. Savoia, "El Negro Alonso," 34.

54. Lane, *Quito,* 33.

55. The Valle Vicioso and the region of Barbacoas were both located to the north of Esmeraldas in what is now Colombia.

Chapter Twelve

Luis de Carvajal the Younger

"May the Lord God of Israel Enlighten Them"

Luis de Carvajal the Younger was the leader of a group of clandestine practitioners of the Jewish faith in New Spain in the late sixteenth century. His
spiritual and biographical writings give us a window into the life and beliefs
of a family that eventually lost all of its members in New Spain to the Inquisition. Luis and his family had migrated to New Spain in 1589 when Luis was
thirteen years old. Family members were arrested twice by the Mexican Inquisition for practicing in secret the Judaism of their forefathers and mothers,
which the Spanish considered a crime. The first time they repented and were
pardoned but, the second time, after recurring in the "crime" of Judaizing,
they were burned at the stake. Author Ilan Stavans states that the family's
odyssey "is emblematic of the fate of the Iberian Jews known as *marranos,*
converts to Christianity during the late fifteenth century who emigrated to the
Americas. Their clash with the religious authorities, and the ensuing drama, a
drama that is about nothing but liberty, became the stuff of myth."[1]

The Holy Office of the Inquisition had begun to function in Spain in 1478,
and King Philip II formally established it in New Spain in 1571, although
bishops in the colony had held inquisitorial powers before that date. The
very first Inquisition had been established by the Catholic Church to investigate heresy in 1184 in France, then in Rome in 1229, and in Spain, as noted
above, in 1478. In all of Europe, following Martin Luther's posting of his
theses against Roman Catholicism in 1517, there was brutal conflict within
Christianity between the Catholic Church and the emerging branches of
Protestantism. And, in Spain, in the years after the Catholic monarchs Isabel
and Ferdinand conquered the final Muslim stronghold of Granada in 1492,
Muslims and Jews were forced to choose between conversion to Catholicism
or leaving the country. Toleration of different religious beliefs was still far in

the future. Historian Alicia Gojman de Backal states that the Spanish Inquisition became the symbol of intolerance, of coercion, and of the entombment of freedom of thought.[2]

Here we will examine briefly the life of Luis de Carvajal the Younger, then look at the history of the Inquisition in New Spain and discuss the Inquisition as representative of the ideas of intolerance of the era. The selections included are from Carvajal's memoirs and from the official documents of his second trial before the Holy Inquisition. The memoirs are believed to be the earliest conserved Jewish manuscripts from the New World and historian and Rabbi Ronnie Perelis calls Carvajal's life story the only surviving "autobiographical account written by a practicing crypto-Jew while still living in the Iberian world . . . within the grasp of the Inquisitors."[3] According to Perelis, Carvajal planned to send his memoirs to his brothers in Italy.[4] However, the Inquisition intervened and, instead, the memoirs were addendums to the records of his second trial and ended up in the Mexican National Archives.[5]

The memoirs have had an eventful recent history. They were stolen from the Archives in 1932 and remained missing until, in early 2017, a New York collector named Leonard Milberg saw them listed in a gallery catalog. Realizing their importance, he had them authenticated, digitized,[6] and repatriated to Mexico where they are now held at the Museum of Anthropology and History in Mexico City.[7]

Luis de Carvajal, the Younger, Biography

Luis was born in 1566 in Benavente, Spain, to Francisca de Carvajal and her husband Francisco Rodríguez de Matos, the fourth of their nine children. Luis's great-great-great grandparents had converted from Judaism to Christianity in 1492 when a royal decree mandated that all Jews either convert or leave Spain. Jews had lived relatively undisturbed in Spain since at least Roman times even while the English had expelled them in 1290 and the French in 1302.[8] Luis and his brother Balthasar studied at the Jesuit school in Medina del Campo where Luis was able to read the Bible (including the Old Testament), which was not normally available to laypeople. When Luis was thirteen, Balthasar told him that he was a New Christian, that is to say a convert, and that Baltasar and other family members followed the old religion in secret. Luis accepted the Law of Moses from that day forward.[9]

In 1580, the family accompanied Luis de Carvajal the Elder, Francisca de Carvajal's brother, to New Spain, where the elder Carvajal had been recently appointed governor of the province of Nuevo León. Not long after, Luis's father, Don Francisco, became sick and never fully recovered, dying in 1584.

The family moved from the coast to Mexico City in 1585. Luis the Younger joined his uncle, the governor, who did not practice the old faith, at the mines of San Gregorio and began a year and a half of service with him. Luis left his uncle's service after his sisters Catalina and Leonor married two wealthy New Christians, relieving the family from the poverty they had suffered after Don Francisco's death.[10]

In early 1589, Governor Carvajal was arrested by the secular authorities for political, nonreligious reasons. Historian Martin Cohen says he was the victim of the crown's policies of "delimiting the conquistadors' power . . . to prevent the rise of a semi-independent feudal-type baronial class."[11] And, as the result of a separate denunciation, young Luis's sister Isabel was arrested by the Inquisition and implicated her relatives. After her testimony, the Office of the Inquisition arrested her mother, her cousin Isabel, Luis the elder, Luis the younger, and even her brother Gaspar, a Catholic priest, who was accused of knowing that Isabel was practicing Judaism but not denouncing her to the Inquisition. Doña Francisca and Isabel were tortured.

In his first audiences in front of the Inquisitors between May and July of 1589, Luis denied practicing Judaism. However, on Aug. 7, 1589, Luis requested an audience and began a confession of Jewish practices, protecting those family members whom he believed had not been accused and implicating no one outside his family.[12] When Doña Francisca was tortured on the rack, her testimony went no further than that of Luis. However, when Isabel was tortured, she implicated all her siblings, resulting in the arrest of Leonor, Catalina, Mariana, and even ten-year-old Ana.[13]

On February 13, 1590, the Inquisitors announced their decisions. Luis's father Francisco and his brother Balthazar were ordered burned in effigy posthumously and in absentia respectively. The other members of the family, who had "repented" were to be reconciled to the Church. With the exception of young Ana, who was placed in the care of the family of a royal official, the remaining family members had to publicly abjure their crimes and were sentenced to wear a yellow vestment called a Sanbenito in public, observe special fasts, be instructed in the Catholic faith, and stay imprisoned in their homes or at work in a hospital, school or church for a period of years.[14]

Luis was assigned to complete his sentence at the San Hipolito Convalescent Hospital in Mexico City. Within a short time, however, Friar Pedro de Oroz arranged for him to be transferred from the hospital (where he had mopped floors) to the Colegio de Santa Cruz de Tlatelolco, where he tutored Indigenous students in Latin, helped Friar Pedro with his research, and had full access to the school's impressive library which was invaluable to him as he began writing his own works. Using the adopted name of Joseph Lumbroso, Luis began writing his memoirs probably in about the year 1591 and made the final entry shortly after October 1594.[15] Historian Richard Green-leaf notes: "His faith, a mixture of orthodox Judaism and Spanish mysticism, led him to write letters, memoirs and testaments which are priceless documents of social and intellectual history. His writings show the extent of the penetration of Jewish erudition into early Mexican culture."[16]

Luis writes in his memoirs that, after several years of penance, he received a letter from his brother-in-law "stating that my release had been granted in writing but that a certain sum had to be paid in Madrid before the decree of freedom became final."[17] He was granted permission to travel around the colony asking for alms[18] and was able to collect the sum needed. On October 24, 1594, the Carvajal family had their freedom restored and could remove the Sanbenito garments. They began planning to leave New Spain for another country where the Inquisition did not hold sway.

However, only a few months later, in January of 1595, two women who had witnessed Luis's participation in Jewish practices denounced him to the Inquisition and he was arrested on February 1st. When Luis learned about the evidence they had against him from a spy and from his writings, he made a 1,500-word confession which, however, maintained that his mother and sisters had not returned to Jewish practices. In spite of this, Doña Francisca, Catalina, Leonor, Isabel, and Ana were arrested in the spring of 1595.

On June 10, 1595, Luis heard his formal accusation from the Inquisition authorities. The inquisitors described him as "a formal relapse as a dogmatizing Judaizante, master and teacher of Judaism"[19] and ordered "that he be relaxed to the authorities and the secular arm"[20] to be burned at the stake. Although the Inquisitors had found out that most of the family had returned to Jewish practices, Luis continued to protect Catalina, Ana, and other people outside the family.

In spite of repeated attempts, the inquisitors were not able to extract much information from Luis that could help them to break up the circle he led of practicing Jews in New Spain.[21] So, on February 6, 1596, the Inquisitors voted to submit Luis to torture, which was carried out for the first time on February 8 and then again on February 9, 10, 12, and 14. While Luis confessed that Ana and Catalina practiced Judaism, he refused to implicate others until the final day when he gave his interrogators a full list. Cohen states that the pain of the confessions must have devastated Luis: "He, the leader and confidant of the secret Judaizers had exposed the cream of the community. He had been unsuccessful in his attempt to withhold information."[22]

But on February 15, Luis refused to ratify his confession. He said, "I protest against the torture because by the love of God His Holiness, I should not have been made to tell lies, and everything I said was a lie from the hour the torture began."[23] Cohen adds, "As Luis well knew, such testimony could mean only a resumption of torture." Around three o'clock in the afternoon, Luis threw himself from the second-floor corridors down onto a courtyard below in an attempt to commit suicide. He injured his right arm and his feet and was handcuffed in his cell to prevent another attempt.[24] On February 16, 1596, seeing no alternative, Luis ratified his confession. His sister Isabel endured the rack and waterboarding until finally completing her confession in September of that same year. Also in September, Luis presented to the authorities his spiritual testament in which he said that he would "live and die" in the Jewish faith.[25]

Five of the nine to be burned at the stake during the auto-da-fé on December 8, 1596, were members of the Carvajal family: Luis, Doña Francisca, Isabel, Catalina, and Leonor. The day began with a Mass at the cathedral followed by a procession to the burning ground at the San Hipólito market. Doña Francisca and her daughters had agreed to convert so they would be garroted before being burned. Although Luis had said he wished to be burned alive, the friar who walked beside him as he was being led to execution maintained that Luis said words at the end that indicated he had converted. Therefore, Luis was also garroted before he was burned. Whether he had actually converted or whether it was in the interest of the authorities to show that he had converted is something that cannot be known.[26]

The Inquisition

While a medieval Spanish inquisition existed in the Kingdom of Aragon as early as 1232, it was not until 1478 that Pope Sixtus IV authorized the establishment of a modern inquisition, first in Seville and later in the other regions of Spain. The Inquisition in Spain and the New World is inextricably linked to Spain's unique situation as home to Christians, Muslims and Jews. Historian Stuart B. Schwartz states:

> Beginning with the Arab conquest of Iberia in the eighth century and continuing through the Middle Ages, the three monotheistic religions of Judaism, Islam, and Christianity survived side by side. . . . Over the centuries, Christian populations had sometimes come under the rule of Muslim lords, Christian princes often ruled Muslim subjects, and depending on the place, Jews lived as subjects of both Christian and Muslim rulers. . . . [But] certainly by the fifteenth century [there was] an increasingly clear story of conflict and of separation as the areas under Muslim control were reduced and as a drive toward religious and political unity took place in the principal Christian kingdoms.[27]

In 1492, Queen Isabel and King Ferdinand issued an edict requiring that all Jews in their kingdoms of Castile and Aragon convert to Christianity or leave and ten years later a similar edict required Muslims to do the same. Jews and Muslims had not previously been subject to the Inquisition, which judged only Christians, but those who chose to remain in Spain after these edicts and who converted to Catholicism would now be under its jurisdiction and subject to punishment if they continued the practices of their former faith. It is thought, for example, that 91.6 percent of those tried by the Inquisition in Valencia between 1484 and 1530 were *conversos* of Jewish origin.[28] Most of those brought before the authorities were reconciled and not arrested again but a certain percentage were released to the secular authorities to be burned at the stake. Historian Jacqueline Holler adds that, in this early period, women accounted for around half of the *conversos* prosecuted "in part because of women's role in maintaining Jewish cultural and religious practices."[29]

Most scholars see the Spanish Inquisition as a political tool used by the monarchs at the end of the fifteenth century to unite their country as the final Muslim lands were coming under Spanish domination. Religion had been seen as an essential uniting force in Europe since the late Roman Empire and by the fourth century, when Christianity became the official religion of the Roman Empire, heresy was considered a crime against both God and the ruler by both religious and civil authorities. By the 1400s it was believed that heresy was a threat to public peace and a serious challenge to both church and state.[30] Historian John Chuchiak states:

> The Inquisition and its defense of Catholic orthodoxy remained essential for the survival of Spain and its worldwide empire, both at home and abroad. The blurring of the separation of church and state in the Spanish empire during this period led to the Spanish Inquisition's and its New World tribunals' continued association of heretics as religious and civil criminals.[31]

The Spanish inquisitors definitely recognized their political role, and it is important to note that they were paid from state coffers.[32] When the Spanish Inquisition committed violent excesses, as happened in 1482, Pope Sixtus protested to the heads of state, Isabel and Ferdinand.[33]

Before Philip II issued his 1569 decree establishing the Holy Office of the Inquisition in New Spain and Peru, similar functions had been carried out first by the clergy of the various religious orders (1522–1535) and later by the bishops (1536–1569).[34] But, under Philip's decree, between 75 percent and 80 percent of the population, the Indigenous people, were excluded from prosecution by the Inquisition. This exemption was inspired by notorious killings of Indigenous leaders committed earlier by some friars and bishops and by the feeling that the short time during which the Indigenous people had been exposed to Christianity was not sufficient to hold them to the same standards as others. Spaniards, other Europeans, and also Mestizos, people of African ancestry, and Asians, were, however, subject to the Inquisition. Historian Solange Alberro considers the inclusion of Africans an example of inconsistency in Spanish policy given Africans' recent and often superficial conversion (similar to that of the Indigenous people) and finds that Africans and individuals defined by the colonizers as Mulattos formed a substantial proportion of those brought before the Mexican Inquisition in the 1600s. Schwartz maintains, however, that, at least in Lima, Blacks, Mestizos, and Mulattos were less than 5 percent of the total Inquisition cases, with Spaniards making up the vast majority.[35]

The total population subject to the Inquisition likely totaled under half a million in all New Spain and Alberro notes, therefore, that the Inquisition in the New World did not have the power to carry out the same function of enforcer of national religious and political unity as it did in Spain.[36] Chuchiak argues that it was designed to control "seditious ideas and heretical propositions spread by foreigners and other dissenters in the colonial milieu." And, he adds that most of the cases before the tribunal concerned witchcraft, blasphemy, sexual offenses (especially bigamy and sodomy), prohibited books, and other similar crimes/sins, not doctrinal heresy per se.[37]

The first *auto-da-fé* held in Mexico City was in 1574 when two pirates were burned at the stake for practicing "Lutheranism," highlighting the struggle of the Catholic Church against Protestantism in the years following the Council of Trent (1545–1563) which had reaffirmed the traditional doctrines of the Church.[38] Over a hundred individuals were sentenced to death for practicing Judaism between 1571 and 1700, some of them burned in effigy. However, Greenleaf says that the Mexican Inquisition "failed to eradicate the judaizantes, who continued to practice the old religion in private and to proselytize. The size of the Jewish or crypto-Jewish community continued to increase in the seventeenth century despite Church and state caveats."[39]

The Inquisition played a role in the formation of what is known as the Black Legend, a series of beliefs about Spain as a place of cruelty and backwardness, which spread throughout the rest of Europe during this period portraying Catholic Spain as inferior to other European countries whose rulers were adopting faiths that were part of the Protestant Reformation. The Black Legend was based in part on Spain's horrific treatment of the Indigenous peoples of the New World, as denounced by Friar Bartolomé de Las Casas. Historian Thomas Madden states that the printing presses of Protestant Europe accused Spain of horrible atrocities in the New World and cast Spain "as a place of darkness, ignorance, and evil."[40] Kamen highlights the role of the Inquisition in the Black Legend when he refers to the "image of Spain as a nation sunk in intellectual torpor and religious superstition, all of it due to the Inquisition."[41]

The Inquisition was also used hundreds of years later by some scholars to portray Latin America as inferior to the United States. The late-nineteenth/early-twentieth-century Inquisition scholar Henry Charles Lea, who taught at major universities in the United States, wrote that Inquisition practices "go far to explain the influences which so long retarded the political and industrial development of the emancipated [Spanish] colonies, for it was an evil inheritance weighing heavily on successive generations."[42]

In the late 1500s, as noted above, the rulers of a number of European countries were joining the various branches of Protestantism that were separating from the Catholic Church. As in Spain, subjects who did not subscribe to the religion of their monarch were often condemned to death. Historian Edward Peters points out that, "Every European state based its legitimacy on religious grounds, and virtually every European state persecuted religious minorities."[43] He adds:

> Repressive legislation on both sides of the Reformation division, dramatic public punishments and executions, exile, and the loss of family and property helped to shape the self-perception of both Catholics and Protestants. . . . Accusations of conspiracy, assassination plots, treason, and blasphemy came to be as characteristic of much sixteenth-century religious self-definition as theological and ecclesiological differences.[44]

During this same period, Elizabeth I of England had Catholic priests executed as Queen Mary before her had executed Protestants.

Although the Black Legend arose in the 1500s, it continued for centuries. Its proponents did not take into account the vociferous debates in Spain and its empire about the natural rights of the peoples they "discovered" in the New World. These debates did not take place among other Europeans who conquered Indigenous peoples and were equally cruel in their treatment of them even if at the time they had no Inquisition in their territories.

So, how should the Inquisition, and in particular the Mexican Inquisition, be evaluated? Green summarizes the discussion in a way that can be applied to the case of the Carvajal family as well, "This is, in the end, the story of how persecution can arise and how it can be avoided; it is a story whose relevance never vanishes, a warning from the past."[45]

In his memoirs, Luis writes in the third person and uses his adopted name Joseph Lumbroso.

THE AUTOBIOGRAPHY AND INQUISITION
TRIAL OF LUIS DE CARVAJAL, THE YOUNGER

Autobiography of Luis de Carvajal, the Younger

[Written in] Mexico City, New Spain, [by] Joseph Lumbroso, of the Hebrew nation, a pilgrim in Occidental India, in devoted recognition of the favors and boons received from the hand of the Most High, who freed him from the gravest perils, in order that they may be known to all who believe in the Most Holy One and await the great mercies that He employs with sinners.

Awakened by the Spirit Divine, Joseph committed these to writing, along with the [story of] his life until the twenty-fifth year of his wandering, in the form of a brief history.

Before beginning he kneels on the ground before the universal God, the Lord of all mercy, and promises, with the God of truth always before him, to portray accurately everything that he writes below.

In the name of God, Adonay Sevaoth, the Lord of Hosts:

Joseph begins his life at the beginning. It should be mentioned that he was born and raised at Benavente, a city in Spain where he lived until the age of twelve or thirteen. There he began to receive instruction in the rudiments of Christianity from a relative, and he completed these studies in Medina del Campo [to which his family moved from Benavente]. There it pleased God's mercy to shed upon him the light by which he recognized His holiness. [It happened] on a special day, which we call the Day of Pardon, a holy and solemn occasion for us, [which falls] on the tenth day of the seventh month. Since God's truth is so clear and pleasant, all that his mother, his older brother, his older sister, and his cousin from that city had to do was to make mention of it to him [and he understood].

Joseph's father and his entire family emigrated to this land of New Spain, though they first planned to cross over into Italy, where all could better serve, worship and love the true God.

. . . [Luis's father died in New Spain probably in about 1585.]

God in his infinite and divine wisdom and mercy ordained that the Inquisition should arrest a widowed sister of theirs. She had been accused [of practicing Judaism] by a heretic who was one of our own people and whom a year before she had tried to indoctrinate into the truth of God. On learning of this, the brothers, struck with fright, decided to flee with their mother and [remaining] sisters, but some God-fearing [Israelites] friends, with whom they discussed the matter, convinced them that it was impossible for them [to take the women along]. After a painful separation which is beyond the power of my words to describe, the brothers therefore went off alone leaving their family exposed to danger, and wending their way to the cadence of their bitter cries and howls. [But] when they reached port, loaded their ship and were ready to embark, the thought of their mother and sisters exposed to mounting dangers overwhelmed them and made them change their plans. Joseph decided to return home and see what was going on, while his brother would remain behind and await word from him.

Two or three days after arriving home, Joseph went to visit his mother in the evening hours. By day they did not dare to be together, because of what they feared might happen. They were about to sit down to dinner when the constables and notaries of the Inquisition knocked on the door. When they opened it the Inquisitional officials set guards there, raised ladders, mounted them and came into the house to arrest Joseph's mother. Though wounded with this cruel enemy's fierce stroke, she donned the garb of modesty, bemoaning her troubles, yet praising the Lord who had sent them. She was then brought to the pitch-black prison by those ministers of malediction and executioners of our lives.

When her two maiden daughters saw their beloved mother sighing with such pain and sadness that she even moved to compassion the cruel and beastly enemies who were taking her away, they anxiously rushed toward her and cried, "Where are they taking you?" We leave to the prudent reader's imagination the feelings of their lamenting mother as she heard these words.

After she was taken away her son Joseph was arrested. They found him behind a door, where he had run for refuge out of fear of the atrocious tyrants. They pounced on him, seized him and carried him to the gloomy, black prison. Joseph uttered nothing except the words, "O God, reveal the truth." . . .

Since the imprisonment of Joseph and his mother dragged on and they remained in the hands of such cruel beasts, their fear made them hide their true identity, and they refrained from confessing publicly that they were keepers of the Lord God's most holy Law. For our affliction and travail has reached such a state that if anyone confesses and affirms [this fact] he is subjected by these heretics to exquisite torture and is [then] burned alive. And fear of this is responsible for their denial of their true identity.

One Friday morning, the Inquisitors, in order to determine whether Joseph and his family were practicing Judaism, summoned Joseph's mother for a hearing, as they had done on many previous occasions. Through a small hole which he and his companion had carved with two sheep bones at the threshold of his cell door, Joseph could watch his mother being led to the court of audience.

When the tyrants saw that she continued to deny [that her family practiced Judaism], they decided to subject her to torture. Preceded by the judges, notary, jailer and constable, she was therefore led to the torture chamber, where the torturer was standing, covered from head to toe with a shroud and white hood.

They immediately ordered the patient sheep to disrobe. They stretched her chaste flesh on the instrument of torture known as the donkey and tied her arms and legs. Then they cruelly twisted the ropes in its iron rings. As the ropes grated her flesh, she heaved the most pitiful sighs, which could be heard by all [the prisoners].

Joseph, on his knees in his cell, heard it all, and that day brought him greater affliction and bitterness than any that had gone before. But he was not without the divine consolation that comes from the hand of the Lord. Blessed be His holy name forever. In the midst of that day of affliction, the Lord permitted him to doze off by the door of his cell. On other days, if he fell asleep for a moment, he awoke melancholy and faint, but not that day.

As soon as he fell asleep, he saw the Lord sending him a man who was a paragon of virtue and patience. He was a fearer of God, one of his own people. In his hands he carried a large and beautiful yam. He showed it to Joseph and said, "Look! What a handsome and beautiful fruit!"

To this Joseph replied, "Indeed."

He gave it to Joseph to smell. Joseph blessed the Lord, creator of all, and said to the man, "Indeed, it smells good, indeed." The man then cut the yam in two and said to him, "Now it smells better."

The man then gave Joseph the interpretation. He said, "Before being imprisoned and racked with torture, your mother was whole and she smelled sweet; she was a fruit of sweet savor before the Lord. But now, when she is cut with torture, she exudes the superior fragrance of patience before the Lord."

With this Joseph awoke and was consoled. May the Most High God, who brings consolation to the afflicted, likewise be adored and extolled. . . .

When Joseph and his family left their prison [duly] penanced and cloaked in the distinctive garb which the enemies of the Law of God require for those who have been convicted of keeping it, the Inquisitors wished to separate the family. They wanted to put each of the women in a different room of a convent that in the company of its idolaters they might suffer twice as much as before. But the Lord in His infinite mercy frustrated this plan. He moved the Inquisitor himself to mention it to Jorge de Almeyda, one of Joseph's brothers-in-law, in whose mouth the Lord put the following reply: "Sir, the action you are contemplating should be well considered before you put it into effect. Do not forget that women are extremely curious and impressionable. The [damaging] influence [of these women] upon the nuns might be very difficult to counteract."

This made quite an impression on the enemy. At the Lord's prompting the Inquisitor changed his mind, and instead of such confinement for life, which is the standard punishment for penitents, he arranged for the women to be given a house where they could all live together—for the sake of the Lord.

Joseph was separated from them and assigned to a hospital, where he was made keeper of the idols—which afflicted him not a little—and employed in other tasks, such as sweeping the floors, which he did after he had moistened them with his tears. But the Lord his God came to his rescue again as He had in all hid previous difficulties.

When Joseph despaired of returning to the company of his mother and sisters—he did not even know how he could ask for such a thing—God on High, who was even more grieved, provided a remedy. He ordained that one of Joseph's brothers-in-law find it necessary to take a trip to Tasco and leave Joseph's mother and sisters alone. He [therefore] went to ask the Inquisitor the favor of allowing Joseph to stay with them while he traveled. This was the first step taken by the Most High to remove Joseph from [what he regarded as] his second captivity, where he sat and wept disconsolately because he was forced to eat forbidden foods. Highly exalted by the Most High, who thus came to Joseph's aid in all his difficulties.

When he returned to his mother and sisters, Joseph found that their enemies' threats and some friends' evil counsel had persuaded them to buy and eat Gentile foods, forbidden by the Law of God. With divine inspiration Joseph changed this. He set before them the example of the saints who preferred to be torn to shreds by cruel tortures rather than eat forbidden foods or even pretend to eat them. But since their hearts were steadfast with their God and Lord—the family had been acting out of fright—little was needed to convince them of their wrongdoing. With many tears and affirmations of their reverence of heaven, they turned again to their God and Lord and added to their merit by rejecting all filthy foods.

As the time drew near for Joseph to return to the hospital where he served, an old monk, a man of great virtue, came to see his mother. The Inquisitor had asked him to be the family's confessor and guardian.

Joseph's mother importuned the monk to secure permission for Joseph to remain on with her and the family. And Joseph received this permission with the requirement that he spend his daytime hours working in a school for Indians [El Colegio de Santa Cruz] which the monk directed. Joseph was given the responsibility of teaching grammar to some of the Indians and helping the monk with his letters and sermons. The Lord his God gave Joseph such favor [in the eyes of] this man that he loved him dearly and cherished him, and not only he, but all his staff as well.

Since the carnivorous wolves had confiscated the family's property and left them destitute, the Lord maintained them in their affliction for four and a half years by having the monk support them from his own pocket and from charities of the Church that was so hostile to them. The Lord's performing a miracle for such sinful and wretched people [as Joseph and his family] is even more striking than His performance of a miracle with the innocent and saintly Daniel. . . .

During this time Joseph received word in letters from his brother-in-law [in Spain], informing him that his liberty . . . had been attained, but for lack of funds, which had to be paid in Madrid, the documents could not yet be [released and] forwarded. . . . Joseph asked the Inquisitor's brother, for whom he was copying [a] notebook to help him get permission to move about freely in order to obtain alms [to pay] for his liberty. By command of the omnipotent Lord God, Joseph was given six months' leave.

Taking . . . letters and the favor of the Lord his God with him, Joseph left his confinement in Mexico City after four years of anguish and affliction. Yet in the midst of it, he was abundantly aided by the Most High. [Now] wherever he went, God's divine majesty gave him grace. In was no small miracle that he moved his very enemies to shower him with their gifts of money, hens, cheese, corn and other items. Laden with these, he would return to the house of his penance, where his mother and sisters still lived.

Whenever Joseph came to a monastery, he was provided with lodging and offered food; but ever mindful of the Law and commandment of his Lord God, he refused the food to avoid defiling himself, saying that he had already eaten. It often happened, when he left the company and board of these men whom he loathed, that he went to eat his bread among the beasts, thinking it better to eat among horses in cleanliness than in uncleanliness at the tables of his well-bred enemies. . . .

Joseph collected more than eight hundred and fifty pesos in alms from the hands of the barbarous Gentiles. May the Lord God of Israel enlighten them and bring them to a recognition of His holiness, that He may be adored and served by all His creatures. His mighty hand moved them to give Joseph these alms so willingly in most places that it was clear that the alms were coming from the Lord. Then Joseph and his mother received word that the brother-in-law . . . had succeeded with the favor of the Most High, in obtaining the family's restoration to liberty. [T]his news arrived in time to serve as celestial medicine for Joseph's mother, for with its joy the Lord revived her from an illness that had her at the brink of death. . . .

On Monday, October 24, 1594, on the command of God Most High, their penitential garb was removed. . . . And because the road along which the Lord God has been leading them has been full of mercies, and His rod has been only the soft scourge of fear, He decreed that on the following Monday, a week after [they had taken off their penitential garb], they should suffer a new blow, one of the most severe yet—though they never suffered any from which the Lord God, in His infinite mercy, did not deliver them in two hours. What this blow was and how it came about are not being recorded for the time being, because the writer is still in lands of captivity, though with the help and favor of the Omnipotent and Almighty Adonay, the God of Israel, he is on the verge of leaving one of the greatest and most dangerous captivities which members of our nation have suffered. Here by the singular kindness of the Lord our God he and his family have been living in a danger no less great than the one which confronted Saint Daniel when he was thrown into the lions' den. The Almighty very miraculously shut the cruel mouth of the [enemies] surrounding him, for had not the Lord our God intervened, he would have immediately been torn to pieces.

Wherefore I humble my heart, worship, and glorify God's most holy name and declare that He is good and very great, and His mercy is eternal. May it help us and all Israel. Amen.

Inquisition Trial

Selected Autos and Proceedings of the Second Trial against Luis de Carvajal the Younger, Reconciled by This Holy Office as a Judaizer, a Relapsed Practitioner of Judaism, and a Formal Heretic, Mexico City, 1594–1596; Source: Archivo General de la Nación, Ramo de Inquisición, vol. 1486, exp. 1. Auto and Proceedings of the Second Trial against Luis de Carvajal the Younger, 1596 [Accusation, June 10, 1595]

Luis de Carvajal the younger, reconciled by this Holy Office, son of Francisco Rodriguez Matos, deceased and condemned, and of Doña Francisca Núñez de Carvajal, reconciled of the generation of New Christians, alias *Joseph Lumbroso.*

As seen by us, the inquisitors against heretical depravity and apostasy in the City and the Archbishopric of Mexico and the provinces of New Spain and its district, by the apostolic and ordinary authority, a lawsuit and criminal case that was pending before us and was pending between Dr. Martos de Bohórquez, the Prosecutor of this Holy Office and accusing member, and the other, the accused defendant, the said Luis de Carvajal the younger, reconciled and changed in name in the Law of Moses, Joseph Lumbroso, who a formal relapse as a dogmatizing Judiazante, master and teacher of Judaism, for which reason the said Prosecuting Attorney denounced and criminally accused him before us, saying that the above-mentioned in previous years was imprisoned in this Holy Office, testifying and accused, despite being a baptized and confirmed Christian, he had guarded and believed in the Old Law and the death of Moses, his rites and ceremonies, and seemingly by exterior trial to be satisfied with the proof and testimony received against him, and that of true heart and faith not feigned he converted to our Holy Catholic Faith, repenting and separating from his errors and heresies, and from his feigned tears and signs that he used in the Public Act of faith that was celebrated in this city this past year of 1590, using with him the leniency and clemency that he did not merit, having been admitted and reconciled to the fold of the Holy Catholic Church, under the promise and solemn judgment that was publicly done then that he not return again to those heresies or to other persons, who abjured and detested [desisted], and submitted himself to the just and severe punishment of fire constituted by relapse, and he had signed his name; and he was like a dog who returns to his own vomit after his abjuration and reconciliation, with the natural ingratitude of Jews and their hardness and perverseness, forgetting the undeserved mercy and benefit that he had received, he returned to his previous beliefs and keeps the Law of Moses, and its rites and ceremonies, that in the milk and hopes of his parents, he was suckled, thinking and believing to be saved in it as in the Good Law given by God to Israel, that promised to those who kept its glory, riches, and worldly goods, and not in our Lord Jesus Christ, whom they do not have as God.

That the said Luis de Carvajal the younger does not believe, nor has he ever believed in Christ our Lord, (and he has) made jests of the Holy Sacraments that were left instituted in his church, and excluding all of that he rejected oral confession and confessed only to God, making laughs and jokes about the Consecrated Host and how His precious and true body was moldy, calling Him inappropriate and strange names concerning His Divinity and Holy Humanity, and others about Our Lady, insulting her dignity; affirming that he was a truly baptized person. He was circumcised, which was ordered by God to Abraham, by means of which men were saved and by no other manner, and it was done in this New Spain, under a palm tree, and he was circumcised with some scissors, with which he arrived at the point of losing his life.

Vote for the Administration of Questioning under Torment in the Case against Luis de Carvajal the Younger, February 6, 1596

In the City of Mexico, Tuesday, 6th of February of the year 1596, being present in the audience chamber of the Holy Office, during the afternoon, in consultation and after having seen the proceedings in the case, the Lord Inquisitors Dr. Lobo Guerrero and Licenciado Don Alonso de Peralta, Dr. Juan de Cervantes the Archdeacon of the Holy Cathedral of this city and the governor of the Archbishopric who serves as the ordinary, and in the presence of the consultants the Lords Dr. Saavedra Valderrama, Dr. Santiago del Riego, and Licenciado Francisco Alonso de Villagra, Judges of the Audiencia and Royal Chancery of this city, and Licenciado Vasco López de Vivero, Corregidor in this city by order of His Majesty, the criminal case against Luis de Carvajal the younger was reviewed, and all were in conformity and voted that it was their opinion that the above-said should be put to questioning under torment *in capit alienum* so that he should state and declare the truth concerning his accomplices and other people who know and continue to guard the Law of Moses, and depending on what should result, the case should be seen again.

Signatures: Dr. Lobo Guerrero, Lic. Don Alonso de Peralta, Mtro. Don Juan de Cervantes, Lic. Saavedra Valderrama, Dr. Santiago del Riego, Lic. Francisco Alonso de Villagra, Lic. Vivero.

Second Vote concerning the Continued Administration of Questioning under Torment in the Case against Luis de Carvajal the Younger, February 14, 1596

In the City of Mexico, during the afternoon of Wednesday the 14th of February of the year 1596, being present in the audience chamber of the Holy Office in consultation and after having seen the proceedings in the case, the Lord Inquisitors Dr. Lobo Guerrero and Licenciado Don Alonso de Peralta, and Dr. Juan de Cervantes, the Archdeacon of the Holy Cathedral of this city and the governor of the Archbishopric who serves as the ordinary, and in the presence of the consultants, Lords Dr. Saavedra Valderrama, Dr. Santiago del Riego, and Licienciado Francisco Alonso de Villagra, Judges of the Audiencia and Royal Chancery of this city, and Licenciado Vasco López de Vivero, Corregidor in this city by order of His Majesty, the criminal case against Luis de Carvajal the younger was reviewed again, concerning the article of whether to continue the questioning under torment which was begun on the 8th of the present month and year, and concerning the diligences made with the accused in the torture chamber, and they voted in the following form:

The Lord Inquisitors Dr. Lobo Guerrero, Dr. D. Juan de Cervantes, the ordinary, and Licenciado Francisco Alonso de Villagra were all in agreement and voted that the torture should not continue, because it is their belief that it is sufficient.

The Lord Inquisitor Licenciado Don Alonso de Peralta, was of the vote and opinion that they should give him three or four more turns of the cords of the rack on his arms.

Their Lords Licenciado Saavedra Valderrama and Dr. Riego were of the vote and opinion that the torture should be continued.

The Lord Corregidor voted that the accused be placed under an order of *Conmitatio* and admonished under pains of punishment to tell the truth.

Signatures: Dr. Lobo Guerrero, Lic. Don Alonso de Peralta, Mtro. Don Juan de Cervantes, Lic. Saavedra Valderrama, Dr. Santiago del Riego, Lic. Francisco Alonso de Villagra, Lic. Vivero.

Before me, Pedro de Mañozca, Secretary

Vote and Definitive Sentence against Luis de Carvajal, the Younger, February 16, 1596

Attending to the acts and merits of the case, the Promotor Fiscal has fully proven his accusation according and how it should be done, and we find and pronounce that he has submitted sufficient proof, in consequence of which we must and do declare that the said Luis de Carvajal, having been and being a practicing Jewish heretic and apostate to our Holy Catholic Faith, an accomplice and one who hides heretical practicing Jews, a false converted Jew, an impenitent, relapsed and pertinacious dogmatist and by this having fallen and incurring the sentence of High Excommunication, and to be combined with this the confiscation and loss of all his goods from the time that he began to commit his crimes of heresy, the proceeds of which we order applied to the Royal Treasury of your Majesty and your Receptor should receive them in your name. We also declare that we must relax [release] and we do relax the person of the said Luis de Carvajal to the Justices and Secular Arm, especially to Licenciado Vasco López de Vivero, Corregidor of this City, so that the punishments should be executed.

Signatures: Dr. Lobo Guerrero, Lic. Don Alonso de Peralta, Mtro. Don Juan de Cervantes, Lic. Saavedra Valderrama, Dr. Santiago del Riego, Lic. Francisco Alonso de Villagra, Lic. Vivero.

Before me, Pedro de Mañozca, Secretary

Judgment and Definitive Sentence of the Corregidor Licenciado Vasco López de Vivero, in the Case against Luis de Carvajal, for the Crime of Relapsing into Judaism after Having Been Reconciled in the Auto-da-fé of 1590; December 8, 1596

Attending to the guilt of the said Luis de Carvajal, I must condemn and order that he be led through the public streets of this city, mounted on a saddled mule. With the voice of a town crier his crimes shall be proclaimed, and he shall be carried to the marketplace of San Hipólito, and in the part and place which has been designated, he shall be burned alive and thrown into the living flames of fire until he is turned to ashes, and of him there will remain no memory. By this means I give my definitive sentence, and thus I pronounce it and order it.

Licenciado Vivero

*Execution of the Sentence against Luis de Carvajal, the Younger,
December 8, 1596*

In the city of Mexico, on the same day, month, and year, in completion of the said sentence, being the said Luis de Carvajal on a saddled horse, was carried through the customary street with the voice of a public crier proclaiming his crime. During the procession, there was a demonstration that the prisoner had been converted and took in his hand a crucifix, and he said some words by which it was understood that he had converted and repented. And due to this, having arrived at the bonfire which was in the marketplace of San Hipólito, he was garroted until he died naturally, and having appeared (dead) he was put on the fire and his body remained burning within the flames until it became a cinder.

Present as witnesses were Balthazar Mexía Salmerón, Chief Constable, and Pedro Rodríguez, and Juan de Budía and Francisco de Benavides, and their lieutenants and many other persons.

Before me, Alonso Bernal, Public Notary

NOTES

1. Ilan Stavans, introduction to *The Martyr: Luis de Carvajal: A Secret Jew in Sixteenth Century Mexico*, by Martin A. Cohen (Albuquerque: University of New Mexico Press, 2001), xix.

2. Alicia Gojman de Backal, "Luis de Carvajal El Mozo. Sus Memorias, correspondencia y su testamento," *Diario Judio*, Feb. 3, 2017, http://diariojudio.com/opinion/luis-de-cavajal-el-mozo-sus-memorias-correspondencia-y-su-testamento/231239/#.

3. Ronnie Perelis, *Narratives from the Sephardic Atlantic: Blood and Faith* (Bloomington, IN: Indiana University Press, 2016), 32–33.

4. Perelis, *Narratives*, 27.

5. Gojman de Bakal, "Luis."

6. The *Memoirs* can be viewed online here: http://digitalcollections.nyhistory.org/islandora/object/nyhs%3A10467#page/1/mode/2up.

7. "Los manuscritos de Luis de Carvajal, germen de la literatura judía en América, al acervo de la BNAH," Instituto Nacional de Antropología e Historia, Mar. 23, 2017. https://www.inah.gob.mx/boletines/6007–los-manuscritos-de-luis-de-carvajal-germen-de-la-literatura-judia-en-america-al-acervo-de-la-bnah.

8. Anna Lanyon, *Fire and Song: The Story of Luis de Carvajal and the Mexican Inquisition* (Crows Nest, New South Wales, Australia: Allen and Unwin, 2011), 7, 9–12.

9. Martin A. Cohen, *The Martyr: Luis de Carvajal: A Secret Jew in Sixteenth Century Mexico* (Albuquerque: University of New Mexico Press, 2001), 30–34.

10. Gojman de Bakal; Cohen "Luis," 7.

11. Cohen, *The Martyr*, 108.

12. Lanyon, *Fire*, 102; Cohen, *The Martyr*, 165.

13. Cohen, *The Martyr*, 170–71.

14. Cohen, *The Martyr*, 174.

15. Cohen, *The Martyr*, 204.

16. Richard Greenleaf, *The Mexican Inquisition of the Sixteenth Century* (Albuquerque: University of New Mexico Press, 1969), 171.

17. Luis de Carvajal, *The Enlightened: The Writings of Luis de Carvajal, el Mozo*, trans. and ed. with intro. Seymour B. Liebman (Coral Gables, FL: University of Miami Press, 1967), 79.

18. Cohen, *The Martyr*, 216–217.

19. John F. Chuchiak IV, *The Inquisition in New Spain, 1536–1820: A Documentary History* (Baltimore: The Johns Hopkins University Press, 2012), 240.

20. Cohen, *The Martyr*, 241.

21. Cohen, *The Martyr*, 242–43.

22. Cohen, *The Martyr*, 244–45.

23. Quoted in Lanyon, 277.

24. Cohen, *The Martyr*, 46.

25. Lanyon, *Fire*, 280–85.

26. Gojman, "Luis," 11; Lanyon, *Fire*, 318; Cohen, *The Martyr,* 259.

27. Stuart B. Schwartz, *All Can Be Saved: Religious Toleration and Salvation in the Iberian Atlantic World* (New Haven and London: Yale University Press, 2008), 43–44, 47.

28. Henry Kamen, *Inquisition and Society in Spain in the Sixteenth and Seventeenth Centuries* (Bloomington: Indiana University Press, 1985), 41.

29. Jacqueline Holler, "'More Sins than the Queen of England' Marina de San Miguel before the Mexican Inquisition," In *Women in the Inquisition: Spain and the New World*, ed. Mary Giles. (Baltimore: Johns Hopkins University Press, 1999), 115.

30. Chuchiak, *The Inquisition*, 3.

31. Chuchiak, *The Inquisition*, 4.

32. Solange Alberro, *Inquisición y sociedad en México 1571–1700* (Mexico: Fondo de la Cultura Económica, 1988), 152, 158.

33. Toby Green, *Inquisition: The Reign of Fear* (New York: St. Martin's Press, 2007), 11.

34. Chuchiak, *The Inquisition*, 8.

35. Alberro, *Inquisición*, 22, 26, 455; Schwartz, *All Can Be*, 129.

36. Alberro, *Inquisición*, 9.

37. Chuchiak, *The Inquisition*, 12, 7.

38. Holler, "More Sins," 119.

39. Richard E. Greenleaf, "Historiography of the Mexican Inquisition: Evolution of Interpretations and Methodologies," in *Cultural Encounters: The Impact of the Inquisition in Spain and the New World*, ed. Mary Elizabeth Perry and Anne J. Cruz (Berkeley: University of California Press, 1991), 266.

40. Thomas F. Madden, "The Real Inquisition: Investigating the Popular Myth," *National Review*, June 18, 2004, 3.

41. Kamen, *Inquisition*, 99.

42. Henry Charles Lea, *The Inquisition in the Spanish Dependencies* (New York: The MacMillan Company, 1908), vii.

43. Edward Peters, *Inquisition* (New York: The Free Press, 1988), 122.

44. Peters, *Inquisition*, 128.

45. Green, *Inquisition*, 14.

Chapter Thirteen

El Inca Garcilaso de la Vega
"Past Greatness and Prosperity"

El Inca Garcilaso de la Vega was the son of a Spanish conquistador and an Incan princess and thus one of the early mestizos of Peru. The first person from the New World to publish a book in Europe, he became a prominent figure in Spanish letters[1] and his works *The Royal Commentaries of the Incas* and *General History of Peru* influenced European and Latin American thought for centuries. Although he spent most of his life in Spain, he never forgot his Peruvian ancestry and added "El Inca" to his name shortly after arriving in Europe.

El Inca Garcilaso was born Gómez Suárez de Figueroa in Cuzco, Peru, on April 12, 1539. His father, Captain Sebastián Garcilaso de la Vega y Vargas, had arrived in Peru with Pedro de Alvarado in 1534, two years after Francisco Pizarro's landing there in 1532. At the time, the Incas were not yet subdued, and there were, as well, fierce battles among the Spaniards. The Captain's companion, Garcilaso's mother, was Isabel Suárez Chimpu Ocllo, niece of the Inca Huayna Capac and granddaughter of Inca Tupac Yupanqui.[2] Garcilaso, like other children of conquistadors and Inca noblewomen, was exposed to both cultures. In 1549, when he was ten years old, his father, following a new rule from Madrid, married a well-born Spanish woman and married Isabel off to a Spanish foot-soldier with a dowry. Garcilaso moved to live in his father's house and visited his mother and her relatives in their homes. From a Spanish tutor, he learned Spanish, Latin, and other skills such as swordsmanship appropriate to the child of an aristocratic Spanish family while from his mother and her relatives he learned Quechua and the traditions and customs of the Incas as well as the origin and history of the Inca Empire. As he grew older, he served as his father's clerk.[3]

In 1560, Garcilaso's father died, and, with the small inheritance left him, the young man sailed for Spain to study. He took part in two military campaigns (in 1564 and 1570) and spent time in an unsuccessful effort to rehabilitate his father's reputation which had suffered after he was suspected of supporting Gonzalo Pizarro's rebellion against the crown. But, after receiving an inheritance from his father's brother in 1570, he spent the rest of his life in study and writing in the village of Montilla and later in the city of Cordoba.[4]

It was in Spain that he took the name of his father and a poet ancestor Garcilaso de la Vega (1503–1536) and also began to call himself "El Inca." Inca Garcilaso's will, which included a list of the books he owned, was discovered in Spain in 1948. Literary scholar Sara Castro-Klaren states that the list showed that "The Inca had clearly immersed himself in the Italian Renaissance, the Christian theological and philosophical tradition, the rediscovery of Greek and Roman culture, and the literature and political thought of his Spanish contemporaries."[5]

Garcilaso's first published work, in Madrid in 1590, was a translation from the Italian into Spanish of *The Dialogues of Love*, a Neoplatonic philosophical work by Judah Abravanel, also known as Leo Hebraeus. This book, although it was later withdrawn from publication by the Inquisition, brought Garcilaso recognition as a major figure in Spanish Renaissance letters. One scholar notes: "With this work, Garcilaso established himself as a European humanist scholar of the highest caliber, yet he called attention to his mestizo status by styling himself 'Inga' on the title page."[6] By daring to call himself mestizo in a full-throated way, he could express the intellectual possibilities gestating in a world that was both Spanish and Indigenous.[7] Neoplatonic philosophy sought to reconcile conflicting schools of thought, and whether it helped to form Garcilaso's ideas or was found by him to embody ideas he already held, it would be reflected strongly in his future writing. His next work, entitled *La Florida del Inca* and published in 1605, was a chronicle of Hernando de Soto's expedition to Florida, based on the recollections of his friend Gonzalo Silvestre, one of the members of that expedition.

Meanwhile, Garcilaso wrote his mestizo classmates in Peru asking for their memories of the stories of Incan life and history, brought together an impressive library of chronicles of the conquistadors and the friars who accompanied them, and began his two-volume work on the Inca civilization in Peru and the conquest of Peru by Spain. Inca Garcilaso said that the first volume, the *Royal Commentaries of the Incas*, was written to fulfill an obligation to his mother's people, and the second, the eventual name of which was *General History of Peru*, written to fulfill an obligation to his father's line. The first volume, completed in 1604, was published in Lisbon in 1609 after approval by the Inquisition, and the second, completed in 1612, was published in 1617 in Córdoba. But Garcilaso died before the *General History* was published—

Figure 13.1. Remains of El Inca Garcilaso de la Vega in the Mosque/Cathedral of Córdoba, Spain
Photo by Katherine Hoyt

on April 23, 1616 (at the age of seventy-seven)—on the same date as William Shakespeare and Miguel de Cervantes.[8]

The selections included in this volume begin with Garcilaso's narration of time spent in his childhood listening to stories of the Inca kings taken from the *Royal Commentaries* and then proceed to his description of Inca agriculture, and of the lives of young knights and heirs of the nobility. From the *General History of Peru*, we read Garcilaso's vision of a mestizo monarchy in Peru.

The *Royal Commentaries*, seen from the time of its publication as an important work, has been read and discussed by innumerable scholars for four hundred years. Scholar Jose Antonio Mazzotti said that "Garcilaso's intention was one of gigantic proportions: to rewrite the history of his people and to expand the borders of the Spanish language in order to create the discourse of a new identity."[9] In Latin America, the book helped inspire the uprising of Tupac Amaru II against the Spanish in 1782 after which the crown ordered it taken out of circulation. It was read in the nineteenth century by liberators Simón Bolívar and José de San Martín and in the twentieth century inspired the *indigenista* movement in Latin America led by such writers as Peruvian José Carlos Mariategui and Mexican José Vasconcelos. Scholar Ricardo Rojas said that no other book of the colonial period had transcended its time so greatly or moved people's spirits so deeply as had the *Royal Commentaries*.[10] In Europe, the French translation of the *Royal Commentaries* of 1633 went through six editions and was popular with the French encyclopedists. John Locke acquired and studied the *Royal Commentaries* when he was in France in the 1670s and makes references to it in his treatises.[11] Historian Karen Spalding notes that "Voltaire drew upon *Royal Commentaries* for his portrait of the enlightened society encountered by Candide in the Americas."[12]

The book has also been the subject of numerous controversies, beginning in the eighteenth century when Scottish historian William Robertson accused Inca Garcilaso of being unable to discriminate between the factual and the fabulous.[13] But historian Sergio Alejandro Herrera points out that Garcilaso himself differentiated between "impertinent" fables and other stories that he included because they were fundamental to the establishment of important institutions or practices of the Incan empire.[14]

Another controversy concerns how much of the Indigenous remained in Inca Garcilaso's writings given that he never returned to Peru after leaving at age twenty and absorbed the philosophy of Renaissance humanism in Europe. However, Garcilaso's reliance on the traditional narratives of the lives and deeds of the Inca rulers that he heard as a child can easily be seen in the *Commentaries*. Mazzotti says that:

> to read the *Commentaries* and only recognize traces of the most prestigious discourses within sixteenth century Humanism is to unintentionally betray . . . particular levels of meaning. . . . These *other* levels of meaning stem from a discursive tradition which is peculiarly Andean, and which, although transformed in the process of transcription into Spanish, retains something of its origins.[15]

Inca Garcilaso compared Cuzco to Rome as the capital of a vast empire. Both had conquered many different tribes and "had excellent laws applied to the good government of the two states," he said.[16] Other writers of the period, including Spaniard Pedro Cieza de Leon, had also compared the Incan Empire to Rome.[17] Historian Sabine MacCormack notes that Garcilaso, in a way similar to the Roman historian Livy, referred to stories about the most distant past as historical fables and that for him they "contained collective memories which, however uncertain and indistinct some of them might be, did outline the principles according to which foundational events unfolded, and the manner in which such events impinged on the present."[18] She adds that explaining events in Peru in light of Roman precedent was a way of incorporating the experience of Andean peoples into human experience "across space and time." She states that "those who criticize these writings for imposing—as they perceive it—alien norms on Andean subject matter should consider the alternative that the Andean world would remain forever separate and secluded from the rest of humanity."[19]

However, some still accused Garcilaso of writing idealized fiction. Mac-Cormack answers this accusation by pointing to "the care with which he consulted earlier historians of the Incas, the effort he expended in collecting his own documentation, and his interest in problems of translation from Quechua into Spanish."[20] Spalding adds that he credited his sources, including those with whom he disagreed.[21] Historian Aurelio Miró Quesada accepts as valid some criticisms of the work, including that of Garcilaso's denial of human sacrifice among the Indigenous people, the disdain he shows for the pre-Inca period, and his description of the supposedly always harmonious conquests made by the Incas.[22]

In the list of works found in Garcilaso's library, we see the name Fizino, which refers to Marsilio Ficino, a neo-platonist philosopher who lived between 1433 and 1499 and was a translator of Plato's works including his late dialogue *Timaeus*. Castro-Klaren points out that Ficino was interested in showing the compatibility of pagan philosophy with Christian theology while Garcilaso wanted to show that Inca religious ideas could lead believers to Christianity. Also, *Timaeus* would have been of particular interest to Inca Garcilaso, because Plato expresses clearly in the work that there is only one world.[23] In the dialogue *Timaeus*, the question is asked and answered thusly: "Are we right in saying that there is only one world, or that they are many and infinite? There must be one only, if the created copy is to accord with the original [pure idea in the mind of the creator]."[24] Something similar is expressed by Inca Garcilaso in the first paragraph of the *Royal Commentaries*:

It seems proper to follow the usual custom of writers and discuss here at the beginning whether there is only one world or many . . . and similar matters which the old philosophers treated very fully and curiously. . . . But trusting in God's infinite mercy, I will say at the outset that there is only one world, and although we speak of the Old World and the New, this is because the latter was lately discovered by us, and not because there are two.[25]

Castro-Klaren notes that:

> The possibility of sustaining that the world was always one and made forever in
> a single unified creation was a point of keen interest to Garcilaso in light of the
> disputations concerning the origin and nature of the New World as well as the
> rapidly growing notion that Amerindians were not quite the same as, were lesser
> than, the inhabitants of the Old World.[26]

The famous argument between Bartolomé de Las Casas and José de
Sepúlveda at Valladolid in 1550 on the nature and rights of the Amerindians
had still not been resolved on the ground even though Pope Paul III in 1537
had said that the Indigenous people were "truly men."[27]

The Neoplatonic philosophy of the *Dialogues of Love* coincided with Garcilaso's hope (as one of the first mestizos of Peru) for what literary scholar
Remedios Mataix calls a loving union between the New and Old Worlds;
another sign of the reconciling power of love as a universal force. Mataix
adds that for Garcilaso the conquest and the resulting *mestizaje* (he himself,
for example) would be evidence of this universal loving union.[28] Historian
D.A. Brading states, however, that "The creation of a Holy Inca Empire,
based on the marriage of conquerors and Inca noblewomen, governed by a
mestizo encomendero class, Christian in religion, ruling a native peasantry
in accordance with the principles of Inca legislation, had failed to emerge."[29]
One cannot help but note, however, that this hopeful vision of an ideal, superior, mestizo union appears again in Jose Vasconcelo's *Cosmic Race*, written
in the twentieth century during the Mexican Revolution. But literary scholar
Aurora Fiengo-Varn says that, by asserting that the Amerindians, in acquiring
the Christian "faith attained a higher degree of perfection than they ever had
before even at the loss of their culture and their lives," Garcilaso "represented
his father's group: the conquerors."[30]

Some, such as noted Spanish literary critic Marcelino Menéndez Pelayo,
in 1905 said that the *Commentaries* was not history at all but rather an imaginary, idealized utopian treatise or novel in the same vein as Plato's *Republic*
or Thomas More's *Utopia*.[31] *Utopia* was published in 1516 and had eleven
editions in circulation at the time Garcilaso began his *Royal Commentaries*.[32]
As Brading points out, Inca Garcilaso "emphasized that all families, sick and
elderly included, received an adequate sustenance."[33] Garcilaso explains further, "They first tilled the part assigned to the Sun and then that of the widows
and orphans and those who were unable to work owing to age or ill health.
The latter were regarded as the poor, and the Inca therefore bade that their
land be tilled for them." This is not dissimilar to More's description of the agricultural system of the island of Utopia: "Under such a system, there's bound
to be plenty of everything, and, as everything is divided equally among the

entire population, there obviously cannot be any poor people or beggars."[34] Both Garcilaso and More set out a political economy based on regard for the needs of the entire population.

The arguments of scholars like Margarita Zamora crediting More's fictional Utopia for influencing Garcilaso are strong. Zamora says, "More's ideal republic was situated in America, somewhere south of the Equator but more significantly, the Utopian sociopolitical model was the only one available at the end of the sixteenth century that presented a contemporary pagan civilization in a favorable light."[35] But, Zamora insists, Garcilaso did not write the *Royal Commentaries* as fiction.[36] While More contrasted a fictional Utopia with European civilization, Garcilaso holds up Tahuantinsuyu (as the Inca Empire was called) as an example of an ideal civilization with a discoverable history. And Inca Garcilaso maintained that the Inca Empire was governed, as was More's Utopia, according to natural law, even though neither place had been exposed to the Christian religion. Brading says that Garcilaso portrayed the Incas "as philosopher-kings, who, much as the Greeks before them, practiced a natural religion, the truths of which were discovered through the exercise of their reason, which is to say, through the operation of the Divine Light in which human intelligence participates."[37] Zamora adds that, while it is true that it failed to develop, El Inca Garcilaso de la Vega's ideal Peru would have been that of a Christian Utopia, "a product of the harmonious integration of the dictates of natural reason and Christian revelation."[38]

In the *General History of Peru*, the second part of Inca Garcilaso's work, he treats the arrival and war making of the Spanish conquistadors against the Incas, the deaths of the two quarreling Inca brothers—Huascar and Atahualpa, the resistance of Manco Inca at Vilcabamba, and the fighting among the Spaniards themselves, including the rebellion against the king by the youngest of the Pizarro brothers, Gonzalo. Literary studies scholar James Fuerst points out that, in spite of the negative consequences for Inca Garcilaso's family of Gonzalo's rebellion (when his father, Capitan Sebastian Garcilaso de la Vega, was accused of aiding Gonzalo's efforts), Inca Garcilaso exalts Gonzalo and his top military advisor Francisco de Carvajal. "In speaking so highly of Gonzalo and Carvajal, Inca Garcilaso was defending sordid characters indeed,"[39] Fuerst says. Why does he do such a thing? Fuerst maintains that he uses Gonzalo Pizarro and Francisco de Carvajal as vehicles for the laying out of his vision of a mestizo Peru—one different from the absolute monarchy of Spain with its viceroys in the New World—a monarchy with a system of corule between Incas and Spaniards.[40]

Fuerst goes on to say that Inca Garcilaso is the first to argue for the possibility of a Peru independent from Spain and to see armed rebellion as a means to that end. He wants to link Spanish and Indigenous elites and institutions and for the monarch (who would be Spanish in the first generation) to take as his wife the highest-ranking Inca princess. This was in contrast to the ideas Friar Bartolomé de Las Casas expressed in his late work *Doce Dudas*, in which he supported the return by the king of Spain of the land of Peru to the Incas (who would rule it as a subject province of the Spanish crown) and also to the ideas of the Indigenous writer Guaman Poma de Ayala, who, while recognizing the permanence of the Spaniards and the value of the Christian religion, wished for Spanish and Indigenous people to live separately.[41] Of course, by the time Inca Garcilaso was writing this, both Gonzalo and Carvajal had been executed and the mestizo kingdom had not developed through union of Spanish and Incas but Fuerst says Garcilaso believed that there might still be ways in the future "through which the two could come together socially, culturally, and politically for their mutual benefit. This is the utopian ideal and progressive postcolonial hope of the *Royal Commentaries*."[42]

In laying out the history of the Inca Empire in the *Royal* Commentaries and the story of the Spanish conquest in the *General History*, Garcilaso provided the basis for a vision of a mestizo Peru which has inspired hope and provoked arguments during many generations in Peru, Latin America, Spain, and the world.

THE ROYAL COMMENTARIES OF THE INCAS (1609) AND *GENERAL HISTORY OF PERU* (1617) OF EL INCA GARCILASO DE LA VEGA

Royal Commentaries of the Incas

Book 1, chapter 1: Whether There Are Many Worlds

Having to treat of the New World, or of the best and most important parts of it, which are the kingdoms and provinces of the empire called Peru, of whose antiquities and of the origin of whose kings we intend to write; it seems proper, and in conformity with the usual custom of authors, to treat here, at the beginning, of the question whether there is one world or many, if it is flat or round, and also whether heaven is flat or round, whether the whole earth is habitable or only the temperate zones, whether there is a way from one temperate zone to the other, whether there are antipodes, and other like matters. The ancient philosophers treated very largely and curiously on these subjects, and the moderns do not fail to argue and write on them, each following the opinion which best pleases him. But as this is not my chief subject, as the powers of an Indian cannot enable him to presume so far, and as experience, since the discovery of what they call the New World, has undeceived us touching most of these doubts, we will pass over them briefly, in order to go on to the other part of my subject, the conclusion of which I am fearful lest I should not reach. I may affirm, however, trusting in the infinite mercy, that, in the first place, there is only one world; and though we speak of the Old World and the New World, this is because the latter was lately discovered by us, and not because there are two, but one only. And to those who still imagine that there are many worlds, there is no answer to be given except that they can remain in their heretical persuasions until they are undeceived in hell. Those who doubt, if there be any such, whether the world is flat or round, may be convinced by the testimony of men who have gone round it.

Book 1, chapter 15: The Origin of the Ynca Kings of Peru

After having sketched out many plans, and taken many roads for entering upon a narrative of the origin of the Yncas, the former native kings of Peru, it seemed to me that the best and clearest way would be to relate what I have often heard, in my childhood, from my mother and from her brothers, uncles, and other relations, touching this origin and beginning. For all that is said on the subject from other sources may be reduced to the same as we shall relate, and it is better that it should be made known in the actual words in which the Yncas have told it, than in those of strange authors. My mother resided in Cuzco, her native town, and almost every week some of the few male and female relations, who escaped the cruelty and tyranny of Atahualpa came to visit her. On the occasion of these visits their usual conversation was on the subject of the origin of the Yncas, of their majesty, of the grandeur of their empire, of their greatness, of their mode of government in peace and war, and of the laws, which they ordained for the good of their subjects. In short, they omitted nothing relating to the flourishing period of their history in the course of these conversations.

From their past greatness and prosperity, they went on to the present state of affairs; they mourned for their dead kings, their lost rule, their fallen state. Such and the like discourses were held by the Yncas and Pallas when they visited my mother, and, at the memory of their lost happiness, they always concluded their conversations with tears and mourning, saying "We are turned from rulers into vassals." During these conversations I, as a boy, came in and out of the place where they were assembled many times and was entertained at hearing them, just as lads always like to hear stories told.

Book 1, chapter 19: Protest of the Author Touching the History

When I had reached a more advanced age, they gave me a long account of their laws and government, comparing them with the new government of the Spaniards. They enumerated the crimes with their punishments in the days of the Yncas, and related how their kings governed in peace and in war, in what manner they treated their vassals, and how they were served by them. Besides, they told me, as to their own son, of all their idolatries, rites, ceremonies, and sacrifices, of their festivals, their superstitions and abuses, and of all their customs, good or evil; as well those relating to their sacrifices, as others. In short, I may declare that they related to me all things connected with their commonwealth; and if I had then written it all down, this history would be more copious. Besides what the Indians told me, I had the opportunity of seeing with my own eyes, a great many of their idolatrous customs, their festivals and superstitions, which were still celebrated even until I was twelve or thirteen years of age. I was born eight years after the Spaniards conquered my country, and, as I have before said, I was brought up in it until my twentieth year, so that I myself saw many things that were practiced by the Indians in the time of their idolatry, and which I shall relate.

But, in addition to what my relations told me, and to what I myself saw, I have heard many other accounts of the conquests and acts of those kings; for as soon as I resolved to write this history I wrote to my old schoolfellows, asking them each to help me by sending me an account of the particular conquest which the Yncas achieved in the provinces of their mothers; for each province has its history, and its knots with their recorded annals and traditions, and thus each province retains a more accurate account of what took place within its borders, than of what happened beyond them. My schoolfellows taking what I had sought from them in earnest, reported my intention to their mothers and relations, who, on hearing that an Indian, a child of their own land, intended to write a history of it, brought out the accounts which they possessed, from the archives, and sent them to me.

Book 1, chapter 21: The Things Which the Ynca
Taught to His Vassals

The [first] Ynca Manco Ccapac, in establishing his people in villages, while he taught them to cultivate the land, to build houses, construct channels for irrigation, and to do all other things necessary for human life; also instructed them in the ways of polite and brotherly companionship, in conformity with reason and the law of nature, persuading them, with much earnestness, to preserve perpetual peace and concord between themselves, and not to entertain anger or passionate feelings towards each other, but to do to one another as they would others should do to them, not laying down one law for themselves and another for their neighbours. He particularly enjoined them to respect the wives and daughters of others; because they were formerly more vicious in respect to women, than in any other thing whatever. He imposed the penalty of death on adulterers, homicides, and thieves. He ordered no man to have more than one wife, and that marriages should take place between relations, so as to prevent confusion in families, also that marriages should take place at the age of twenty years and upwards, that the married couples might be able to rule their households, and work their estates. He directed the tame flocks, which wandered over the country without a master, to be collected, so that all people might be clothed with their wool, by reason of the industry and skill which had been taught to the women by the Queen Mama Occllo Huaco. They were also taught to make the shoes which are now used, called *usata*. A Curaca, which is the same as a Cacique in the language of Cuba and San Domingo, and means lord of vassals, was appointed over every nation that was subjugated. The Curacas were chosen from among those who had done most in conquering the Indians, for their merit, as being most affable, gentle, and pious, and most zealous for the public good, They were constituted lords over the others, that they might instruct them as a father does his children, and the Indians were ordered to obey them, as sons obey their parents.

He ordered that the harvests gathered by each village, should be preserved in common, so that each might be supplied with what it required, until arrangements could be made for giving an allotment of land to each Indian. Together with these precepts and laws, he taught the Indians the worship of his idolatrous religion. The Yncas selected a spot for building a temple where they might sacrifice to the Sun, persuading the people that it was the principal God whom they should worship, and to whom they should give thanks for the natural benefits which he conferred on them by his light and heat. For they saw that these properties of the Sun caused their crops to grow and their flocks to multiply, and produced the other mercies which they received every day: and they were instructed that their worship and service were more especially due to the Sun and Moon, for having sent their children to take them from the wild life they had hitherto led, and to bring them to a more civilised condition.

Book 5, chapter 1: How They Divided the Land Amongst the Vassals

As soon as the Ynca had conquered any kingdom or province and established his Government amongst the inhabitants according to his laws and idolatrous customs, he ordered that the cultivated land capable of yielding maize should be extended. For this purpose he caused irrigation channels to be constructed, which were most admirable, as may be seen to this day; both those that have been destroyed, the ruins of which are yet visible, and those still in working order. The engineers led the irrigation channels in directions required by the lands to be watered; for it must be known that the greater part of this land is barren as regards corn-yielding soil, and, for this reason, they endeavored to increase its fertility as much as possible. As the land is under the torrid zone it requires irrigation. The Yncas supplied the water with great ingenuity, and no maize crop was sown without being also supplied with water. They also constructed channels to irrigate the pasture land, when the autumn withheld its rains, for they took care to fertilise the pastures as well as the arable land, as they possessed immense flocks. These channels for the pastures were destroyed as soon as the Spaniards came into the country but the ruins may be seen to this day. Having made the irrigation channel, they levelled the fields and arranged them in squares, so that they might get the full benefit of the water.

On the sides of the mountains where there was good soil, they made terraces so as to get level ground, as may be seen at this day round Cuzco and all over Peru. These terraces or *andenes* consisted of three walls of strong masonry, one in front and two at the sides, slightly inclining inwards, as are all their walls, so as to sustain the weight of the earth, which was filled in until it reached the top of the walls. Over the first *anden* they constructed another narrower one, above that another still smaller. Thus they gradually covered the whole mountain, levelling the ground after the manner of a flight of stairs, and getting the use of all the land that was suitable for sowing, and that could be irrigated. Where there were masses of rock, the rocks were removed and earth was brought from elsewhere to make terraces, so that even such a site might be made useful and not lost. The first terraces were of a size conformable to the position of the site, capable of containing a hundred to two or three hundred *fanegas* [about 1.1 acre each], more or less; and the second were smaller; and so they went on diminishing in size as they ascended, until the highest only gave room for two or three rows of maize. In many places they led an irrigation channel for fifteen or twenty leagues, to irrigate only a few *fanegas* of maize land, that it might not be lost.

Having thus increased the quantity of arable land, they measured all that was contained in each province, every village by itself, and then divided it into three parts. The first part was for the Sun, the second for the King, and the third for the people. These divisions were always carefully made, in order that the people might have sufficient land for their crops; and it was a rule that they should rather have more than was requisite than too little. When the people of a village or province increased in number, a portion was taken from the lands of the Son and of the Ynca for the vassals. Thus the King only took for himself and for the Sun such lands as would otherwise remain desert and without an owner. Most of the *andenes* belong to the Sun and to the Ynca, because the sovereign had ordered them to be made.

Besides the maize lands which were irrigated, other unirrigated tracts were portioned out, in which they sowed pulses and other crops of much importance, such as those they call *papas* [potatoes], *ocas* [Oxalis tuberosa], and *añus* [Tropaeolum tuberosum]. These also were divided into three parts: for the people, the Sun, and the Ynca. But as they were not fertile, from want of irrigation, they did not take crops off them more than once or twice, and then portioned out other lots, that the first might lie fallow. In this way they cultivated their poor lands, that there might always be abundance. The maize lands were sown every year, because, as they were irrigated and manured like a garden, they were always fertile. They sowed a seed like rice with the maize, called *quinua*, which is also raised on the cold lands.

Book 5, chapter 2: The Arrangement They Adopted for Tilling the Land

They also established a regular order in the tilling and the cultivating of the land. They first tilled the fields of the Sun; then those of the widows, orphans, aged, and sick, for all these persons were classed as poor, and, as such, the Ynca ordered that their fields should be tilled for them. In each village, or in each ward, if the village was large, there were men deputed to look after the lands of persons who were classed as poor. These deputies were named *Llacta-camayu*, which means "officers of the village." They superintended the ploughing, sowing, and harvesting; and at such times they went up into towers the night before, that were built for the purpose, and after blowing through a trumpet or shell to secure attention, cried with a loud voice that on such a day such and such lands of the poor would be tilled, warning those, whose duty it might be, to repair thither. The inhabitants of each district were thus apprised on what lands they were to give assistance, which were those of their relations or nearest neighbours. Each one was expected to bring food for himself of what he had in his house, for those who were unable to work were not required to find food for those who could. It was said that their own misery sufficed for the aged, sick, widows, and orphans, without looking after that of their neighbours. If the disabled had no seed, it was provided from the stores, of which we shall speak presently. The lands of soldiers who were employed in the wars were also tilled in this way, like those of widows and orphans; and while the husbands were serving in the wars, their wives were looked upon as widows during their absence. Great care was taken of the children of those who were killed in the wars, until such time as they were married.

After the lands of the poor and distressed had been tilled, the people worked on their own lands, the neighbors assisting each other. They then tilled the fields of the *Curaca*, which were the last that received attention in each village or district. In the time of Huayna Ccapac, an Indian superintendent in the province of Chachapoyas was hanged because he caused the land of a *Curaca*, who was a relation of his, to be tilled before that of a widow. He was punished as a breaker of the rules established by the Ynca for the tilling of the land, and the gallows was set up on the land of the *Curaca*. The Yncas ordered that the lands of their vassals should take precedence over their own because they said that from the prosperity of his subjects was derived their faithful service to the King; for if they were poor and in need, they would not be able to serve well either in peace or war.

The last fields that were cultivated were those of the King. All the people tilled the lands of the Ynca and of the Sun in common, and they went to them with great joy and satisfaction, dressed in the clothes which they wore on their grandest festivals. These garments were covered with plates of gold and silver, and the people also wore plumes of feathers on their heads. When they ploughed (which was the labour they most enjoyed) they sang many songs, composed in praise of their Yncas, and they went through their work with joy and gladness, because it was in the service of their God and of their King.

Book 6, chapter 24: How the Knights Were Armed and How They Were Examined

The word *Huaracu* belongs to the general language of Peru, and is equivalent to what in Spanish would indicate the arming of a knight. For this word signified the granting of the insignia of manhood to the youths of the blood royal, and the clothing of them in the habiliments of war as well as of peace. Without these insignia they were not considered eligible for the one office or the other, and as the books on knighthood would have it, they were virgins unable to bear arms. In order to receive these insignia, which we shall describe further on, the youths who were prepared to enter upon the career of arms, had to pass through a very rigorous novitiate. They were examined in all the labours and emergencies that are likely to arise in war, whether under prosperous or adverse circumstances.

In order that the whole ceremony may be clearly understood, it will be well to describe every part of it in detail; for, considering that the people are so barbarous, it certainly contained many things well worthy of attention. The festival was an occasion of great rejoicing for the common people, and of much honour and majesty for the Yncas, as well the aged who had been proved in war, as the youths who were then to undergo the novitiate. For the honour or shame that the novices acquired in the trial was shared by their relations, and as the Yncas were all of one common parentage, the good or evil that befell each member was felt by the whole family, although those most nearly related were most affected.

Each year, or every second year, according to circumstances, the Ynca youths were submitted to the military ordeal. They were assembled in a house built for that purpose, which stood in the quarter called the Collcampata. I have myself seen it, and I have even beheld a portion of the ceremonies, but in those days they might more properly be described as shadows of the past, as regards their magnificence and reality. In this house there were aged Yncas, experienced in the arts of peace and war, who were the instructors of the novices, and who examined them in the things we shall presently mention and in others which have slipped from my memory. For six days the novices had to endure a very rigorous fast, during which time they were given nothing but a few grains of raw maize and a jar of plain water, without anything else whatever. . . . After the fast, having been indulged with rather more food, the novices were examined in the agility of their persons. . . . On another day the novices were divided into two equal bodies. One was ordered to remain in the fortress, and the other to go outside, and to fight one against the other, one striving to take the fortress, and the other to defend it. After the contest had lasted the whole day, they changed rounds on the following day, those who had been defenders taking the place of assailants. . . .

Book 6, chapter 26: When the Prince Became a Novice He Was Treated with More Severity than the Others

Every day one of the captains or managers of the ceremonies delivered a harangue, in which the ancestry of the Yncas, the deeds of former kings, in peace and war, and those of other heroes of the blood royal, were called to mind. In these discourses the novices were urged to practice all the moral philosophy to which these Indians had attained; they were told of the bravery and stout-heartedness they ought to display in the wars for enlarging the bounds of the empire, of the patience and long-suffering in work, whereby they should prove their ardour and generosity; of the clemency, piety and meekness that was due to the poor and the subdued enemy, of the right and justice they should administer by doing no injury to any one, and above all of the liberality and magnificence that must be seen in all of them, as children of the Sun, who had descended from heaven. The novices were made to sleep on the ground, to eat little and bad food, to go barefoot, and to practice all the other austerities that might tend to make them good soldiers.

The eldest son of the Ynca, the heir to the empire, also entered upon this ordeal when he had arrived at an age to perform the exercises, and it must be understood that he was examined with the same severity as the others. No distinction whatever was made in his case, by reason of his exalted rank, except that the pennon [pennant] intended for the swiftest in the race was given to the Prince as being his right as heir to the kingdom. But in all the other exercises, in fasting, military discipline, skill in making arms and shoes for himself, sleeping on the ground, faring ill, and going barefoot, he was in no way privileged. If there was any difference, the Prince was treated with even more rigour than the others, for it was said that he who was to be king should excel his fellows as well in the height and dignity of his rank as in all other things. It was thought that, in prosperity and in adversity the royal person should be above all others, whether in the gifts of his mind or in matters relating to bodily skill, especially in warlike exercises. They said that the Prince deserved to reign more on account of these accomplishments than because he was the firstborn of his father. They also held that it was very necessary for kings and princes to endure the toils of war that they might know how to value and reward those who served under them. During the whole time that the noviciate lasted, which was from one new moon to the next, the prince was dressed in the vilest and most wretched clothes that can be imagined, and appeared in public in these rags on all necessary occasions. They affirmed that he was clothed in rags in order that when he became a powerful king he might not despise the poor, but remember that he had once been one of them, and be their friend, so as to merit the title of *Hacchacuyac*, which they gave to their kings. The meaning of the word is "lover and benefactor of the poor." After the ordeal the princes were considered worthy of the insignia of royalty, and held to be true Yncas, children of the Son. Then the mothers and sisters of the youths came and put shoes of reeds on their feet, in token of their having passed through the sharp ordeal of the military exercises.

Book 7, chapter 2: The Heirs of the Chiefs Were Brought up at Court

Those Kings also ordered that the heirs of the Lords of vassals [from lands subject to the Inca] should be brought up in the court and reside there until they succeeded to the lordships, that they might be well-instructed, and habituated to the customs and breeding of the Yncas. They were treated by the Yncas as friends, that they might love and zealously serve them in future years for the sake of old memories. They were called *Mitmac* because they were settlers. This was also done to ennoble the court by the presence of so many lordly heirs from all parts of the empire.

This rule ensured the learning of the general language with more good will and less trouble; because the servants who accompanied the young lords to the court took back to their own country some knowledge of the court language, and spoke it with much pride amongst their own people, it being the language of a race that was held to be divine. This gave rise to much jealousy among their countrymen, who also desired to learn it. Those who acquired a little knowledge communicated more frequently and freely with the governors and ministers of justice and revenue who held office in their districts. Thus, with gentleness and ease, and without the special teaching from master, the people learnt and spoke the general language of Cuzco over a region little less than one thousand three hundred leagues [one league equals around three miles] in extent, which was subjugated by these kings.

Besides the motive of adding grandeur to their court by the presence of so many princes, those Ynca Kings had another reason for this policy. This was to secure the provinces from rebellions. The empire was of vast extent, and many provinces were four to five and six hundred leagues from the capital. Among them were populous and very warlike nations, such as those of Quito and Chile, and others who, from their distance and the fierceness of their dispositions, might be expected to rise and attempt to throw off the imperial yoke. And, although one might not succeed alone, they might make a league [alliance] together and trouble the empire on all sides, thus endangering the supremacy of the Yncas. They adopted, as a remedy against these evils and others which might arise in so vast an empire, the plan of obliging all the heirs to live at court, where they were treated with kindness and attention, according to their respective importance and merits, whether the Ynca was present or absent. The princes gave detailed accounts of these special favours to their fathers, sending them dresses [garments] from the Yncas, which were very highly esteemed. Thus the Ynca Kings strove to oblige their vassals and induce them to be loyal for the sake of these benefits. Even when the chiefs were so ungrateful as not to recognize these favours, they at least repressed their evil feelings, seeing that their sons and heirs were at the court as hostages for their fidelity. Owing to this sagacious policy, and to the uprightness of their rule, the Yncas had their dominions in such a state of peace that, during the whole period of their sway, there were scarcely any rebellions to punish and suppress.

General History of Peru

Book 4, chapter 40: What Carvajal Wrote and Said to Gonzalo Pizarro on the Question of His Becoming King of Peru

[Opposed to the Crown's New Laws of 1542, which limited the encomiendas, or allotments of Indigenous people, to the lifetime of the recipient, Gonzalo Pizarro and his followers rebelled against the King in 1546. Some of his men, including his military strategist Francisco de Carvajal, urged Pizarro to declare himself king of Peru, which he refused to do, desiring instead to be named governor. Here Carvajal explains to Pizarro what he thinks he should do.]

"[D]eclare yourself king; and take the government for yourself without waiting for another to give it to you, and put a crown on your head; and allocate whatever land is unoccupied among your friends and supporters; and as what the king gives is temporary for two lives, you give it as a perpetual title and make dukes and marquises and counts, such as there are in all the countries of the world, so that they will defend your lordship in order to defend their own estates.

"Set up military orders with the same names and titles as those in Spain and other saints as patrons and such insignia as you think fit. Give the knights of the orders revenues and pensions to keep themselves and live at ease, as military knights do everywhere. With all this I have said in brief Your Lordship will attract to your service all the Spanish chivalry and nobility in this empire, fully rewarding all those who conquered it and who have served Your Lordship, which is not now the case. And to attract the Indians and make them so devoted that they will die for Your Lordship as they would for their Inca kings, take one of their princesses, whichever is closest to the royal line, to wife, and send ambassadors to the forests where the heir to the Incas is [at Vilcabamba] and bid him to come forth and recover his lost majesty and state, asking him to offer you as your wife any daughter or sister he may have. You know how much this prince will esteem kinship and friendship with you, and you will gain the universal love of all the Indians by restoring their Inca and at the same time make them genuinely willing to do whatever their king orders them on your behalf, such as bringing supplies, abandoning the villages, holding the roads against your enemies—in short all the Indians will be on your side, and if they do not help your enemies with supplies and porters, no one can prevail against you in Peru. Their prince will be satisfied with the title of king and the fact that his vassals obey him as they used to do; and he will govern his Indians in peace as they did in the past, while your Lordship and your officials and captains govern the Spaniards and have charge of military affairs, requiring the Inca to tell the Indians to do whatever you command. Thus you will be sure that the Indians do not deceive you or act as double spies, as they now do, serving first one side and then the other.

"In addition, Your Lordship will receive from the Inca not only all the gold and silver the Indians produce in this empire, for they do not regard it as treasure or wealth, but also all the treasure of the kings their ancestors which they have hidden, as is well known. All this will be given and delivered to Your Lordship both on account of your relationship with the Inca and because of his restoration to his former majesty. With all the gold and silver they were reputed to have Your Lordship can buy the whole world, if you want to be master of it. And pay no attention if they say you are a traitor to the king of Spain; you are not, for as the saying goes, no king is a traitor.

This land belonged to the Incas, its natural lords, and if it is not restored to them, you have more right to it than the king of Castile, for you won it at your expense and risk, together with your brothers. Now, by restoring it to the Inca, you are simply doing what you should by natural law; and in seeking to govern it yourself as its conqueror and not as the vassal and subject of another, you are doing what you owe to your reputation, for anyone who can become king by the strength of his arm should not remain a serf for lack of spirit. It all depends on the first step and the first declaration. I beg Your Lordship carefully to consider the import of what I have said about ruling this empire in perpetuity, so that all those who live and shall live here may follow you. Finally I urge you whatever may happen to crown yourself and call yourself king, for no other name befits one who has won an empire by his strength and courage. Die a king. I repeat many times, die a king and not a vassal, for whoever lets a wrong be put on him deserves worse." . . .

Book 4, chapter 41: The Respect of Gonzalo Pizarro for the Royal Service

Gonzalo wished to avoid a decision about assuming the title of king for his natural respect for his prince was stronger than the pleas of his friends, and he never lost hope that His Imperial Majesty would grant him the confirmation of his governorship of Peru, on the grounds that he and his brothers had won it, and in return for his personal services, realizing that he knew all those who had served His Majesty in Peru and was in the best position to reward them. All these things were arguments in favor of the award of the governorship, in addition to the fact that the emperor had issued a grant to the marquis his brother [Francisco] by which he could appoint his successor as governor, and he had in fact appointed Gonzalo. . . .

Pizarro thought that he not only deserved a pardon for the past, but the award of the governorship anew; for it is a natural habit among men of war to esteem their own deeds, even if they are guilty ones. As Pizarro had not dared to venture on an undertaking so much to his advantage, as his friends maintained, the common people attributed it to lack of sense, and not to excess of respect toward his king. They regarded him as mean spirited and mocked his lack of judgment. The historians have respected this, because they were given a distorted version, and do not say what really happened. For it was the common opinion of those nearest to Gonzalo Pizarro who knew him best that he was a man of good judgement, who never caviled or deceived or made false promises or spoke evasively. He was simple, sincere, noble, and good, and trusted in his friends, who destroyed him, as the historians themselves say.

Book 8, chapter 21: The Last of This History

Having begun this history with the commencement and origin of the Inca kings in Peru, and having noticed at length their conquests and generous deeds, their lives, their government in peace and war, and the idolatrous religion they had in heathen times—all of which were performed at length in the first part of these *Commentaries*, with divine aid—we fulfilled the obligation we felt toward our mother country and our maternal stock. In the Second Part, as we have seen, a long account was given of the deeds and heroic actions that the brave and valiant Spaniards performed in conquering that wealthy empire, wherein we have fulfilled, even though not completely, our paternal obligations, which we owe to our father and his illustrious and generous companions. It now seems to me proper to conclude this work. . . . I hope [it] will have been as great a service to the Spaniards who won the empire as to the Incas who formerly possessed it.

The Divine Majesty, Father, Son, and Holy Ghost, three persons and one single true God, be praised *per omnia saecula saiculorum*, who has granted me the great mercy of allowing me to reach this place.

NOTES

1. Margarita Zamora, "Garcilaso Inca de la Vega (1539–1616)," in *Narradores Indígenas y mestizos de la época colonial (siglos XVI–XVII): Zonas andina y Mesoamérica*, ed. Rocío Cortés and Margarita Zamora (Lima: Centro de Estudios Literarios Antonio Cornejo Polar, 2016), 227.

2. José Antonio Mazzotti, *Incan Insights: El Inca Garcilaso's Hints to Andean Readers*, trans. Barbara M. Corbett (Madrid: Iberamérica, 2008), 11.

3. Karen Spalding, introduction to *Royal Commentaries of the Incas and General History of Peru*, by Garcilaso de la Vega, El Inca, trans. Harold V. Livermore (Indianapolis: Hackett, 2006), XV–XVI.

4. Mazzotti, *Incan*, 12; Spalding, introduction, xviii.

5. Sara Castro-Klaren, "Writing the Andes," in *A Companion to Latin American Literature and Culture*, ed. Sara Castro-Klaren (Hoboken: Blackwell Publishing, 2008), 130.

6. "Garcilaso Inca de la Vega (1539–1616)," *Selections from the Library of José Durand*, South Bend: University of Notre Dame, Rare Books and Special Collections, accessed May 20, 2020, https://rarebooks.library.nd.edu/exhibits/durand/biographies/garcilaso.html.

7. Max Hernandez, *Memoria del Bien Perdido: conflicto, identidad y nostalgia en el Inca Garcilaso de la Vega* (Lima: Instituto de Estudios Peruanos, 1993), 159.

8. Spalding, introduction, xviii, xix. It was the same date but not the same day because of calendar differences.

9. Mazzotti, *Incan*, 9.

10. Ricardo Rojas, "Prologo a 'Comentarios Reales de los Incas,'" in *Los Garcilasistas: Antología*, ed. Cesar Toro Montalvo (Lima: Editorial San Marcos, 1987), 187.

11. James W. Fuerst, "Locke and Inca Garcilaso: Subtexts, Politics, and European Expansion," in *Inca Garcilaso and Contemporary World-Making*, ed. Sara Castro-Klarén and Christian Fernández (Pittsburgh: University of Pittsburgh Press, 2016), 272.

12. Spalding, introduction, xxvi.

13. Cited in Margarita Zamora, *Language, authority, and Indigenous history in the Comentarios reales de los incas* (Cambridge: Cambridge University Press, 1988), 4.

14. Sergio Alejandro Hererra Villagra, "Ideologías, identidades y mentalidades en la obra de 'Tres Autores Andinos,' Peru, Siglos XVI y XVII," *Diálogo Andino—Revista de Historia, Geografía y Cultura Andina* 40 (diciembre 2012), 27.

15. Mazzotti, *Incan,* 14.

16. Garcilaso de la Vega, El Inca, *Royal Commentaries of the Incas and General History of Peru*, trans. Harold V. Livermore, ed. Karen Spalding (Indianapolis: Hackett, 2006), 64.

17. Sabine MacCormack, "The Incas and Rome," in *Garcilaso Inca de la Vega: An American Humanist, a Tribute to Jose Durand*, ed. Jose Anadon (Notre Dame: Notre Dame University Press, 1988), 9.

18. Sabine MacCormack, "History, Historical Record, and Ceremonial Action: Incas and Spaniards in Cuzco," *Comparative Studies in Society and History* 43, no. 2 (April 2001): 335.

19. Sabine MacCormack, *On the Wings of Time: Rome, the Incas, Spain, and Peru* (Princeton: Princeton University Press, 2007), xvii–xviii.

20. MacCormack, "The Incas," 12.

21. Spalding, introduction, xxvi.

22. Aurelio Miro Quesada, *El Inca Garcilaso* (Lima: Fondo Editorial de la Pontifica Universidad Católica del Perú, 1994), 253–255.

23. Sara Castro-Klaren, "'For It Is but a Single World,'" *Inca Garcilaso and Contemporary World-Making*, ed. Sara Castro-Klaren and Christian Fernandez (Pittsburgh: University of Pittsburgh Press, 2016), 195–198.

24. Quoted in Castro-Klaren, "For It Is," 195.

25. Garcilaso de la Vega, El Inca, *Royal Commentaries of the Incas and General History of Peru, Part One*, trans. with Intro. Harold V. Livermore (Austin: University of Texas Press, 1966), 9.

26. Castro-Klaren, "For It Is," 197–98.

27. Lewis Hanke, *All Mankind Is One: A Study of the Disputation between Bartolomé de Las Casas and Juan Ginés de Sepúlveda in 1550 on the Intellectual and Religious Capacity of the American Indians* (DeKalb: Northern Illinois University Press, 1974), 21.

28. Remedios Mataix, "Biografía Del Inca Garcilaso de la Vega." Biblioteca Virtual Miguel de Cervantes: http://www.cervantesvirtual.com/portales/inca_gar cilaso_de_la_vega/autor_apunte/, accessed May 23, 2020.

29. D. A. Brading, "The Incas and the Renaissance: The Royal Commentaries of Inca Garcilaso de la Vega." *Journal of Latin American Studies* 18 (1986): 22.

30. Aurora Fiengo-Varn, "Reconciling the Divided Self: Inca Garcilaso de la Vega's Royal Commentaries and his Platonic views of the conquest of Peru," *Revista de Filologia y Lingüística* 29, no. 1 (2003): 122, 126.

31. Marcelino Menendez Pelaya, *Orígenes de la novela* (Madrid: 1905), quoted in Zamora, *Language*, 5.

32. Zamora, *Language*, 130.

33. Brading, "The Incas," 15.

34. Thomas More, *Utopia*, trans. and intro. by Paul Turner (London: Penguin Books, 2003), 65.

35. Zamora, *Language*, 131.

36. Zamora, *Language*, 153.

37. Brading, "The Incas," 14.

38. Zamora, *Language*, 164.

39. James W. Fuerst, *New World Postcolonial: The Political Thought of Inca Garcilaso de la Vega* (Pittsburgh: University of Pittsburgh Press, 2018), 153.

40. Fuerst, *New World*, 154–55.

41. Fuerst, *New World*, 174–76.

42. Fuerst, *New World*, 176.

Chapter Fourteen

Felipe Guamán Poma de Ayala
"Indians Should Not Be Abused"

Felipe Guamán Poma de Ayala, author of *The First New Chronicle and Good Government*, was born in the Peruvian Andes city of Huamanga (modern Ayacucho) sometime between 1535 and 1550.[1] His massive manuscript, a petition to King Philip III for improved treatment for the Indigenous people, is one of the very few works penned by a Native writer in the early colonial period without the assistance of a Spanish translator or scribe.[2] In 2007, the *New Chronicle* was named part of the UNESCO Memory of the World Register[3] as a document of world significance and outstanding universal value.

Poma de Ayala was descended on his father's side from nobility of the Yarovilca, a people conquered by the Incas,[4] and his mother, he said, was a daughter of the Inca Tupac Yupanqui, who ruled the Incan empire from 1471 to 1493. He learned Christian doctrine and to read and write in Spanish and Quechua as a boy. In the period 1569–1570, he participated (probably as an interpreter) in a campaign to put down the Indigenous Takiy Unquy movement[5] that practiced the old religion and preached resistance to Spanish ways. He later came to regret his participation in that repression.[6] He also condemned the policies of Spanish Viceroy Francisco de Toledo, who resettled natives to make labor more available for the Spanish landowners. Literary historian Raquel Chang-Rodriguez notes that the title of the first part of his work, *The First New Chronicle*, implies that previous chronicles had been European justifications of the conquest and the early decades of colonization while his would be the first of a new type of chronicle. The title of the second part, *Good Government*, documents the evils of the colonial government and how it should be replaced by his improved model.[7]

In the years before writing *The First New Chronicle and Good Government*, Poma traveled around Peru documenting the lives of the Indigenous inhabitants. It probably took him over a decade to write the entire book, which consists of 1,200 pages, including 398 full-page drawings. He finished the final draft with additions and changes around 1616[8] and sent the book to King Philip III of Spain in the hope that it would serve him as the guide for his governance of Peru. A letter to the king notifying him that the book was on its way has been discovered by scholars. It is likely that Guaman Poma died in 1616 not long after sending the book to Spain.[9]

It is not known if the king himself saw the book, but it did arrive at the Spanish court. It came into the hands of the Ambassador of Denmark to Spain, Cornelius Lerche, who donated it to the Danish Royal Library between 1650 and 1662, and it first appears in a catalog of that library in 1729. Since it was part of a closed collection, it was perfectly conserved over the centuries. It was rediscovered by German historian and librarian Richard Pietschmann in 1908.[10] A facsimile edition of the work was published in France in 1936, and in 1980 scholars Rolena Adorno and John V. Murra published a critical edition. In recent years there has been much attention to Poma and his writing, and in 2001 a digital facsimile of the entire work was published online by the Danish Royal Library with Rolena Adorno as editor.[11]

Until recently, the only available English version of the work was Christopher Dilke's 1978 abridged translation entitled *Letter to a King*. However, in 2006, David Frye published a new abridged translation and, in 2009, a complete translation of the first third of the work by Roland Hamilton was released. The selections in this volume are taken from the Frye edition as they are from parts of Poma's work not included in Hamilton's translation.

The First New Chronicle and Good Government is divided into three parts: 1) a recounting of ancient Andean history, 2) the story of the Spanish conquest, and 3) Poma's suggestions for reform of the colonial system. The book is important because it is the work, not of a Spanish conquistador (such as Bernal Diaz del Castillo who wrote of the conquest of Mexico) or of a person of mixed blood who lived the life of the elite in Lima and Spain (as did El Inca Garcilaso de la Vega) but rather of a provincial Indian nobleman who lost his land in legal battles and knew firsthand the struggles of his people.[12] Adorno writes that "to unmask the excesses of colonialism and to defend the cultural and historical dignity of his race were the literary tasks to which Guamán Poma applied himself."[13]

Poma's drawings are among the only surviving illustrations of preconquest Indian life and contain a wealth of information for scholars. But the drawings also were used by Poma to graphically denounce the mistreatment of the Indigenous people and to show concrete aspects of what he sees as the misgovernment of the Viceroyalty of Peru by colonial civil and religious authorities.

Within the *First New Chronicle and Good Government*, we find geography, anthropology, theology, history, and politics. Literary scholar Sara

Castro-Klaren calls it "a feat that remains unequalled in the history of co-lonial or modern letters." She adds that "he learned doctrine by attending sermons, law by frequenting the courts, and drawing by apprenticing himself to various churchmen and artists."[14] We see what Poma accepted of European culture, the Christian religion, for example, and what he rejected, principally the treatment of the Indigenous people. Anthropologist David Frye points out that Poma condemned the Spanish order "as contrary to the very Christian principles that the Spanish themselves claimed to follow."[15] We are interested here in Poma's political writings on colonial reform because it is that part which can be considered normative political theory, i.e. his views on how a society, in this case colonial Peru, should be ordered. He believed that the king of Spain should govern his various territories through local Indigenous rulers, even offering himself as a deputy to carry out the policies he recom-mended for Peru. Poma wished for the Indigenous people to live separately from the Spaniards, recuperate their lands so that they could grow crops, and reverse an alarming decrease in their numbers.

Included here are a letter from Poma to the king, a description of the abuses of the Spanish *corregidores* (who were the district governors under the vice-roy of Peru), advice to the *corregidores* and to the authorities under them, recommendations to the king on the management of the dangerous mercury mines, advice to priests and bishops on how to behave justly, an imaginary meeting of Poma de Ayala with King Philip in which the king asks him ques-tions about how to resolve problems in Peru and Poma answers, and finally a recommendation to Christians of the world to read his book and heed his advice.

The First New Chronicle and Good Government can be seen as an example of a universal genre of literature of advice to rulers, often called "mirror of (or for) princes." Historian Robert Dankoff, in his introduction to *Kutadgu Bilig* (written in the eleventh century by the Turko-Islamic writer Yusuf Khass Hajib), says, "We find mirrors for princes wherever there is a tradition of autocratic state organization. There are examples from the ancient Near East, from China, India, the Islamic Near East, from the ancient Greek tyrannies, and from medieval Europe."[16]

Students of Western political thought are likely to study twelfth-century writers John of Salisbury (British) and Giles of Rome (French), and the Ital-ians Christine de Pizan (fifteenth century) and Niccolo Machiavelli (sixteenth century). Spanish writers of "mirror" literature included Antonio Guevara, Jeronimo Osorio, Felipe de la Torre, Marco Antonio de Camos y Requesens, and Jeronimo Merola. Fadrique Furio Ceriol wrote to Philip II with advice, while the works of Pedro Ribadeneyra, Juan de Mariana, and Juan de Santa Maria were dedicated, like the book by Poma de Ayala, to Philip III.

Figure 14.1.   Guamán Poma's drawing of himself presenting his book to King Philip III and answering his questions. Folio 975, Nueva corónica y buen gobierno (1616)
Courtesy of the Royal Danish Library, Copenhagen, Denmark

Literary scholar Mercedes Lopez-Baralt points out that Poma fulfilled the qualifications for an advisor to the king as laid out by Furio Ceriol. Furio states that, if the ruler has many lands under his governorship, he should seek advisors not only from among his countrymen but also from among those in his subject territories.[17] Poma listed his qualifications to be the King's advisor: he had impeccable aristocratic credentials from the pre-Incan and Incan nobility, and he had served the king by working with the colonial administration in several situations. He may very well have read similar advice manuals in Lima. Scholars believe that copies of works by the Spaniard Antonio Guevara, the Italian Francesco Patrizi, and German Johann Boemus could have been in libraries there. Enrique Garces, who spent many years in Peru, translated a work by Francesco Patrizi in 1591, which he dedicated to the aging Philip II.[18] Whether or not he read these earlier works, Poma de Ayala's *First New Chronicle and Good Government* can be classed among them as part of the genre of mirror for princes literature within the field of political thought.

Beyond this, a number of Peruvian scholars have called Poma de Ayala a precursor of later ideas on freedom, equality, and universal education. Scholar Juan Andía Chávez states that Poma demanded from the authorities all that was necessary for the continued existence of his people and insisted that the law be applied equally to all. He demanded the return to the Amerindians of the lands that had been taken away by the Spaniards and Andía notes that this demand has been considered by some as a precursor of the call for land reform in Latin America.[19] Historian Juan José Vega emphasizes that Poma de Ayala insisted on education for all girls and boys. He notes that Poma, breaking with Incan and European practices of elite patriarchal education, supported universal education for both sexes with schools in even the smallest villages.[20] Andia summarizes by saying that Poma de Ayala can be seen as one of the first great precursors in the struggle for universal human rights.[21]

Conservative Peruvian writers have tried to diminish his stature. In the 1940s, Raul Porras Barrenechea called him a resentful Indian, full of hate, possibly enlivened by alcohol, who wanted to replace one despotism with another even older despotism.[22] Porras' countryman, historian José Varallanos, however, writing in 1979, stated that it was time to resurrect Poma de Ayala as a great patriot, rescuing him from among the "dead leaves of history" and from the social and racial discrimination against him as an Indian.[23] But literary scholar Jaime Vargas Luna calls attention to the contradictions between Poma's desire to preserve the customs, cultures and populations of the Indigenous people while collaborating with the Spanish crown in the extirpation of the old religion in the crushing of the Takiy Unquy movement.[24]

Scholar Jean-Philippe Husson points out that Poma de Ayala believed that the Spaniards were foreigners in Peru and as such had no right to its riches. It was the Indigenous people who had rights to the land, to minerals under the soil, and to Peru's cultural heritage. Poma felt that while the Indigenous society of Peru could be criticized because it lacked Christianity, that defect did not have negative consequences for the rest of Peruvian civilization. In contrast, the Spaniards, although they were formally Christian, conducted themselves in a way that made them unworthy of salvation.[25] And, while a fervent Christian, Poma de Ayala was very critical of parish priests (while praising Franciscans and Jesuits). Literary scholar Marcel Velázquez Castro notes that he believed that the priests preferred to keep the Indigenous people illiterate in order to take advantage of their labor and sexually oppress the Indian women. His remedy was literacy for both men and women.[26]

Poma de Ayala strongly denounced the Spanish corruption of Indigenous women, criticizing those who, under the flag of Christianity, came to transform Amerindian women into sinners. This contributed to the convulsion of the Andean world, putting it "upside down." Poma's solution was complete segregation of Indigenous people and Spaniards, which would promote the ancestral way of life of the Andean people. This, scholar Sara Vicuña Guengerich notes, was in direct contrast to the view of El Inca Garcilaso de la Vega, who believed that a stable colonial society could only emerge from the fusion of the Andean and European cultures.[27]

Because Poma de Ayala has in recent years become such an iconic figure as a Peruvian Indian, the discovery of several documents in Italy in the 1990s that indicated that a mestizo Jesuit priest rather than Guamán Poma was the author of the *New Chronicle and Good Government* caused a tremendous stir in Peru and around the world. According to the documents, which were discovered in a private library in Naples, the mestizo Jesuit priest Blas Valera, who had supposedly died in Spain in 1597, instead returned to Peru, where he worked until 1618 before going back to Spain and dying there in 1619. The documents asserted that while in Peru he wrote the *New Chronicle and Good Government* using the name of Guamán Poma de Ayala.[28] The documents were found in the library of teacher and journalist Clara Miccenelli.[29] University of Bologna Anthropology Professor Laura Laurencich-Minelli was given access to the documents and has published extensively about them.

The first of the two Miccinelli manuscripts to be published was *Historia et rudimenta linguae Piruanorum* (History and Primer of the Language of the Peruvians). The document details the biography and beliefs of Blas Valera and was supposedly written by Italian missionaries Juan Antonio Cumis and Juan Anello Oliva in two periods, in 1610 and in 1637–8.[30] The second manuscript, *Exsul immeritus Blas Valera populo suo* (Blas Valera, Unjustly Exiled, to His Followers), is dated "Alcalá, Spain, 1618." It is in Latin and purports to be the handwritten will and testament of Blas Valera himself.[31] Laurencich explains that the two documents assert things that challenge history in a number of ways, including the assertion that Valera did not die in Spain in 1597.[32]

As the controversy over the documents continued over the years, three positions emerged: first, that the documents are authentic; second, that they are modern forgeries; and third, that they were forgeries from the seventeenth or the eighteenth century, the product of bitter battles within the Jesuit order over the evangelization of the Indies. At a conference held in Rome in September of 1999, scholars and experts on different sides of the issues presented papers. Technical expert Luigi Altamura, hired by Laurencich-Minelli, reported that all of the documents were written in a natural organic flowing fashion that is very distinct from that of forgeries.[33] Tests of the inks and colors used in the documents showed results indicating that all the pigments except titanium dioxide were consistent with those used in the seventeenth century.[34] And more recent research has shown that the Peruvian Incas were using titanium dioxide from a local mine on wooden drinking cups beginning in the early 1500s.[35]

However, when the documents were presented to the Asociación Société des Américanistes in Paris for review and publication, they were rejected as "highly suspicious."[36] Expert Juan Carlos Estenssoro, who examined the documents for the Asociación, stated that while the papers were from the correct period, they had marks of seals in the wrong places and were apparently envelopes that were being recycled to perpetrate a fraud. He also stated that the Quechua text would not have been understandable by a Quechua speaker because the syntax was Spanish.[37]

However, these technical matters are less significant than the problem of the lack of correspondence between the known beliefs of Guamán Poma and Blas Valera. Blas Valera was a mestizo whose mother was from the Chachapoyas ethnic group. He believed that the Indigenous people of Peru could be best brought to Christianity by preserving aspects of their Inca religion, which he felt was similar to Christianity, and he was suspected by the Inquisition of founding a neo Inca-Christian movement. Adorno says that Guamán Poma, on the other hand, condemned the new mestizo race constantly and obsessively, held an orthodox view of Catholic priests and their campaigns against Amerindian religion and rites, and held the Chachapoyas in fierce contempt. He railed against corrupt and lecherous priests but not against the goal of evangelization. On mestizos Adorno says, "Guamán Poma's resounding condemnation of *mestizaje* constitutes one of the basic premises of his work's conceptualization."[38] She states that these beliefs are expressed throughout the *New Chronicle* and also in legal documents and drawings that are separate from that major work. She adds that it is impossible to dismiss the enormous energy of the two great forces motivating *New Chronicle*: the desire to extirpate idolatry and the fear of the disappearance of the Andean race caused by *mestizaje* (the mixing of Spanish and Indian).[39]

Finally, Blas Valera biographer Sabine Hyland lays out the reasons why she believes that the Naples documents are what she calls "true lies," that is, later forgeries but also dating from the seventeenth century. She first examines the critiques by Estenssoro finding them "hardly . . . sufficient to label the document a modern forgery."[40] She also provides evidence against Adorno's accusations of anachronistic text and summarizes by stating that none of the arguments that the documents are a modern forgery are "capable of withstanding scrutiny."[41] She goes on to say that the documents present a very real mystery because while there is evidence that they are "genuine seventeenth-century artifacts," they contain "obvious falsehoods." She therefore agrees with anthropologist R. Tom Zuidema and others that they are "authentic documents containing falsehoods that express the frustrations and desires of certain Jesuits in Peru."[42] She believes that Anello Oliva wrote the parts of *Historia et Rudimenta* that were ascribed to him and probably at least part of *Exsul Immeritus*, which was supposedly written by Blas Valera, noting that Valera's signature on that latter document does not match his only surviving signature from the time of his novitiate. She adds, "One major question remaining is whether these documents were one man's anguished vision or part of a larger Jesuit movement."[43]

The New Chronicle and Good Government appears to have survived a bizarre and unexpected attack on its authenticity and it maintains its status as a major work of advocacy for the rights of his own people by a notable seventeenth century Indigenous man, Felipe Guamán Poma de Ayala. Whereas Porras de Barrenechea called him "a resentful Indian," D. A. Brading says he "must surely figure as the chief native disciple of Bartolomé de Las Casas, his hopes for Peru a faithful application of the doctrines of the great Dominican. Where else in colonial literature can we encounter so powerful an affirmation of the . . . exaltation of the poor and downtrodden?"[44]

THE FIRST NEW CHRONICLE AND GOOD GOVERNMENT BY GUAMÁN POMA

A Letter from Don Felipe Guamán Poma de Ayala to His Majesty King Philip:

Many times I have doubted, Your Sacred Royal Catholic Majesty, whether to accept this enterprise, and many more times after taking it up I have wished to go back, judging my intentions to be reckless and finding my capacities insufficient to the task of finishing it, in accordance with its reliance on histories written in no script whatsoever, but solely on *quipus* [knotted cords used for record keeping] and on the reports and accounts of the oldest Indian men and women elders and eyewitnesses, that they may swear to it, and that any sentence that may be passed be thereby valid.

And thus I spent countless days and years amidst discourses that go back to the beginning of this kingdom, until, overcome by my advanced years, I accomplished this age-old desire, which was always to investigate, despite the crudeness of my wit, my blind eyes, little sight, little learning, and my lack of a graduate degree, a doctorate, a master's, or even Latin. Yet, as the first in this kingdom with the occasion and the ability to serve Your Majesty, I resolved to write about the history, descendants, and famous deeds of the first kings, lords, and captains, our grandfathers; and about the nobles and the lives of the Indians, their generations, and their descent from the first Indians—the *Wari Wiracocha Runa* and *Wari Runa* (the descendants of Noah of the Flood), the *Purun Runa*, and the *Auca Runa.*

I would also write about the twelve Incas, their idolatries and errors, about their wives, the queens; about the princesses, noblewomen, wives of nobles, and captains general; and about the dukes, counts, marquises, and other Indian petty authorities. And about the contest between the legitimate Inca, Topa Cusiwalpa Wascar Inca, and his bastard brother Atawalpa Inca; and about his captains general and majors, Chalco Chima Inca, Awa Panti Inca, Quisquis Inca, Quiso Yupanqui Inca, and Manco Inca, who defended himself from the damage inflicted by the Spaniards in the days of the Emperor.

And then about the conquest of this your Kingdom of the Indies of Peru; about the uprisings against your Royal Crown by Don Francisco Pizarro, Don Diego de Almagro, Gonzalo Pizarro, Carvajal, Francisco Hernández Girón, and the other captains and soldiers; and about your first Viceroy, Vasco Núñez de Vela; and about Viceroy Don Antonio de Mendoza of the Order of Santiago, Viceroy Don Martin Enriquez, Viceroy Don Luis de Velasco of the Order of Santiago, Viceroy Don Gaspar Zúñiga y Acevedo, Count of Monterrey, and Viceroy Marquis Don Juan de Mendoza y Luna.

And about the lives of your *corregidores* [district governors], notaries, deputies, *encomenderos* [holders of rights to Indians and their labor] and parish priests; about the mine owners, the Spanish travelers who stay in the [royal way stations], and the roads, rivers, boundaries, and the whole Kingdom of Peru of the Indies; about the inspectors and judges; and about the noble *caciques* [Indian leaders or chiefs], the poor common Indians, and other matters.

To this end, I have toiled to obtain the most truthful accounts I could taking the essence from all the people who were brought to me; even though they came from many different places, I finally reduced all their accounts to the most common opinion. I selected the language and the wording, whether in Castilian, Aymara, Colla, Puquina Conde, Yunca, Quechua, Inca, Wanca, Chinchaysuyu, Yauyo, Andesuyu, Condesuyu, Collasuyu, Cañari, Cayanpi, or Quito. I have labored hard to complete this book, with the hope of presenting it to you. It is entitled *First New Chronicle of the Indies of Peru, Profitable to Faithful Christians*, written and illustrated by my hand and wit in such a way that the variety and inventiveness of the pictures and illustrations, to which Your Majesty is inclined, may lighten the weight and trouble of a script that is lacking in invention and in the ornamentation and polished style found among the great talents. As an example and for the conservation of the Holy Catholic Faith and correcting errors and profit for the infidels through the salvation of their souls, as an example and corrective for the Christians, whether they be priests or *corregidores*, *encomenderos*, mine owners, or Spanish travelers, noble *caciques* or common Indians, may Your Majesty benignly receive this humble small service, together with my great hope; for me, this will be a blessed and restful reward for my toil.

In the Province of Lucanos, on the first of January of 1613

Your humble subject,

Don Felipe de Ayala,

Author

History of the *Corregidores* of This Kingdom and Their Lives

They live as absolute rulers with little fear of justice or of God, throughout the kingdom. One of them will extract thirty thousand pesos from a [district] and become rich before he leaves, harming the poor Indians and the [Indian] nobles, scorning them, and taking away their offices and duties, in this kingdom.

Since the time when these *corregidores* were created by Don Francisco de Toledo [viceroy, 1569–1581], they have caused terrible damage to these kingdoms of Peru. By the time they finish their terms and leave their [districts], they amass fortunes of more than fifty thousand pesos, at the cost, and to the detriment, of the poor Indians throughout this kingdom. And there is no remedy: in this way the Indians are coming to an end.

The *corregidores*, claiming to defend the poor Indians of this kingdom from the damage done by the padres, the priests of the Indian parishes, the *encomenderos*, and the other Spaniards such as stewards, travelers, and judges in this kingdom, take and steal everything for themselves, without giving anything to the Indians.

The *corregidores* get involved in commerce and trade and many other things, and for these purposes they take money from the community treasuries and the tribute collections, or they borrow money from the village priests. The noble *caciques* do not defend against this, because the *corregidores* befriend them and become godparents of their children. The priests and the *corregidores* then praise them: "Oh Don Pedro! What a noble chief you are!"

They are friends in this kingdom. Other nobles are afraid that the *corregidor* will mistreat them or, will take away the ruling offices that God and His Majesty gave them, or will accuse them with false information, and so they keep quiet about what goes on and pretend not to notice.

The *corregidores*, priests of the Indian parishes, *encomenderos*, stewards, and other Spaniards who go about among the Indians, all act as absolute lords with little fear of God and justice. They do terrible harm and damage to the poor nobles and Indians of this kingdom.

The *corregidores* who are honorable and Christian, and who fear God and His Majesty, earn their salary cleanly and are satisfied with it; they do not get into trouble by having too many friends, and they have no enemies. It there are no charges against them, their enemies have to keep quiet. Their purses fill with coins, they give good accounts of themselves to the royal court, and they deserve new assignments as *corregidores*. . . .

Corregidores, Deputy *Corregidores*, Commissioner Judges, Notaries [etc.]

Christian Readers: Know that God's good justices—judges who are honorable—should want to get through their terms of office in the [districts] without lawsuits. They should take with them, in good stead, the small amount that they have earned, but not all that they have stolen: let them leave behind everything except for their poverty, and not feel ashamed. They should be able to look the viceroy and his court in the face and be honored. Those who do ill should be offered no other position in this kingdom. Judges will then keep to a clean path and have many friends, while their enemies will be mocked and will weep. You will come out laughing, as did the *corregidor* and judge Gregorio López de Puga—a licentiate, a brave judge, and a Christian, who was no Creole but rather was born in Spain and studied in Salamanca. There had been so many lawsuits among the other *corregidores*, one *corregidor* against another, that he asked me (as a level-headed, wise, and well-read man) how he might get through his terms without such suits. I answered him in the way I have described above.

Here, then, is my advice, which you may take if you want to go through your term without lawsuits and leave your office with your purse filled with coins while the poor Indians mourn [your departure].

First of all, you should do your work as God ordained. Be a good Christian, fear God, and favor the poor of Jesus Christ.

Second, you should be a brave judge, and display justice and a lion's eyes and teeth to the Spaniards, *encomenderos*, padres, and priests of the Indian parishes.

Third, do not punish anyone without sufficient evidence, and never do so at the bidding of *encomenderos* or priests, and never do anything simply because the priests will it. If you were to do so, you would be ruined. Rather, they have always been terrible enemies, like knives, inciting the Indians with the harm they cause and bringing up charges when *corregidores* are audited at the ends of their terms. Therefore, *corregidores*, tell each of them to go say their Masses and their prayers for the dead: "Say the Mass, toll the church bells, and hear confessions, as the Holy Council [of Trent] has ordained you do." If each one would stick to his own office and benefice, all would be well and he would be honored. . . .

Recommendation to the King about the Mercury Mines

The mercury mines[45] of Huancavelica are where the poor Indians are so harshly punished, where they are tortured and so many Indians die; it is there that the noble *caciques* of this kingdom are finished off and tortured. The same is true in all the other mines: the silver mines of Potosí, the silver mines of Chocllo Cocha, the gold mines of Carabaya, and the other mines elsewhere in this kingdom. The owners and stewards of the mines whether Spaniards, *mestizos*, or Indians, are such tyrants, with no fear of God or justice, because they are not audited and are not inspected twice a year. And thus there is no remedy.

All of this abuse and shaming is done to them under the excuse that a few Indians are missing from the forced labor draft. These punishments are carried out against the [Indian] lords of the land in this kingdom, who hold their titles by His Majesty. They are punished most cruelly, as if they were thieves or traitors. Because of these troubles, they have died in shame, and there is no remedy. . . .

And [the mine owners] keep Indian cooking women in their residences; they use cooking as a pretext for taking concubines. They and their stewards force their way on some of the daughters of their servants' wives by sending their husbands off to the mines at night, or by sending them somewhere far away. And they oblige the Indians to accept corn or meat or corn beer or cheese or bread at their own expense, and they deduct the price from their labor and their workdays. In this way the Indians end up very poor and deep in debt, and they have no way to pay their tribute.

There is no remedy for all this, because any *corregidor*, governor, or judge who enters comes to an agreement with [the mine owners], and all [the owners] join forces in bribing him. When he sees the gold with his own eyes, he would rather tell them to kill all the poor Indians. Even the protector of the Indians is useless; he is, instead, against the Indians. He does not defend them against these torments from hell, nor does he warn Your Majesty or your royal court about the harms done to the poor Indian.

Your Majesty should know: where do the mine owners get the means to dress up all in silk and gold and silver, other than from the labor of the poor Indians and from what they steal from Your Majesty? Therefore, it would be good that these mine owners be inspected every six months and audited and held to account, and that the mines be inspected. . . .

[The Indians] leave their towns to avoid going to the mines, where they would suffer torments and martyrdom. To avoid suffering the demonic pains and torments of that inferno, some flee the mines, while others flee the highway that would bring them to the mines, to keep from dying a sudden death. Those who go would rather die than live, and they beg to be finished off once and for all, because, when they get the mercury poisoning, they dry up like sticks, they get asthma, and they cannot live by day or by night. They last a year or two like that, and then they die.

Therefore, for my part, I recommend that Your Majesty have your governor and your court report to you, write to you, and inform you, so that some Christian might stand up for the poor of Jesus Christ, in order that this might be remedied and that all the ills and harm done in the mines of this kingdom might cease to grow. . . .

The Priests of This Kingdom

The priests who stand in for God and his saints—the cleric St. Peter, the Mercedarian friar of Our Lady of Mercy, the lord St. Francis, St. Dominic, St. Augustine, and the hermits St. Paul, the first hermit, and St. Anthony—do not do as those blessed souls did. Instead, they tend towards greed for silver, clothes, the things of the world, the sins of the flesh, and appetites and wrongs that cannot be put into writing, though the good reader will immediately know that they are well worth exemplary punishments. They should be punished by the Holy Inquisition, and the blame for this state should be laid to their prelates and superiors. Their sins harm the Spaniards, and even more so the New Christians, who are the Indians and blacks. How can a priest who has a dozen children set a good example for the Indians of this kingdom?

The priests of the Indian parishes are very bad-tempered, despotic, and proud, and they are filled with disdain, which causes the Indians to keep away from them in fear. These priests forget that our Lord Jesus Christ made himself poor and humble, so that he might attract the poor sinners, gather them in, and bring them into his holy church, and from there bring them to His kingdom of heaven. . . .

The priests of the Indian parishes trade and do business, in their own persons and through others, causing great damage; and they do not pay. With the pretext of paying [their debts], they employ many Indians, and there is no remedy, throughout the kingdom.

The priests oversee the making of cloth . . . to sell, claiming that the cloth is for their prelates. They tell their managers to order the poor Indians to make the cloth, employing them without paying them anything at all, throughout the kingdom. . . .

The only thing that you must do, Christian priests, is commend yourselves to God.

The second thing is to read these chapters, and cease being fierce. Humble yourselves before your prelates; do not be despotic lords; do not meddle in doing justice when that is not your place; do not enter into government, nor give orders from a post of justice or of the noble *caciques* and *corregidores*. Do not go beyond the Holy Council [of Trent], beyond all that was decreed by God in the Ten Commandments, the Holy Gospel, and the good works of mercy, and beyond all His Majesty's decrees. Do not go beyond the Testaments.

Be satisfied with your salary and altar fees. Pay what you owe for your food. You must pay for hay, firewood, other products, and the labor of the contracted Indians.

Do not introduce the living soul of a woman into your consecrated house without pondering that you are a priest. Do not let your other sins be known in public, for you are setting a bad example for Christians.

Do not fight with everyone in the village, nor with any poor Indian man or woman, as you do, taking up arms—a sword—against laymen soldiers and attacking them like highwaymen on the open roads, taking away the Indians' estates and stealing their women, their daughters, and everything they own, even though you have never been charged with these crimes. . . .

On this occasion, let me reply to His Lordship [the bishop], and let me say:

I beg Your Lordship be pleased to hear my plea for justice, that Your Lordship might discover the truth. Send us the reverend fathers from the Company of Jesus, or the reverend friars and fathers from the Order of St. Francis (but from no other religious order), for six months. If we are wrong, and we end up quarreling with these saintly religious men, these servants of Jesus Christ, then punish us. Otherwise, Your Lordship will discover the whole truth, will do service to God and justice to us, and will favor the poor Indians. Your Lordship may see the crimes and the insolence with which [the priest] treats the Spaniards; what might he not do with my Indians, helpless and poor as they are? . . .

Thus you must consider and put an end to this. For there are no *encomenderos* nor lords of this land other than us, the legitimate owners of the land by the rights of God and by justice and its laws. With the exception of the king, there is no other Spaniard who has the right: all are foreigners (*mitmacs*) in our land, and they are under our command and lordship, which was given to us by God. Consider, Christian.

His Majesty Questions, the Author Replies

His Royal Catholic Majesty questions the author Ayala to learn everything there is to know about the kingdom of the Indians of Peru, for good government and justice, for remedying troubles and misfortunes, for the poor Indians of the kingdom to multiply, and for the reform and good example of the Spaniards, *corregidores*, justices, priests of the Indian parishes, *encomenderos*, noble *caciques*, and petty authorities.

Hearing His Majesty's questions, the author replies and speaks with His Majesty, saying:

"Your Royal Catholic Majesty, you should listen closely to me. When I have finished, please ask me questions. I am delighted to give you my report on everything in the kingdom, for the memory of the world and Your Majesty's greatness."

Your Royal Catholic Majesty, I will communicate with Your Majesty regarding the service of God our Lord and regarding the service to your royal crown and the increase and welfare of the Indians of this kingdom, because some people report lies to you, others report the truth, and others give their reports in order to get Your Majesty to grant them a position as bishop, dean, canon, president, *Audiencia* judge, or some other rank and post.

I, as the grandson of the king of Peru, would like to serve Your Majesty; to meet with you face to face; to speak and communicate about these things in your presence. But I cannot travel so far, being eighty years old and infirm. [Internal references hint that Poma was somewhat younger.] I hope that you will be pleased with my thirty years of working in poverty, leaving my house, children, and estates to serve Your Majesty. Therefore, we will meet through writing and sending letters. So, Your Majesty, please ask me questions, and I will reply to them in this way.

His Majesty asks: "Don Felipe, author Ayala, tell me how the Indians of this kingdom had multiplied even before there was an Inca."

I say to Your Majesty that, in those times, the Inca alone was king, though there were also dukes, counts, marquises, and great noble lords. But they lived under the laws and commandments of the Incas, and because they had a king, they peacefully served in this kingdom; they multiplied, and had estates, plenty to eat, and their own children and wives.

"Tell me, author, why do the Indians not multiply now? Why are they becoming poor?"

I will say to Your Majesty, first, that they do not multiply because all the best women and maidens are taken by the priests of the Indian parishes, *encomenderos, corregidores,* Spaniards, stewards, deputies, and officers, and their servants. That is why there are so many little mestizos and mestizas in this kingdom. They claim that the women have lovers as a pretext for taking them and their estates from the poor. Because of all these things, all these offenses and harms, the Indians hang themselves, as the *Changas* did in Andahuayllas—that was a small mountain range, once filled with Indian men and women; they preferred to die once and for all rather than face all the harm that was being done to them.

Tell me, author, how will the people multiply?

I say to Your Majesty, just as I have written: the priests, *encomenderos, corregidores,* other Spaniards, and noble *caciques* should live as Christians, as Your Majesty has ordained, and not go beyond that. They should let [the people] enjoy their wives and estates, and should leave their maidens alone. There should not be so many kings and justices over the people, and they should let the people multiply, or else be severely punished and removed from their offices and benefices.

Tell me, author, how will the Indians become rich?

Your Majesty should know that they should keep community estates (which they call *sapsi*), with fields planted with corn, wheat, potatoes, peppers, *macno*, cotton, and grapes, [as well as] textile workshops, dye works, coca fields, and fruit orchards. The maidens and widows should spin and weave—ten women working on one piece of cloth. On one portion of the community land (*sapsi*), they should keep Castilian cattle. Each Indian man and woman should have a piece of an estate from their community land (*sapsi*).

Overseeing this, in every province there should be an administrator with a salary set at one seventh [of the income from the community lands]—one main overseer for each province. Whenever there is need, Your Majesty would be able to borrow money and take your royal fifth from the commoners.

With this, the Indians of this kingdom will become rich people. God and Your Majesty's royal crown will be served in this kingdom; and the Indians will increase in this kingdom.

Tell me, author: how can the absent Indians in that kingdom be gathered in?

I say to Your Majesty that, in every province, these Indian men, women and children should be gathered into some old pueblo, for they are lost. Give them cropland and bounded pastures, so that they may serve God and Your Majesty. Let them be called your royal crown Indians, and let them pay taxes and tribute, and hold no other office. Their administrator, the noble *cacique*, should be subject to you. No one but the administrator should take a salary from what they pay, in keeping with the Indians' wishes; the rest [of their taxes] should be applied to the service of your royal crown. In this way, [the absent Indians] will be gathered in throughout the kingdom....

Your Majesty should order, under strict penalties, that the [Indigenous] nobles and Indians should not be abused, and that no Indian boy under the age of twenty should be sent into the gallery of any mercury, silver, or gold mine, nor to smelt ore or work in the mercury ovens, because they are tender of age, mere boys. They quickly come down with mercury poisoning, and there is no way to heal them; they die, and the Indians come to an end.

. . . Likewise, Your Majesty should decree that stores of food and water be kept in the mine galleries throughout this kingdom. Then, if [the miners] become caught inside, they may have the help of God, food, and water, so that they can work day and night to clear the mountain and make an opening. In this way those who are trapped in mines may be saved in this kingdom.

. . . [End of the King's questions.]

See here the Christians of the world: some will weep; others will laugh; others will curse. Others will commend me to God. Others, out of sheer wrath, will throw away this book; others will want to hold this book and *Chronicle* in their hands, to restrain their spirits, consciences, and hearts, and to live by the law of God—the Ten Commandments, the holy gospel, and everything decreed by the Holy Mother Church of Rome, the most Holy Father Pope, and everything that His Majesty decrees. You should know that there is only one God and one king and his justice. The proud, like Lucifer, will be punished in this world—or, if not, in the next world, by the punishments of God. . . .

Therefore, I beg for you to restrain yourselves and for each of you to see what it is that you are. If you are a gentleman or an *hidalgo*, you will seem very goodly. But if you are a commoner, a Jew, or a Moor, mestizo, or mulatto, as God created you, do not pretend to be a gentleman by force. Noble *caciques* are of long lineage: commoner Indians, do not pretend to be lords. Rather, let each one appear according to his nature, as God created him and ordained in the world.

Thus, this *Chronicle* is for the whole world and all of Christendom. Even the infidels should read it, for the good justice, public order, and law of the world.

NOTES

1. Rolena Adorno and Franklin Pease state that Poma de Ayala was born around 1535 while David Frye uses the 1550 date. See Rolena Adorno, "Early Peruvian recorded daily life under the rule of Spanish conquistadores," *The New World* 1 (Spring 1990), 1; Franklin Pease, prólogo to *Nueva Corónica y Buen Gobierno* by Felipe Guamán Poma de Ayala (Lima: Fondo de la Cultura Económica, 2005), x; and David Frye, introduction to *The First New Chronicle and Good Government (Abridged)*, by Felipe Guamán Poma de Ayala. Selected, translated and annotated by David Frye (Indianapolis: Hackett Publishing Co., 2006), viii.

2. Carlos García-Bedoya M., "Guaman Poma: de la visión de los vencidos a la fundación del discurso letrado andino," in "Más allá de los 400 años: Guamán Poma de Ayala revisitado," ed. Rocío Quispe-Agnoli and Carlos García-Bedoya. *Revista de Investigación de la Facultad de Letras y Ciencias Humanas*, 91, no. 133 (March 2020): 36.

3. Rocio Quispe-Agnoli, 'Escribirlo es nunca acabar': cuatrocientos cinco años de lecturas y silencios de una *Opera Aperta* colonial andina," in "Más allá de los 400 años: Guamán Poma de Ayala revisitado," ed. Rocío Quispe-Agnoli and Carlos García-Bedoya. *Revista de Investigación de la Facultad de Letras y Ciencias Humanas* 91, no. 133 (March 2020): 6.

4. Jaime Vargas Luna, "Felipe Guamán Poma de Ayala (¿1556?/1556?-¿1615/1644?)," *Narradores indigenas y mestizos de la época colonial (siglos XVI–XVII): Zonas andina y mesoamericana,* ed. Rocío Cortés and Margarita Zamora. (Lima: CELACP, 2016), 270.

5. Pease, prólogo, x.

6. Adorno, "Early Peruvian," 1.

7. Raquel Chang-Rodriguez, "Sobre los cronistas indígenas del Perú y los comienzos de una escritura hispanoamericana," *Revista Iberoamericana* 48, núm. 120–121 (julio-diciembre 1982): 546.

8. Rolena Adorno, "New Biographical Information about Guaman Poma," A Witness unto Itself: The Integrity of the Autograph Manuscript of Felipe Guamán Poma de Ayala's El primer nueva corónica y buen gobierno (1615/1616). Copenhagen: The Royal Library, 2002. http://wayback-01.kb.dk/wayback/20101105080508/http://www2.kb.dk/elib/mss/poma/docs/adorno/2002/index.htm.

9. Annick Benavides, "Guaman Poma and the First New Chronicle and Good Government," *First American Art Magazine* (Summer 2017): 34. https://firstamericanartmagazine.com/faam-no-15-summer-2017/.

10. Rolena Adorno, "'(Re)discovery' and Provenance," A Witness unto Itself: The Integrity of the Autograph Manuscript of Felipe Guamán Poma de Ayala's El primer nueva corónica y buen gobierno (1615/1616). Copenhagen: The Royal Library, 2002. http://wayback-01.kb.dk/wayback/20101105080508/http://www2.kb.dk/elib/mss/poma/docs/adorno/2002/index.htm.

11. The digital facsimile of Poma's work on the web page of the Danish Royal Library can be found here: http://www.kb.dk/permalink/2006/poma/info/en/front

page.htm. The first of the parts selected for this volume begins at: http://www.kb.dk/ permalink/2006/poma/8/en/text/?open=id2971082.

12. Serafin M. Coronel-Molina, forward to *The First New Chronicle and Good Government: On the History of the World and the Incas up to 1615*, by Felipe Guamán Poma de Ayala, trans. and ed. by Roland Hamilton (Austin: University of Texas Press, 2009), xiv.

13. Adorno, "Early Peruvian," 2.

14. Sara Castro-Klaren, *The Narrow Pass of Our Nerves: Writing, Coloniality and Post-Colonial Theory* (Frankfurt: Vervuert, 2011), 153.

15. Frye, annotation, *The First New*, 143.

16. Robert Dankoff, introduction to *Wisdom of Royal Glory: A Turko-Islamic Mirror for Princes*, by Yusuf Khass Hajib (Chicago: University of Chicago Press, 1983), 3.

17. Mercedes Lopez-Baralt, "La iconografía de vicios y virtudes en el arte de reinar de Guamán Poma de Ayala: Una contribución Americana a la literatura de regimine principium," in *Historia y ficción en la narrativa hispano-americana*, ed. Roberto González Echeverría (Caracas: Monte Avila Editores, 1984), 73.

18. Ronald W. Truman, *Spanish Treatises on Government, Society and Religion in the Time of Philip II* (Leiden: Brill, 1999), 23.

19. Juan Andía Chávez, *El cronista Felipe Guamán Poma de Ayala: Un precursor de los derechos humanos* (Lima: Centro de Investigación Empresorial, 2002) 64, 65, 126, 142.

20. Juan José Vega, *Guamán Poma: el precursor* (Lima: Derrama Magisterial, 1988) 15–16. Poma says, *"Que los dichos maestros han de enseñar [a leer y escribir] . . . a los niños, niñas, mozos y las doncellas . . . para que sean cristianas . . . y si pudiera en pueblo grande o chico haya escuela. . . ."* [These teachers must teach (how to read and write) to the boys, girls, young men and maidens . . . so that they will be Christians . . . and if possible there should be a school in every large or small town." Vol. II, 543, of the *Nueva corónica y buen gobierno*. Quoted in Andia, *El cronista*, 74.

21. Andía, *El cronista*, 142.

22. Raul Porras Barrenechea, "El Cronista Indio Felipe Huaman Poma de Ayala (1534–1515?)," *Mercurio Peruano* 227 (Feb. 1946): 97–99.

23. José Varallanos, *Guamán Poma de Ayala: Cronista precursor y libertorio* (Lima: G. Herrera, Editores, 1979), 203.

24. Vargas Luna, "Felipe Guamán," 270.

25. Jean-Philippe Husson, "La defensa de la nación indo-peruana, objetivo primordial de Felipe Guamán Poma de Ayala," *Revista de Crítica Literaria Latinoamericana*, 42, no. 84 (2016): 40, 42.

26. Marcel Velázquez Castro, "Figuras del mal gobierno: 'españoles soberbiosos e indias putas' en la obra de Guamán Poma de Ayala," in "Más allá de los 400 años: Guamán Poma de Ayala revisitado," ed. Rocío Quispe-Agnoli and Carlos García-Bedoya. *Revista de Investigación de la Facultad de Letras y Ciencias Humanas* 91, no. 133 (March 2020): 293, 295.

27. Sara Vicuña Guengerich, "Virtuosas o corruptas: Las mujeres indígenas en las obras de Guamán Poma de Ayala y el Inca Garcilaso de la Vega,*" Hispania*, 96, no. 4 (December 2013): 673.

28. Laura Laurencich-Minelli, "Presentación del documento Exsul immeritus Blas Valera populo suo," in *Guamán Poma y Blas Valera: Tradición Andina e Historia Colonial*, ed. Francesca Cantu (Rome: Instituto Italo-Latinoamericano, 2001), 111–2.

29. Francesca Cantú, introduction to *Guamán Poma y Blas Valera: Tradición Andina e Historia Colonial*, ed. Francesca Cantu (Rome: Instituto Italo-Latinoamericano, 2001), 15–16.

30. Ivan Boserup and Mette Kia Krabbe Meyer, "The Illustrated Contract between Guamán Poma and the Friends of Blas Valera: A Key Miccinelli Manuscript Discovered in 1998," in *Unlocking the Doors to the Worlds of Guamán Poma and his Nueva corónica*, ed. Rolena Adorno and Ivan Boserup (Copenhagen: The Royal Library Museum Tusculanum Press, 2015), 20.

31. Boserup and Meyer, "Illustrated," 20.

32. Laurencich, "Presentación," 111–12.

33. Luigi Altamura, "Relazione di consulenza concernente la verifica di scritture," in *Guamán Poma y Blas Valera: Tradición Andina e Historia Colonial*, ed. Francesca Cantu (Rome: Instituto Italo-Latinoamericano, 2001), 144.

34. A. Bertoluzza, C. Fagnano, M. Rossi, and A. Tinti, "Primi resultati dell'indagine spettroscopica micro-raman sui documenti miccinelli," *Guamán Poma y Blas Valera: Tradición Andina e Historia Colonial*, ed. Francesca Cantu (Rome: Instituto Italo-Latinoamericano, 2001), 189.

35. Adam Rogers, "How the Inca Discovered a Prized Pigment: A centuries-old history of titanium white," *Smithsonian Magazine*, June 2021, 18.

36. Jesús Bustamante García, "Falsificación y revisión histórica: Informe sobre un supuesto nuevo texto colonial andino," *Revista de Indias* LVII, num. 210 (1997): 564.

37. Juan Carlos Estenssoro, "¿Historia de un fraude o un fraude histórico?" *Revista de Indias* LVII, num. 210 (1997): 567–8, 573.

38. Rolena Adorno, *Guamán Poma: Writing and Resistance in Colonial Peru*, Second edition (Austin: University of Texas Press and Institute of Latin American Studies, 2000), xli.

39. Rolena Adorno, "Contenidos y contradicciones: la obra de Felipe Guamán Poma y las aserveraciones de Blas Valera," paper read at the international colloquium "Guamán Poma de Ayala y Blas Valera: tradición andina e historia colonial," organized by the Instituto Italo-Latinamericano in Rome, September 29, 1999. http://ensayistas.org/filosofos/peru/Guamán/adorno.htm. This paper was presented at the conference but was not included in the book of papers from that conference published in 2001. Other writers who make similar points about the contrast between the views of Poma and Valera are R. Tom Zuidema, "Guamán Poma, Blas Valera y los escritos jesuitas sobre el Perú," in *Guamán Poma y Blas Valera: Tradición Andina e Historia Colonial*, ed. Francesca Cantu (Rome: Instituto Italo-Latinoamericano, 2001), 370; and Xavier Albó, "La *Nueva corónica y buen gobierno*: ¿obra de Guamán Poma o de jesuitas?" *Anthropológica* 16, num. 16 (1998): 327–29.

40. Sabine Hyland, *The Jesuit and the Incas* (Ann Arbor, University of Michigan Press, 2004), 215.

41. Hyland, *The Jesuit*, 215–21.

42. Hyland, *The Jesuit*, 227–28.

43. Hyland, *The Jesuit*, 225, 32.

44. D. A. Brading, *The First America: The Spanish Monarchy, Creole patriots, and the Liberal State 1492–1867* (Cambridge: Cambridge University Press, 1991), 165.

45. Mercury was used to extract gold from ore, but it is so toxic that thousands of Indigenous mercury miners died.

Chapter Fifteen

Alonso de Sandoval

"The Souls of Blacks Are as Important as Those of Whites"

Alonso de Sandoval, a Jesuit priest, wrote a treatise on slavery and in particular the slave trade as a manual for missionaries to the thousands of enslaved Africans taken to Cartagena, Colombia, by European enslavers in the first half of the seventeenth century. His 1627 treatise, which he called *De instauranda Aethiopum salute* (although this title appears only on the cover of the second 1647 edition), is noteworthy as the first Spanish-American writing that looks at the historical, philosophical, and cultural aspects of the encounter between Africans and Europeans in a New World context.[1] The work is also important in the field of African studies, providing valuable information about the origins, cultures, and languages of the enslaved people.[2]

Biography

Sandoval was born in 1576 in Seville but was taken to Lima, Peru, when he was seven years old when his father was named accountant of the Royal Treasury there. Tristan Sanchez, Alonso's father, held several important posts in the New World beginning in the 1540s and was a key official under three viceroys.[3] Sanchez had several children with his first wife in Lima and, after his return to Spain and her death, married Alonso's mother María de Aguilera and had several more children including Alonso before returning to Lima with the whole family in 1583. Alonso studied at the San Pablo Jesuit School which was considered one of the best in the Americas at that time. He officially joined the Company of Jesus in 1593 and was ordained a priest in 1600. Six of his eleven siblings also chose the religious life, with two rising to high posts in their religious orders.[4]

Answering a call for priests to work in the new Jesuit province of Nueva Granada (now Colombia) by its Provincial General, Sandoval began work in Cartagena in 1605, ministering to the enslaved Africans disembarking there before they were sent to other parts of the Spanish Empire. Early in his ministry, Sandoval asked for an assistant, and in 1610 Pedro Claver was assigned to work with him. While Claver was called the "slave of the slaves" and was eventually canonized by the Catholic Church, his interests and abilities were different from those of Sandoval. Claver biographer Arnold Lunn writes that "Whereas Claver was only interested in slaves, Sandoval was interested in slavery."[5] Except for a two-year stay from 1617 to 1619 in Lima, during which time he was able to do research for his book, and several missionary trips to other areas in Colombia, Sandoval would spend the rest of his life in Cartagena.[6] In 1619, he published his translation from Portuguese into Spanish of the biography of St. Francis Xavier by Joao de Lucena.[7] In 1620, he was named procurator general of the Jesuit province and, in 1623, head of the Jesuit school.[8] Sandoval was never approved to profess the fourth and highest vow in the Jesuit order (that of obedience to the Pope) in spite of the recommendation of his superior. In 1627, the first edition of his treatise on slavery with the long title *Naturaleza, policía sagrada i profana, costumbres i ritos, disciplina i catecismo evangelico de todos etíopes* was published in Seville.

Sandoval saw as his first obligation to the arriving enslaved Africans, after treating the sick and providing some clothes to the naked, the teaching of Catholic doctrine followed by baptism. The Africans were supposed to have been baptized before they left African ports but Sandoval found that, while the majority had had some water splashed on them, they did not know the reason for it. Sandoval instructed the enslaved Africans according to their levels of knowledge and baptized those who were willing.[9] However, the diocesan clergy objected to the Jesuits taking over baptisms saying that baptizing was their role. Sandoval and the Jesuits took the case to court and won not only the case but the admiration of the local clergy for their work among the mistreated Africans.[10]

One of Sandoval's major problems was communication with the enslaved because of the many different languages that they spoke. While he eventually learned several African languages, he used numerous interpreters and kept their names and languages in a little book that he carried with him. He had to use two interpreters to communicate with speakers of some languages because no one was available who spoke both their language and Spanish. Sandoval said he was eventually able to distinguish more than seventy African tongues.[11]

In 1647, he published a revised, longer version of his treatise on slavery in Madrid and may have been planning a third but, in 1650 he contracted a serious illness from which he died two years later. His associate Pedro Claver died in 1654. With both of its principal advocates now dead, most of the enthusiasm of the Cartagena Jesuits for their mission to the enslaved Africans was lost.[12]

The Philosophers and Slavery

Slavery has been defended and attacked by philosophers and theologians for many centuries. Aristotle (384–322 BCE), wrote that "it is clear that, just as some are by nature free, so others are by nature slaves, and for these latter the condition of slavery is both beneficial and just."[13] In contrast, early Christianity appealed to the poor and to slaves with ideas such as those of St. Paul (ca 1–64 CE) who wrote, "There is no longer Jew or Greek, there is no longer slave or free man, there is no longer male or female. For all of you are one in Christ Jesus."[14] Historian Frank Tannenbaum adds, "[I]n their brotherhood as children of one God, the bondsman and the master are equal in his sight. This does not involve a repudiation of slavery, but rather an assertion that spiritually they are equal."[15]

A great codification of traditional Spanish law known as Las Siete Partidas took place under King Alfonso the Wise between 1263 and 1265 in the midst of the wars to expel the Muslims from Spain and at a time when captives were often enslaved. Tannenbaum (writing in 1946) explains:

> *Las Siete Partidas* was framed within this Christian doctrine, and the slave had a body of law, protective of him as a human being, which was already there when the Negro arrived and had been elaborated long before he came upon the scene. And when he did come, the Spaniard may not have known him as a Negro, but the Spanish law and *mores* knew him as a slave and made him the beneficiary of the ancient legal heritage.[16]

Thus, when black African slavery emerged, the slave remained a person and was never treated by the law as mere property. Slaves received the sacraments of the Church including marriage and, in theory, married couples could not be separated. Cases of mistreatment, while numerous, were also frequently brought before the courts in Spanish and Portuguese America. Purchase of freedom was common.[17]

The theologian and philosopher Francisco de Vitoria (1483–1546), who taught at the University of Salamanca in Spain, had complex ideas on African slavery. He stated that enslavement based on trickery was not justified. But he said that purchasers of slaves did not have the obligation to investigate to determine if a slave was legitimately captured in war and one could purchase a person who was a slave in his, the slave's, own country. He also felt that slavery as a commutation of the death penalty was legitimate.[18] Historian Hebe Mattos de Castro notes that in the seventeenth century, while skin color and place of origin were never sufficient justifications for enslavement, capture in a just war was considered a legitimate justification.[19]

Tannenbaum emphasizes that slavery developed with a different moral and legal basis in the British colonies, including the West Indies and what became the United States. The British, he says, had not known slavery for centuries and had no laws to govern it. Therefore, the power of the master was absolute. Blacks became identified with slavery and were, in the main, denied the privileges of Christianity. Tannenbaum adds, "In fact, the Negro [in the British colonies] was considered a slave by nature."[20]

Along with Sandoval, there were numerous other clergymen in colonial Spanish and Portuguese America who denounced the slave trade, slavery, or aspects of them. They included, among the Spanish, Dominican Friar Alonso Montúfar, Archbishop of Mexico City; Friar Bartolomé Frías de Albornoz, also a Dominican, who taught law at the University of Mexico; Dominican Friar Tomás de Mercado, an important theorist and writer who studied in Mexico; Luis de Molina, a noted Jesuit theologian who never came to the New World; and among the Portuguese, Jesuit Miguel García, who opposed his fellow Jesuit Manuel da Nóbrega, a defender of slavery in Brazil; and Jesuit Antonio Vieira, a missionary, preacher and diplomat. Like Sandoval, most of these clergymen condemned aspects of slavery and the slave trade while not supporting abolition. The exceptions could be Albornoz, whose book *Arte de contratos* (1573) was put on the Inquisition's list of forbidden books and who slavery historian David Brion Davis noted "had the outlook of a genuine abolitionist"[21] and certainly the Capuchin friars Francisco José de Jaca and Epifanio de Moirans, who served in Venezuela and condemned both the slave trade and the institution of slavery.[22]

The Society of Jesus was founded by Pope Paul III in 1540 with the papal bull *Regimini militates ecclesiae* sixty years before Alonso de Sandoval was ordained. Under the leadership of founder Ignatius Loyola, the Jesuits were expected to be strong advocates for a strict Catholic orthodoxy at a time when the Protestant Reformation was gaining strength. However, literary scholar Margaret Olsen states that, while Jesuits were orthodox in doctrine, when circumstances demanded it, "They were happy to step in with their own erudition and experiences to forge new ways of doing things."[23] While their members generally came from elite families and they were confessors and teachers of nobility, they also ministered to prisoners, the poor and the sick.[24] Olsen notes that in the Americas they became thoroughly immersed in the cultures of the inhabitants, adding that they had a "willingness to approach Indigenous culture with relative objectivity . . . [and a] disposition to adapt the instruction of Christianity to the needs and capacity of the convert."[25]

The Jesuits were influenced by both Scholasticism and Renaissance humanism. Scholasticism, which experienced its high point in the thirteenth century with St. Thomas Aquinas, was in decline at the beginning of the sixteenth century. But during that century, it experienced a resurgence with the teachings of Spanish theologians Vitoria, Molina, and Francisco Suarez. Aquinas's use of the ideas of Aristotle and emphasis on the roles of reason and intellectual debate in areas of faith were particularly attractive to the Jesuits. At the same time, Jesuits were influenced by the Renaissance humanism's emphasis on returning to ancient sources which for them included the Bible and the writings of the early Church. In line with the teachings of founder Loyola, Jesuits gave importance to the individual Christian's relationship with God, an idea that also accorded with humanism.[26]

From the time of their founding, Jesuits traveled around the world to spread Christianity to Japan, China, India and the Americas. They exhibited their openness to other cultures printing in 1629 in Lima 1,400 copies of catechisms and prayer leaflets in African languages to use with both enslaved and free Africans there.[27] However, their writings indicate that they remained convinced of European superiority and intolerant of all religions except Catholic Christianity.[28] Olsen states that "Missions like those of the Guaraní in Paraguay (1610–1767) [the subject of a 1986 movie], for example, demonstrated an amazing level of cultural relativity and openness to Indigenous reality." She adds, however, that some critics have called those missions an attempt to create a society under Jesuit governance where they could put their own philosophy into practice.[29]

But there was an even greater contradiction. Olsen notes that Sandoval's work, the only writing from early Spanish America that deals with African slavery and which presents slaves as members of the Catholic Church, comes from a member of the Jesuit Order which held thousands of African slaves at that time. The profits from African slave labor were used to support missions to the Indigenous but even more contradictory was the fact that the profit from African slave labor on Jesuit haciendas was used to support the college that was promoting a mission for African slaves![30]

Thus, just as the Spanish monarch had decided that slavery was an economic necessity for his empire, the Jesuits made the same decision for their missionary enterprise in spite of the obvious and severe moral contradictions.

De instauranda Aethiopum salute

Sandoval wrote his book based on his conversations with the enslaved Africans themselves, with captains of slave ships, and with travelers, and on correspondence with Jesuits who lived and worked in Africa. To this he added his substantial reading of learned books while in residence in Lima.[31]

The work was probably completed in 1620. In 1623 and 1624, Sandoval sent the manuscript to prominent church figures to obtain their endorsement and received official church approval in January of 1627.[32] The book finally came off the presses in Seville later in 1627. It was well received and served as a "missionary handbook" for those working with Africans throughout the Spanish Empire.[33] Sandoval completed a revised and expanded edition which was published in Madrid in 1647. Surviving copies of the 1627 and 1647 editions of the book exist in a number of libraries.[34]

After its widespread use during the lifetime of Sandoval and Claver, *De instauranda Aethiopum salute* quickly fell into oblivion and was virtually ignored for three centuries, probably because it put the slave trade and slavery itself in such a harsh light.[35] Northern European Protestant countries did not pick it up to use against Catholic Spain as they did with the works of Las Casas because they were engaged in the slave trade as well. It was not until 1956 that an edition of the 1627 version, edited by Jesuit scholar Angel Valtierra, was published in Bogota on the three-hundredth anniversary of the death not of Sandoval, but of St. Peter Claver.[36] Another edition of the 1627 version of the work, edited by historian Enriqueta Vila Vilar, was published in 1987, shortly after the Colombian government honored Fathers Sandoval and Claver and Brother Nicolas González, "in an effort," as Olsen notes, "to acknowledge the past reality of slavery and its impact on Colombia" and to honor the efforts of the three men to alleviate the slaves' suffering.[37] The selection used here is from historian Nicole Von Germeten's 2008 abridged translation into English of the 1956 edition.[38]

Sandoval titled his work *De instauranda Aethiopum salute* or "How to restore the salvation of the Ethiopians" for several reasons. The title refers to the ancient Christian heritage of Ethiopia of which Sandoval would been aware. It evokes fellow Jesuit Jose de Acosta's work *De procuranda indorum salute* (On procuring Indian health) which proposed missionary strategy for the conversion of Indigenous Americans.[39] While other early writers used Ethiopia as a synonym for all of sub-Saharan Africa, Sandoval, in an attempt to raise up his mission to enslaved African in the Americas, expands the reference even further to include parts of the Arab world, South Asia, including India, and parts of East Asia, such as the Philippines and the Moluccas. In this way, as Olsen states, he portrays the work of Jesuit missionary St. Francis Xavier and other Jesuits as having been undertaken almost exclusively among "Black" peoples.[40] Von Germeten adds that Sandoval wants to prove that his mission carries out Xavier's goals and "represents the Jesuits' most important endeavor."[41]

Sandoval begins his book by examining different aspects of African life and customs. Von Germeten notes that, "By starting his narration in Africa, not America or Europe, Sandoval acknowledges that African slaves had a history and a culture before they came in contact with European slave traders."[42] Just as other missionary friars such as Franciscan Friar Bernardino de Sahagún had studied Indigenous language, customs, and traditions in order to better convert the Native peoples to Christianity, so Sandoval, as historian Robin Blackburn states, "developed the idea that he would be able to save more of these Africans if he knew more of their customs and fears."[43] Some of his descriptions of Africans and their customs are more mythological than anthropological such as his citing of Roman historian Pliny the Elder (23–79 CE) who Sandoval said described some Ethiopians as having heads with no eyes because these were lodged in their shoulders.[44] However, other descriptions, including that of the principal city of the Popo kingdom, included here, seem to be based on actual observations. Literary scholar Christopher Dennis notes that the representation of the African as monstrous and as coming from the devil justifies the work of conversion to Christianity while the ethnographic descriptions serve to identify, categorize, and appropriate the bodies of the Africans in order to save their souls.[45]

In attempting to resolve the question of why Africans were black, Sandoval examines various theories. Not knowing about melanin and genetics, he discards the theory proposed by some scholars of his time that it is because of the extreme heat of the sun because, he states, when Africans move to Europe, they do not give birth to white children. He accepts instead reasons based on two biblical stories about Adam and his son Cain and Noah and his son Ham but does not seem to make a firm decision between them.[46] Historian Catalina Ariza Montañez states that for Sandoval, blackness is a divine mark of imperfection to punish the descendants of Ham and is translated into less mental capacity as demonstrated by the African customs he considered savage and Africans' non-Christian religious beliefs.[47] But María Eugenia Chaves Maldonado emphasizes that this radically subaltern condition did not disqualify these human beings from being subjects of salvation and adds that conversion and baptism would "whiten" their souls and guarantee their redemption, if not in this life, then in the next.[48] Sandoval believed that humans were born free and equal as he states: "We all know that when He created the world, God Our Lord did not populate the earth with masters and slaves. . . . We also know that it was not until time passed and people became malicious that they began to tyrannize over the liberty of others." Anthropologist Eduardo Restrepo adds that, while for Sandoval there may be distinctions and hierarchies between nations and individuals, he does not see them as derived directly from the color of their skin.[49]

But, at the same time, Sandoval accepts that it is convenient for there to be servants and slaves and natural that some should rule and others be subject to them.[50] Restrepo states that Sandoval notes differences in abilities among Africans but attributes these to their conditions of life rather than to their nature.[51] He notes that, at the same time, Sandoval did not believe that slavery was against natural law if and when it came about under justifiable circumstances.[52]

These apparently contradictory views are on a par with Sandoval's varying portrayal of Africans and Europeans. He says, "In nature's forge, the prince and the plebian are crafted in the same way" and notes that the Africans "have wars and make peace, they marry, buy and sell, barter and exchange just like we do." But he also says, "The European land . . . is the most noble, virtuous, magnificent, and civilized part of the world." At the same time as Sandoval places African slaves at the bottom of the economic and social hierarchy in his book, he insists throughout the work that Africans are equal in spiritual capacity to Europeans. Historian Vincent P. Franklin states, "For Sandoval, slavery is an external situation of the body that does not affect the soul. All men are equal, not because they are all men, or all human; but because they all have eternal souls."[53] In other words, inequality and slavery are human creations and, in spite of them, humans are equal in the sight of God. Olsen says that "Sandoval is asking the white European and New World *criollo* to meet the black African on a common ground of spirituality."[54]

We have seen that while Sandoval denounces the slave trade and the mistreatment of slaves, he does not denounce slavery in so many words. In places he indicates that the benefits of conversion to Christianity may fully compensate for the suffering under slavery. Lunn writes (in 1935) that, from a Catholic premise, one must concede that slavery was a boon to the slave, or at least to the slave who was baptized and saved.[55] Von Germeten states, "To Sandoval, slavery is allowable if slave traders and masters abide by certain rules. The crucial rule is that slaves must become good Christians and everyone who deals with slaves in any way . . . must take responsibility for this."[56] However, Chaves points out that in the first two centuries of Spanish colonization, evangelization was turned into a tool that permitted the conquerors to justify their pillage and genocide of the Indigenous population and the capture and enslavement of Africans.[57]

Sandoval accepts the justifications for slavery put forward by the learned theologians and philosophers saying that he "will leave the final justification of slavery to legal and ecclesiastical authorities, especially the Jesuit Luis de Molina." But he has concerns about them. With relation to the position that a person can be legitimately captured and enslaved in a just war, Sandoval writes that a slave trader had told him that "half the wars fought between blacks would not take place if the Spanish did not go there to buy slaves." Enslavement as punishment for crimes or offenses was also widely accepted, and Sandoval accepts it in cases of conviction for serious crimes. But he questions it in the case where a king is a tyrant over his subjects, saying, "This is not justice but absolute power."

Sandoval notes that the population of Indigenous people in the Americas had been greatly reduced by overwork and disease and that enslaved Africans were brought in to replace them. He does not seem to question the justice of this, but he does question why, given that the hardworking slaves are making the Spaniards rich, they do not properly care for them: "[I]nstead of sheltering them, curing their illnesses, and defending them, because slaves bring them wealth and honor, the Spanish abandon them."

Sandoval is clear when he writes about treatment of slaves, describing in vivid detail the conditions on the slave ships during the two month voyage across the Atlantic. He also describes the mistreatment then inflicted on the enslaved by their new owners, noting that every day cases of abuse were brought before the courts. Sandoval exhorts slave owners to give their enslaved workers the care they themselves would like to receive and to punish them only as they would their own children. Sandoval emphasizes, however, that the punished worker must be submissive even if the punishment is undeserved.[58]

Franklin emphasizes that Sandoval's entire work "is concerned with the justification of the ministry to the [African] slaves, not with dramatizing the horrors of slavery and the slave trade.[59] But justifying this ministry was challenging work because, as historian Norman Meiklejohn states, many churchmen at the time contended that Africans "were incapable of comprehending the Christian religion" and, instead of blaming their own poor pedagogy, asserted that the Africans were of low intelligence.[60] Sandoval asserts that instead of insisting that Black people cannot understand Christian concepts, "we must look for proper interpreters and translators." Sandoval had to admit that the enslaved had the spiritual capacity to become Christians because he believed in one origin for all of humanity.[61]

Olsen comments about the difficulties surrounding communication and understanding between Sandoval and his African pupils:

> The clash between colonialist and subaltern systems of meaning in human interaction is a phenomenon with which Sandoval is intimately familiar. His own daily communications with Africans expose him to perpetual misunderstandings that arise from linguistic and cultural differences. . . . One may criticize the Jesuit for embracing a missionary praxis that could be seen not only as a violent imposition of religion but also for being condescending in his willingness to simplify the gospel. But one must also appreciate, independently of his motivations, the degree to which Sandoval struggles to bridge difference and minimize intercultural misunderstanding, especially through his use of interpreters.[62]

But there is another serious question for Sandoval to resolve. He consistently insists that all people have free will and that the slaves should not be baptized unless they freely consent. In this he coincides with the opinion of Bartolomé de Las Casas that the Indigenous should not be converted by force. But Von Germeten states that neither of these writers ever "perceived another choice for non-Christians than accepting Christianity. This meant that, in their opinion, the inhabitants of two continents had no right to continue the way of life they had known before violent contact with Europeans."[63] However, Sandoval does contemplate occasional rejection of the Christian faith. He says: "Sometimes, very rarely, the slaves do not want to be baptized. They refuse to leave their sect and false law. But usually, like bestial people who live among us, such as captured Moors or Englishmen, the slaves simply do not understand our language." In other words, he believes there will be some who will reject Catholic doctrine, but that they will be few if the right language is used.

Von Germeten exposes another possible contradiction in Sandoval's thought. She states that "Sandoval exoticizes African beliefs and practices, despising them for their difference from Christianity" but at the same time he "mentions African festivals, parades, and celebrations . . . highlighting the variety of African involvement in the Catholic Church." Sandoval also writes about an African brotherhood sponsored by the Jesuits in Cartagena.[64] This would seem to be an example of the Jesuit willingness to allow a certain amount of syncretism or mixture of traditions in the Catholicism of their missions around the world. Dennis postulates that in Sandoval we note an effort to mediate between Africans and Europeans in order to unite them in a Christian utopia.[65]

Sandoval, Olsen argues, allows in his writing for numerous places "in which the African becomes a historical or discursive actor or subject in the text."[66] She notes that there were religious workers in the Americas who were willing to "approach the Other in a radically new way that is more . . . culturally accommodating" and that will leave a written record "more likely to include the discursive participation of the Amerindian or African."[67] Sandoval writes about a virtuous black woman in Huamanga, Peru, saying that, "Everyone wants to speak to her because she lovingly discusses Our Lord and her speech fills her listeners with divine love." However, literature scholar Larissa Brewer-García points out that while Sandoval describes the lives of thirteen holy Africans as a way to show that they could accept Christianity and approach sanctity, he is careful to tell the stories in a way that confirms their servile position in seventeenth century Spanish American society.[68]

In the end, Sandoval's position on the justice of slavery remains contradictory. Vila Vilar sums it up by asking if Sandoval refrained from expressing a clear opinion because he was not entirely sure that slavery was unjust or because he thought that, if he denounced the institution of slavery openly, his book would never receive the permissions needed for publication, or if it was perhaps for both reasons.[69] The conversion of Africans was of the greatest importance to him and he saw as necessary the publication of a manual for the achieving of that goal. The final verdict on the justice of the institution of slavery he would leave to others.

ALONSO DE SANDOVAL'S
DE INSTAURANDA AETHIOPUM SALUTE

To the Christian Reader: The Purpose of This Book

Christian reader, many learned books have been written to help people spiritually. We should also try to help the Ethiopians,[70] who because of their color, are commonly called blacks. This book's goal is to encourage the desire to help the Ethiopians, a nation with a small role on the world stage but a designated place in God's plan. Some will say that, in Christ's robes, the black and white threads are intertwined, and the souls of blacks are as important as those of the whites. And thus my work is unnecessary, because all souls are the same. I respond that the blacks' fate is so sad and dark, and slavery is so unbearable, that I must describe both of these conditions here in order to inspire compassion, in hopes of helping overcome these difficulties and improving their fate. The souls of the blacks are no less precious than those of whites, nor did they cost less of the blood of the Lamb of God shed for all.

The title *De instauranda Aethiopum salute* means "How to restore the salvation of the blacks," because its primary and fundamental goal is not to motivate people to go to their lands to convert them (although this is a secondary goal) but instead to go to the ports where the slaves disembark. These slaves are incorrectly judged to be Christians, so we must ask them if they have been baptized. If they have not, we must instruct them. Once they have been well instructed, we can baptize them and restore their spiritual health, which has been lost.

This tract is divided into four books. The first describes the extended empire of the Ethiopians, in the West as well as the East, and its many nations and diverse customs. I present this description to inspire those who work in spiritual labor to join in this glorious task. The second book describes the unsurpassed misery and unhappiness endured by Ethiopian slaves and the great need for this ministry. The third book explains how to teach them. The first book will delight, the second inspire, and the third teach. Because I especially want to motivate the sons of the Company of Jesus [the Jesuits], my fathers and sons, to join this holy ministry, I added a fourth book, in which I discuss the great esteem that the Company itself has always had for this ministry. . . .

I pray to the Divine Majesty that this work will inflame the hearts of the ministers of the Church so that they will reach out to the forgotten, miserable slaves. They deserve charity; let this charitable fire burn brightly. . . .

Book 1. Chapter 2. The nature of Ethiopians, commonly called "blacks"

Throughout the world, color seems to depend on the climate of the land where a given person lives. This theory is supported by what we know of the East and West Indies, the coast of Africa, and even China, where people in Canton are black like those in Fez [Morocco]. People who live in the inland provinces of China are white because they live in a cold land. The same applies to Spain, where some are dark and others are blond or red-haired like the Germans. Scholars say that Ethiopians are black because the extraordinary heat of the sun in their hot lands burns off the first layer of their skin. They also say that the land is full of serpents, basilisks, dragons, unicorns, and other beasts. The black inhabitants curse the sun for burning them so harshly.

I believe these opinions have some basis in fact, but if climate causes skin color, Spaniards who live in Africa and are married to Spanish women will engender black children. And, vice versa, blacks living in Europe will give birth to white children. However, obviously experience belies this supposition. One could infer, not without some basis, that the black skin of the Ethiopians not only comes from the curse Noah put on his son Ham but also in an innate or intrinsic part of how God created them, so that in this extreme heat, the sons engendered were left this color, as a sign that they descend from a man who mocked his father, to punish his daring. Thus the Ethiopians descend from Ham, the first servant and slave that there ever was in the world, whose punishment darkened the skin of his sons and descendants.

Others have a very different theory, one I agree with, even if what I have just finished saying seems a sound philosophy. This last theory says that Adam cursed his son Cain for the shamelessness he showed in treating Adam with so little reverence, that Cain lost his nobility and even his personal freedom and became a slave, along with all of his children. This was the first servitude in world history. Although Cain was of light-skinned lineage, he was born dark. Thus blacks are also born as slaves, because God paints the sons of bad parents with a dark brush.

Book 1. Chapter 14. The customs, nature, morals, false religion, and gentile ceremonies of the Ethiopian kingdoms

The main city of the Popo kingdom [Benin] is enclosed by walls and moats two leagues in circumference. The city gates are guarded so that no people can leave without registering what they are carrying. Along the roads, at every league stands a guardhouse, where all goods must again be registered, so that it seems impossible for anything to be hidden, lost, or stolen. The houses in the city are made of clay and roofed in straw. Every night, men patrol the streets to make sure none of the roofs catch on fire and burn down the city. The palace is a city of its own, because it houses all of the important people. Although it is not built of stone, it has many corridors, doorways, and well-built wooden pillars, decorated in brass figures of men, animals, and birds[71] that are so well made that one of our silversmiths could not do it so well. The streets are very large and populated with people who usually walk around nude. One must have a license to wear clothes, which all the married women have. The men usually wear blankets around their loins, and some wear cotton cloths down to their knees. Over these they wear a lighter cloth, from their chests to the floor, made of very soft cotton. . . .

The kingdom is governed by a cabinet of wise men. Each shows his office by the color of his clothes. Some wear white, others yellow, others blue or green. The judges lead the cabinet, listening to various debates and conflicts. . . . The noblest people show the king the most respect, obedience, and reverence because they believe him to be immortal. It is illegal to say anything about the king dying, because he is like a ruling deity, although every man must die, including every king in the world. The king rarely leaves his house and is only seen occasionally in the market, where the people are allowed to look at him. The markets are marvelous, full of many unusual, costly items presented in a well-ordered way. In conclusion, the king is so respected and his subjects are so at the mercy of his will that every week they tell him everything that has happened in the kingdom, including the details of all births and deaths. No matter how difficult his commands seem to be, they always carry them out.

At certain times of the year, the king honors the dead with festivals that last for three days, when they sacrifice sixteen thousand souls, men and women. They sacrifice them by opening up their stomachs and hanging them from trees to be eaten by vultures. . . . When the sacrifice is over, a great procession is made all over the kingdom. Crippled people have their own procession, as do invalids, the blind, the mute, and the deaf. All the disabled and sick people come together, and the king feeds them well.

Book 1. Chapter 17. General points relating to slavery among the Guinean blacks and at other ports

The debate among scholars on how to justify the arduous and difficult business of slavery has perplexed me for a long time. I could have given up on explaining it and just ignored it in this book. However, I am determined to discuss it, although I will leave the final justification of slavery to legal and ecclesiastical authorities, especially the Jesuit Luis de Molina.[72] I will only mention here what I have learned after many years of working in this ministry. The readers can formulate their own ideas on the justice of this issue.

We have just said that black slaves usually come here from the ports of Cacheu, Guinea, the Cape Verde Islands, Sao Tomé Island, and Luanda in Angola. In reference to the slaves that come from Cape Verde Island, we should not worry about enslaving these blacks, because this island is not an Ethiopian island. Cape Verde is the main slave-trading port where slaves come from other parts of Africa. When the slaves arrive here, they have already been bought and sold three or four times. . . .

It is likely that many of the slaves that come from the Guinean rivers, especially Cacheu, a major slave-trading port, are enslaved illegally. When a merchant or ship owner comes to this port, they sell merchants their goods, normally printed cloth from India used for cloaks. They also sell wine, iron, and garlic to the Portuguese who live there, who are called *tangomaos*, in exchange for blacks. They also have agents, called carriers, whose job is to go inland with these goods to find blacks to exchange for the goods. This is how black slaves end up in Cacheu. . . . Slaves are captured in many different ways, and this disturbs the slave traders' consciences. One slave trader freely told me that he felt guilty about how the slaves he had bought in Guinea had come to be enslaved. Another slave trader, who had bought three hundred slaves on foot, expressed the same concerns, adding that half the wars fought between blacks would not take place if the Spanish did not go there to buy slaves. . . .

Book 1. Chapter 18. The slave ships

We all know that when He created the world, God Our Lord did not populate the earth with masters and slaves. . . . We also know that it was not until time passed and people became malicious that they began to tyrannize over the liberty of others. Solomon said that the poor man and the king, the monarch and the shepherd, were born with the same fate and under the same laws. In nature's forge, the prince and the plebian are crafted in the same way, and gentlemen are not born with more elegant clothes than peasants. Nobles do not have more eyes, feet, or arms than commoners. All of us live under the sky, the sun shines on us all, and we breathe the same air and endure the same elements. Both the king and the slave strive for liberty.

The Gospels of Mark and of Matthew say: Go all over the world, preach the Gospel to everyone regardless of lineage or condition, and make no distinction among men. The Company of Jesus values a noble soul more than a noble body. We care more for a man's soul than for his status and fortune. God does not distinguish men in this way, nor should we so judge and measure them. True liberty comes from avoiding sin, and the greatest wealth comes from being virtuous. The redemption and blood of Christ, who bled for all of us, also equalizes us. A man's low condition and status do not prevent him from having value, nor does a grand lineage make him especially praiseworthy. Only faith matters, because slave and freeman are the same to Christ, and each one will receive a good or evil reward depending on what they have done in life. Servitude does not take this away, and liberty does not guarantee it, because both have the same importance to the Lord. There is no difference between the merits of a slave who serves well and those of a freedman who enjoys his liberty, because everyone should serve Christ. Servitude can be glorious, because God bought all of us equally with the blood of his holy son. All faithful workers, black or white, free or enslaved, have the same value. . . .

Only God knows if these blacks are enslaved justly, but after they have been captured, they are put in brutal prisons. They remain in chains until they arrive at the port of Cartagena or another port. The slave ships have shelves built into their holds in order to transport three, four, five, and even six hundred or more slaves or however many it takes to fill the ship. Normally twelve to fourteen ships with this many black slaves in each ship enter this port [Cartagena] alone every year. . . . Shackled in chains, they endure misery and misfortune for two months. They receive only the most disgusting food and drink and thus become very sad and melancholy believing they will be rendered into fat and eaten. One third [of the slaves] die during the voyage. I know individuals who have endured this journey. They say they are extremely cramped, nauseous, and mistreated. They are shackled at the neck along a chain of six-by-six slaves, or two-by-two, fettered at the ankle. They are imprisoned in the ships, lying with one person's head at another person's feet. They are locked in the hold and closed off from the outside so that they cannot see the sun or moon. . . . The slaves look forward to eating once every twenty-four hours, although they get no more than a half cup of corn or crude millet and a small cup of water. Other than that, they get nothing else besides beating, whipping, and cursing. Many people I know have experienced this. . . .

Book 2. Chapter 2. The evils of nature and fortune endured by the blacks

We now describe the terrible things that happen to slaves—men and women condemned to a life more suited to beasts. Their masters beat them until their skin falls off and they die from the cruel blows and horrible torture. Masters will do this for any trivial infraction. Or they terrorize them until they die, rotten and full of worms. Every day the courts hear cases with accounts of this kind of abuse. Many times I have seen things with my own eyes that make my heart cry out with shame. No one could see a poor black man covered in terrible wounds from beatings done for no reason whatsoever without feeling moved to pity. If slaves do not show up for work one day, their masters will shackle yokes with four cruel spikes in them to their heads. Anyone would be enraged by the fact that just a few days ago a noble and important lady killed her black slave woman, and then she killed another two slaves, for a total of three murders. . . .

Everyone knows that the Spaniards abused the Indians so that in many provinces there are very few Indians left. In other places they have disappeared entirely. The blacks came here to replace these Indians. Huge numbers of slaves come here to work on Spanish land and to mine gold to make the Spanish rich. The slaves sustain the Spanish through their hard work, sweat, and industry. But instead of sheltering them, curing their illnesses, and defending them, because slaves bring them wealth and honor, the Spanish abandon them. They will not waste four *reales* to help a sick slave but instead leave them carelessly to die, rotting in their own excrement.

Book 2. Chapter 3. The blacks' spiritual suffering

God, who is a merciful father, asks those who have power over others to care for them. Thus masters are obliged to care for their slaves. . . . Why not give slaves enough food to live? Why not provide them with adequate shelter? Why not cure them when they are sick? . . .

Book 2. Chapter 4. How slaves should serve their masters, and how masters should serve their slaves

Masters must open their eyes and see their obligations: they are masters, not absolute lords living outside of the law, nor are they kings commanding their slaves. They must exert their power in moderation. When they act immoderately, their slaves have good reason to ask: "How can a Christian act like this?" On the other hand, slaves should know that they must be obedient to both strict, cruel masters and kind, gentle, and friendly masters. If a servant has a clear conscience he will attain God's grace and friendship. He must have patience to endure the sadness and pain caused by his master's unjust fury that comes even when he does his work well. . . .

Saint Paul has this to say to servants who are punished just for doing their work: "Continue working without complaining, because you know you will be rewarded by God in heaven." [Colossians 3:22–24] In other words, masters on earth do not appreciate, your work, but God will not forget to reward you for all you have done for his love. If you are not compensated on earth for your work, you will be compensated in heaven. . . . Servants must serve their masters as if their masters were God, because God wants servants to be obedient. Masters that are fair rule over their servants in God's name and command their servants in a way that pleases God. God is an absolute lord, but he does not rule like a tyrant; instead, he is like a father who commands his servants with love, tenderness, and friendliness.

Book 2. Chapter 5. Quotes from sacred scripture about how masters should treat slaves

The holy apostle Paul says: If a person does not care for his own, especially his servants, he rejects the faith and is worse than an infidel [1 Timothy 5:8]. A master who acts carelessly is not faithful to divine law and Christian faith. . . . The master should be very careful in anything he does with regard to his slaves' bodies and souls. He should make sure they know the Christian doctrine and how to follow the Church's rules. They should go to Mass and observe official fasting days if at all possible. They should take confession and communion at the proper times, following the guidance of their confessor. Masters should try to figure out if their slaves are not Christian and try to help them. Anything related to the soul is very important, but the body also has needs that masters must fulfill fairly. They must provide a fair daily wage or decent food, clothing, and shelter. They should remember the Golden Rule—do unto others as you would have done unto you—and love their slaves as they love themselves. . . .

Saint Augustine ranked the love we must feel for others: love God first, then your parents, then your children, and lastly your slaves—unless your slaves behave better than your children.

Book 2. Chapter 6. Our Lord God values the blacks and his ministry

Many churchmen work to bring Christianity to the Indians, and I envy them for working on such a glorious task, but their enthusiasm also discourages me, because our work with the blacks is just as important. No one speaks in their defense and no one runs to help them. I believe I am not exaggerating in saying that the poor blacks are more desperate than the Indians. . . .

Book 2. Chapter 14. Motivation to remedy the miseries of such cursed souls

God has given me the responsibility to reach out to the poor and dejected of the world. God's message is to help the poor, shelter those in need, and bring together the outcasts to share the good news of the Gospel with those who need it. Trust me: working with the Spanish by teaching and confessing them is a more luxurious ministry, but it is dangerous, insecure, and not as beneficial for us. Those that help the rich nobles and people who live in luxury take on their very heavy burdens of conscience. These poor blacks do not have burdens for us to carry; they carry fewer burdens than we do, so we can easily carry both their burdens and our own. . . .

Book 3. Chapter 3. Of the blacks' potential to understand our holy faith

Our Lord God, the Catholic Church, the pope, the monarchs of Castile and Portugal, and the Company of Jesus have all shown that they value black people, because they work to convert and save them in Ethiopia, Guinea, Congo, and the Philippines. I believe that black people are worthy of all this effort. The time spent teaching them and administering the sacraments to them is not wasted. Those who say that these people are barbarous and rustic, lacking the potential to understand our faith, should remember that the apostles also preached to those whom they now call incapable of understanding the faith. In those days, they did not understand more nor were they any smarter than they are now. If the apostles and other saintly men found them to be so barbaric and believed that they wasted their time preaching to them, they would not have bothered to give them the good news of the Gospel. If the glorious Saint James the Great had judged the Spanish to be stubborn and rustic, he never would have gone to them to preach the gospel. Even after he made a huge effort, he did not convert more than ten Spaniards. But even though we are not apostles, we convert many more people, which shows that the African nations have the potential to be Christian. . . .

First, these blacks are not the beasts that some people like to think they are. Those people *want* them to be incapable of Christianity. The blacks should not be considered infants, either. They are adult men, and as such they should be baptized after being instructed and giving their free consent. When we instruct them, we have to consider what nation they come from and how much they might understand, because every nation differs. Second, these people cannot understand us as quickly as Spaniards do, so pastors and ministers must teach them slowly and spend a great deal of time on their catechism. However, they do possess free will and exercise it in all of their actions, like any other human being. They have wars and make peace, they marry, buy and sell, barter and exchange just like we do. Sometimes, very rarely, the slaves do not want to be baptized. They refuse to leave their sect and false law. But usually, like bestial people who live among us, such as captured Moors or Englishmen, the slaves simply do not understand our language.

I conclude by rebuking those who say that the blacks are incapable of receiving the sacraments and living by God's law or that blacks cannot understand these concepts. Instead, motivated by charity and zeal for the glory of the Lord and the desire to help abandoned souls, we must look for proper interpreters and translators. I confess that when a black person speaks to me in his language, I do not understand a word and seem more *bozal* [backward, rustic] than he does when I speak to him in my language. I believe that all people confess the same. Why do we think that a black person should understand our language? Why do we use their ignorance as an excuse to avoid working with such needy and hopeless people?

When a black slave lives for a long time among the Spaniards, he can show similar understanding and devotion to our own. Some of them are even more virtuous than the average Spaniard, and many black slaves live completely pure lives. One man who lives in the city of Quito [Ecuador] is so rude and uncivilized that he hardly understands our language, but he is so saintly and good that his master set him free. He is now employed as a humble lay brother for the Franciscan friars, and he frequently takes the sacraments. Everyone knows that he has done many miracles, and the people revere and honor him like a saint. In the city of Huamanga in Peru, all the noble and devout ladies honor a virtuous black woman. She is admitted to the parlors of all the noble houses. Everyone wants to speak to her because she lovingly discusses Our Lord and her speech fills her listeners with divine love. Her masters revere her so much that they do not treat her like a slave but worship her as a saint. She governs over their house. God honors those who serve him. In plain black vessels, he stores the precious liquor of the virtues and his divine grace.

Book 3. Chapter 5. The value of these baptisms

I do not believe that they give their consent to be baptized [before leaving the African ports], and I see much proof that they do not willingly receive baptism or understand that this water is a holy thing. They are not explicitly asked for their consent. If someone asks them if they want to have this water poured on them so they can be like whites, and so on, I am certain that they not only reject this but detest this water and all other things connected to the whites from the bottom of their hearts. Whites are their worst enemies: they take the slaves from their homelands, separate them from their parents and siblings, take away their liberty, put them in chain gangs, shackles, and prisons, and then confine them in a ship to take them to distant lands, without hope of returning to their own. They are badly fed and treated and threatened with poor examples. It is much more likely that God has lost them rather than gained them with holy baptism—no surprise, considering the imprisonment and abuse that takes place. . . . The absurd answers we get when we ask the slaves if they understood their baptism or what was meant when their heads were washed are another form of proof that they do not receive legitimate, voluntary baptisms in their lands and are even unaware that they were baptized at all.

Book 4. Chapter 1. How the ministry to the blacks is proper work for the Company of Jesus

The founding of the Company of Jesus and the opening of communication with the Ethiopians are like twins born in the same womb: the Company was born as an instrument of their salvation. God gave the Company the goal of bringing them salvation as well as helping others in Rome, Italy, Spain, or Europe, and in all the rest of the world. God calls us to be soldiers in the Company of Jesus to wander through these barbarous and remote black nations, to save the people, and to bring them into his service. Our destiny is to teach the doctrine to humble, low, crude people and care for them as if they were children.

Book 4. Chapter 15. The motives and reasons why the Company of Jesus has, in the Indies, devoted itself to the salvation of the blacks

It is very true that our principal function in the Indies is to work with Indians, as stated in our constitutions. But it is also absolutely certain that very important work must be done for the black slaves that serve us in these parts. Without doubt, the purpose of the Company of Jesus here is to help the natives, but we should also help the blacks, especially in the places where there are no Indians. After all, black slaves came here to supplement the lack of Indians to serve us here on earth. They are also here for us to help them spiritually. They are our slaves and not free people like the Indians. Therefore, we must make a greater effort to help them because, as I have clearly shown, the blacks are in much greater need than the Indians. It is more difficult to instruct the blacks than the Indians, and thus they offer the hope of a greater reward. Our sacred Company has already truthfully declared that it equally values working for the salvation of both the blacks and the Indians, and all the ecclesiastical privileges that are conceded to the Indians are also conceded to the blacks and vice versa.

NOTES

1. Margaret Olson, *Slavery and Salvation in Colonial Cartagena de Indias* (Gainesville: University Press of Florida, 2004), 2.

2. María Cristina Navarrete Pelaez, "Las Cartas Annuas jesuitas y la representación de los etíopes en el siglo XVI," in *Genealogías de la Diferencia: Tecnologías de la salvación y representación de los africanos esclavizados en Iberoamérica colonial*, ed. María Eugenia Chaves Maldonado (Bogotá: Editorial Pontificia Universidad Javeriana, 2009), 29.

3. Enriqueta Vila Vilar, introducción to *Un tratado sobre la esclavitud*, by Alonso de Sandoval, (Madrid: Alianza Editorial, 1987), 26, 28.

4. Nicole Von Germeten, introduction to *Treatise on Slavery: Selections from De instauranda Aethiopum salute* by Alonso de Sandoval, S.J., ed. and trans. Nicole von Germeten (Indianapolis: Hackett Publishing Company, 2008), ix; Christopher Dennis, "El 'Negro' en dos textos Colombianos y el 'blanqueo' de su alma," *Chasqui* 36, no. 1 (May 2007): 4.

5. Arnold Lunn, *A Saint in the Slave Trade: Peter Claver (1581–1654)* (New York: Sheed and Ward, Inc., 1935), 101.

6. Vila Vilar, introducción, 31

7. Copies of this book are held in the National Library of Spain, and in the libraries of the Universities of Seville and Barcelona.

8. Navarrete, "Las Cartas," 30.

9. Angel Valtierra, S.J., *Peter Claver: Saint of the Saints*, trans. Janet H. Perry and L. J. Woodward (Westminster, Maryland: The Newman Press, 1960), 315.

10. Norman Meiklejohn, "Alonso de Sandoval, the First Advocate of Black Studies in America," in *Latin America: A Historical Reader*, ed. Lewis Hanke (Boston: Little, Brown and Company, 1974), 159.

11. Vila, introducción, 32; Valtierra, *Peter Claver*, 316; Vincent P. Franklin, "Alonso de Sandoval and the Jesuit Conception of the Negro," *The Journal of Negro History* 58, no. 3 (July 1973): 351.

12. Von Germeten, introduction, xxiii.

13. Aristotle, *The Politics of Aristotle*, trans. Ernest Barker (London: Oxford University Press, 1958), 14.

14. St. Paul, "The Letter to the Galatians, 3:28," *The New Testament, St. Joseph New Catholic Version* (New Jersey: Catholic Book Publishing Corp., 2015), 298.

15. Frank Tannenbaum, *Slave and Citizen: The Negro in the Americas* (New York: Vintage Books, 1946), 47.

16. Tannenbaum, *Slave*, 48

17. However, writing about purchase of freedom in early eighteenth-century Central America, Russell Lohse notes that while the Siete Partidas proclaimed that all loved liberty, "[i]n many cases, rights ostensibly guaranteed by law became reduced to privileges or 'favors' dispensed according to the master's will." Russell Lohse, "Deathbed and Other Whispered Promises: Masters, Slaves, and Contested Manumission in Colonial," *Colonial Latin American Review* 27, no. 4): 461.

18. Ann M. Pescatello, "The *Leyenda Negra* and the African in Sixteenth and Seventeenth Century Iberian Thought," *The Catholic Historical Review* 66, no. 2 (April 1980): 175–76.

19. Hebe Mattos de Castro, "Esclavización y mancha de sangre en el mundo atlántico del siglo XVII: discursos y trayectorias," trans. María Eugenia Chaves Maldonado, in *Genealogías de la diferencia: Tecnologías de la salvación y representación de los africanos esclavizados en Iberoamérica colonial*, ed. Maria Eugenia Chaves Maldonado (Bogotá: Editorial Pontificia Universidad Javeriana, 2009) 90.

20. This, he says, impacted the way abolition occurred in the two areas: peacefully in Latin America and through war in North America. Tannenbaum, *Slave*, 42, 100–101, 82, 107, viii.

21. David Brion Davis, *The Problem of Slavery in Western Culture* (Ithaca: Cornell University Press, 1966), 190.

22. Margaret Olsen, *Slavery and Salvation in Colonial Cartagena de Indias* (Gainesville: University Press of Florida, 2004), 19.

23. Olsen, *Slavery*, 32.

24. Olsen, *Slavery*, 33; Von Germeten, introduction, xvi.

25. Olsen, *Slavery*, 33.

26. Olsen, *Slavery*, 36–37.

27. Luis Martin, *The Intellectual Conquest of Peru: The Jesuit College of San Pablo, 1568–1767* (New York: Fordham University Press, 1968), 51. San Pablo also became a center for the distribution of Sandoval's book.

28. Olsen, *Slavery*, 41; Von Germeten, introduction, xxi.

29. Olsen, *Slavery*, 34.

30. Olsen, *Slavery*, 16–17.

31. Navarrete, "Las Cartas," 26.

32. Alonso de Sandoval, *Naturaleza, policía sagrada i profana, costumbres i ritos, disciplina i catecismo evangélico de todos etíopes* (Sevilla: Francisco de Lira, Impresor, 1627), 2. https://catalogoenlinea.bibliotecanacional.gov.co/client/es_ES/search/asset/71933.

33. Franklin, "Alonso," 352.

34. The volumes of the 1627 edition at the National Library of Colombia in Bogotá and at the National Library of France have been digitized and posted online. They can be viewed here: https://catalogoenlinea.bibliotecanacional.gov.co/client/es_ES/search/asset/71933 and here: https://gallica.bnf.fr/ark:/12148/bpt6k73763z. There are also copies at the Library of the University of Seville in Spain, at the Library of Con-

gress in Washington, DC, and at the Library of the University of Cagliari in Sardinia, Italy. The National Library of Spain in Madrid has digitized its copy of the 1647 edition and posted it online at: http://bdh-rd.bne.es/viewer.vm?id=0000092806&page=1 as has the Library of the University of Heidelburg at: https://digi.ub.uni-heidelberg. de/diglit/sandoval1647bd1/0003/image. Other copies of the 1647 edition are located at the National Library of Chile, the National Library of France, the New York Public Library, and at several university libraries including Oxford, Yale, the Colegio de México, and the University of Minnesota.

35. Olsen, *Slavery*, 58.

36. Alonso de Sandoval, *De instauranda Aethiopum salute. El Mundo de la esclavitud negra en América*, ed. with intro by Ángel Valtierra (Bogotá: 1956), Olsen, *Slavery, 7.*

37. Olsen, *Slavery*, 9.

38. Von Germeten, introduction, xxix.

39. Larissa Brewer-García, "Hierarchy and Holiness in the Earliest Black Hagiographies: Alonso de Sandoval and His Sources," *The William and Mary Quarterly* 76, no. 3 (July 2019): 480–481.

40. Olsen, *Slavery*, 60.

41. Von Germeten, introduction, xviii.

42. Von Germeten, introduction, xv.

43. Robin Blackburn, *The Making of New World Slavery: From the Baroque to the Modern, 1492–1800* (London and New York: Verso, 2010), 154.

44. Quoted in Dennis, "El 'Negro,'" 7.

45. Dennis, "El 'Negro,'" 66.

46. Alonso de Sandoval, S.J., *Treatise on Slavery: Selections from De Instauranda Aethiopum salute*, ed., trans., intro. Nicole von Germeten (Indianapolis: Hackett Publishing Company, 2008 [1627]), 20–21.

47. Catalina Ariza Montañez, "El viaje dantesco de los etíopes: la construcción del ser esclavo en el período colonial," in *Genealogías de la diferencia: Tecnologías de la salvación y representación de los africanos esclavizados en Iberoamérica colonial*, ed. María Eugenia Chaves Maldonado (Bogotá: Editorial Pontificia Universidad Javeriana, 2009), 284.

48. María Eugenia Chaves Maldonado, "La creación del 'Otro' colonial: Apuntes para un estudio de la diferencia en el proceso de la conquista americana y de la esclavización de los africanos," in *Genealogías de la diferencia: Tecnologías de la salvación y representación de los africanos esclavizados en Iberamérica colonial*, ed. María Eugenia Chaves Maldonado (Bogotá: Editorial Pontificia Universidad Javeriana, 2009), 205, 207.

49. Eduardo Restrepo, "El negro en un pensamiento colonial de principios del siglo XVII: diferencia, jerarquía y sujeción sin racialización," in *Genealogías de la diferencia: Tecnologías de la salvación y representación de los africanos esclavizados en Iberoamérica colonial*, ed. María Eugenia Chaves Maldonado (Bogotá: Editorial Pontificia Universidad Javeriana, 2009), 174.

50. Sandoval *Treatise*, 75–76.

51. Restrepo, "El Negro," 158.

52. Restrepo, "El Negro," 161.

53. Franklin, "Alonso," 356.

54. Olsen, *Slavery*, 23.

55. Lunn, *A Saint*, 99.

56. Von Germeten, introduction, 50.

57. Chaves, "La creación," 232.

58. Ariza, "El viaje," 268.

59. Franklin, "Alonso," 369.

60. Meiklejohn, "Alonso," 160.

61. Dennis, "El 'Negro,'" 8.

62. Olsen, *Slavery*, 146.

63. Von Germeten, introduction, xv. Some scholars interpret Las Casas as believing that the Indigenous had the right to reject Christianity and continue to practice their old religions.

64. Nicole Von Germeten, notes to *Treatise on Slavery: Selections from De instauranda Aethiopum salute* by Alonso de Sandoval, S.J., ed. and trans. Nicole von Germeten (Indianapolis: Hackett Publishing Company, 2008), 31; Von Germeten, introduction, xii–xiii.

65. Dennis, "El 'Negro,'" 15.

66. Olsen, *Slavery*, 4.

67. Olsen, *Slavery*, 26. An outstanding example of this is Sahagún who compiled 14 volumes of information from the Native people of New Spain, far beyond what he needed for conversion purposes.

68. Brewer-García, "Hierarchy," 477–478, 480.

69. Vila Vilar, introducción, 31.

70. Sandoval often, as here, uses the term Ethiopian to refer to Africans in general.

71. These brass figures were stolen in the nineteenth century from Benin City and taken to museums in Europe and elsewhere. The Metropolitan Museum in New York announced in June of 2021 that it was returning two brass figures (often called bronzes) to Nigeria where Benin City is located. Sarah Bahr, "Met Museum Announces Return of Two Benin Bronzes to Nigeria," *New York Times* (June 9, 2021) https://www.nytimes.com/2021/06/09/arts/design/met-museum-benin-bronzes-nigeria.html.

72. Luis de Molina (1535–1600), an influential Jesuit theologian, argued that all human beings had free will and also that people could be enslaved in war.

Bibliography

INTRODUCTION

"Andean Civilizations," Arizona Museum of Natural History: Cultures of the Ancient Americas. Accessed June 13, 2021. https://www.arizonamuseumofnaturalhistory .org/explore-the-museum/exhibitions/cultures-of-the-ancient-americas/andean -civilizations.

Bahr, Sarah. "Met Museum Announces Return of Two Benin Bronzes to Nigeria." *New York Times* (June 9, 2021) https://www.nytimes.com/2021/06/09/arts/design/ met-museum-benin-bronzes-nigeria.html.

Burkholder, Mark A., Monica Rankin, and Lyman L. Johnson. *Exploitation, Inequality, and Resistance: A History of Latin America since Columbus.* Oxford: Oxford University Press, 2018.

"Cities of Caral-Supe (Peru) and Levoca (Slovakia) added to UNESCO's World Heritage List." *UNESCO News and Events* (June 28, 2009) https://whc.unesco .org/en/news/534/.

de la Torre Rangel, Jesús. *Alonso de la Veracruz: amparo de los indios. Su teoría y práctica jurídica.* Aguascalientes: Universidad Autónoma de Aguascalientes, 1998.

Díaz, Mónica. *Indigenous Writings from the Convent: Negotiating Ethnic Autonomy in Colonial Mexico.* Tucson, University of Arizona Press, 2010.

Dussel, Enrique. "1492: The Discovery of an Invasion." Translated by Gary McEoin. *CrossCurrents* 41, no. 4 (Winter 1991–92): 437–52.

———."Origen de la filosofía política moderna: Las Casas, Vitoria y Suarez." *Caribbean Studies* 33, no. 2 (Jul–Dec, 2005): 35–80.

"First City in the New World? Peru's Caral suggests civilization emerged in the Americas 1,000 years earlier than experts believed." *Smithsonian Magazine* (August 2002). https://www.smithsonianmag.com/history/first-city-in-the-new -world-66643778/.

Fuentes, Carlos. *The Buried Mirror: Reflections on Spain and the New World.* Boston: Houghton Mifflin Company, 1992.

Gershon, Livia. "Mexico City Marks 500th Anniversary of the Fall of Tenochtitlán." *Smithsonian Magazine Smart News* (May 24, 2021). https://www.smithsonianmag.com/smart-news/mexico-city-marks-500th-anniversary-fall-tenochtitlan-180977794/.

Golomb, Jason. "Why the Nasca lines are among Peru's greatest mysteries," *National Geographic History and Culture—Reference.* Accessed June 13, 2021. https://www.nationalgeographic.com/history/article/nasca-lines?loggedin=true.

Mallon, Florencia E. "The Promise and Dilemma of Subaltern Studies: Perspectives from Latin American History." *The American Historical Review* 99, no. 5 (Dec. 1994): 1491–1515.

Malpass, Michael A. *Ancient Peoples of the Andes.* Ithaca: Cornell University Press, 2016.

Mann, Charles C. *1491: New Revelations of the Americas Before Columbus.* New York: Alfred A. Knoff, 2005.

Martínez-Dávila, Roger L. Josef Díaz, and Ron D. Hart. *Fractured Faiths: Spanish Judaism, the Inquisition, and New World Identities.* Santa Fe: New Mexico History Museum, 2016.

"Mexico Demands Apology from Spain and the Vatican over Conquest." *BBC News* (March 26, 2019). https://www.bbc.com/news/world-latin-america-47701876.

Restall, Matthew and Kris Lane. *Latin America in Colonial Times.* Cambridge: Cambridge University Press, 2011.

Sabine, George H. and Thomas Landon Thorson. *A History of Political Thought.* Orlando, Holt, Rinehart and Winston, Inc., 1973.

Sandweiss, Daniel H., Ruth Shady Solís, Michael E. Moseley, David K. Keefer, and Charles R. Ortloff. "Environmental Change and Economic Development in Coastal Peru between 5,800 and 3,600 Years Ago." *Proceedings of the National Academy of Sciences of the United States of America* 106, no. 5 (2009).

Souza, Jonas Gregorio de, Denise Pahl Schaan, Mark Robinson, Antonia Damasceno Barbosa, Luiz E. O. C. Aragão, Ben Hur Marimon Jr., Beatriz Schwantes Marimon, Izaias Brasil da Silva, Salman Saeed Khan, Francisco Ruji Nakahara and José Iriarte. "Pre-columbian earth-builders settled along the entire southern rim of the Amazon." *Nature Communications* (March 27, 2018). https://www.nature.com/articles/s41467-018-03510-7#citeas.

Spivak, Gayatri Chakravorty. "Can the Subaltern Speak?" *Marxism and the Interpretation of Culture.* Edited by Cary Nelson and Lawrence Grossberg. Urbana and Chicago: University of Illinois Press, 1988.

"Voyages: The Trans-Atlantic Slave Trade Database." Voyages Database, Emory University. Last modified 2009. https://slavevoyages.org/assessment/estimates.

Whitaker, Arthur P. "The Origin of the Western Hemisphere Idea." *Proceedings of the American Philosophical Society* 98, no. 5 (Oct. 15, 1954): 323–26.

CHAPTER 1: THE KAQCHIKEL MAYA: "GO TO WHERE YOU WILL SEE YOUR MOUNTAINS"

The Annals of the Cakchiquels. Original text with translation, notes, and introduction by Daniel Brinton. Philadelphia: Brinton's Library of Aboriginal American Literature, Number VI, 1885. http://www.gutenberg.org/files/20775/20775–h/20775–h.htm.

The Annals of the Cakchiquels and Title of the Lords of Totonicapan. Translated from the Cakchiquel Maya by Adrián Recinos and Delia Goetz. Norman, OK: University of Oklahoma Press, 1953.

Carmack, Robert M. *Quichean Civilization: The Ethnohistoric, Ethnographnic and Archeological Sources.* Berkeley: University of California Press, 1973.

———. *The Quiché Mayas of Utatlán: The Evolution of a Highland Guatemala Kingdom.* Norman, OK: University of Oklahoma Press, 1981.

Hammond, Norman. "Inside the Black Box: Defining Maya Polity." In *Classic Maya Political History: Hieroglyphic and Archeological Evidence,* edited by T. Patrick Culbert. Cambridge: Cambridge University Press, 1996, 253–84.

Hill, Robert M. II. *Pictograph to Alphabet—and Back: Reconstructing the Pictographic Origins of the Xajil Chronicle.* Philadelphia: American Philosophical Society, 2012.

Kaqchikel Chronicles: The Definitive Edition. Translation and exegesis by Judith M. Maxwell and Robert M. Hill II. Austin: University of Texas Press, 2006.

Knight, Alan. *Mexico: From the Beginning to the Spanish Conquest.* Cambridge: Cambridge University Press, 2002.

Lovell, W. George. "Surviving Conquest: The Maya of Guatemala in Historical Perspective," *Latin American Research Review* XXII, 2 (1988): 25–57.

Manuscrito Cakchiquel: ó sea memorial de Tecpan-Atitlan (Solola) Historia del antiquo reino del Cakchiquel, dicho de Guatemala. Written in Cakchiquel by don Francisco Ernantez Arana Xahila Xahila and continued by don Francisco Diaz Gebuta Queh, 1604. Schoenberg Center for Electronic Text and Image. Library of the University of Pennsylvania. http://sceti.library.upenn.edu/sceti/codex/public/PageLevel/index.cfm?WorkID=839.

Nicholson, H. B. *Topiltzin Quetzalcoatl: The Once and Future Lord of the Toltecs.* Boulder: University of Colorado Press, 2001.

Recino, Adrián and Delia Goetz. Introduction to *The Annals of the Cakchiquels and Title of the Lords of Totonicapan,* translated by Adrian Recino and Delia Goetz, 3–42. Norman, OK: University of Oklahoma Press, 1953.

Sherman, William L. "Some Aspects of Change in Guatemalan Society, 1470–1620." *Spaniards and Indians in Southeastern Mesoamerica: Essays on the History of Ethnic Relations,* edited by Murdo J. MacLeod and Robert Wasserstrom. Lincoln: University of Nebraska Press, 1983.

Smith, Anthony Douglas. *The Ethnic Origins of Nations.* Oxford, UK: Basil Blackwell, Inc., 1986.

Wilson, Walter T. "Urban Legends: Acts 10:1–11:18 and the Strategies of Greco-Roman Foundation Narratives." *Journal of Biblical Literature* 120 (Spring 2001): 77–99.

Wren, Linnea H., and Peter Schmidt. "Elite Interaction during the Terminal Classic Period: new evidence from Chichen Itza," In *Classic Maya Political History: Hieroglyphic and Archeological Evidence*, edited by T. Patrick Culbert, 199–225. Cambridge: Cambridge University Press, 1996.

CHAPTER 2: CHRISTOPHER COLUMBUS: "TOOK POSSESSION OF THAT ISLAND FOR THE KING AND QUEEN"

Alexander VI, Pope. "Inter caetera Divinae." In *Church and State through the Centuries*. Edited and translated by Sidney Z. Ehler and John Morrall. New York: Biblo and Tannen Publishers, 1967.

Bergreen, Laurence. *Columbus: The Four Voyages*. New York: Viking, 2011.

Colón, Cristóbal. *Viajes de Cristóbal Colon*. Biblioteca Digital Hispánica (Madrid: Biblioteca Nacional de España, 1552) Abstracted from the log of Columbus by Bartolomé de Las Casas and written in his hand. http://bdh-rd.bne.es/viewer.vm?id=0000042224&page=1 Or http://www.bne.es/en/Catalogos/BibliotecaDigitalHispanica/Inicio/index.h,tml Search for *Viajes de Cristobal Colon*. Choose item. Click on "View work." The selection included here begins on page 16.

Columbus, Christopher. *The Diario of Christopher Columbus's first Voyage to America 1492–1493*. Translated with notes by Oliver Dunn and James E. Kelley, Jr. Norman: University of Oklahoma Press, 1989.

——— .*The Log of Christopher Columbus*. Translation and introduction by Robert H. Fuson. Camden, Maine: International Marine Publishing Company, 1987.

——— ."Letter to Luis de Santangel." In *Select Documents Illustrating the Four Voyages of Columbus*, edited and translated by Cecil Jane. London: Hakluyt Society, 1930.

——— . *Personal Narrative of the First Voyage of Columbus to America from a Manuscript Recently Discovered in Spain*. Translated and Preface by Samuel Kettell. Boston: Thomas B. Wait and Son: 1827. http://babel.hathitrust.org/cgi/pt?id=hvd.32044005032289;seq=7;view=1up;num=i.

Columbus, Ferdinand. *The Life of the Admiral Christopher Columbus by His Son Ferdinand*. Translated and annotated by Benjamin Keen. New Brunswick: Rutgers University Press, 1959.

Discussion on the special theme for the year: "The Doctrine of Discovery: its enduring impact on Indigenous peoples and the right to redress for past conquests." Permanent Forum on Indigenous Issues of the UN Economic and Social Council, May 10, 2012, http://unpfip.blogspot.com/2012/05/recommendations-of-permanent-forum.html.

Fadel, Leila. "Columbus Day or Indigenous Peoples' Day," *Morning Edition*, NPR, October 14, 2019, https://www.npr.org/2019/10/14/769083847/columbus-day-or-Indigenous-peoples-day.

Fernández-Armesto, Felipe. *Columbus on Himself.* Indianapolis: Hackett Publishing Company, Inc., 2010.

González, Maria del Refugio. "El Descubrimiento de America y el derecho." In *El Descubrimiento de America y su impacto en la historia*, edited by Leopoldo Zea. 95–112. Mexico, DF: Fondo de la Cultura Económica, 1991.

Greenblatt, Stephen, *Marvelous Possessions: The Wonder of the New World.* Chicago: University of Chicago Press, 1991.

Machemer, Teresa. "Christopher Columbus Statues Beheaded, Pulled Down Across America." *Smithsonian Magazine*, June 12, 2020. https://www.smithsonianmag.com/smart-news/christopher-columbus-statues-beheaded-torn-down-180975079/.

Miller, Robert J. "The International Law of Colonialism: A Comparative Analysis." *Lewis & Clark Law Review* 15, no. 4 (2011): 847–922.

Morison, Samuel Eliot. *Admiral of the Ocean Sea: A Life of Christopher Columbus.* Boston: Little, Brown and Company, 1942.

Paul, Heike. *Christopher Columbus and the Myth of 'Discovery': The Myths that Made America.* Bielefeld, Germany: Transcript Verlag, 2014.

Sale, Kirkpatrick. *Christopher Columbus and the Conquest of Paradise.* London: I. B. Taurus and Co. Ltd., 2006.

Saito, Natsu Taylor "Reflections on Homeland and Security." *The New Centennial Review* 6, no. 1 (Spring 2006): 243–67.

Seed, Patricia. "Taking Possession and Reading Texts: Establishing Authority of Overseas Empires." *William and Mary Quarterly* 8, no. 2 (1992): 183–209.

Toensing, Gale Courey. "Indigenous delegates ask Pope to repudiate Doctrine of Discovery." *Indian Country Today* (Dec. 21, 2009). https://indiancountrytoday.com/archive/indigenous-delegates-ask-pope-to-repudiate-doctrine-of-discovery.

Wilford, John Noble. *The Mysterious History of Columbus: An Exploration of the Man, the Myth, the Legacy.* New York: Alfred A. Knopf, 1991.

World Council of Churches Executive Committee, Statement on the doctrine of discovery and its enduring impact on Indigenous Peoples. February 17, 2012. http://www.oikoumene.org/en/resources/documents/executive-committee/bossey-february-2012/statement-on-the-doctrine-of-discovery-and-its-enduring-impact-on-Indigenous-peoples.html.

Zamora, Margarita. "Abreast of Columbus: Gender and Discovery," *Cultural Critique* no. 17 (Winter, 1990–1992): 127–49.

CHAPTER 3: ANTONIO DE MONTESINOS: "ARE THEY NOT HUMAN BEINGS?"

Aspinall, Dana E. Introduction to *Montesino's Legacy: Defining and Defending Human Rights for 500 Years,* edited by Edward C. Lorenz, Dana E. Aspinall, and J. Michael Raley. Lanham, MD: Lexington Books, 2014.

Beuchot, Mauricio. "Fray Antón de Montesino: Su novedad," In *El grito y su eco: El sermón de Montesino,* edited by Ricardo de Luis Carballada, 87–94. Salamanca: Editorial San Esteban, 2011.

"Carta de Fernando el Católico a Diego Colon, 20 marzo 1512," Cited in Juan Manuel Perez. *Sermón de Antonio de Montesinos*. Accessed May 17, 2020. http://jubileo .dominicos.org/kit_upload/file/Jubileo/materiales-2010/Sermon-de-Antonio-de -Montesinos-Esquema-3.pdf.

"Fr. Antón de Montesinos, O.P.," *Personajes Dominicanos*. Accessed May 17, 2020. www.dominicos.org/grandes-figuras/personajes/anton-de-montesinos.

Figueras Vallés, Estrella. "Las contradicciones de la conquista española en América: El Requerimiento y la evangelización en Castilla del Oro." In *Orbis incognitvs: avisos y legajos del Nuevo Mundo: homenaje al profesor Luis Navarro Garcia*, edited by Fernando Navarro Antolín, 375–83. Huelva, Spain: Universidad de Huelva, 2007.

Friede, Juan. "Las Casas and Indigenism in the Sixteenth Century" In *Bartolome de Las Casas: Toward an Understanding of the Man and His Work*, edited by Juan Friede and Benjamin Keen, 127–234. DeKalb: Northern Illinois University Press, 1971.

Hanke, Lewis. "Free Speech in Sixteenth-Century Spanish America." *The Hispanic American Historical Review* XXVI, no. 2. (May 1946): 135–46.

Isabel I de Castilla. *Testamento y Codicilo*. Medina del Campo: Villa de las Ferias. Accessed May 17, 2020. www.delsolmedina.com/testamentoTexto-22.htm.

Las Casas, Bartolomé de. Volume III, chapter 3. *Historia General de Las Indias*. National Library of Spain in Madrid.

———. *History of the Indies*. Translated and edited by Andreé Collard. New York: Harper & Row, 1971.

Little, Ambrose Mary. "The Foundation of Human Rights in Natural Universals." In *Montesino's Legacy: Defining and Defending Human Rights for 500 Years*, edited by Edward C. Lorenz, Dana E. Aspinall, and J. Michael Raley. Lanham, MD: Lexington Books, 2014.

McKenna, Charles H. "Francisco de Vitoria: Father of International Law." *Studies: An Irish Quarterly Review* 21, no. 84 (Dec. 1932): 635–48.

Medina Escudero, Miguel Angel. "¿Estos no son hombres? El profetismo de los primeros dominicos en América." Accessed May 17, 2020. https://docplayer .es/406775–Estos-no-son-hombres-el-profetismo-de-los-primeros-dominicos-en-america.html.

Peck, Douglas T. "Lucas Vásquez de Ayllón's Doomed Colony of San Miguel de Gualdape. *The Georgia Historical Quarterly* 8, no. 2 (Summer 2001): 183–98.

Pereña, Luciano. *La idea de la justicia en la conquista de America*. Madrid: Editorial MAPFRE: 1992.

Pierce, OP, Brian. "Seeing, Touching and Speaking the Truth: The First Dominicans in the Americas." *Spirituality* 13, nos. 72 and 73 (2007).

Poole, Stafford. "Iberian Catholicism Comes to the Americas." In *Christianity Comes to the Americas—1492-1776*, edited by Charles H. Lippy, Robert Choquette and Stafford Poole. New York: Paragon House, 1992.

Schroeder, Henry Joseph."Antonio Montesino." *The Catholic Encyclopedia*. Vol. 10. New York: Robert Appleton Company, 1911. Accessed May 20, 2020. http://www .newadvent.org/cathen/10534b.htm.

Watner, Carl. "'All Mankind Is One': The Libertarian Tradition in Sixteenth Century Spain." *The Journal of Libertarian Studies* VIII, no. 2 (Summer 1987): 293–309.

CHAPTER 4: BARTOLOMÉ DE LAS CASAS: "THIS IS AGAINST ALL DIVINE AND HUMAN LAWS"

Adorno, Rolena. *The Polemics of Possession in Spanish American Literature.* New Haven: Yale University Press, 2007.

Biermann, Benno M. "Bartolomé de Las Casas and Verapaz." In *Bartolomé de Las Casas in History: Toward an Understanding of the Man and His Works,* edited by Juan Friede and Benjamin Keen, 443–86. DeKalb, IL: Northern Illinois University Press, 1971.

Bolívar, Simón. "The Jamaica Letter." In *The Political Thought of Bolivar: Selected Writings,* edited by Gerald E. Fitzgerald, 27–44. The Hague: Martinus Nijhoff, 1971.

Borges, Pedro. *Quién era Bartolomé de Las Casas.* Madrid: Ediciones Rialp, S.A., 1990.

Cárdenas Bunsen, José. "Consent, Voluntary Jurisdiction and Native Political Agency in Bartolomé de Las Casas' Final Writings." *Bulletin of Spanish Studies* XCI, no. 6 (2014): 719–817.

Castro, Daniel. *Another Face of Empire: Bartolomé de Las Casas, Indigenous Rights, and Ecclesiastical Imperialism.* Durham: Duke University Press, 2007.

Clayton, Lawrence A. *Bartolomé de Las Cass: A Biography.* Cambridge: Cambridge University Press, 2012.

Comas, Juan. "Historical Reality and the Detractors of Father Las Casas." In *Bartolomé de Las Casas in History: Toward an Understanding of the Man and His Work,* edited by Juan Friede and Benjamin Keen, 487–538. DeKalb: Northern Illinois University Press, 1971.

Dussel, Enrique. "Origen de la filosofía política moderna: Las Casas, Vitoria y Suarez," *Caribbean Studies* 33, no. 2 (Jul–Dec, 2005), 35–80.

———. "The Discovery of an Invasion." Translated by Gary McEoin. *CrossCurrents* 41, no. 4 (Winter 1991–92), 437–52.

Giménez Fernandez, Manuel. "Fray Bartolomé de Las Casas: A Biographical Sketch." In *Bartolomé de Las Casas in History: Toward an Understanding of the Man and His Work,* edited by Juan Friede and Benjamin Keen, 67–126. DeKalb, IL: Northern Illinois University Press, 1971.

Gutiérrez, Gustavo. *Las Casas: In Search of the Poor of Jesus Christ.* Translated by Robert R. Barr. Maryknoll, NY: Orbis Books, 1993.

Hanke, Lewis. *All Mankind Is One: A Study of the Disputation between Bartolomé de Las Casas and Juan Ginés de Sepúlveda in 1550 on the Intellectual and Religious Capacity of the American Indians.* DeKalb: Northern Illinois University Press, 1974.

———. *Aristotle and the American Indians: A Study in Race Prejudice in the Modern World.* Bloomington: Indiana University Press, 1959.

Keen, Benjamin. "Introduction: Approaches to Las Casas, 1535–1970." In *Bartolomé de Las Casas in History: Toward an Understanding of the Man and His Work,* edited by Juan Friede and Benjamin Keen, 3–66. DeKalb: Northern Illinois University Press, 1971.

Knight, Franklin W. Introduction to Bartolomé de Las Casas, *An Account, Much Abbreviated, of the Destruction of the Indies*, edited by Franklin W. Knight, xi–l. Indianapolis: Hackett Publishing Company, 2003.

Las Casas, Bartolomé de. *Apologia fratris Bartholomaei a Casaus adversus Genesium Sepulvedam.* Départament des manuscrits, Bibliotheque nationale de France. Las Casas' translation into Latin of his presentation at Valladolid held at the National Library of France. http://gallica.bnf.fr/ark:/12148/btv1b9080777g/f4.image The sections included here begin on this page: http://gallica.bnf.fr/ark:/12148/btv1b9080777g/f6.image.

———. *Apología o declaración y defensa universal de los derechos del hombre y de los pueblos.* Translated into Spanish from the Latin and edited by Vidal Abril Castelló, María Asunción Sánchez Manzano, Salvador Rus Rufino, Jesús Angel Barreda García, Isacio Pérez Fernández, and Miguel José Abril Stoffels. Salamanca: Junta de Castilla y León Consejería de Educación y Cultura, 2000.

———. *A Short Account of the Destruction of the Indies.* Translated by Nigel Griffin, London: Penguin Books, 1992.

———. Juan Ginés de Sepúlveda, Domingo de Soto, *Aquí se contiene una disputa, o controversia: entre el Obispo don fray Bartholomé de las Casas, . . . y el doctor Ginés de Sepúlveda.* Seville: 1552. Pamphlet containing the minutes of the Sepúlveda and Las Casas debate, at the James Ford Bell Library at the University of Minnesota. https://umedia.lib.umn.edu/item/p16022coll185:2191?q=Las+Casas

———. *History of the Indies.* Translated and edited by Andrée Collard. New York: Harper "& Row, 1971.

———. *In Defense of the Indians: The Defense of the Most Reverend Lord Don Fray Bartolomé de Las Casas, of the Order of Preachers, Late Bishop of Chiapa, Against the Persecutors and Slanderers of the Peoples of the New World Discovered Across the Seas.* Translated from the Latin and edited by Stafford Poole. DeKalb, IL: Northern Illinois University Press, 1992.

———. *The Only Way.* Edited by Helen Rand Parish, Translated by Frances Patrick Sullivan, S.J. New York: Paulist Press, 1992.

Losada, Angel. "The Controversy between Sepúlveda and Las Casas in the Junta of Valladolid." In *Bartolomé de Las Casas in History: Toward an Understanding of the Man and His Work,* edited by Juan Friede and Benjamin Keen, 279–308. DeKalb, IL, Northern Illinois University Press, 1971.

Mayer, Alicia. "El pensamiento de Bartolomé de las Casas en el discurso sobre el indígena. Una perspectiva comparada en las colonias americanas," *Historia Mexicana* 63, no. 3 (January–March 2014): 1121–79.

Menéndez Pidal, Ramón. *El Padre Las Casas: Su Doble Personalidad.* Madrid: Espasa-Calpe, S.A., 1963.

Mires, Fernando. *En nombre de la cruz: discusiones teologícas y políticas frente al holocausto de los indios, período de conquista.* San Jose, Costa Rica: Editorial DEI, 1989, Segunda Edición.

Motolinía, Fray Toribio de. "The Franciscan Reply to the Emperor, 1555," in *Letters and People of the Spanish Indies: Sixteenth Century.* Translated and edited by James Lockhart and Enrique Otte, 218–47. Cambridge: Cambridge University Press, 1976.

Orique, O.P., David T. "Vox legis in Bartolomé de Las Casas' *Brevísima relación de la destrucción de las Indias.*" In *Montesinos' Legacy: Defining and Defending Human Rights for 500 Years.* Edited by Edward C. Lorenz, Dana E. Aspinall, and J. Michael Raley. New York: Lexington Books: 2014.

Pagden, Anthony. Introduction to Bartolomé de Las Casas, *A Short Account of the Destruction of the Indies.* Edited and translated by Nigel Griffin, viii–xli. London: Penguin Books, 1992.

Parish, Helen Rand. Preface and introduction to *The Only Way* by Bartolomé de Las Casas. New York: Paulist Press, 1992.

Pérez Fernández, Isacio. *Bartolomé de Las Casas: Viajero por dos mundos.* Cuzco: Centro de Estudios Regionales Andinos Bartolomé de Las Casas: 1998.

Poole, Stafford. Preface to *In Defense of the Indians: The Defense of the Most Reverend Lord Don Fray Bartolomé de Las Casas, of the Order of Preachers, Late Bishop of Chiapa, Against the Persecutors and Slanderers of the Peoples of the New World Discovered Across the Seas*, by Bartolomé de Las Casas. Translated and edited by Stafford Poole, ix–xxvi. DeKalb, IL: Northern Illinois University Press, 1992.

Solodkow, David. "The Rhetoric of War and Justice in the Conquest of the Americas: Ethnography, Law, and Humanism in Juan Ginés de Sepúlveda and Bartolomé de Las Casas." In *Coloniality, Religion, and the Law in the Early Iberian World*, edited by Santa Arias and Raul Marrero-Fente, 181–200. Nashville: Vanderbilt University Press, 2014.

Vickery, Paul. *Bartolomé de Las Casas: Great Prophet of the Americas.* Mahwah, NJ: Paulist Press, 2006.

Von Vacano, Diego. "Las Casas and the Birth of Race," *History of Political Thought.* Vol. XXXIII, No. 3 (Autumn 2012): 401–26.

Yañez, Agustin. *Fray Bartolomé de Las Casas: El Conquistador conquistado.* Mexico: Editorial Planeta Mexicana, 2001.

CHAPTER 5: ALONSO DE LA VERA CRUZ: "THE SPANIARDS CANNOT HAVE JUST DOMINION"

Aspe Armello, Virginia. "El viejo al nuevo mundo: El tránsito de la noción de dominio y derecho natural de Francisco de Vitoria y Alonso de la Veracruz." *Revista Española de Filosofía Medieval* 17 (2010): 143–55.

Beuchot, Mauricio, "Escolástica, humanismo y derechos humanos en la conquista según Fray Alonso de la Vera Cruz." *Revista de Filosofía* 21 (1995): 83–92.

Blethen, John F. "The Educational Activities of Fray Alonso de la Vera Cruz in Sixteenth Century Mexico." *The Americas* 5, no. 1 (July 1948): 31–47.

Burrus, E. J. "Alonso de la Veracruz's Defence of the American Indians (1553–1554)," *The Heythorp Journal* 4, issue 3 (July 1963), 225–53.

Burrus, Ernest J. "Alonso de la Vera Cruz (d. 1584), Pioneer Defender of the American Indians," *The Catholic Historical Review* LXX, no. 4 (Oct. 1984): 531–46.

Castañeda, Carlos E. "The Coming of the Augustinians to the New World," *Records of the American Catholic Historical Society of Philadelphia* 6, no. 4 (Dec. 1949): 189–196.

De la Torre Rangel, Jesús. *Alonso de la Veracruz: amparo de los indios. Su teoría y práctica jurídica.* Aguascalientes: Universidad Autónoma de Aguascalientes, 1998.

De la Vera Cruz, Alonso. *The Writings of Alonso de la Vera Cruz: Vol. II. Defense of the Indians: Their Rights,* Original Latin texts with English translation by Ernest J. Burrus. St. Louis: Jesuit Historical Institute, 1968.

———. *De dominio infidelium et iusto bello, Sobre el dominio de los infieles y la guerra justa.* Translation from the Latin with notes by Roberto Heredia Correa. México: Universidad Nacional Autónoma de México, 2007.

Ennis, Arthur. "Fray Alonso de la Vera Cruz, O.S.A. (1507–1584): A Study of His Life and His Contribution to the Religious and Intellectual Affairs of Early Mexico, Chapt. I–III." *Augustiniana* 5, no. 1/2 (April 1955): 64–67.

———. "Fray Alonso de la Vera Cruz, O.S.A. (1507–1584): A Study of His Life and His Contribution to the Religious and Intellectual Affairs of Early Mexico, Chapt. IV." *Augustiniana* 5, no. 3 (August 1955): 241–67.

———. "Fray Alonso de la Vera Cruz, O.S.A. (1507–1584): A Study of His Life and His Contribution to the Religious and Intellectual Affairs of Early Mexico, Chapt. VI and VII." *Augustiniana* 7 (1957): 149–95.

Gómez Robledo, Antonio. "Alonso de la Veracruz: Vida y Muerte." In *Homenaje a fray Alonso de la Veracruz en el cuarto centenario de su muerte (1584–1984),* edited by Mauricio Beuchot. 43–52. México: Instituto de Investigaciones Jurídicas, 1986.

———. "El Problema de la Conquista en Alonso de la Veracruz." *Historia Mexicana* 23, no. 3 (January–March, 1974), 379–407.

Gözler Çamur, Elif. "Civil and Political Rights vs. Social and Economic Rights: A Brief Overview." *Journal of Bitlis Eren University Institute of Social Sciences,* 6, no. 1 (June 2017): 205–14.

Gracia, Jorge J. E. "Hispanic Philosophy: Its Beginning and Golden Age." *Hispanic Philosophy in the Age of Discovery,* edited by Kevin White. 3–27. Washington, DC: Catholic University of America Press, 1997.

Gutiérrez, Gustavo. *Las Casas: In Search of the Poor of Jesus Christ.* Translated by Robert R. Barr. Maryknoll, NY: Orbis Books, 1993.

Heredia Correa, Roberto. Introducción to Alonso de la Vera Cruz, *Sobre el dominio de los indios y la guerra justa.* Translated by Roberto Heredia, Antonio Gómez, and Paula López. 24–76. México: Facultad de Filosofía y Letras UNAM, 2004.

———. "Breve historia del texto" in introducción to *De dominio infidelium et iusto bello, Sobre el dominio de los infieles y la guerra justa,* by Fray Alonso de la Vera Cruz. Translation and notes Roberto Heredia Correa. XIII–XL. México: Universidad Nacional Autónoma de México, 2007.

Pagden, Anthony. *The Fall of Natural Man: The American Indian and the Origins of Comparative Ethnology.* Cambridge: Cambridge University Press, 1982.

Quijada, Monica. "From Spain to New Spain: Revisiting the Potestas Populi in Hispanic Political Thought." *Mexican Studies/Estudios Mexicanos* 24, no. 2 (Summer 2008): 185–219.

Quijano Velasco, Francisco. *Las repúblicas de la Monarquía: Pensamiento constitucionalista y republicano en Nueva España, 1550–1610.* México: Instituto de Investigaciones Históricas UNAM, 2017.

Rubial García, Antonio, "Fray Alonso de la Veracruz, agustino. Individualidad y corporativismo en la Nueva España del siglo XVI." In *Innovación y tradición en Alonso de la Veracruz,* edited by Carolina Ponce Hernández, 79–101. México: UNAM, Facultad de Filosofía y Letras, 2007.

Skinner, Quentin. *The Foundations of Modern Political Thought, Volume Two: The Age of Reformation.* Cambridge: Cambridge University Press, 1978.

Velasco Gómez, Ambrosio. "La filosofía de Alonso de la Veracruz a 500 años de la conquista." *Revista Portuguesa de Filosofía* 75, no. 2 (2019): 1030, 1024.

CHAPTER 6: ISABEL DE GUEVARA: "THIS WAS MEN'S WORK"

Carta de Isabel de Guevara a la princesa gobernadora, Juana de Austria, exponiendo los trabajos hechos por las mujeres para ayudar a los hombres en el descubrimiento y conquista del Río de la Plata, pidiendo repartimientos para su marido Pedro de Esquivel. Archivo Histórico Nacional, DIVERSOS-COLECCIONES, 24, N.18. Portal de Archivos Españoles, http://pares.mcu.es/ParesBusquedas20/catalogo/description/1339358.

Gálvez, Lucía. *Mujeres de la Conquista.* Colección Mujeres Argentinas. Buenos Aires: Editorial Planeta Argentina, 1990.

Groussac, Paul. *Mendoza y Garay: Las Dos Fundaciones de Buenos Aires, 1536–1580.* Buenos Aires: Casa Editora de Coni Hermanos, 1916, 2nd edition.

Langa Pizarro, Mar. "Mujeres en la expedición de Pedro de Mendoza: Cartas, crónicas y novelas; verdades, mentiras, ficciones y silencios," *America sin nombre* 15 (2010): 15–29.

Larreta, Enrique. *Tenía que suceder: Las dos fundaciones de Buenos Aires.* Buenos Aires: Espasa-Calpe, S.A., 1944.

Lopreto, Gladys. "La Carta de Isabel de Guevara (Siglo XVI): La mujer y la conquista." *Páginas de Estudio* (blog), written 1996, posted Feb. 28, 2011. http://pginasdeestudio.blogspot.com/2011/02/carta-de-isabel-de-guevara-siglo-xvi.html.

Ludmer, Josefina. "Tretas del Debil." In *La sarten por el mango,* edited by Patricia Elena González and Eliana Ortega, 47–54. Ríos Piedras, Puerto Rico: Ediciones Huracán, 1984.

Marrero Fente, Raul. "De retórica y derechos: estrategias de la reclamación en la carta de Isabel de Guevara," *Hispania* 79, no. 1 (Mar. 1996): 1–7.

Martin, Luis. *Daughters of the Conquistadores: Women of the Viceroyality of Peru.* Dallas: Southern Methodist University Press, 1989.

Peña, Enrique. *Documentos relativos a la expedición de don Pedro de Mendoza y acontecimientos ocurridos en Buenos Aires desde 1536 a 1541.* Buenos Aires: Imprenta Angel Curtolo, 1936.

Quispe-Agnoli, Rocío. "Discursos coloniales escritos y agencia femenina: la 'Carta a la Princesa Juana,'" *Cuaderno Internacional de Estudios Humanísticos y Literatura*, Edición Especial Monográfica—Más allá del Convento 5 (2005–2006), 81–91.

Quispe-Agnoli, Rocio. "Secular Women Writers in the New World," *The Routledge Research Companion to Early Modern Spanish Women Writers*, edited by Nieves Baranda and Anne J. Cruz, 329–345. London: Routledge, 2017.

Scott, Nina M. *Madres del Verbo / Mothers of the Word: Early Spanish-American Women Writers, A Bilingual Anthology.* Albuquerque: University of New Mexico Press, 1999.

Szurmuk, Mónica. "Gesto autobiográfico: Historia y narrativo de viajes de Isabel de Guevara." In *Modalidades de representación del sujeto auto/biográfico feminino*, edited by Magdalena Maiz and Luis H. Pena. Mexico City: Grafo Print Editores, SA. 1997.

CHAPTER 7: COUNCIL OF HUEJOTZINGO: "OUR FATHERS KNEW NO TRIBUTE"

Aguilera, Carmen. "The Matrícula de Huexotzinco: A Pictorial Census from New Spain," *Huntington Library Quarterly* 59, no. 4 (1996): 529–41.

Anderson, Arthur J. O., Frances Berdan, and James Lockhart. "The Historical-Anthropological Potential of Nahuatl Documentation." In *Beyond the Codices: The Nahua View of Colonial Mexico*, edited and translated by Arthur J. O. Anderson, Frances Berdan, and James Lockhart, 1–12. Berkeley: University of California Press, 1976.

Assadourian, Carlos Sempat. "The Colonial Economy: The Transfer of the European System of Production to New Spain and Peru," *Journal of Latin American Studies* 24 (1992, Quincentenary Supplement): 55–68.

Barlow, Robert. "El Derrumbe de Huexotzinco." *Cuadernos Americanos* 7, número 3 (mayo-junio 1948): 147–60.

Brito Guadarrama, Baltazar. *Códice Chavero de Huexotzingo: Proceso a sus oficiales de república.* México: Instituto Nacional de Antropología e Historia, 2008 [1578].

———. *Códice Guillermo Tovar de Huejotzingo, Libro I: Estudio introductorio.* Puebla: Gobierno del Estado de Puebla/Secretaría de Cultura, 2011 [1566].

"Carta del Cabildo de Huejotzingo, 1560." *Cartas de Indias* (Madrid: Ministerio de Fomento, 1877), 1006–11. Accessed May 17, 2020. http://www.bibliotecavirtual deandalucia.es/catalogo/consulta/registro.cmd?id=1039364.

Council of Huejotzingo. "An Indian Town Addresses the King," in *Letters and People of the Spanish Indies: Sixteenth Century*, translated and edited by James Lockhart and Enrique Otte. Cambridge: Cambridge University Press, 1976.

Davies, Nigel. *Los Señores Independientes del Imperio Azteca.* Mexico: Instituto Nacional de Antropología e Historia, 1968.

Díaz, Mónica. *Indigenous Writings from the Convent: Negotiating Ethnic Autonomy in Colonial Mexico.* Tucson, University of Arizona Press, 2010.

"Facsimile U." *Cartas de Indias.* Mexico: Grupo Editorial Miguel Angel Porrua, 2008.

García Granados, Rafael and Luis MacGregor. *Huejotzingo: La ciudad y el convento franciscano.* México: Secretaría de Educación, 1934.

Gibson, Charles. *The Aztecs under Spanish Rule: A History of the Indians of the Valley of Mexico, 1519–1810.* Stanford: Stanford University Press, 1964.

Hébert, John R. and Barbara M. Loste. Introduction to *Huexotzinco Codex.* Facsimile of the 1531 Huexotzinco Codex in the Harkness Collection of the Library of Congress, Washington, DC. XIII–IV. Mexico: Ediciones Multiarte, SA de CV, 1995. https://babel.hathitrust.org/cgi/pt?id=uc1.31210010190401;view=1up;seq=2.

Herrera M., María del Carmen and Marc Thouvenot. "Tributarios en la escritura indígena de la Matrícula de Huexotzinco." *Dimensión Antropológica* 22, vol. 65 (Septiembre/Diciembre 2015): 125–161.

Lockhart, James, and Enrique Otte, "Petitions, Correspondence, and Other Formal Statements," in *Letters and People of the Spanish Indies, Sixteenth Century.* Translated, edited, and commentary by James Lockhart and Enrique Otte, 160–65. Cambridge: Cambridge University Press, 1976.

Mallon, Florencia E. "The Promise and Dilemma of Subaltern Studies: Perspectives from Latin American History." *The American Historical Review* 99, no. 5 (Dec. 1994), 1491–1515.

Matrícula de Huexotzingo 1560, Bibliotheque Nacionale de France, Mexicain 387. https://gallica.bnf.fr/ark:/12148/btv1b7200005f/f7.image.

Menegus Bornemann, Margarita. "Encomienda, tributos y señores naturales," in *Historia colonial de México: Instauración y desarrollo del sistema de encomiendas,* edited by Isabel Fernández Tejado, 103–137. México, DF: Universidad Iberamericana, 1995.

Noguez, Xavier. Introduction to *Huexotzinco Codex*, Facsimile of the 1531 Huexotzinco Codex in the Harkness Collection of the Library of Congress, Washington, DC. (Mexico, DF: Ediciones Multiarte, SA de CV, 1995) 91–103. https://babel.hathitrust.org/cgi/pt?id=uc1.31210010190401;view=1up;seq=89.

Prem, Hans. *Matricula de Huexotzinco, MS. Mex. 385, Bibliotheque Nationale, Paris.* Graz, Austria, 1974.

Sarabia Viejo, María Justina. *Don Luis de Velasco, virrey de Nueva España, 1550–1564.* Sevilla: Escuela de Estudios Hispano-Americanos, 1978.

Schwartz, Stuart B., *Victors and Vanquished: Spanish and Nahua Views of the Conquest of Mexico.* Boston: Bedford/St. Martin, 2000.

Slicher van Bath, B. H. "The calculation of the population of New Spain, especially for the period before 1570." *Boletín de Estudios Latinoamericanos y del Caribe* 24 (junio 1978): 67–95.

Spivak, Gayatri Chakravorty. "Can the Subaltern Speak?" *Marxism and the Interpretation of Culture,* edited by Cary Nelson and Lawrence Grossberg, 24–28. Urbana and Chicago: University of Illinois Press, 1988.

Spores, Ronald. "Mixteca Cacicas" in *Indian Women of Early Mexico,* edited by Susan Schroeder, Stephanie Wood, and Robert Haskett, 185–199. Norman: University of Oklahoma Press, 1997.

CHAPTER 8: BERNARDINO DE SAHAGÚN: "I ASSEMBLED ALL THE LEADERS"

Anderson, Arthur J. O. "Variations on a Sahaguntine Theme." In *Florentine Codex, Part I Introductions and Indices*, edited and translated by Arthur J. O. Anderson and Charles E. Dibble, 3–8. Salt Lake City: University of Utah Press, 1982.

———. "Sahagún: Career and Character." In *Florentine Codex, Part I Introductions and Indices,* by Bernardino de Sahagún, edited and translated by Arthur J. O. Anderson and Charles E. Dibble, 29–41. Salt Lake City: University of Utah Press, 1982.

Baudot, Georges. "The Last Years of Fray Bernardino de Sahagún (1585–1590): The Rescue of the Confiscated Work and the Seraphic Conflicts. New Unpublished Documents." In *Sixteenth-Century Mexico: The Work of Sahagún*, edited by Munro S. Edmonson, 165–187. Albuquerque: University of New Mexico Press, 1974.

Browne, Walden. *Sahagún and the Transition to Modernity.* Norman: University of Oklahoma Press, 2000.

Calnek, Edward E. "The Sahagún Texts as a Source of Sociological Information." In *Sixteenth-Century Mexico: The Work of Sahagún*, edited by Munro S. Edmonson, 189–204. Albuquerque: University of New Mexico Press, 1974.

Castro-Klaren, Sara. "Produciendo a Sahagún: El problema de la autoría en Sahagún, Pablo de San Buena Ventura, Antonio Valeriano, Alonso Vegerano, Martín Jacobita y otros, Sahagún y los neo-Tlacuilos." *Revista de Crítica Literaria Latinoamericana* 43, no. 86 (2nd semestre 2017): 89–110.

Dibble, Charles E. "Sahagún's Historia" in *Florentine Codex, Part I Introductions and Indices*, by Bernardino de Sahagún, edited and translated by Arthur J. O. Anderson and Charles E. Dibble, 9–23. Salt Lake City: University of Utah Press, 1982.

Edmonson, Munro S. Introduction to *Sixteenth-Century Mexico: The Work of Sahagún*, edited by Munro S. Edmonson, 1–15. Albuquerque: University of New Mexico Press, 1974.

Garibay, Angel Maria K. *Historia de la Literatura Nahuatl. Segunda parte: El trauma de la conquista (1521–1750).* Second edition. Mexico, DF: Editorial Porrua, S.A., 1971.

Keber, John. "Sahagún and Hermeneutics: A Christian Ethnographer's Understanding of Aztec Culture." In *The Work of Bernardino de Sahagún: Pioneer Ethnographer of Sixteenth Century Aztec Mexico*, edited by J. Jorge Klor de Alva, H. B. Nicholson, and Eloise Quiñones Keber, 53–63. Austin: University of Texas Press, 1988.

Klor de Alva, J. Jorge. "Sahagún and the Birth of Modern Ethnography: Representing, confessing, and inscribing the native other." In *The Work of Bernardino de Sahagún: Pioneer Ethnographer of Sixteenth Century Aztec Mexico,* Edited by J.

Jorge Klor de Alva, H. B. Nicholson, and Eloise Quiñones Keber, 31–52. Austin: University of Texas Press, 1988.

Leon-Portilla, Miguel. *Bernardino de Sahagún: First Anthropologist.* Translated by Mauricio J. Mixco. Norman: University of Oklahoma Press, 2002.

———. "The Problematics of Sahagún: Certain Topics Needing Investigation" in *Sixteenth-Century Mexico: The Work of Sahagún,* edited by Munro S. Edmonson, 235–55. Albuquerque: University of New Mexico Press, 1974.

López, Austin, Alfredo. "The Research Method of Fray Bernardino de Sahagún: The Questionnaires." In *Sixteenth-Century Mexico: The Work of Sahagún,* edited by Munro S. Edmonson, 111–49. Albuquerque: University of New Mexico Press, 1974.

Nicolau D'Olwer, Luis. *Fray Bernardino de Sahagún (1499–1590).* Translated by Mauricio J. Mixco. Salt Lake City: University of Utah Press, 1987.

Sahagún, Bernardino de. *General History of the Things of New Spain: Florentine Codex.* Translated by Arthur J. O. Anderson and Charles E. Dibble. Salt Lake City: University of Utah Press, 1982.

———. *Historia general de las cosas de la Nueva España: Códice Florentino.* Biblioteca Medicea Laurenziana, Florence, Italy. Copy and paste this link in your browser: http://mss.bmlonline.it/?search=Bernardino%20de%20Sahag%C3%BAn

———. *Historia General de las Cosas de Nueva España,* edited by Juan Carlos Temprano. Madrid: Editorial Historia 16, 1990.

Sullivan, Thelma D. "The Rhetorical Orations or Huehuetlatolli Collected by Sahagún." In *Sixteenth-Century Mexico: The Work of Sahagún,* edited by Munro S. Edmonson, 79–109. Albuquerque: University of New Mexico Press, 1974.

Temprano, Juan Carlos. Introducción to *Historia General de las Cosas de Nuevo España,* by Bernardino de Sahagún, edited by Juan Carlos Temprano. Madrid: Editorial Historia 16, 1990.

CHAPTER 9: THE INCA TITU CUSI YUPANQUI: "THE NATURAL LORDS THAT USED TO RULE PERU"

Andrien, Kenneth J. *Andean Worlds: Indigenous History, Culture, and Consciousness under Spanish Rule, 1532–1825.* Albuquerque: University of New Mexico Press, 2001.

Bauer, Brian S. and Javier Fonseca Santa Cruz, and Mirian Araóz Silva. *Vilcabamba and the Archaeology of Inca Resistance.* Los Angeles: Cotsen Institute of Archaeology, 2015.

———. Madeleine Halac-Higashimori, and Gabriel E. Cantarutti. *Voices from Vilcabamba: Accounts Chronicling the Fall of the Inca Empire.* Louisville, CO: University Press of Colorado, 2016.

Bauer, Ralph. Introduction to *An Inca Account of the Conquest of Peru, by Titu Cusi Yupanqui.* Translated, introduced, and annotated by Ralph Bauer. Boulder: University of Colorado Press, 2005.

Bingham, Hiram. "In the wonderland of Peru—rediscovering Machu Picchu: The work accomplished by the Peruvian Expedition of 1912, under the auspices of Yale University and the National Geographic Society." *National Geographic*, March 31, 2013—reprinted from the April 1913 edition. https://www.nationalgeographic .com/magazine/article/machu-picchu-peru-inca-hiram-bingham-discovery.

———. "The Ruins of Espiritu Pampa, Peru." *American Anthropologist* 16, no. 2 (Apr–Jun, 1914): 185–99.

Blair, Laurence. "Peru's last Inca city reveals its secrets: 'It's genuinely a marvel.'" *The Guardian,* Sept. 28, 2018. https://www.theguardian.com/world/2018/sep/28/ perus-last-incan-city-reveals-its-secrets-its-genuinely-a-marvel.

Castillo, Moisés R. "Estrategias de Resistencia y de crítica en el Perú colonial: La 'Relación de Titu Cusi Yupanqui y los 'Coloquios de la verdad' de Pedro de Quiroga." *Latin American Literary Review* 40, no. 80 (July–Dec. 2012): 123–26.

Chang-Rodríguez, Raquel. *La apropiación del signo: Tres cronistas indígenas del Perú.* Tempe: Center for Latin American Studies, Arizona State University, 1988.

———. "Rebelión y religión en dos crónicas del Perú de ayer." *Revista de Crítica Literaria Latinoamericana* 14, no. 28 (1988): 175–92.

———. *Violencia y subversión en la prosa colonial hispanoamericana, siglos XVI y XVII.* Madrid: José Porrúa Turanzas, S.A., 1982.

———. "Writing as Resistance: Peruvian History and the *Relación* of Titu Cusi Yupanqui," In *From Oral to Written Expression: Native Andean Chronicles of the Early Colonial Period,* edited by Rolena Adorno, 41–64. Syracuse: Maxwell School, 1982.

Guillén Guillén, Edmundo. *Visión peruana de la Conquista: La Resistencia Incaica a la invasión española.* Lima: Editorial Milla Batres, 1979.

———. *La Guerra de Reconquista Inca: Historia épica de como los Incas lucharon en defensa de la soberanía del Perú o Tawantinsuyo de 1536–1572.* Lima: R.A. Ediciones e.i.r.l., 1994.

Herrera Villagra, Alejandro, "Titu Cusi Yupanqui: diálogo, comunicación y traducción en la redacción de epístolas entre la mascapaicha quechua y la corona española. Vilcabamba, 1560–1570. Revisitado," *Yuyay Taqe: Los Incas en su tiempo y en el nuestro,* edited by Roberto Ojeda Escalante and Alejandro Herrera Villagra, 69–117. Cuzco: Universidad Andina del Cusco, 2019.

Horswell, Michael J. "Negotiating Apostasy in Vilcabamba: Titu Cusi Yupanqui Writes from the Chaupi." *The Romanic Review* 103, no. 1–2 (2012): 81–110.

Jákfalvi-Leiva, Susana. "De la voz a la escritura: La Relación de Titu Cusi (1570)." *Revista de Crítica Literaria Latinoamericana* 19, no. 37 (1993): 259–77.

Julien, Catherine. "Francisco de Toledo and His Campaign against the Incas." *Colonial Latin American Review* 16, no. 2 (Dec. 2007): 243–72.

———. Introduction to *History of How the Spaniards Arrived in Peru,* by Titu Cusi Yupanqui. Edited and translated by Catherine Julien, vii–xxix. Dual-Language Edition. Indianapolis: Hackett Publishing Company, Inc. 2006.

Kubler, George. "A Peruvian Chief of State: Manco Inca (1515–1545)." *The Hispanic American Historical Review* 24, no. 2 (May 1944): 271–74.

Las Casas, Bartolomé de. *Obras completas 11.2 Doce dudas.* Madrid: Alianza, 1992 (1564).

————. *History of the Indies*. Translated by Andrée M. Collard. New York: Harper & Row, 1971.

Legnani, Nicole Delia. "A Necessary Contextualization" to *Titu Cusi: A 16th Century Account of the Conquest*, by Titu Cusi Yupanqui. Translated and edited by Nicole Delia Legnani. Cambridge: Harvard University Press, 2005.

————. Introduction to *Titu Cusi: A 16th Century Account of the Conquest*, by Titu Cusi Yupanqui. Translated and edited by Nicole Delia Legnani. Cambridge: Harvard University Press, 2005.

No, Song. "La heterogeneidad suterada: Titu Cusi Yupangui. *Revista de Crítica Literaria Latinoamericana* 31, no. 62 (2005): 85–96.

Post, Ben. "Titu Cusi Yupanqui (ca. 1526–1570)." In *Narradores Indígenas y mestizos de la época colonial (siglos XVI–XVII)*, edited by Rocío Cortés and Margarita Zamora, 177–202. Lima: Centro de Estudios Literarios Antonio Cornejo Polar, 2016.

Regalado de Hurtado, Liliana. Estudio preliminar to *Instrucción al Licenciado Don Lope García de Castro (1570)*, by Inca Titu Cusi Yupanqui. Lima: Fondo Editorial de la Pontifica Universidad Católica del Perú, 1992.

Roy, Hélene. "El discurso neo-inca y su significado político: Vilcabamba entre sumisión, sincretismo y resistencia." *Revista de Crítica Literaria Latinoamericana* 40, no. 80 (2014): 87–101.

Salomon, Frank. Preface to *Titu Cusi: A 16th Century Account of the Conquest*, by Titu Cusi Yupanqui. Translated and edited by Nicole Delia Legnani. Cambridge: Harvard University Press, 2005.

Spalding, Karen. "Notes on the Formation of the Andean Colonial State." In *State Theory and Andean Politics: New Approaches to the Study of Rule*, edited by Christopher Krupa and David Nugent, 213–233. Philadelphia: University of Pennsylvania Press, 2015.

Titu Cusi Yupanqui. *An Inca Account of the Conquest of Peru*. Translated, introduced, and annotated by Ralph Bauer. Boulder: University of Colorado Press, 2005.

Titu Cussi Yupangui, Diego de Castro. *Relación de la conquista del Perú y hechos del Inca Manco II*, edited by Horacio H. Urteaga and biography by Carlos A. Romero. Lima: Imprenta San Marti y Ca., 1916.

Townsend, Camilla. "Burying the White Gods: New Perspectives on the Conquest of Mexico." *The American Historical Review* 108, no. 3 (June 2003): 659–687.

Wachtel, Nathan. *The Vision of the Vanquished: The Spanish Conquest of Peru through Indian Eyes: 1530–1570*. Translated from the French by Ben and Sian Reynolds. New York: Harper & Row Publishers, 1977.

CHAPTER 10: PEDRO SARMIENTO DE GAMBOA: "THE HORRIBLE TYRANNY OF THE INCAS"

Adorno, Rolena. *The Polemics of Possession in Spanish American Narrative*. New Haven: Yale University Press, 2007.

Barros Franco, José Miguel. "Los últimos años de Pedro Sarmiento de Gamboa." *Boletín de la Academia Chilena de la Historia* no. 90 (1997/1998): 53–69.

Bauer, Brian S. and Decoster, Jean-Jacques. Introduction to *The History of the Incas*, by Pedro Sarmiento de Gamboa. Translated and edited by Brian S. Bauer and Vania Smith, 1–34. Austin: University of Texas Press, 2007.

Bauer, Ralph. Introduction to *An Inca Account of the Conquest of Peru* by Titu Cusi Yupanqui. Translated and annotated by Ralph Bauer, 1–56. Boulder: University of Colorado Press, 2005.

Carrillo, Francisco. *Cronistas del Peru Antiguo: Enciclopedia Histórica de la Literatura Peruana, Vol. 4.* Lima: Editorial Horizonte, 1989.

Cartwright, Mark. "Inca Civilization." *Ancient History Encyclopedia*, last modified Sept. 2014, https://www.ancient.eu/Inca_Civilization/.

Clissold, Stephen. *Conquistador: The Life of Don Pedro Sarmiento de Gamboa.* London: Derek Verschoyle, 1954.

Covey, R. Alan. "Chronology, Succession, and Sovereignty: The Politics of Inka Historiography and Its Modern Interpretation." In *Comparative Studies in Society and History* 48, no. 1 (Jan. 2006): 169–99.

González Díaz, Soledad. "Del Génesis a los Andes: la cronología del incario en la *Historia de los Incas* de Pedro Sarmiento de Gamboa." *Estudios Atacameños* no. 51 (2015): 153–175.

———. "A Three-Century Journey: The Lost Manuscript of the History of the Incas by Pedro Sarmiento De Gamboa." *The Americas* 78, no. 3 (2021): 467–91.

Hanke, Lewis. "Viceroy Francisco de Toledo and the Just Titles of Spain to the Inca Empire: The Defense of the Spanish Title to Peru." *The Americas* 3, no. 1 (July 1946): 3–19.

Julien, Catherine. "Francisco Toledo and His Campaign against the Incas." *Colonial Latin American Review* 16, no. 2 (Dec. 2007): 243–72.

———. *Reading Inca History.* Iowa City: University of Iowa Press, 2000.

Las Casas, Bartolomé de. *Obras completas 11.2 Doce dudas.* Madrid: Alianza, 1992 (1564).

Levillier, Roberto. *Don Francisco de Toledo, Supremo Organizador del Perú: su vida, su obra (1515–1582, Tomo I: Años de andanzas y de guerras (1515–1572).* Madrid: Espasa-Calpe, 1935.

MacCormack, Sabine. "History, Historical Record, and Ceremonial Action: Incas and Spaniards in Cuzco." *Comparative Studies in Society and History* 43, no. 2 (April 2001): 329–363.

Markham, Clements R. Introduction" to *Narratives of the Voyages of Pedro Sarmiento de Gamboa to the Straits of Magellan* by Pedro Sarmiento de Gamboa, ix–xxx. Translated by Clements R. Markham. New York: Burt Franklin, Publisher, 1895.

Means, Philip Ainsworth. *Fall of the Inca Empire and the Spanish Rule in Peru: 1530–1780.* New York: Charles Scribner's Sons, 1932.

———. "Sarmiento de Gamboa, Captain Pedro." In *Biblioteca Andina, Part I, The Chroniclers, or, the Writers of the Sixteenth and Seventeenth Centuries Who Treated of the Pre-Hispanic History and Culture of the Andean Countries.* New Haven: Transactions of the Connecticut Academy of Arts and Sciences, no. 29

(1928): 462–478. Posted October 19, 2017. https://archive.org/details/b29827322/page/n3/mode/2up.

Millones Figueroa, Luis. "Colonial Andean Texts in English Translation." *Latin American Research Review* 44, no. 2 (2009): 181–192.

Mumford, Jeremy Ravi. *Vertical Empire: The General Resettlement of Indians in the Colonial Andes.* Durham: Duke University Press, 2012.

Pease G.Y., Franklin. *Las Crónicas y Los Andes.* Mexico: Fondo de Cultura Económica, 2010 [1995].

Porras Barrenechea, Raúl. "Pedro Sarmiento de Gamboa [1532–1592?]." In *Los Cronistas del Peru (1528–1650) y Otros Ensayos,* edited, prologue, and notes by Franklin Pease, 362–366. Lima: Biblioteca Clásicos del Perú, 1986 [1962].

Sarmiento de Gamboa, Pedro. *History of the Incas.* Translated and edited by Clements Markham. London: Hakluyt Society, 1907 [1572].

———. *The History of the Incas,* Translated and edited by Brian S. Bauer and Vania Smith with introduction by Brian S. Bauer and Jean-Jacques Decoster. Austin: University of Texas Press, 2007.

———. *Viage al Estrecho de Magallanes por el Capitán Pedro Sarmiento de Gamboa en los Años 1579 y 1580.* Madrid: Imprenta Real de la Gazeta, 1786. http://www.cervantesvirtual.com/obra-visor/viage-al-estrecho-de-magallanes-por-el-capitan-pedro-sarmiento-de-gamboa-en-los-anos-de-1579-y-1580-y-noticia-de-la-expedicion-que-despues-hizo-para-poblarle--0/html/.

Spalding, Karen. "Notes on the Formation of the Andean Colonial State." In *State Theory and Andean Politics: New Approaches to the Study of Rule,* edited by Christopher Krupa and David Nugent, 213–33. Philadelphia: University of Pennsylvania Press, 2015.

Zuidema, R. T. *The Ceque System of Cuzco: The Social Organization of the Capital of the Inca.* Leiden: E.J. Brill, 1964.

CHAPTER 11: ALONSO DE ILLESCAS: "SUSPEND THE EXPEDITION"

Angulo, Alberto. *Moros en la costa: Vivencia afrocolombiana en la cultura colectiva.* Bogotá: Docentes Editores, 1999.

Beatty-Medina, Charles. "Alonso de Illescas (1530s-1590s): African, Ladino, and Maroon Leader in Colonial Ecuador," *In the Human Tradition in the Black Atlantic,* edited by Beatriz Gallotti Mamigonian and Karen Racine, 9–22. Lanham, MD: Rowman & Littlefield, 2010.

———. "Between the Cross and the Sword: Religious Conquest and Maroon Legitimacy in Colonial Esmeraldas," In *Africans to Spanish America: Expanding the Diaspora,* edited by Sherwin K. Bryant, Rachel Sarah O'Toole, and Ben Vinson, 95–113. Urbana, IL: University of Illinois Press, 2012.

——— ."Caught between Rivals: The Spanish African Maroon Competition for Captive Indian Labor in the Region of Esmeraldas during the Late Sixteenth and Early

Seventeenth Centuries," *The Americas* 63, no. 1 (The African Diaspora in the Colonial Andes, July 2006): 113–36.

———. "Maroon Chief Alonso de Illescas' Letter to the Crown, 1586." In *Afro-Latino Voices: Narratives from the early modern Ibero-Atlantic world, 1550–1812*, edited by Kathryn Joy McKnight and Leo J. Garofalo, 30–33. Indianapolis: Hackett Publishing Company, 2009.

Blackburn, Robin. *The Making of New World Slavery: From the Baroque to the Modern, 1492–1800*. London and New York: Verso, 2010.

Bowser, Frederick P. *The African Slave in Colonial Peru, 1524–1650*. Stanford, CA: Stanford University Press, 1974.

Cabello Balboa, Miguel. "Verdadera Descripción de la Provincia de Esmeraldas [1583]." In *Descripción de la Provincia de Esmeraldas*, edited with notes and introduction by José Alcino Franch, 31–106. Madrid: Consejo Superior de Investigaciones Científicas, 2001.

Davidson, David M. "Negro Slave Control and Resistance in Colonial Mexico, 1519–1650." In *Maroon Societies: Rebel Slave Communities in the Americas*, edited by Richard Price, 82–103. Baltimore: Johns Hopkins University Press, 1979.

Espinoza, Alonso de. "Alonso de Espinoza a la Audiencia de Quito, 22 mayo 1585," In *Documentos para la historia de la Audiencia de Quito, Vol. 4,* edited by José Rumazo Gonzalez, 11–12. Madrid: A. Aguado, 1948.

Franch, José Alcino. Introducción to *Descripción de la Provincia de Esmeraldas*, edited with notes and introduction by José Alcino Franch, 9–30. Madrid: Consejo Superior de Investigaciones Científicas, 2001.

Franco, José L. "Maroons and Slave Rebellions in the Spanish Territories." In *Maroon Societies: Rebel Slave Communities in the Americas*, edited by Richard Price, 35–48. Baltimore: Johns Hopkins University Press, 1979.

Franklin, Vincent P. "Alonso de Sandoval and the Jesuit Conception of the Negro." *The Journal of Negro History* 58, no. 3 (July 1973): 349–60.

Garofalo, Leo. "The Shape of a Diaspora: The Movement of Afro-Iberians to Colonial Spanish America." In *Africans to Spanish America: Expanding the Diaspora*, edited by Sherwin K. Bryant, Rachel Sarah O'Toole, and Ben Vinson III, 27–49. Urbana: University of Illinois Press, 2012.

Hall, Gwendolyn Midlo. *Slavery and African Ethnicities in the Americas: Restoring the Links*. Chapel Hill: University of North Carolina, Press, 2005.

Illescas, Alonso de. *Alonso de Illescas a la Corona, 24 febrero 1586*. Seville: Archivo General de Indias, Escribania 922b, folio 11, 1586.

———. "Letter from Don Alonso de Illescas, a Black Man in Esmeraldas [1586]," Introduction and translation by Charles Beatty-Medina. *Afro-Latino Voices: Narratives from the Early Modern Ibero-Atlantic World, 1550–1812*, edited by Kathryn Joy McKnight and Leo J. Garofalo, 34–37. Indianapolis: Hackett Publishing Co., 2009.

King, James Ferguson. "Negro History in Continental Spanish America," *The Journal of Negro History* 29 1 (Jan. 1944): 7–23.

Klein Herbert S. and Ben Vinson III. *African Slavery in Latin America and the Caribbean*. New York and Oxford: Oxford University Press, 2007.

Landers, Jane. "Maroon Women in Colonial Spanish America: Case Studies in the Circum-Caribbean from the Sixteenth through the Eighteenth Centuries." In *Beyond Bondage: Free Women of Color in the Americas*, edited by David Barry Gaspar and Darlene Clark Hine, 3–18. Champaign: University of Illinois Press, 2004.

Lane, Kris. *Quito 1599: City and Colony in Transition*. Albuquerque: University of New Mexico Press, 2002.

Las Casas, Bartolomé de. *The Only Way*. Edited by Helen Rand Parish and translated by Frances Patrick Sullivan, S.J. New York: Paulist Press, 1992.

Lienhard, Martin. *Disidentes, rebeldes, insurgentes: Resistencia indígena y negra en América Latina, Ensayos de historia testimonial*. Madrid: Iberoamérica, 2008.

"Los tres mulatos de Esmeraldas" de Andrés Sánchez Galque, Museo del Prado https://www.museodelprado.es/coleccion/obra-de-arte/los-tres-mulatos-de-esmeraldas/1224cef3–e625–4ea6–9c27–2ae81d789e14 (Accessed July 20, 2021).

Pescatello, Ann M. "The *Leyenda Negra* and the African in Sixteenth and Seventeenth Century Iberian Thought." *The Catholic Historical Review* 66, no. 2 (April 1980): 169–183.

Ratcliff, Anthony. "'Black Writers of the World, Unite!' Negotiating Pan-African Politics of Cultural Struggle in Afro-Latin America." *The Black Scholar* 37, no. 4, (Rethinking Pan-Africanism for the 21st Century, Winter 2008): 27–38.

Rout, Jr. Leslie B. *The African Experience in Spanish America*. Princeton: Markus Wiener Publishers, 2003.

Rueda Novoa, Rocio. *Zambaje y Autonomía: Historia de la gente negra de la provincia de Esmeraldas Siglos XVI–XVIII*. Esmeraldas, Ecuador: Municipalidad de Esmeraldas, Taller de Estudios Históricos, 2001.

Sánchez-Godoy, Rubén A. "We Never Could Understand Why the Black Man Did Not Come to Us': Early African-Amerindian Subjectivities in Miguel Cabello Balboa's *Verdadera Descripción de la Provincia de Esmeraldas* (1583)." *Comparative Literature Studies* 49, no. 2 (Special Issue: Comparative Perspectives on the Black Atlantic, 2012): 167–85.

Savoia, Rafael. "El Negro Alonso de Illescas y sus descendientes (entre 1553–1867)." In *Actas del Primer Congreso de Historia del Negro en el Ecuador y sur de Colombia*, edited by Rafael Savoia, 29–61. Quito: Centro Cultural Afro-Ecuatoriano, 1988.

Szazdi, Adam. "El trasfondo de un cuadro: 'Los Mulatos de Esmeraldas' de Andrés Sánchez Galque." *Cuadernos Prehispánicos* 12 (1986–1987): 93–142.

Tannenbaum, Frank. *Slave and Citizen: The Negro in the Americas*. New York: Vintage Books, 1946.

Vila Vilar, Enriqueta. Introducción to *Un tratado sobre la esclavitud*, by Alonso de Sandoval. Edited by Enriqueta Vila Vilar, 3–40. Madrid: Alianza Editorial, 1987.

Von Germeten, Nicole. Introduction to *Treatise on Slavery: Selections from De instauranda Aethiopum salute*, by Alonso de Sandoval, S.J. Translated by Nicole von Germeten, ix–xxx. Indianapolis: Hackett Publishing Company, 2008.

Voyages Database. 2009. *Voyages: The Trans-Atlantic Slave Trade Database* https://slavevoyages.org/assessment/estimates. Emory University.

Wade, Peter. "The Cultural Politics of Blackness in Colombia." *American Ethnologist* 22, no. 2, (May 1995): 341–57.

Wheat, David. "The First Great Waves: African Provenance Zones for the Transatlantic Slave Trade to Cartagena de Indias, 1570–1640." *The Journal of African
History* 52, no. 1 (2011): 1–22.

CHAPTER 12: LUIS DE CARVAJAL THE YOUNGER:
"MAY THE LORD GOD OF ISRAEL ENLIGHTEN THEM"

Alberro, Solange. *Inquisición y sociedad en México 1571–1700.* Mexico: Fondo de
la Cultura Económica, 1988.
Carvajal, Luis de, the Younger. "The Autobiography of Luis de Carvajal, the
Younger." Translated by Martin Cohen. *American Jewish History* 55, no. 3 (1966):
282–318.
———. *The Enlightened: The Writings of Luis de Cavajal, el Mozo.* Translated and
edited with introduction by Seymour B. Liebman. Coral Gables, FL: University of
Miami Press, 1967.
Carvajal, Luis de, El Mozo. *Memorias.* México: Biblioteca Nacional de Antropología
e Historia (BNAH). Before 1596. http://digitalcollections.nyhistory.org/islandora/
object/nyhs%3A10467#page/1/mode/2up.
Chuchiak, John F. IV, ed. and trans. *The Inquisition in New Spain—1536–1820: A
Documentary History.* Baltimore: The Johns Hopkins University Press, 2012.
Cohen, Martin A. Introduction to "The Autobiography of Luis De Carvajal, the
Younger." *American Jewish Historical Quarterly* 55, no. 3 (1966): 277–81.
Cohen, Martin A. *The Martyr: Luis de Carvajal: A Secret Jew in Sixteenth Century
Mexico.* Albuquerque: University of New Mexico Press: 2001 [1973].
Gojman de Backal, Alicia. "Luis de Carvajal El Mozo. Sus memorias, correspon-
dencia y su testamento." *Diario Judio*, February 3, 2017. http://diariojudio
.com/opinion/luis-de-carvajal-el-mozo-sus-memorias-correspondencia-y-su-testa
mento/231239/.
Green, Toby Green. *Inquisition: The Reign of Fear.* New York: St. Martins Press,
2007.
Greenleaf, Richard E. *The Mexican Inquisition of the Sixteenth Century.* Albuquer-
que: University of New Mexico Press, 1969.
———. "Historiography of the Mexican Inquisition: Evolution of Interpretations and
Methodologies." In *Cultural Encounters: The Impact of the Inquisition in Spain
and the New World,* edited by Mary Elizabeth Perry and Anne J. Cruz, 248–276.
Berkeley: University of California Press, 1991.
Holler, Jacqueline. "'More Sins than the Queen of England' Marina de San Miguel
before the Mexican Inquisition." In *Women in the Inquisition: Spain and the New
World,* edited by Mary Giles, 209–28. Baltimore: Johns Hopkins University Press,
1999.
Hordes, Stanley M. "The Inquisition and the Crypto-Jewish Community in Colonial
New Spain and New Mexico." In *Cultural Encounters: The Impact of the Inquisi-
tion in Spain and the New World,* edited by Mary Elizabeth Perry and Anne J. Cruz,
207–220. Berkeley: University of California Press, 1991.

Kamen, Henry. *Inquisition and Society in Spain in the Sixteenth and Seventeenth Centuries.* Bloomington: Indiana University Press, 1985.

Lanyon, Anna. *Fire and Song: The Story of Luis de Carvajal and the Mexican Inquisition.* Crows Nest, NSW, Australia: Allen and Unwin, 2011.

Lea, Henry Charles. *The Inquisition in the Spanish Dependencies.* New York: The MacMillan Company, 1908.

"Los manuscritos de Luis de Carvajal, germen de la literatura judía en América, al acervo de la BNAH," Instituto Nacional de Antropología e Historia, Mar. 23, 2017. https://www.inah.gob.mx/boletines/6007–los-manuscritos-de-luis-de-carvajal-germen-de-la-literatura-judia-en-america-al-acervo-de-la-bnah.

Madden, Thomas F. "The Real Inquisition: Investigating the Popular Myth." *National Review,* June 18, 2004. http://www.nationalreview.com/article/211193/real-inquisition-thomas-f-madden.

Perelis, Ronnie. *Narratives from the Sephardic Atlantic: Blood and Faith.* Bloomington, IN: Indiana University Press, 2016.

Peters, Edward. *Inquisition.* New York: The Free Press, 1988.

Schwartz, Stuart B. *All Can Be Saved: Religious Tolerance and Salvation in the Iberian Atlantic World.* New Haven: Yale University Press, 2008.

Stavans, Ilan. Introduction to *The Martyr: Luis de Carvajal: A Secret Jew in Sixteenth Century Mexico*, by Martin A. Cohen, ixx–xxiv. Albuquerque: University of New Mexico Press, 2001 [1973].

Toro, Alfonso. *The Carvajal Family: Jews and the Inquisition in New Spain in the Sixteenth Century.* Adaptation by Frances Hernández. El Paso: Texas Western Press, 2002.

CHAPTER 13: EL INCA GARCILASO DE LA VEGA: "PAST GREATNESS AND PROSPERITY"

Brading, D. A. "The Incas and the Renaissance: *The Royal Commentaries* of Inca Garcilaso de la Vega." *Journal of Latin American Studies* 18 (1986): 1–23.

Castro-Klaren, Sara. "Writing the Andes." In *A Companion to Latin American Literature and Culture,* edited by Sara Castro-Klaren, 117–36. Hoboken: Blackwell Publishing, 2008.

———. "'For It Is But a Single World,'" In *Inca Garcilaso and Contemporary World-Making*, edited by Sara Castro-Klaren and Christian Fernández, 195–228. Pittsburgh: University of Pittsburgh Press, 2016,

Fiengo-Varn, Aurora. "Reconciling the Divided Self: Inca Garcilaso de la Vega's Royal Commentaries and his Platonic view of the conquest of Peru," *Revista de Filologia y Lingüística* XXIX, no. 1 (2003): 119–28.

Fuerst, James W. "Locke and Inca Garcilaso: Subtexts, Politics, and European Expansion," *Inca Garcilaso and Contemporary World-Making*, edited by Sara Castro-Klarén and Christian Fernández, 269–96. Pittsburgh: University of Pittsburgh Press, 2016.

———. *New World Postcolonial: The Political Thought of Inca Garcilaso de la Vega.* Pittsburgh: University of Pittsburgh Press, 2018.

"Garcilaso Inca de la Vega (1539–1616)" In *Selections from the Library of José Durand.* South Bend: University of Notre Dame, Rare Books and Special Collections. Accessed May 20, 2020. https://rarebooks.library.nd.edu/exhibits/durand/biographies/garcilaso.html.

Hernández, Max. *Memoria del Bien Perdido: Conflicto, identidad y nostalgia en el Inca Garcilaso de la Vega.* Lima: Instituto de Estudios Peruanos, 1993.

Hererra Villagra, Sergio Alejandro. "Ideologías, identidades y mentalidades en la obra de 'Tres Autores Andinos:' Peru. Siglos XVI y XVII." *Diálogo Andino—Revista de Historia, Geografía y Cultura Andina* 40 (diciembre 2012): 21–46.

MacCormack, Sabine. "History, Historical Record, and Ceremonial Action: Incas and Spaniards in Cuzco." *Comparative Studies in Society and History* 43, no. 2 (April 2001): 329–36.

———. "The Incas and Rome." In *Garcilaso Inca de la Vega: An American Humanist, a Tribute to Jose Durand*, edited by Jose Anadon, 8–31. Notre Dame: Notre Dame University Press, 1988.

———. *On the Wings of Time: Rome, the Incas, Spain, and Peru.* Princeton: Princeton University Press, 2007.

Mataix, Remedios. "Biografía Del Inca Garcilaso de la Vega." Biblioteca Virtual Miguel de Cervantes. Accessed May 23, 2020. http://www.cervantesvirtual.com/portales/inca_garcilaso_de_la_vega/autor_apunte/.

Mazzotti, Jose Antonio. *Incan Insights: El Inca Garcilaso's Hints to Andean Readers.* Translated by Barbara M. Corbett. Madrid: Iberoamerica, 2008.

Miro Quesada, Aurelio. *El Inca Garcilaso.* Lima: Fondo Editorial de la Pontífica Universidad Católica del Perú, 1994.

More, Thomas. *Utopia.* Translated with introduction by Paul Turner. London: Penguin Books, 2003.

Ricardo Rojas, "Prologo a 'Comentarios Reales de los Incas,'" in *Los Garcilasistas: Antología*, edited by Cesar Toro Montalvo, 180–87. Lima: Editorial San Marcos, 1987.

Spalding, Karen. Introduction to *Royal Commentaries of the Incas and General History of Peru*, by Garcilaso de la Vega, El Inca. Translated by Harold V. Livermore. Indianapolis: Hackett, 2006.

Vega, Garcilaso de la, El Inca. *Royal Commentaries of the Incas and General History of Peru*, Vol. I and II. Translated by Harold V. Livermore. Austin: University of Texas Press, 1966.

———. *Royal Commentaries of the Incas and General History of Peru.* Translated by Harold V. Livermore, edited with an introduction by Karen Spalding. Indianapolis: Hackett Publishing Company, Inc., 2006.

Vega, Garcilasso de la, the Ynca. *The Royal Commentaries of the Yncas, Volumes I and II.* Translated with notes and introduction by Clements R. Markham. London: Hakluyt Society, 1869. Internet Archive. Last modified November 4, 2016. https://archive.org/details/firstpartofroyal01vega/page/n4.

Varner, John Grier. *El Inca: The Life and Times of Garcilaso de la Vega.* Austin: University of Texas Press, 1968.

Zamora, Margarita. *Language, Authority and Indigenous history in the Comentarios Reales de los Incas.* Cambridge: Cambridge University Press, 1988.

———."Garcilaso Inca de la Vega (1539–1616)," In *Narradores Indígenas y mestizos de la época colonial (siglos XVI–XVII): Zonas andina y Mesoamérica,* edited by Rocío Cortés and Margarita Zamora, 225–64. Lima: Centro de Estudios Literarios Antonio Cornejo Polar, 2016.

CHAPTER 14: FELIPE GUAMÁN POMA DE AYALA: "INDIANS SHOULD NOT BE ABUSED"

Adorno, Rolena. "Contenidos y contradicciones: la obra de Felipe Guamán Poma y las aserveraciones de Blas Valera." Paper read at the international colloquium "Guamán Poma de Ayala y Blas Valera: tradición andina e historia colonial," organized by the Instituto Italo-Latinamericano in Rome, September 29, 1999. Proyecto Ensayo Hispánico. Last modified 2015. http://ensayistas.org/filosofos/peru/Guamán/adorno.htm.

———. "Early Peruvian recorded daily life under the rule of Spanish conquistadores," *The New World: A Smithsonian Quincentenary Publication* 1: 2 (Spring 1990): 8–9.

———. *Guamán Poma: Writing and Resistance in Colonial Peru.* Austin: University of Texas Press, Second Edition, 2000.

———. *Guamán Poma and His Illustrated Chronicle from Colonial Peru: From a Century of Scholarship to a New Era of Reading.* Copenhagen: Museum Tusculanum Press, 2001.

———. A Witness unto Itself: The Integrity of the Autograph Manuscript of Felipe Guamán Poma de Ayala's El primer nueva corónica y buen gobierno (1615/1616). Copenhagen: The Royal Library, 2002. https://tidsskrift.dk/fundogforskning/articleview/40691/45983.

Albó, Xavier. "La Nueva corónica y buen gobierno: ¿obra de Guamán Poma o de jesuitas?" *Anthropologica* 16, no. 16 (1998): 307–48.

Altamura, Luigi. "Relazione di consulenza concernente la verifica di scritture." In *Guamán Poma y Blas Valera: Tradición Andina e Historia Colonial,* edited by Francesca Cantu, 143–69. Rome: Instituto Italo-Latinoamericano, 2001.

Andía Chávez, Juan. *El cronista Felipe Guamán Poma de Ayala: Un precursor de los derechos humanos.* Lima: Centro de Investigación Empresarial, 2002.

Benavides, Annick. "Guaman Poma and the *First New Chronicle and Good Government,*" *First American Art Magazine* (Summer 2017): 28–34.

Bertoluzza, A., Fagnano, C., Rossi, M. and Tinti, A. "Primi resultati dell'indagine spettroscopica micro-raman sui documenti miccinelli." In *Guamán Poma y Blas Valera: Tradición Andina e Historia Colonial,* edited by Francesca Cantu, 181–190. Rome: Instituto Italo-Latinoamericano, 2001.

Boserup, Ivan, and Krabbe Meyer, Mette Kia. "The Illustrated *Contract* between Guamán Poma and the Friends of Blas Valera: A Key Miccinelli Manuscript Discovered in 1998." In *Unlocking the Doors to the Worlds of Guamán Poma and his Nueva corónica*, edited by Rolena Adorno and Ivan Boserup, 19–64. Copenhagen: The Royal Library Museum Tusculanum Press, 2015.

Bustamante García, Jesús. "Falsificación y revisión histórica: Informe sobre un supuesto nuevo texto colonial andino." *Revista de Indias* LVII, núm. 210 (1997): 563–565.

Cantú, Francesca. Introduction to *Guamán Poma y Blas Valera: Tradición Andina e Historia Colonial*, edited by Francesca Cantu. Rome: Instituto Italo-Latinoamericano, 2001.

Castro-Klaren, Sara. *The Narrow Pass of Our Nerves: Writing, Coloniality and Post-Colonial Theory*. Frankfurt: Vervuert, 2011.

Chang-Rodriguez, Raquel. "Sobre los cronistas indígenas del Perú y los comienzos de una escritura hispanoamericana." *Revista Iberoamericana* XLVIII, núm. 120–121 (julio–diciembre, 1982): 533–548.

Coronel-Molina, Serafin M. Forward to Felipe Guamán Poma de Ayala. *The First New Chronicle and Good Government: On the History of the World and the Incas up to 1615*. Translated and edited by Roland Hamilton. Austin: University of Texas Press, 2009.

Dankoff, Robert. Introduction to *Wisdom of Royal Glory: A Turko-Islamic Mirror for Princes*, by Yusuf Khass Hajib. Chicago: University of Chicago Press, 1983.

Estenssoro, Juan Carlos. "¿Historia de un fraude o un fraude histórico? *Revista de Indias* LVII, núm. 210 (1997): 566–578.

Frye, David. Introduction to *The First New Chronicle and Good Government (Abridged)*, by Felipe Guamán Poma de Ayala, vii–xxxi. Selected, translated and annotated by David Frye. Indianapolis: Hackett Publishing Co., 2006.

Hamilton, Roland. Introduction to *The First New Chronicle and Good Government: On the History of the World and the Incas up to 1615*, by Felipe Guamán Poma de Ayala, xvii–xxiv. Translated and edited by Roland Hamilton. Austin: University of Texas Press, 2009.

Husson, Jean-Philippe. "La defensa de la nación indo-peruana, objetivo primordial de Felipe Guamán Poma de Ayala." *Revista de Crítica Literaria Latinoamericana* 42, no. 84 (2016): 39–52.

Hyland, Sabine. *The Jesuit and the Incas*. Ann Arbor: University of Michigan Press, 2004.

Laurencich-Minelli, Laura. "Presentación del documento *Exsul immeritus Blas Valera populo suo*." In *Guamán Poma y Blas Valera: Tradición Andina e Historia Colonial*, edited by Francesca Cantu, 111–42. Rome: Instituto Italo-Latinoamericano, 2001.

Lopez-Baralt, Mercedes. "La iconografía de vicios y virtudes en el arte de reinar de Guamán Poma de Ayala: Una contribución Americana a la literatura de regimine principium." In *Historia y ficción en la narrativa hispano-americana,* edited by Roberto González Echeverría. Caracas: Monte Avila Editores, 1984.

Pease, Franklin. Prólogo to *Nueva Corónica y Buen Gobierno* by Felipe Guamán Poma de Ayala. Lima: Fondo de la Cultura Económica, 2005.

Poma de Ayala, Felipe Guamán. *The First New Chronicle and Good Government: On the history of the World and the Incas up to 1615.* Translated and edited with introduction by Roland Hamilton. Austin: University of Texas Press, 2009.

———. *The First New Chronicle and Good Government* (Abridged). Selected, translated, and annotated with introduction by David Frye. Indianapolis: Hackett Publishing Co., 2006.

———. *El primer nueva corónica y buen gobierno* (1615/1616). (Copenhagen: The Royal Library, GKS 2232 4°) Autograph manuscript facsimile, annotated transcription, documents, and other digital resources, last updated 2001. http://www.kb.dk/permalink/2006/poma/info/en/frontpage.htm.

Poma, Huaman. *Letter to a King: A Peruvian Chief's Account of Life Under the Incas and Under Spanish Rule.* Translated, arranged, and edited with introduction by Christopher Dilke. New York: E.P. Dutton, 1978.

Porras Barrenechea, Raul. "El Cronista Indio Felipe Huaman Poma de Ayala (1534–1515?)," *Mercurio Peruano,* No. 227, February 1946.

Quispe-Agnoli, Rocio "'Escribirlo es nunca acabar': cuatrocientos cinco años de lecturas y silencios de una *Opera Aperta* colonial andina." In "Más allá de los 400 años: Guamán Poma de Ayala revisitado," edited by Rocío Quispe-Agnoli and Carlos García-Bedoya. *Revista de Investigación de la Facultad de Letras y Ciencias Humanas,* 91, no. 133 (March 2020): 5–34.

Rogers, Adam. "How the Inca Discovered a Prized Pigment: A centuries-old history of titanium white." *Smithsonian Magazine* (June 2021): 18.

Truman, Ronald W. *Spanish Treatises on Government, Society and Religion in the Time of Philip II.* Leiden: Brill, 1999.

Varallanos, José. *Guamán Poma de Ayala: Cronista precursor y libertario.* Lima: G. Herrera, Editores, 1979.

Vargas Luna, Jaime. "Felipe Guamán Poma de Ayala (¿1536?/1556?-¿1615/1644?)." In *Narradores indigenas y mestizos de la época colonial (siglos XVI–XVII): Zonas andina y mesoamericana,* edited by Rocío Cortés and Margarita Zamora, 269–96. Lima: CELACP, 2016.

Vega, Juan José. *Guamán Poma: el precursor.* Lima: Derrama Magisterial, 1988.

Velázquez Castro, Marcel. "Figuras del mal gobierno: 'españoles soberbiosos e indias putas' en la obra de Guamán Poma de Ayala," In "Más allá de los 400 años: Guamán Poma de Ayala revisitado," edited by Rocío Quispe-Agnoli y Carlos García-Bedoya. *Revista de Investigación de la Facultad de Letras y Ciencias Humanas* 91, no. 133 (March 2020): 279–304.

Vicuña Guengerich, Sara. "Virtuosas o corruptas: Las mujeres indígenas en las obras de Guamán Poma de Ayala y el Inca Garcilaso de la Vega." *Hispania* 96, no. 4 (December 2013): 672–83.

Zuidema, R. Tom. "Guamán Poma, Blas Valera y los escritos jesuitas sobre el Perú." In *Guamán Poma y Blas Valera: Tradición Andina e Historia Colonial,* edited by Francesca Cantu, 365–86, Rome: Instituto Italo-Latinoamericano, 2001.

CHAPTER 15: ALONSO DE SANDOVAL: "THE SOULS OF BLACKS ARE AS IMPORTANT AS THOSE OF WHITES"

Aristotle. *The Politics of Aristotle*. Translated by Ernest Barker. London: Oxford University Press, 1958.

Ariza Montañez, Catalina. "El viaje dantesco de los etíopes: la construcción del ser esclavo en el período colonial." In *Genealogías de la diferencia: Tecnologías de la salvación y representación de los africanos esclavizados en Iberoamérica colonial*, edited by María Eugenia Chaves Maldonado, 244–89. Bogotá: Editorial Pontificia Universidad Javeriana, 2009.

Brewer-García, Larissa. "Hierarchy and Holiness in the Earliest Black Hagiographies: Alonso de Sandoval and His Sources." *The William and Mary Quarterly* 76, no. 3 (July 2019): 477–508.

Chaves Maldonado, María Eugenia. "La creación del 'Otro' colonial: Apuntes para un estudio de la diferencia en el proceso de la conquista americana y de la esclavización de los africanos." In *Genealogías de la diferencia: Tecnologías de la salvación y representación de los africanos esclavizados en Iberamérica colonial*, edited by María Eugenia Chaves Maldonado, 178–243. Bogotá: Editorial Pontificia Universidad Javeriana, 2009.

Davis, David Brion. *The Problem of Slavery in Western Culture*. Ithaca: Cornell University Press, 1966.

Dennis, Christopher. "El 'Negro' en dos textos Colombianos y el 'blanqueo' de su alma." *Chasqui* 36, no. 1 (Mayo 2007): 3–17.

Franklin, Vincent P. "Alonso de Sandoval and the Jesuit Conception of the Negro." *The Journal of Negro History* 58, no. 3 (July 1973): 349–60.

Lohse, Russell. "Deathbed and Other Whispered Promises: Masters, Slaves, and Contested Manumission in Colonial Nicaragua." *Colonial Latin American Review* 27, no. 4: 452–468.

Lunn, Arnold. *A Saint in the Slave Trade: Peter Claver (1581–1654)*. New York: Sheed and Ward, Inc., 1935.

Martin, Luis. *The Intellectual Conquest of Peru: The Jesuit College of San Pablo, 1568–1767*. New York: Fordham University Press, 1968.

Mattos de Castro, Hebe. "Esclavización y mancha de sangre en el mundo atlántico del siglo XVII: discursos y trayectorias," translated by María Eugenia Chaves Maldonado. In *Genealogías de la diferencia: Tecnologías de la salvación y representación de los africanos esclavizados en Iberoamérica colonial*, edited by María Eugenia Chaves Maldonado, 88–116. Bogotá: Editorial Pontificia Universidad Javeriana, 2009.

Meiklejohn, Norman. "Alonso de Sandoval, the First Advocate of Black Studies in America," In *Latin America: A Historical Reader*, edited by Lewis Hanke, 154–163. Boston: Little, Brown and Company, 1974.

Navarrete Pelaez, María Cristina. "Las Cartas Annuas jesuitas y la representación de los etíopes en el siglo XVI." In *Genealogías de la Diferencia: Tecnologías de la salvación y representación de los africanos esclavizados en Iberoamérica colonial*, edited by María Eugenia Chaves Maldonado, 22–57. Bogotá: Editorial Pontificia Universidad Javeriana, 2009.

Olsen, Margaret. *Slavery and Salvation in Colonial Cartagena de Indias.* Gainesville: University Press of Florida, 2004.

Paul, Saint. "The Letter to the Galatians," *The New Testament, St. Joseph New Catholic Version.* New Jersey: Catholic Book Publishing Corp., 2015.

Pescatello, Ann M. "The *Leyenda Negra* and the African in Sixteenth and Seventeenth Century Iberian Thought." *The Catholic Historical Review* 66, no. 2 (April 1980): 175–176.

Restrepo, Eduardo. "El negro en un pensamiento colonial de principios del siglo XVII: diferencia, jerarquía y sujeción sin racialización," In *Genealogías de la diferencia: Tecnologías de la salvación y representación de los africanos esclavizados en Iberoamérica colonial,* edited by María Eugenia Chaves Maldonado, 118–76. Bogotá: Editorial Pontificia Universidad Javeriana, 2009.

Sandoval, Alonso de. *De instauranda Aethiopum salute. El Mundo de la esclavitud negra en América,* edited with introduction by Ángel Valtierra. Bogotá: Biblioteca de la Presidencia de Colombia, 1956 [1627].

———. *De Instauranda Aethiopum Salute: historia de Aethiopia, naturaleza, policía sagrada y profana, costumbres, ritos y cathecismo evangélico, de todos los Antíopes.* Madrid: Alonso de Paredes, 1647. Located in the Biblioteca Nacional de España in Madrid. Can be viewed online at: http://bdh-rd.bne.es/viewer.vm?id=0000092806&page=1.

———. *Naturaleza, policía sagrada i profana, costumbres i ritos, disciplina i catecismo evangélico de todos etíopes.* Sevilla: Francisco de Lira, Impresor, 1627. Located in the Biblioteca Nacional de Colombia in Bogotá. Can be viewed online at: https://catalogoenlinea.bibliotecanacional.gov.co/client/es_ES/search/asset/71933.

———. *Treatise on Slavery: Selections from De Instauranda Aethiopum salute.* Edited and translated with introduction by Nicole Von Germeten. Indianapolis: Hackett Publishing Company, 2008 [1627].

———. *Un tratado sobre la esclavitud.* Transcribed with introduction by Enriqueta Vila Vilar. Madrid: Alianza Editorial, 1987 [1627].

Tannenbaum, Frank. *Slave and Citizen: The Negro in the Americas.* New York: Vintage Books, 1946.

Valtierra, S.J., Angel. *Peter Claver: Saint of the Saints.* Translated by Janet H. Perry and L. J. Woodward. Westminster, Maryland: The Newman Press, 1960.

Vila Vilar, Enriqueta. Introducción to *Un tratado sobre la esclavitud* by Alonso de Sandoval. Transcribed with introduction by Enriqueta Vila Vilar. Madrid: Alianza Editorial, 1987.

Von Germeten, Nicole. Introduction to *Treatise on Slavery: Selections from De instauranda Aethiopum salute* by Alonso de Sandoval, S.J. Edited and translated by Nicole von Germeten, ix–xxx. Indianapolis: Hackett Publishing Company, 2008.

Index

Page references for figures are italicized.

About the Author

Katherine Hoyt holds a PhD in political theory from Rutgers University and is the author of *The Many Faces of Sandinista Democracy* from Ohio University Press. Her work is informed by eighteen years living in Latin America and many years of nonprofit education and advocacy work on Latin American issues in the United States.

www.ingramcontent.com/pod-product-compliance
Lightning Source LLC
Chambersburg PA
CBHW050627280326
41932CB00015B/2552